Revolt in Southern Rhodesia
1896–97

A Study in African Resistance

REVOLT IN SOUTHERN RHODESIA
1896–97

A Study in African Resistance

T. O. Ranger

Northwestern University Press
Evanston

© T. O. Ranger 1967

LIBRARY OF CONGRESS CATALOGUE CARD NUMBER 67–25663

Printed in Great Britain

To the memory of Sketchley

Contents

List of Plates

List of Maps

Preface

IN HIS account of the Ndebele and Shona resistance to the imposition of colonial rule in Southern Rhodesia the Russian scholar, Professor A. B. Davidson expressed the hope that the next contribution made to the study of the subject would be from African historians using oral sources. This book is not, unhappily, a fulfilment of this hope. I am not an African historian and remain excluded from many of the insights into Ndebele and Shona society which are needed for a truly balanced account of the meeting of black and white in Southern Rhodesia. Nor have I been able to make extensive use of oral sources. In Southern Rhodesia in the early 1960s, when I was working on this book, old men were still reluctant to talk to strangers, black or white, about their part in the risings of seventy years ago; moreover I was myself barred from entering the African rural areas where much of the information is to be found. In these circumstances I have collected and used only enough oral material to be convinced of its value. The reminiscences of the descendants of 'Mapondera', leader of the northeastern rising of 1900, have a solidity and relevance which has convinced me of the importance of seeking out in the same way the families of other rebel leaders; the Rozwi tradition which was collected for me by Mr Solomon Nengubo enabled me to make sense of an important but obscure episode, the attempt at the end of 1896 to revive the Rozwi empire. With Professor Davidson I look forward to the day when a comprehensive deployment of such evidence will revolutionize our vision of the risings and their significance.[1]

Meanwhile what justification is there for another lengthy account of the risings? Professor Davidson was obliged to use the abundant secondary material available—official inquiries, press reports, the reminiscences of white participants, later secondary studies. I have been fortunate to enjoy access to the very large archival

[1] A. B. Davidson, *Matabele i Mashona v Bor'be Protiv Angliyskoy Kolonizatsii, 1888–1897*, Moscow 1958.

collection in the National Archives, Salisbury, Southern Rhodesia. And it is upon these extensive manuscript sources that this book is based. A description of them will be found in a note at the end of this book, but one thing must be said here. Extensive though these sources are, they are in many ways obviously unsatisfactory. For one thing, the material which is genuinely illuminating about African society and its participation in the risings is scattered amongst a great mass of material which is not concerned with, or if concerned with not perceptive about, Africans at all. Even in the files dealing with the risings by far the greater bulk of the material is concerned with such matters as the supply of boots to the police and army; the fortifications of the Salisbury or Bulawayo laager; letters of condolence to bereaved relatives. But a much more serious problem is the inevitably suspect nature of those documents which do relate to the African side of the fighting. It will be one of my arguments, for example, that official beliefs about African society were mostly ill founded and yet I am dependent upon material produced by these officials for my own reconstruction. Moreover a good deal of the evidence comes, as one would expect, from spies, or from prisoners under interrogation, or from evidence given in preliminary examinations into charges of murder. Given the problems of language and given the pressures to which all these informants were exposed, it is plain that the material needs to be used with very great care.

These are problems, however, which are by no means insuperable, nor are they peculiar to African history. Those scholars who have made brilliant reconstructions of the role of the mob in the French revolution or of inarticulate peasant movements in southern Europe have necessarily had to rely also upon the police files, and their example demonstrates what can be gleaned from such sources. I have become convinced in relation to my own material that at least there was no deliberate, centrally directed attempt to falsify or to produce a particular picture for public consumption. The trials of rebels in Southern Rhodesia were not show trials in that sense, and so far from anybody being in a position to manipulate them to produce a certain result nobody at the time pulled together the evidence given in them to produce a coherent picture of any kind. There is, of course, the distortion of ignorance and the distortion of prejudice; sometimes, as we shall see, the distortion of self-glorification. No doubt the oral material when it is available will suffer from the same sort of distortions and have to be used with the same care.

The character of most of my evidence, however, has made me more than ever reliant on the insights into Ndebele and Shona history and society which have been provided by other scholars, by anthropologists and oral historians, archaeologists and archival historians. This book has derived more than usual from the work of colleagues in Salisbury; from Mr Donald Abraham's work on the oral traditional history of the Shona; from Mr Richard Brown's work on Ndebele history in the nineteenth century; from Dr Kingsley-Garbett's work on the spirit mediums of contemporary Mashonaland; from Professor George Fortunes' work on Shona language and literature and his interest in the Mwari cult; from Mr Nathan Shamuyarira's knowledge of twentieth-century African political history in Southern Rhodesia; above all from the encouragement and stimulation of Dr Eric Stokes. It has also derived a very great deal from the interest of my students in Salisbury, some of whom worked on oral and others on archival material on my behalf, who explored with me the caves where chief Makoni made his last stand in August 1896 and who challenged in argument my first interpretations. I am especially grateful to Miss Rachel Thomson and Mrs Marylee Wiley for assistance in the Archives and to Mr Solomon Nengubo for oral research. Mr Aeneas Chigwedere is now embarking on research of his own into aspects of the risings in Mashonaland which is to be hoped will realize the expectations of Professor Davidson.

In this combination of archival research and the insights of other students of African society in Southern Rhodesia lies the justification for a new study of the Ndebele and Shona risings. The significance of such a study, if it does succeed in throwing new light, is not confined, I think, to Southern Rhodesian history alone, crucial though the risings were to the development of that history. There is today a very widespread interest in the so-called 'primary resistances' to European rule in Africa and a lively historical debate about their significance; their links with the pre-colonial past; and their links with later nationalist politics. We may expect in the near future the publication of a number of studies dealing with particular manifestations of resistance—the Zulu rebellion and the Maji-Maji rising in Tanganyika, for instance; of generalizing articles; and of symposia pulling together material on a whole

variety of resistances. It is in the context of this interest that this
book is written. The Ndebele and Shona risings were in some ways
✓the most spectacular manifestation of resistance in East and
Central Africa, and for this reason information about them is
significant to the study of the phenomenon as a whole. In this
respect I should acknowledge the debt I owe to my colleagues in
the University College, Dar es Salaam, at which this book has
been written. Through my discussions with Dr John Lonsdale, who
has worked on resistances in Kenya, with Dr John Iliffe, who is
now making a full-scale study of the Maji-Maji rising in Tan-
zania, and with Dr John McCracken, who is concerned with the
similar period in the history of Malawi, I have been able to see my
own study in a wider and more valuable context.

There is one final debt to acknowledge. This project was conceived in affection and admiration for the African people of
Southern Rhodesia. My interest in it was stimulated by my friendship with more people than it is possible to name. Some of them,
however, must be mentioned. I owe much to Ndabaningi Sithole
and Stanlake Samkange, themselves historians and interpreters of
their country's past: to George Nyandoro, descendant of one of the
most formidable Shona leaders of 1896–7; to Herbert Chitepo,
whose poem on the end of the old order in Manyika is a valuable
way into the late nineteenth-century history of eastern Mashonaland; to Mrs Mwendapole, proud descendant of 'Mapondera' who
collected and made available to me her family memories of that
rebel leader; to Basil Nyabadza and Eric Magwasa who were my
guides to Gwindingwi caves and to the history of the Makoni area;
to Mr Chifamba, who introduced me to the old songs of the risings
which came back into nationalist politics in the 1960s; and to
many more. To them, through its dedication to Sketchley Samkange, my dear friend and introducer to African life, who died
before the unhappy division in the nationalist movement and who
symbolizes to me its essential unity, I dedicate this book.

Dar es Salaam, June 1966   T.O.R.

CHAPTER ONE

The Shona and Ndebele Past

IN MARCH 1896 throughout the greater part of the province of
Matabeleland whites living outside the towns were suddenly
attacked and killed; in June 1896 similar attacks were made with
equal suddenness over large areas of the province of Mashonaland.
These attacks took the British South Africa Company administration, which had been governing Mashonaland since 1890 and
Matabeleland since 1893, completely by surprise. When the Acting
Chief Native Commissioner, Matabeleland, was asked for his
opinion in March 1896 about the causes of the Ndebele rising, he
answered with a frank admission of incomprehension. 'This outbreak was got up as a matter of fact so quickly', he wrote, 'and in
opposition to all our native lore, that we feel almost unable to
venture any further opinion on natives at all; except this—that
they are not for one moment to be trusted.' When the western and
central Shona rose there was an even greater incredulity. 'I may
remark', wrote Marshall Hole, the Resident Magistrate of Salisbury, 'that this sudden departure on the part of the Mashona
tribes has caused the greatest surprise to those who from long
residence in the country thought they understood the character
of these savages and to none more than to the Native Commissioners themselves. . . . With true kaffir deceit they have beguiled us
into the idea that they were content with our administration of the
country and wanted nothing more than to work for us and trade
with us and become civilized; but at a given signal they have cast
aside all pretence and simultaneously set in motion the whole of
the machinery which they have been preparing.'[1]

This white unreadiness gave the rebels their opportunity to
launch a sudden and co-ordinated attack. But more than this—
in the willingness of Marshall Hole and others to be 'beguiled into
the idea that they were content with our administration' there was
contained a profound misunderstanding of the reaction of the

[1] Acting C.N.C. to Acting Administrator, 30 Mar. 1896, A 10/1/1; report
by Marshall Hole, 29 Oct. 1896, A 1/12/36.

African peoples of Southern Rhodesia to colonial rule, a misunderstanding which was at the root of the tensions between white and black. This misunderstanding arose, as some of the Native Commissioners came to see later, partly out of white ignorance of the history of the Shona and the Ndebele and of the continuing significance of the pre-colonial past to these peoples. 'We had underrated the Mashonas,' confessed 'Wiri' Edwards, the first Native Commissioner of Mrewa in central Mashonaland. 'We knew nothing of their past history, who they were or where they came from, and although many of the Native Commissioners had a working knowledge of their language, none of us really understood the people or could follow their line of thought. We were inclined to look down on them as a downtrodden race who were grateful to the white man for protection.'[1]

Whites believed that the Shona peoples would not rebel because they believed that the Shona had no roots, no sense of history; no sense of religion, the feeblest of political institutions—in short, no way of life worth fighting and dying for. Whites believed that the Ndebele would not rebel because they believed that Ndebele society, no matter how centralized and effective it had been in the past, had also been so arbitrary and oppressive that it had been abhorrent to most of those involved in it. Whites believed that the Shona welcomed Company rule as a protection against the Ndebele; and that the mass of the Ndebele welcomed Company rule as a protection against their own institutions. They were wrong in all these beliefs, of course, vastly under-estimating the attachment of the Shona peoples to their traditional institutions and the continuing prestige of the Ndebele system. In order to understand the risings we must first seek to correct these errors and to look at the African past of Southern Rhodesia as it is beginning to emerge from the work of modern scholars.

The view held by whites of Shona society in the 1890s can best be amplified by extracts from contemporary comments. The Shona were held to be relatively recent arrivals in Rhodesia, only shallowly rooted there and with no effective memory of their previous history. 'Either owing to the intense stupidity of the Mashona or his knowing nothing', wrote the Native Commissioner, Salisbury, in January 1896, 'I have been able to discover very little of his origin or history. . . . Unlike the Zulus the Mashonas have no

[1] Reminiscences of 'Wiri' Edwards, ED 6/1/1.

folk lore and are content to enjoy today and think nothing of yesterday, or tomorrow either for that matter. . . . I do not think it is much more than 100 years since this country was first occupied or invaded by Mashonas.' Shona chiefs were credited with almost no power. 'There is no such thing as a chief in my area,' wrote the Native Commissioner, Hartley, in December 1895 from the kraal of paramount chief Mashiangombi, who was to become the main leader of the rising in western Mashonaland. 'Those who are called chiefs have not the slightest authority; they are defied even in their own kraals.'[1]

Nor did whites think that the Shona had any sense of religion or possessed any religious organization. 'Among the Mashonas there are only very faint traces of religion,' wrote the Jesuit missionary, Father Hartmann, in 1894. 'They have hardly any idea of a supreme being. . . . The Mashonas are united as a common wealth by nothing except the unity of their language.' So far did the Jesuit fathers at Chishawasha believe the Shona to be from religious maturity that they thought it necessary first to instruct them in 'natural religion' before broaching the great truths of Christianity.[2]

The reaction of settlers, missionaries and administrators alike to these unfortunate people was one of contempt and dislike. A Bulawayo diarist summed up general white attitudes when he noted in June 1896: 'No one likes the Mashonas, dirty, cowardly lot. Matabele bloodthirsty devils but a fine type.' 'Father Biehler is so convinced of the hopelessness of regenerating the Mashonas,' wrote Lord Grey from Chishawasha in January 1897, 'whom he regards as the most hopeless of mankind . . . that he states that the only chance for the future of the race is to exterminate the whole people, both male and female, over the age of 14! This pessimistic conclusion', Grey continued, 'I find it hard to accept.' But even he could find nothing more to say for the Shona than that they had 'been governed and controlled entirely through the influence of fear—they have the habits of a whipped cur and not infrequently bite through terror the hand outstretched to help them'.[3]

[1] Monthly report, Salisbury, Jan. 1896, N 1/1/9; half yearly report, Hartley, Dec. 1895, N 1/1/3.

[2] *Reports on the Administration of Rhodesia, 1892–4*, p. 82.

[3] Grey to Lady Grey, 23 Jan. 1897, GR 1/1/1; diary of F. R. de Bertodano, entry for 21 June 1896, BE 3/2.

White views were well summed up by Marshall Hole. 'The Mashona race has always been regarded as composed of disintegrating groups of natives, having no common organization and owing allegiance to no single authority, cowed by a series of raids from Matabeleland into a condition of abject pusillanimity and incapable of planning any combined or pre-meditated action.'[1]

That something was wrong with these views was made abundantly clear by the 'combined' and 'pre-meditated' action of the Shona rising itself. In fact almost everything was wrong with them. We do not know a very great deal about Shona history even now, but certain things have become clear. Among the mixed peoples who spoke dialects of Shona in the 1890s there were many who had been resident in much the same area for centuries and who had a well preserved and institutionalized memory of their history. The Shona linguistic area had been the scene of at least two remarkable attempts at political centralization—the confederacies of the Mutapas and of the Rozwi Mambos. The authority of the paramount chiefs had survived the collapse of these confederacies in most of Mashonaland. The Shona peoples had evolved, moreover, two remarkable and developed religious systems which were widely influential in the 1890s, And, finally, the effect of Ndebele raids upon the Shona of Mashonaland has been much exaggerated.

We must look at these points in more detail. Two things need to be made clear first, however. The word Shona does not carry with it any precise tribal or ethnic connotation; nor does it relate only to the peoples who lived in the area now known as Mashonaland. It is a linguistic term used to describe a group of dialects spoken throughout what is now Southern Rhodesia and in parts of adjacent territories. These dialects—Kalanga, Karanga, Zezuru, Korekore, Manyika, Ndau—do not have precise ethnic connotations either. Thus when we speak of the Shona people we mean all those who spoke dialects of Shona over this wide area; when we talk of the Zezuru peoples we mean those who spoke the Zezuru dialect and who lived in a particular district of the Shona liguistic area. So defined, Shona peoples were involved in the so-called Ndebele rising in the province of Matabeleland, as well as in the so-called Shona rising in the province of Mashonaland, and what is said below about Shona history is relevant, therefore, to the risings in both provinces. We may as well note here, indeed, that

[1] Marshall Hole, op. cit.

the names Matabeleland and Mashonaland are thoroughly misleading; the political division which they imply did not exist before the nineteenth century; the Ndebele did not live throughout
Matabeland but only in a central district of it, and the Shona lived
in wide areas outside Mashonaland.[1]

'There appears to be a sufficiently marked cultural as well as
linguistic uniformity' among the Shona peoples, so Dr Kuper tells
us, 'to distinguish them from the neighbouring Nguni and Sotho
of Southern Africa as well as from Bantu tribes north of the
Zambesi'. But if there is a Shona culture, a way of life, it has
emerged from a most complex series of conquests, assimilations and
movements of peoples. 'Historically', writes Father Devlin, 'the
Mashona have been formed by a criss-cross dove-tailing of bits of
tribes who broke apart and then came together again centuries
later, each part bringing new blood with it. Their myth and ritual
is much concerned with the assimilation of invaders by earlier
inhabitants.' This complex history has provided, as we shall see,
a sort of common environment for large numbers of Shona-speaking
peoples over large areas for considerable periods of time, which
makes it improper to speak of a 'Shona past' or a 'Shona way of
life'. But we should emphasize here that in the 1890s, as today,
there was still a great variety of practice and belief among the
speakers of Shona and that we must make the same apology as Dr
Kuper in her ethnographic survey of the Shona: 'Inevitably in a
brief survey such as this details and variations of custom are omit-
ted, and a more uniform picture is presented than actually
occurred.'[2]

In looking at Shona history thus generally it will be best to
begin with the two centralizing experiments which brought together under one hegemony the majority of the Shona-speaking
peoples. 'The Mashonas were not a war-like people', wrote one of
the Native Commissioners of the 1890s. 'They were not a nation
under one supreme head as were the Matabele. They were a
multitude of different tribes or clans, each with its own paramount
chief and territorial boundaries. . . . There may once have been a

---

[1] The only recent general survey of the Shona is Hilda Kuper, 'The Shona',
in H. Kuper, A. J. B. Hughes and J. Van Velsen, *The Shona and Ndebele of
Southern Rhodesia*, London, 1955.

[2] Kuper, op. cit. C. Devlin, 'The Mashona and the Portuguese' and 'The
Mashona and the British', in *The Shield*, May and June 1961.

Kingdom of Monomatapa, but I hae ma doots.' Such caution was reasonable in the 1890s when the Mwene Mutapa confederation was still shrouded in myth of both African and European making. Today, however, as the result of work done on relevant Portuguese documents, on newly available oral tradition, and on archaeological remains, we can say that there certainly was a kingdom of Mwene Mutapa; that it developed into an 'empire' or 'confederacy' covering most of what later became Mashonaland and a great area of Portuguese East Africa; that it was one of the most successful African Iron Age states; and that it was created by and largely ruled over Shona-speaking peoples.[1]

The Mwene Mutapa dynasty was established in the country to the south of the Zambesi, in what is now north-east Mashonaland, as the result of the conquest of the Tavara tribes of that area by Shona speakers from the south—the so-called Korekore—in the fifteenth century. These Shona conquerors came from an area already in trading contact with the outside world and developing political and technological sophistication. Well placed to make contact with the long-established trade of the coast, their new kingdom expanded, made conquests, and was imitated until it became the centre of a widely spread and elaborate system with which the Portuguese soon came into contact in the sixteenth century. From their accounts of it, it was clearly a state system, of considerable sophistication. The kingdom of Mwene Mutapa, writes Mr Gann in the most recent account of it, turned into 'an empire over many other tribes, who were allowed to keep their own chiefs but were obliged to forward tribute. In exchange the king's subjects received protection from their enemies, as well as gifts; the royal court perhaps acted as the centre of a vast system of tributary exchange which functioned without money. . . . The Monomotapas in time managed to build up a great tribal confederacy. Hoe-cultivation and small-scale industries like weaving, gold-mining, pottery and the production of ironware built up a

[1] Reminiscences of 'Wiri' Edwards, ED 6/1/1. The most recent account of research is, B. M. Fagan, *Southern Africa*, London, 1965. Fagan writes of a 'Shona empire' based on Great Zimbabwe and dating from the thirteenth or fourteenth century for the history of which 'we must rely almost wholly on archaeological evidence'. The assumption here is that the newcomers who introduced technological and political techniques also introduced the Shona language which then became the language of both themselves and the older populations.

surplus; trade in luxury goods enhanced the country's wealth. As time went on, powerful men could afford richer clothes, finer ornaments and better weapons than their followers. . . . The king himself used great nobles in his household which formed the nucleus of a rudimentary state organization. He also received asssistance from a body of tribal intellectuals, part royal spirit mediums and part official historians, who were supposed to voice the will of ancestral kings, and maintain the traditions of their race. There was too a host of office bearers, described by a Portuguese chronicler of the sixteenth century as the governor of the kingdoms, the captain-general, the chief major-domo, the chief musician, the captain-general of the vanguard in wartime, the king's right hand, the chief wizard, the king's doorkeeper, 'and numerous other officers of lower rank whom it would be unending and tedious to enumerate'. All these dignitaries held land and vassals, but they resided at the King's court. . . . Local government remained in the hands of minor chiefs and headmen.'[1]

The Mutapa's power was partly economic, partly spiritual— 'everything points', so Fagan tells us, 'to the power of the Shona and Rozwi chiefs having been based on their intermediary powers or on their control of the powerful *mhondoro* (tribal spirits), upon whose messages to *Mwari* depended the fortune of the community'. The Mutapa was surrounded by ritual and prohibitions; the dead Mutapas were honoured at the great royal graves, tended by their own posthumous court. And the rites which surrounded the Mutapa were emulated by the rulers of the provinces or the principalities of his 'empire'.

For some time, then, the Mutapa's court, within its stone-walled stockade 'in the somewhat eerie escarpment country, where ghostly white "fever trees" and grotesque baobabs grow among the *mopane*', was the focus of the economic, administrative and spiritual life of very many of the Shona-speaking peoples. There congregated Arab or Swahili traders from the coast, messengers from the provinces, 'the sons of the nobles of his kingdom' picking up an education by serving as pages, soldiers and their commanders. But the system, impressive and effective in its day, had many

[1] L. H. Gann, *A History of Southern Rhodesia*, London, 1965, pp. 9–10. See also D. P. Abraham, 'The early political history of the Kingdom of Mwene Mutapa (850–1589)' in *Historians in Tropical Africa*, Salisbury, 1962, and 'The Monomatapa dynasty' in *Native Affairs Department Annual*, No. 36, 1959.

weaknesses and these were soon revealed by the pressure put on the Mutapas by the Portuguese. The Mutapas were caught between Portuguese demands and the resistance to these of their vassals; if they accommodated themselves to the Portuguese they faced rebellion; if they accommodated themselves to the demands of most of their subjects and attempted to exclude Portuguese influence they faced the military strength of this early colonial power. Soon their system began to fall apart. 'In the seventeenth century, writes Professor Oliver, 'the Monomotapas became Portuguese puppets, and their outlying provinces hived away from their allegiance. By the eighteenth century there was little trace of their former empire, by the nineteenth, none.'[1]

Yet even in the late nineteenth century the fact of the existence of the Mutapa empire was still of some significance. The religious system with which it has been closely associated was still influential, as we shall see, and the spirits of dead Mutapas continued to command respect even when the live titular Mutapa was reduced 'to provincial status in Thawara country west of Tete'. And under the pressures of the new colonial incursion in the 1890s even the titular Mutapa was able to serve as the focus for considerable movement of resistance throughout the nuclear area of the old empire and its eastern provinces. The then Mutapa claimant was one Chioco Dambamutupe and his influence was treated with more respect by the Rhodesian authorities than that of a mere provincial Tavara chief even if with less respect than that of an emperor. 'Choko, a powerful chief in Portuguese territory, was at the head of the whole affair', wrote the Native Commissioner, Mrewa, in 1898 when there was a movement of unrest in the Rhodesian Korekore and Tavara areas. 'Before the occupation of the country by the British South Africa Company, Choko's country came right down to the border of Maramba in this district and in fact until quite lately the natives in Fungwi paid tribute to him. . . . As far as I can make out he was chief of the Korekori and for years he has given the Portuguese a lot of trouble and they have been too weak to tackle him.' A month or so later Colonel Leverson, who was at work delimiting the Rhodesian-Portuguese boundary, ran into Chioco's hostility. 'The natives about here stand in great awe' of Chioco, wrote Leverson, 'some well-informed people telling me that his territory extended as far south as the Mazoe and into the British sphere of influence'.

[1] R. Oliver, 'Exploring the History of Africa', *Encounter*, Mar. 1963.

And in May 1901, when this unrest had broken out into open violence, the Rhodesian administration went so far as to send a secret emissary into the territory of their Portuguese colonial colleagues in order to try to persuade Chioco to use his influence to end the disturbances.[1]

Even the idea of the power of the Mutapa was not, then, a completely dead concept in the 1890s. But much more vital and important was the memory of the second of the great Shona centralizing experiments—the empire of the Rozwi Mambos. The Rozwi confederacy came to an end only in the 1830s; it was still fresh in the memory of old men in the 1890s; and, as we shall see, its legacy played an important part in the risings of 1896-7, which broke out largely in those areas where the Rozwi supremacy had been effective. The origins of the Rozwi state system date back to the fifteenth century and for a time it co-existed with the Mutapa confederacy with which it had many and complex inter-relationships. But its real period of power and prosperity came in the second half of the seventeenth and the eighteenth century, when it wrested control of external trade from the declining Mutapas and emerged as the only strong state in the Shona speaking area. The Rozwi confederacy was based in what later became Matabeleland and western Mashonaland, where was located its capital, the great assemblage of stone enclosures and walls now known as Great Zimbabwe. In the late seventeenth and eighteenth century Rozwi authority was recognized also by the central and eastern Shona peoples, but it did not extend to Korekore or Tavara country, the old heartland of the Mutapa kingdom.

A state based on much the same principles of organization as the Mutapa kingdom, its achievements in its period of power outshone those of its predecessor. Where the Mutapas had been undermined by the Portuguese, the Rozwi Changamire dynasty drove them out of what is now Southern Rhodesia. The Rowzi brought the tradition of stone building to a high degree of elaboration. building the most impressive structures at Great Zimbabwe and further royal residences at Khami, Dhlo-Dhlo, Naletale and the rest. The achievements symbolized by those buildings were considerable. A developed economic system, a stable political regime, a

[1] Edwards to C.N.C., 1 Aug. 1898, NSI 1/1/1; Leverson to Secretary, Administrator, 15 Oct. 1898, Colonial Office, Confidential Prints, Southern Africa, No. 574, pp. 130–2; Gilson to Flint, 22 Apr. 1901, A 11/2/12/13.

complex administrative hierarchy—all these were thought by white Rhodesians in the 1890s to be unthinkably beyond the capabilities of black Rhodesians, so that the stone ruins were ascribed to a long vanished race of white colonizers. Our knowledge that these achievements were essentially Shona ones and that the society which created them was enjoying what Basil Davidson calls 'a time of comfortable and slow peace' not much more than fifty years before the risings, necessarily puts the Shona peoples in a different context for us than that in which they were seen in the 1890s.[1]

In this period of peace Zimbabwe enjoyed, so its excavator Mr Roger Summers tells us after a cautious examination of the evidence, 'so advanced a culture that it was virtually a city'. 'The Rozwi monarchs', he suggests, 'organized their production and managed their exports for their own personal profit as capably as the nineteenth-century Randlords. One may venture to guess, from the poor material culture of the mining villages and the frequency of traces of mining accidents, that the mine-girls of pre-history got no more share in their chief's profits than the modern mine-worker does today.' Mr Summers is no doubt right to remind us that the 'complex social organization, which clustered around Zimbabwe', its prosperity and its rich material culture, were the fruits of a system conducted in the interests of the few and super-imposed on the way of life of the many. But during the high period of the Rozwi peace there seems no reason to doubt that its benefits were widespread. The famous hunter, F. C. Selous, writing in 1893 of the paramountcies of central Mashonaland, drew a picture of the country as it must have been 'some fifty years ago'. 'The peaceful people inhabiting this part of Africa must then have been at the zenith of their prosperity. Herds of their small but beautiful cattle lowed in every valley and their rich and fertile country doubtless afforded them an abundance of vegetable food.' The Shona paramounts were then 'rulers of large and prosperous tribes . . . whose towns were for the most part surrounded by well built and loop-holed stone walls . . . Hundreds of thousands of acres which now lie fallow must then have been under cultivation . . . while the sites of ancient villages are very numerous all over the

[1] See R. Summers, *Zimbabwe, A Rhodesian Mystery*, Cape Town, 1963; K. R. Robinson, 'The archaeology of the Rozwi', in *The Zambesian Past*, eds. E. T. Stokes and R. Brown, Manchester, 1966.

open downs.' This picture of Shona peace and prosperity may possibly have been overdrawn by Selous for the sake of the contrast with the disturbances which followed, but it is probably substantially true.[1]

At any rate in the 1830s the time of peace came to an end and the Shona time of troubles began. Among the Nguni-speaking peoples to the south who had hitherto not been politically centralized a great upheaval had been taking place in the first decades of the nineteenth century. This upheaval had produced the Zulu state which was organized on a military principle very different from the system of the Mutapas or the Rozwi. It had also produced a number of splinter groups from the Zulu state or fugitive groups from the surrounding peoples who now made use of the new military tactics and weapons of the Zulu to push into the older areas of political centralization and to conquer and subdue their peoples. The first such invasion of the Rozwi area came in 1830 or 1831 when the so-called Ngoni under the leadership of Zwangendaba broke into the territory of the confederation, looting and destroying as they went. The *zimbabwes* of the Rozwi Mambos were fired and ransacked and the reigning Mambo himself killed. In 1898 one of the first Native Commissioners took down from an old survivor of Zwangendaba's *impi* his memories of this invasion. 'Of all the countries we passed through,' the old man recalled, 'there was one which struck us as most desirable. This was the country in which a people called the Abalozwi lived. They built their villages in granite hills which they fortified with stone walls. Their chief, Mambo, put up a stubborn fight and then fled into the very hilly granite country, making it difficult for us to subdue him and his people.' Zwangendaba and his men laid siege to the last stronghold of the Mambo, the hill of Taba Zi Ka Mambo which was to play so significant a part in 1896. 'They threw down beads and skins and hoes and offered us cattle and sheep to go away and leave them in peace . . . but we were not to be propitiated . . . Next day they came out again on the rocks and directed us to stand below a certain strange overhanging rock. It looked like a big balcony giving standing room to about 200 men. Hereon were

[1] F. C. Selous, *Travel and adventure in South East Africa*, London, 1893; R. Summers, 'Was Zimbabwe civilized?' and 'Notes on the economic bases of the Rhodesian Iron Age cultures', in *Conference of the History of the Central African Peoples*, Lusaka, 1963.

gathered the Mambo and his counsellors, jabbering and chattering like a lot of monkeys. This rock stands about a hundred feet above where we were standing with a sheer drop, and it is here that Mambo threw himself down in our midst to fall dead and mangled at our feet . . . The next day we found that these people had deserted that part of the country during the night and as we wished to continue our trek northward we packed up and took up the trail leaving Mambo's mangled remains where he had fallen and named the hills the Intaba zi ka Mambo, by which name they are known even unto the present day.' That vision of the last Mambo and his counsellors 'jabbering and chattering like a lot of monkeys' is eloquent of the contempt with which the military Nguni peoples from the south—Ngoni and Ndebele alike—regarded the very different institutions of Rozwi and Shona monarchy.[1]

Zwangendaba passed on but the Ndebele of Mzilikazi were hot on his heels, also in flight from the upheavals of the south, and attempts to revive the Rozwi empire were crushed by Ndebele might. Instead there developed the military state of the Ndebele which is described below. The Rozwi aristocracy scattered, some to the north, others seeking refuge among the peoples of western and central Mashonaland. By the 1890s it was difficult to find any material traces of the old Rozwi system, always excepting the now ruined and deserted *zimbabwes*. 'How many people,' asked an early Native Commissioner, 'know who the Rozwi are, or where they live and what influence they exert in the land over which they once ruled supreme?'[2]

The Rozwi did undoubtedly continue to exert influence into the 1890s and an influence which was of not inconsiderable import- ance in 1896. The memory of Rozwi dominance was still vivid among the Shona peoples in the 1890s. A court case of 1897 brings this out well. In that year one Manyanga was being tried for extortion and sedition. A Karanga witness from the Fort Victoria district explained that he had paid the tribute demanded by the accused because he was 'a MuRozi belonging to the BaRosi country. The BaRosi's are the big people of the country. We are afraid of the BaRosi because they sometimes attack us with an impi like the Matabele and kill us'. Clearly the memory of Rozwi supremacy did not seem impossibly remote in the 1890s. Native

[1] Citsha's story, WE 3/2/6.
[2] Notes by Native Commissioner Weale, ibid.

Commissioners in Mashonaland, charged in 1895 with the duty of recording information on the history of the Shona, reported that all they could gather were stories about the Rozwi and their allegedly supernatural powers. Moreover, some of the Rozwi aristocracy continued to exercise a considerable direct influence, living scattered amongst the peoples of western and central Mashonaland but often standing in a relationship of ritual superiority to their chiefs.[1]

These, then, were the two great attempts to superimpose a central authority over the complexity of Shona society. Both had been broken by the 1890s. What remained were the provincial units, the paramountcies or the principalities, to use Mr Abraham's terminology. The paramountcies of western and central Mashonaland, which were the essential political units of the late nineteenth century and which were so heavily involved in the risings of 1896–7, were thought at that time to be of very recent origin. Certainly there had been many movements of people within Mashonaland during the nineteenth century and no doubt the boundaries of the paramountcies and still more the composition of their populations had undergone change. Nevertheless it is possible to trace the history of some of these units continuously from the sixteenth or seventeenth centuries and to find the titles of their rulers occurring regularly in Portuguese sources as advisers or provincial or tributary kings of the Mutapa. Some of them no doubt pre-dated the rise of the Mutapa confederacy, becoming provinces of that empire and then of the Rozwi empire in turn, and surviving the downfall of both to regain independent status in the nineteenth century. Others were founded during the Mutapa period by the outward thrust of groups of Shona or Korekore aristocrats from the Mutapa kingdom which proceeded to conquer a new area and to introduce into it, on a reduced scale, the institutions of the parent state. This happened, for instance, with the paramountcy of Barwe which in the 1890s still functioned as a political unit under its paramount, the Makombe, and which was established by a Korekore conquest in the late fifteenth or early sixteenth century. Others yet again were founded by the intrusion into the area of powerful groups who set up their own little conquest states on the model of the Mutapa dependencies or who took over already existing entities. The paramountcy of Maungwe under the Makoni was

[1] Evidence of Umqueba, Oct. 1897, HC/M, No. 306.

established by such an invasion; the Mutassa dynasty took over the old 'principality' of Manyika by such an intrusion.[1]

Once established they became the essential units of Shona political life. Barwe, Maungwe, Manyika, Mbire under chief Soswe, Nohwe under chief Mangwende, Boca under chief Marange, Budja under chief Mtoko—over the centuries these paramountcies pursued a complex course of rivalry and alliance, of war and trade with each other, with the Portuguese and with any other visitors to central and eastern Mashonaland. As we have seen, whites in the 1890s thought that their rulers, the paramount chiefs, possessed no real power. This was certainly a mistake. They all preserved rituals of 'kingship', dating perhaps from before the Mutapas and the Rozwi but profoundly influenced by the ceremonial of those empires. In Barwe in the first half of the nineteenth century, according to a Portuguese account of that period, the installation of the Makombe was still attended by the rituals of ceremonial incest, ordeals, and so on, which had characterized the accession of the Mutapa. The accession of the Makoni of Maungwe was accompanied by the ceremony of the 'royal' fire. In Manyika the Mutassa chiefs were still exposed to the danger of ritual killing in the nineteenth century—a present-day Manyika poet has given us this version of their accession instructions: 'Should famine come upon this land we will strike off your head. Know then that we desire rain, deal lovingly with all your councillors, spread no slander about men. Enrich the poor, and whosoever it may be, show mercy to all who enter into this your citadel.' The Mangwende of Nohwe was not allowed to leave his paramountcy, nor come face to face with another paramount, for fear of the effects of the emanations of royal spiritual energy. Through all the fighting of 1896-7, though hunted by the white forces, the Mangwende never passed outside the boundaries of his land. The paramountcies did not reproduce, of course, the elaborate bureaucratic hierarchy of the Mutapas but they did have hereditary officers responsible for ceremonial functions and in a variety of other ways showed what Professor Oliver calls 'vestigial traces of a strongly centralized political structure.'[2]

So far from being rootless and without a sense of history, then, the peoples and especially the aristocracies of these paramountcies

---

[1] D. P. Abraham, 'The early political history of the Kingdom of Mwene Mutapa', op. cit.; 'The Principality of Maungwe', *NADA*, 1951.

[2] 'Account of the Succession of the Makombe', *NADA*, 1954.

could relate themselves to two or three centuries of a traditionally known past. The paramounts, thought of as so powerless, in fact exercised a profound, extensive and subtle influence through their relationship with the previous occupiers, with the dead, and with the land. 'The power of the Shona chiefs was relatively limited compared with that of the Ndebele kings,' writes Dr Kuper. 'They did not have centralized and disciplined age regiments whereby they could exercise military control . . . tribal advisers exercised constant restraint on the behaviour of the chiefs.' Nevertheless, she points out, Shona chiefs 'are treated with very considerable respect, and to some extent with reverence'. 'The Mashona chief has never been credited with great power over his people', wrote Native Commissioner Edwards in 1899, wise in the experience of the risings, 'but although he has not had the tyrannical power of some native chiefs in other territories he has a moral power as head of his tribe which we are getting to understand better every day and he can use this power for either good or evil just as he thinks it will suit him best.' The central and western Shona paramounts were not Ndebele kings; but if, as Professor Oliver has written, the Mwene Mutapa and the Rozwi Mambos were Divine Kings, the paramounts were divine kings writ small.[1]

Perhaps the best way to achieve a sympathetic insight into what was involved in the institution of chieftainship in these paramount-cies is from Mr Herbert Chitepo's remarkable poem, *Soko Risina Musoro*, which describes the last days of the Mutassa paramountcy before the coming of colonial rule. Mutassa's court drummer, Curu, speaks to the assembled people of the paramount. 'He who stands here is the Night-Walker, whom you know, he it was who led us here and gave us the blessings of a country. We knew him—that he had the heart of a lion. All men were astonished to see him, they turned to look upon him, twice, thrice, and yet a fourth time. All men feared him and numbered his blessings. They knew that even God had made choice of him.' 'In the years gone by', says Curu again, now addressing the Mutassa himself, 'the earth trembled when trodden by the foot of King Mutassa, and the crops of the earth came out to greet you and to satisfy your family. The voice of your prayers was carried by the wind and was followed by the rain clouds.' 'You are the lion", says another councillor. 'You are the foe of the land, you are the bull in this our kraal. You

[1] N. C. Mrewa, Annual Report for year ending 31 March 1899, *NSI* 1/1/1.

are the one who has the power to pray to those who are ahead in the nameless place. We are your children, O King, we are the fruit of the stem of the great tree, the tree of the Lion.' And the old paramount himself remembers the time 'when I sat upon the throne governing all the land. I ruled, but I ruled with the power that comes from my fore-fathers, the power without beginning, which I thought was endless. We fought battles and were victorious, and returned home with gold and riches.'[1]

The Shona paramounts of the 1890s still enjoyed the 'power without beginning' which they, too, thought was endless. They also enjoyed, though on a very much reduced scale, something of the 'gold and riches' which had been the economic support of the great empire. In the 1890s the gold trade with Tete, which had been one of the sources of strength of the Mutapa, was still continuing in north, east and much of central Mashonaland. It was no longer the monopoly of the ruler of a powerful empire, able to exploit long-distance trade for the support of his semi-urbanized capital. But individual paramounts were able to control the trade in their own areas and to derive considerable advantage from it. The Shona paramount, Dr Kuper tells us, was 'the wealthiest man in his tribe' and 'also supposed to be the most generous'. The hospitality which he offered, the state which he kept, was dependent partly on fines, tribute labour, gifts of 'royal' game, and so on. It was also often dependent, as was the supply of firearms for his warriors, on the trade with Tete.

Reports of the 1890s show us the trade in operation; Goanese and half-caste traders basing themselves on the kraal of the paramount, as once the Arabs and Swahili had based themselves at the Mutapa's court, with their agents going out to the kraals of the various headmen and giving in return for gold, cloth, beads and above all guns. 'A good deal of alluvial gold was washed by the natives from the two rivers, Mazoe and Nyadiri', an early Native Commissioner tells us. 'It was, I may say, the attraction for the Goanese traders who annually visited the Fungwe. Each of the different headmen had their own gold washing sites on the rivers Mazoe and Nyadiri. The whole kraal or group of kraals would move there for two months every year, usually the months of September and October, for gold washing. The women did most of the washing, assisted by the children. . . . This yearly washing

[1] H. C. Chitepo, *Soko Risina Musoro*, Oxford, 1958.

of gold had been going on from time immemorial, hundreds of women were yearly employed, the gold won must have been quite considerable. The greater portion went to Tete.' In 1895 two English traders were able to verify 'the accounts they had often heard of the Portuguese trading with the natives in gold dust. On the Gwetera river they saw huge circular pits in the dry sandy bottom of the river where the natives wash for gold. The usual method employed by the merchants at Tete . . . is to employ about a dozen intelligent natives (often half castes) under the charge of a head man. The head man takes down trading goods, perhaps to the value of some hundreds of pounds, mainly consisting of beads, white limbo and guns. . . The head man selects his headquarters and giving his subordinates each a certain complement of goods despatches them to the different kraals situated on the gold bearing parts. At the expiration of the washing season when the heavy rains silt the river beds . . . the headman collects his men, collects what gold they have traded and returns to Tete. Martins and his fellow traders have often netted as much as 20 or 30 lbs. weight of gold in one season.'[1]

Whatever the disturbances of the nineteenth century they had neither destroyed the deeply rooted authority of the paramounts nor completely dislocated the long established pattern of trade. Nor had they destroyed the religious systems of the Shona of the existence of which the whites were so incredulous. The universal missionary belief that the Shona had no sense of the divine or of the religious life was extraordinarily beside the mark. As Dr Kuper tells us, 'the Shona have an elaborate cult, unusual in southern Africa, centring in the Supreme Being, Mwari'. It would in fact be more accurate, at any rate for the nineteenth century, to say that the Shona peoples had two elaborate religious systems centring in Mwari. The concept of Mwari—or Mlimo as he came to be called in Matabeleland—as the high God was common throughout the Shona area but there were significantly different systems for making approaches to him. The two developed systems were the system of the spirit mediums, or the *Mondoro* cult; and the cult of the oracular deity, usually known as the Mwari or Mlimo cult. Mr Abraham has argued that the two systems originally formed one coherent system of belief and practice; that the monarchies

---

[1] Reminiscences of 'Wiri' Edwards, op. cit.; report by Col. Frank Rhodes, 11 June 1895, LO 5/2/43.

of both the Mutapa dynasty and the Rozwi Mambos were supported by spirit mediums and by priests of Mwari. My own
view of the evidence leads me rather to suppose that the system of
the spirit mediums was particularly associated with the Mutapas
and the Mwari cult particularly associated with the Rozwi kings,
and that despite the innumerable connections between them they
were, and remained, distinct systems. Certainly in the 1890s each
system had its own geographical area, though the two overlapped.
The Mwari cult was effective among the Shona peoples of what
was by then Matabeleland and of western Mashonaland but did
not exist in organized form further east; while the system of the
spirit mediums was effective in north, east, and central Mashonaland and in parts of western Mashonaland but did not operate in
Matabeleland. The differences between them were considerable
ones but the mediumistic element in the Mwari cult, the fact that
some of the spirit mediums were the vehicles not of dead ancestors
but of nature spirits or manifestations of Mwari, and the long
history of interaction of the two state and religious systems made
it easy for them to cooperate in 1896.[1]

The system of the spirit mediums expresses the common African
idea of the increased power of the dead, of their ability to communicate more freely with the divine, and of their role as protector of
the land and the people. The dead were thought of as forming
what Mr J. V. Taylor in his recent study of African religious
thought calls 'the tender bridge' between the living and the divine.
Mr Chitepo, in the poem already quoted, has a striking expression
of this idea in a Shona context, when he has one of his Manyika
councillors describe the place where the nation makes its rituals
of approach to the dead ancestors, in these terms. 'In ancient days
all things were there. For there it was that heaven and earth were
wont to meet. Every year we used to gather there, we the creatures
of the earth, and they, the elders who led the way over the river in
between, which divides the creator from his creatures.'[2]

This dividing river was crossed for many of the Shona peoples
through the spirit mediums. The spirit medium was a man or a
woman believed to be regularly possessed by an important ancestor

[1] D. P. Abraham, 'The roles of Chaminuka and the Mhondoro cults in
Shona Political History', in *The Zambesian Past*, Manchester, 1966, eds. E. T.
Stokes and R. Brown.
[2] J. V. Taylor, *The Primal Vision*, London, 1963, Chitepo, op. cit.

spirit. When in a trance such a medium spoke with the voice of the ancestor, became, for all essential purposes, the ancestor; in this way the living and the dead could literally converse. The living would approach the dead for advice, for intercession with the divine on behalf of the people; the dead would tell the living of their past and something of the world outside life. The claims of the spirit medium, when thus considered, are breathtaking ones, and whites in the 1890s unanimously agreed in regarding them as conscious frauds. More recent investigators have concluded that it is true of them as of the priest-diviners of Ghana that they 'are for the most part honest men. The phenomenon of dissociated personality, upon which their claim to veneration is based, is genuine and impressive. The priests themselves reverence it and submit to severe discipline in its service.' The Shona spirit medium who takes himself and his position seriously observes rules of austerity to fit himself to be 'the purse' filled with the treasure of the dead; and some of the mediums have impressed students with their sense of vocation and service to the traditional values of their community.[1]

Under the Mutapa dynasty this system of spirit mediums was closely associated with the monarchy. The spirits who thus manifested themselves were those of important men—ancestors of the king himself, or perhaps of past representatives of the original owners of the soil. It was regarded as an essential part of the duties of the King, as of the paramount chief on a smaller scale, to maintain contact with these powerful dead on behalf of the nation. It was from them, indeed, that he derived 'the power that has no beginning'; and it was to them that he must make propitiation and intercession on behalf of the people he ruled. The Mutapa monarchy observed a cult of the royal graves, the reigning monarch visiting the graves of his predecessors before any major expedition or initiative, just as the king of Barotseland was still doing in the 1890s. When later, in the decline of the Mutapa monarchy, the royal graves were demolished, the mediums continued to operate and to 'represent' the past monarchs. Under the Mutapas there were mediums not only for important royal ancestors but also for past owners of the soil or noted rain-makers, like Dzivaguru, the

[1] M. J. Field, *Search for Security*, London, 1960. The fullest studies of the spirit mediums are, M. Gelfand, *Shona Ritual*, Cape Town, 1959, and *Shona Religion* Cape Town, 1962.

famous rain-maker of the conquered Tavara. The medium of
Dzivaguru, based at the cult shrine in the foothills of the Mavura-
dona mountains, became almost the chief ritual officer of the
Mutapa kingdom and through him the conquerors assured themselves of 'peace with the land'.

The same sort of system existed in the various paramountcies
or principalities which grew up around the Mutapa kingdom. The
founder of the paramountcy usually became the senior spirit of the
area and his medium the senior spirit medium; other significant
ancestors would also have mediums and in the same way as the
assimilation of the Dzivaguru cult important nature-spirits or rain-
makers would find representation in this hierarchy of mediums.
Thus there grew up what Mr Abraham calls a double 'status category of political implication; a lower category of spirits at tribal
level and an upper category of supra-tribal spirits connected with
the royal dynasties' or with powerful rain-makers. This double
hierarchy of spirits and mediums survived the collapse of the
Mutapa dynasty so that, long after the secular Mutapa had been
confined to his Tavara enclave, the mediums of important Mutapas
of the past, or of spirits like Dzivaguru or Chaminuka, were still
powerful in wide area of east, central and western Mashonaland.[1]

When the Mutapa kingdom was still functioning, these mediums
had clearly played an important political as well as a ritual role—
the two were inextricable. They at once guaranteed and limited
the power of the king; just as mediums at the tribal level guaranteed and limited the power of the chief. In this way the senior
mediums acted as a centralizing and stabilizing factor and this to
some extent they continued to do after the collapse of the secular
institutions of the kingdom. The senior mediums of the paramountcies, some of whom possessed a more extensive area of influence than any tribal chief, were of course continually involved
in tribal politics. And over and above them were the great mediums
of Mutota and Chingoo, Dzivaguru and Chaminuka and Nehanda,
who commanded respect over very large areas and were the nearest thing to a 'national' focus that the Shona of Mashonaland
possessed. We shall discuss in more detail later the exact extent to
which the senior mediums were influential and effective in the
1890s and their significance in the risings. We can say here that
despite all the qualifications which can be made, the situation in

[1] D. P. Abraham, op. cit.

central and eastern Mashonaland in the 1890s was not unlike that described by Mr Ogot in a recent article on the Luo. 'No political superstructure, such as a federation or a con-federation existed. But many of the famous prophets, who acted as counsellors to the chiefs, and whose main function was to look after the spiritual well-being of the tribe, and to prescribe moral standards against which the policies of individual chiefs had to be judged, were known and consulted all over Luo-land. This tended to emphasize the unity of the Luo as a group.'[1]

The Mwari cult was based upon a different notion of how the living could establish contact with the divine. The High God in this view of him is active and immanent. 'Mwari is spiritual owner of the earth and creator of mankind,' writes Dr Kuper. 'He intervenes actively in human affairs . . . He is not a remote ancestor . . . and is not concerned with purely personal affairs but only with matters of tribal importance; he punishes acts, such as incest, which are considered contrary to nature and the perpetuation of the tribe, with pestilence and famine. He manifests himself in such great natural phenomena as volcanic eruptions and lightning.' 'Mwari was a genuine conception of deity', writes Father Christopher Devlin, 'an invisible supreme being.' Something of the content of this concept of deity and of the significance of the High God to those who worshipped him can be seen from a praise poem of the Mwari cult, collected by Professor Fortune.

> Praise,
> Lion of praise!
> Lion who laughs at
> My little spear, though I throw it far.
> But he sees everything, even in Tswana country;
> He gathers fruit afar,
> And comes back when his children are longing for him.
>
> Lion of praise!
> Mwali with the single breast
> Sucked by all the tribes; [i.e. provider of rain].
> His needle is not for sewing blankets
> But sews up rocks with ease. [i.e. master of the lightning].

[1] Ogot, 'British Administration in the Central Nyanza District of Kenya, 1900–60', *Journal of African History*, Vol. IV, No. 2, 1963.

Mwali is a great one;
A great Mukwakwa fruit tree without sap,
Which is eaten by his children in the rainy time;
A Mupani tree without a hollow which saved the tired
squirrel. (i.e. He provides comfort in all seasons and suc-
cour in unexpected ways).

Lion of praise,
Lion of laughter, Great Mbedzi.[1]

This praise-song proclaims an altogether unusual sense of the
closeness of the creator and of his concern with the welfare of his
people. In this system of religious thought, indeed, the role of the
dead as a bridge between the living and the divine was not empha-
sized; it was believed that Mwari spoke directly to the living, not
only in the thunder and the wind, but as a voice, heard most
frequently in caves amidst the rocks, and that he could be approached by the living with sacrifice and supplication. But though
the dead did not play an important part as intermediaries, intermediaries there were between Mwari and the great majority of those
who worshipped him. The worship of Mwari in what was to become
Matabeleland and adjacent areas developed into an elaborate and
esotoric cult; the place or places at which the god chose to manifest
himself became oracular shrines served by an organized priesthood.
The organization of the cult at its central shrine is thus described
by Blake-Thompson and Summers. 'Mwali speaks through or in-
spires the utterances of the chief officer of the cult, the Mouth; he
receives petitions from another high officer, the Ear, and information from a less important officer, the Eye.' The external organization of the cult was in the hands of the last named, and was in
itself complex. In every district in which the influence of the cult
was dominant there were Wosana or Manyusa, messengers to
Mwari from the chiefs and people of the district and from Mwari
back to them again. These messengers made at least an annual
visit to the central shrine or shrines, taking with them cattle and
gifts as offerings for rain or fertility or relief from misfortunes of
various kinds. At the shrine reports on the situation in the districts

[1] Kalanga praise-song, collected from Mr Masola Kumile by Professor
George Fortune, who has very kindly made it available to me. Kuper, op. cit.
Devlin, op. cit.

were made to Maziso, the Eye; petitions addressed to Nzewe, the Ear; and answers received from Muromo, the Mouth.[1] Whites in the 1890s regarded this cult apparatus as an elaborate and conscious swindle, designed to extort gifts from the credulous. More recent commentators have been more sympathetic, pointing out that the criticisms levelled at the cult 'apply equally to any form of institutional religion, especially those which are esoteric'. It is worth bearing in mind what Shona informants in the Inyati area told the missionary, Elliott, in the 1890s. A priest of Mwari was known because he was 'touched' by the god and subject to trances or convulsions; but he was also known by superior virtue. 'If he honours others and is upright and good we know he is sent from Mngwali.' Elliott himself pointed out that 'these "sons of god" are in quite a different class to the ordinary bone-thrower'. There can be no doubt that the white insistence in the 1890s in regarding the Mwari priesthood as sinister and fraudulent 'witch-doctors' prevented any real understanding of the role of the cult.[2]

This elaborate organization obviously lent itself to the support of an experiment in political centralization. 'The organization of the cult is identical with that of the courts of important African chiefs,' write Blake-Thompson and Summers. 'The addressing of petitions to one official, the issue of edicts by another, a secret intelligence service and a numerous court were common form'. It is clear that the value of working with, or controlling, this elaborate hierarchy was fully appreciated by the Rozwi Mambos. It was for this reason, Summers has suggested, that they based themselves at Great Zimbabwe, which was evidently the site of the chief Mwari shrine. 'Zimbabwe was a *religious* centre. All the miscellany of buildings on the Hill and in the valley were attracted here because of the special sanctity of the site. Some were undoubtedly royal dwellings, others administrative buildings or even trading places, but they crowded round the sacred area just as King, Parliament, Government, trade and commerce all crowd round the Royal

[1] J. Blake-Thompson and R. Summers, 'Mlimo and Mwari: notes on a Native Religion in Southern Rhodesia', *NADA*, 1956; H. Franklin, 'Manyusa', *NADA*, 1932.

[2] J. Blake-Thompson and R. Summers, op. cit; W. A. Elliott, 'The Mashuna' in D. Carnegie, *Among the Matabele*, London, 1894. See also J. B. Richards, 'The Mlimo', *NADA*, 1942, where it is asserted that 'the principles on which the belief in Mlimo are founded are no more "superstition" than the old Hebraic belief extant in the time of Moses'.

Church of Westminster Abbey.' The so-called eastern enclosure at Zimbabwe was the site of the Mwari cult activities; there the chief officers of the cult and the divine king of the Rozwi confederation joined in the ceremonies which assured the welfare of the monarchy and its subjects. 'This', writes Summers, 'was the true centre of the whole complex and the most sacred spot in the whole Rozwi confederacy. . . . It is, even in its sadly ruined state, the very epitome of a vanished people and a forgotten culture.'[1]

Control of the two great cult offices of the Mouth and the Ear was left by the Rozwi in the hands of what Father Devlin calls 'older Shona (or Karanga) peoples'; but the Eye, Maziso, came to be controlled by Rozwi of the royal clan. In political terms 'the third office was the most powerful because it was the effective link between the temple and the people; it supervised the external organization of the cult'. In this way the Rozwi monarchy controlled the 'secret intelligent service' of the cult, and in this way also added to its military and political authority 'a sort of spiritual domination' over many of the Shona peoples.[2]

As the influence of the senior spirit mediums survived the collapse of the Mutapa confederacy, so the influence of the Mwari cult survived the destruction of the Rozwi monarchy by the Swazi and Ndebele. We shall discuss later the question of its relationship with the Ndebele state and the exact extent of its influence in the 1890s. Here we need only note that the cult still enjoyed prestige throughout its old area of operation; that its prestige was still linked with that of the Rozwi; and that these two facts were of great importance in the risings in both Matabeleland and Mashonaland.

We have seen something now of the Shona past. What we have seen—this long history, this complex of religious and political institutions and beliefs, this pattern of economic activity, these notions of prestige and communal well-being—adds up to a Shona 'way of life' or perhaps to Shona 'ways of life'. So far from being meekly prepared to succumb to the first colonial pressures, this 'way of life' had been putting up a resolute and successful resistance to them over centuries. For centuries Portuguese power and Portuguese ideas had been pressing in on the eastern and central Shona peoples. Portuguese power had been successfully repulsed by the

[1] Blake-Thompson and R. Summers, op. cit.; R. Summers, *Zimbabwe, A Rhodesian Mystery*.   [2] C. Devlin, op. cit.

military strength of the Rozwi confederation. Portuguese ideas fared no better. A Jesuit historian has described the fate of the Portuguese missionary effort amongst the Shona. 'What was the result of these hundred years of devoted effort? Almost nothing. It was one of the most complete failures of missionary history. During these years when missionaries were struggling to Christianize the Zambesi valley and the north-east of Mashonaland, Xavier's work on the Fishery coast on the southern tip of India was being continued, and Christianity remains vigorous to this day. . . . Japan too had its Christian converts during these years, some of whom remained faithful through one of the worst persecutions in history, and through two centuries of isolation, until Christian missionaries found them again in the middle years of the nineteenth century. . . . None of these regions bears comparison with this part of Africa, where, though there were no notable external trials, the Christian faith which had been taught so long and so devotedly perished so completely and so soon.' In the 1890s the same stubborn resistance was being put up; everywhere in Mashonaland missionary 'beginnings were slow and painful'; in three year's work prior to the rising the Roman Catholic mission at Chishawasha could record only two baptisms, and their experience was common to all. 'A closer acquaintance with the Mashona', confessed a Jesuit missionary in 1897, 'shows at all events that they have but little willingness to become Christians.' He put it down to 'their depraved habits and their low intelligence', but it was rather a manifestation of loyalty to their own concepts of society and the divine; a steady passive resistance which was to turn in 1896 into an armed attack upon the missions and their few converts as well as upon all other whites.[1]

To say that there was a broad Shona 'way of life' and that this was still being defended in the 1890s is not to claim that this 'way of life' had survived everywhere in the old Shona-speaking areas, intact in all its aspects. Clearly in part the Ndebele had done what the Portuguese had failed to do—destroyed in the area of Ndebele settlement the structure of Shona society and assimilated many Shona speakers into their own system. We will say more about the role of the Shona peoples in the Ndebele state proper later. But

[1] W. F. Rea, S.J., 'The Missionary Factor in Southern Rhodesia', *Historical Association of Rhodesia and Nyasaland, Local Series*, 7, 1962; Viator, S.J., 'A visit to Chishawasha', *Zambesi Mission Record*, Vol. 1, No. 1, 1898.

here we will examine how far the Ndebele incursion had affected Shona society in those parts of Matabeleland outside the area of Ndebele settlement and in Mashonaland.

The area of Ndebele settlement, in which alone the institutions of the Ndebele state functioned fully, was relatively compact; certainly it covered a much smaller area than either the old Mutapa or the old Rozwi confederation. Outside that area the Ndebele did not attempt to build up societies on the Ndebele pattern. But whites in the 1890s believed that Shona life was affected everywhere in Southern Rhodesia by the regular Ndebele raids on the surrounding peoples; raids, it was held, which had depopulated the greater part of the Shona territories and undermined Shona society.

A few only of the innumerable statements to this effect will suffice. In 1890, for example, Jameson wrote from the Pioneer Column, which had then reached Chibi's country, to report 'how delighted these unfortunate Banyai are to welcome the coming in of the White Man in force sufficient to put an end to all this murder and slave raiding. Further on in Mashonaland Mr Selous tells me that there are entire tracts of country absolutely depopulated by the Matabele and even where the people remain they have been so impoverished by the Matabele impis that the latter no longer think it worth while to make their excursions to the northeast.' Further experience did not modify these views. In 1893, just before the Ndebele war, the Chartered Company's secretary, Rutherfoord Harris, told the London Office that it was estimated that the Ndebele had killed 100,000 Shona during the last 70 years; this estimate having been arrived at on the basis of 'the very large number of deserted villages and deserted valleys'. At much the same time Father Hartmann, S.J., wrote to the press claiming that 'if no stop is put to these raids it will go on until the Mashonas are exterminated. . . . The Mashonas are a complete wreck physically, intellectually and also morally. In my constant intercourse with them I hear it oftentimes said that if the white men do not protect them they will emigrate from the country.' And at the very end of 1893 Selous published his famous, *Travel and Adventure in South East Africa*, in which he drew a terrible picture of devastation. 'The poor Mashunas, unskilled in war and living, moreover, in small communities scattered all over the country,' he wrote of the Mashonaland plateau country north of

Salisbury, 'without any central government, fell an easy prey to the invader, and very soon every stream in their country ran red with their blood, while vultures and hyaenas feasted undisturbed amidst the ruins of their devastated homes. Their cattle, sheep and goats were driven off by their conquerors and their children . . . were taken for slaves. . . . In a few years there were no more Mashunas left in the open country, the remnant that had escaped massacre having fled into the mountainous districts to the south and east of their former dwellings, where they still live.' If these reports were correct it would not have mattered much how long established and complex the Shona 'way of life' had been since the Shona would almost have ceased to exist as an organized society.[1]

It seems clear, however, that these assertions were wildly overstated. That there were destructive and cruel Ndebele raids upon Shona peoples and that the prosperity and security of Shona life in the 1890s was woefully reduced from the high days of the Rozwi confederation are both true. But it is not true that the Shona speaking peoples had been almost wiped out or that they had become totally demoralized. We must distinguish, in discussing this question, between the Shona peoples who lived within the radius of constant Ndebele activity, and those who lived outside it. There is no doubt that very many Shona speaking people in a great circle around the area of Ndebele settlement were exposed to constant Ndebele visitations and demands. The Kalanga of the south west of Matabeleland; the Karanga of the Fort Victoria area; the Zezuru of Hartley and Charter and southern Lomagundi; the Rozwi, Tonga and other groups to the north of Inyati; all these fell into this category. But what did this Ndebele activity actually involve for these peoples?

We can get some idea from the reminiscences of one of the Ndebele raiders himself, as recorded in 1898. 'The next few years,' he said, speaking of the period following Mzilikazi's arrival in the country, 'were very exciting, for we were always out raiding and subduing the neighbouring tribes and collecting tribute from their chiefs. If they submitted and acknowledged our King's sovereignty and if they gave cattle freely we left them alone but if they refused we fought them and burnt their kraals and took their young

---

[1] Jameson report to the *Cape Times*, 17 Aug. 1890, LO 5/2/3; Hartmann article, 1893, LO 5/2/29; Harris to London Office, 27 Sept. 1893, LO 5/2/30; F. C. Selous, op. cit.

people into slavery. . . . After we had discovered the country of the Maswina and their people our King partitioned it off into districts and each of our chiefs would be allotted his district in which he would collect the King's tribute, and then the raids ceased except when some Maswina chief misbehaved himself or refused to pay tribute.' This records a violent process, certainly, and no doubt one bitterly unpopular with its victims, but it does not record a process of continued and arbitrary slaughter.

The impression given by these reminiscences of the increasing regularity of Ndebele relations with neighbouring peoples and the creation of some sort of system of tribute and submission is supported by other evidence. In 1904, for instance, the Tonga chief, Pashu, who lived in the Sebungwe area of Matabeleland, resisted the collection of hut tax by the administration and refused to admit the force of their argument that it was a fair return for protection from the Ndebele. 'Pashu stated that while under Mzilikazi's rule they were continually carried off, yet after Lobengula's accession he was left unmolested so long as he paid his tribute of skins, feathers, etc., to the King.' Moreover, the evidence suggests that under Lobengula even if a chief refused to pay tribute the punishment imposed was not necessarily arbitrary and wholesale. The famous case of the killing of chief Lomagundi in 1891, for instance, is worth examining. The chief had refused any longer to acknowledge Lobengula's supremacy or pay tax. A small *impi* was sent to his area; its commander first visited the senior spirit medium of the paramountcy and obtained her approval of the punishment of the chief; then the chief's kraal was attacked and he and his people killed. Jameson's chief reaction was one of surprise that so few people had been killed; the action, he reported, was 'in accordance with Lobengula's laws and customs'. And laws and customs of a sort rather than random brutality did govern Ndebele relations with their tributaries.[1]

Moreover the consultation of the senior spirit medium brings out another aspect of Ndebele relations with their Shona tributaries. The Ndebele made no attempt to re-model Shona political or religious institutions in the tributary areas, but rather in many cases entered into relations of varying kinds with Shona paramounts and mediums. Shona society in these areas was certainly

[1] Citsha's statement, 1898, WE 3/2/6; report of C.N.C. Matabeleland, May 1904, LO 5/5/26; for Lomagundi see CT 1/15/1 and LO 5/2/16.

exposed to severe strains by the Ndebele demands but in essentials it continued as it had done in the past—much poorer than in the days of peace; humiliated by Ndebele supremacy, exposed to a system which though observing some sort of rules was nevertheless capricious, but surviving. In these circumstances the Shona peoples showed characteristic adaptability; it was even possible, as the example of chief Chilimanzi shows, to exploit the Ndebele power for one's own ends and to preserve a precarious independence. Manowe, son of chief Chilimanzi, was a great hunter and in that capacity a firm favourite with Lobengula. On his father's death he contested the succession to the paramountcy with his uncle, gaining both Lobengula's backing and that of the majority of his people to whom he explained 'that to maintain themselves as a separate people they would have to adopt a policy of their own, especially as their country bordered onto Matabeleland proper. . . . Manowe's position was a very difficult one,' wrote the first Native Commissioner of his area, 'for the Matabele on their way into Mashonaland on their raids inevitably passed through his country first, and although they looked upon him as a Mashona, yet he kept his tribe neutral as far as the Mashona were concerned, assisting neither side, never allowing his men to accompany Matabele impis on a raid or permitting them to assist the Mashonas to defend themselves against the Matabele. He was thus rewarded by the Matabele by not being molested or taxed, and he avoided the enmity of his Mashona neighbours in that he never assisted the Matabele against them and often warned them of their coming surreptitiously.' [1]

Outside this ring of tributary territories co-existing with the Ndebele state in some sort of regular relationship were areas into which the Ndebele continued to make periodic raids for loot and which did not recognize their supremacy. But these raids have been greatly exaggerated as factors of disintegration. In later years, at any rate, few Shona communities suffered heavy losses of life or property as a result of raids which they were organized to survive. Our Ndebele warrior himself admits that 'these people all cleared into the granite ranges and hills to build their strongholds and kept a keen watch on our movements. They also developed a sort of code of calls and ways of sounding their drums and sent messengers to keep one another informed of our every

[1] Mnyenyezi's story of Chilimanzi, WE 3/2/6.

movement. So it became very difficult to take them by surprise as time went on.' Once again the evidence supports this. One of the paramounts exposed to Ndebele attacks, for example, was chief Kunzwi-Nyandoro, who had incurred Ndebele enmity while living in the Hartley area and had moved with his people to the Salisbury district. Father Hartmann has left us an account of a Ndebele raid on Kunzwi's people. As soon as the alarm was given the people herded their animals into a great cave on the side of a steep hill, 'in an inconceivably short space of time' and 'without the least sign of any panic or confusion'. Indeed, the Jesuit reported, they were 'all in very good spirits'. Our Ndebele raider confirms the effectiveness of such tactics and the difficulty of storming such Shona strongholds—'in such cases we bided our time', he says, 'and trusted to our luck to catch them unawares on some future occasion'.[1]

Chief Kunzwi-Nyandoro, indeed, is an excellent example of the point I am making. If anyone should have been 'a complete wreck', it was he. He and his people had moved from the north-east of Mashonaland to the west and back again to the central plateau, having to fight their way and exposed to a series of Ndebele raids. Yet Kunzwi-Nyandoro, in his stronghold and on his guard, retained all the attitudes and pride of a Shona paramount, exerting a powerful authority over his people, respecting the spiritual eminence of the Dzivaguru and Chaminuka mediums, and savouring his 'independence' above everything. In 1897, when called upon to surrender, Kunzwi would not come to negotiate and 'said it was unbecoming for a King to leave his kraal'. And however absurd it seemed to the whites, it was still as kings that the Shona paramounts saw themselves in the 1890s.[2]

Finally, there were extensive areas of central and eastern Mashonaland which remained either largely or completely unaffected by Ndebele raids. The most impressive testimony to this comes from the officers of the Company, as they learnt on the spot in 1890 and 1891 the true facts of the Mashonaland situation. The first Administrator, Colquhoun, and the first commander of police, Pennefather, had been instructed that the Company's claim to Mashonaland depended upon concessions from Lobengula

---

[1] Citsha's story, ibid; 'The History of the Zambesi Mission', *Zambesi Mission Record*, Vol. 3, No. 32.
[2] Grey to Rhodes, 19 June 1897, Rhodes House, Mss. Afr. s. 228, C. I, Vol. 1.

and that his effective sovereignty extended throughout the territory. But once in Mashonaland they both became convinced that the true situation was very different. 'Lobengula's claims . . . I have understood to extend at least as far east as the Sabi river,' wrote Colquhoun in September 1890. 'I consider, however, that if any inquiry were made on the spot, this claim would be most difficult to establish, and it would be undesirable to have the question raised. . . . Between the Sabi and Ruzarwe rivers there are chiefs who acknowledge *no one's authority*. They have certainly *never* been under Matabele authority, nor have they ever seen any Matabele. . . . Selous has maintained, and maintains as you know, that (a) east of Sabi and (b) north and east of the Hunyani the Matabele have no real claim whatever, and that such claims *would not stand investigation.*' Pennefather came to similar conclusions. 'After making personal acquaintance with the country and the natives,' he wrote, 'I am strongly of the opinion that Lobengula's impis have not raided further than 32° east.' And in October 1890, Selous, sent by Colquhoun to make good the Company's title by treaties with 'independent' Shona chiefs, wrote satirically that he was 'off to get mineral concessions and come to a friendly understanding with several native chiefs living to the south and east of furthest Mashonaland, of whom neither Lo Bengoola, Dr Harris nor Dr Jameson have ever yet heard'.[1]

The paramounts to whom Selous was sent included Makoni of Maungwe, Soswe of Mbire, Mtoko of Budja, and Marange of Boca. Treaties were also made with the Mangwende of Nohwe and Mutassa of Manyika. These paramounts were certainly not basking in peace and prosperity in the 1890s. The eighteenth century 'golden age' was over. If they were not under pressure from the Ndebele they were certainly under pressure from renewed Portuguese activity and especially they were involved in the series of wars sparked off by the ambitions of the remarkable Goanese adventurer, Gouevia. They, too, had abandoned their well-built stone kraals in the valleys for strongholds in the granite hills. But there was certainly no question of their being exterminated without white protection or being forced to emigrate from the paramountcies which still formed the total and sufficient objects of their ambitions. Among them, at any rate, the Shona 'way

[1] Colquhoun to Rhodes, 27 Sept. 1890, CT 1/3/3; Pennefather to Colquhoun, 11 Oct. 1890, CT 1/1/3; Selous to Harris, 4 Oct. 1890, CT 1/20/3.

of life' was certainly not dead in the 1890s, and despite their poverty they were not totally unprepared to defend it since the disorders of the nineteenth century had meant an increased flow of firearms into the area.

We have now made all the qualifications necessary to the white views of Shona society in the 1890s. We must be careful to avoid errors in the other direction. Shona society proved itself in 1896 and 1897 to be capable of coordinated and determined resistance. The potentiality was there but there were formidable difficulties in the way of its realization. With all their history, all their shared participation in the great centralization experiments, for all their devotion to the way of life to which they had been accustomed, the Shona paramounts were extremely disunited in the 1890s. The constant fighting which went on between them was, indeed, a part of the way of life which they cherished. Because of this some considerable changes were needed before they could be brought together into rebellion. We shall see later how this was done. But we must end this account of Shona history with an illustration of Shona division. In May 1892 Captain Lendy left Salisbury with a police patrol to visit the paramounts of the Salisbury district. His report gives a vivid picture of the disunity of men who four years later were allied against the whites. Paramount chief Chishawasha came in to complain against paramount chief Kunzwi-Nyandoro for an assault committed before the arrival of the whites in the country; paramount chief Marondera was similarly involved in allegations of raids and counter-raids with chief Chiduku; chief Mbelewa 'seems to live in constant fear of being raided by Makoni's people'. Lendy's appearance on the scene was taken as an opportunity to gain an advantage over traditional rivals rather than as an occasion to offer united resistance. Chishawasha thus triumphed over Kunzwi-Nyandoro, telling him that 'he had been to the white man about the case and that he would come and wipe him out'. It was hardly surprising that Lendy did not foresee the challenge of 1896, for many changes were to take place in the next four years.[1]

The Ndebele state was very different from the Rozwi and Mutapa confederations. It centred around an active and authori-

[1] Lendy to Jameson, 23 June 1892, A 1/9/1.

tarian monarch rather than the sacred but restricted figure of the divine king. It was highly centralized military system rather than a diffuse bureaucratic one. It made no attempt to set up a 'trading empire', and although it was in contact with traders from the south it did not depend for its power and prosperity, as had the older systems, upon control of wide networks of external trade. The Ndebele were not craftsmen, nor did they have a reputation for divination, prophecy and rain-making, and feared and respected Shona skills in these respects. Pre-eminently the Ndebele King was a national military leader and the Ndebele were warriors and cattle-keepers. The atmosphere of the great kraal of the Ndebele King was utterly different from the atmosphere of a complex ritual, bureaucratic and commercial centre like Great Zimbabwe. Monolithic, authoritarian, militaristic, it was in many ways a less attractive system than the old confederations, but there was no doubt that it was a highly efficient one.[1]

The character of the Ndebele state had been largely determined by its history. 'Its beginnings were small', writes Mr Brown, 'and its expansion rapid.' The first Ndebele King, Mzilikazi, left his homeland as a Zulu general fleeing from the anger of Shaka with a following of only a few hundred. 'Subsequently other fugitives from Zululand, some with and some without previous ties to Mzilikazi, had to be incorporated, as well as thousands of Sotho and Tswana captives.' The Ndebele horde was heterogenous enough, then, when it arrived in the 1830s in the country of the Rozwi Mambos. Thereafter it assimilated 'large numbers of former inhabitants of the Rozwi empire' and 'absorbed a steady stream of captives from the medley of tribes periodically raided by Matabele war bands'. Faced with the problem of unifying these various groups in one system, the Ndebele Kings modified Zulu institutions and produced their own strikingly successful military state.[2]

This state derived its unity and discipline almost exclusively from the institution of monarchy. 'The fiction was that the king

---

[1] For the Ndebele state see, A. J. B. Hughes and J. Van Velsen, 'The Ndebele' in *The Shona and Ndebele of Southern Rhodesia*, 1955; A. J. B. Hughes, *Reconstruction of the Ndebele Society under European control*, unpublished typescript deposited in 1956 at the Rhodes Livingstone Institute, Lusaka; A. J. B. Hughes, *Kin, Caste and Nation among the Rhodesian Ndebele*, Lusaka, 1956; R. Brown, 'Aspects of the Scramble for Matabeleland' in *The Zambesian Past*, eds. E. T. Stokes and R. Brown, Manchester, 1966.   [2] R. Brown, op. cit.

was the source of all authority, and that all land, cattle, and people belonged to him. He was the supreme commander of the army and the supreme judge. All major decisions should be made by him, and only he had the power of life and death over his subjects. He was the centre of the great annual ceremony of the Inxwala, the First Fruits Ceremony . . . which was the biggest ceremony of the Ndebele nation and which everyone tried to attend. . . . The king was informed of every detail of what happened in his country; of casualties or births among his herds of cattle, of domestic incidents among his people, of the arrival and movements of Europeans, and so on'. 'This idea', wrote Father Hartmann in 1893, 'that every one of the nation is gravitating towards their chief, brings in a forcible way home to them that they are a compact mass, a force of collected strength, and therefore invincible.' [1]

The Ndebele king was not merely the 'fictional' centre of the state; both Mzilikazi and Lobengula were also its actual directors, possessing a remarkable grasp of administrative detail, and informed, through the device of placing the queens in the various regimental kraals, of all important developments. Both were men of outstanding ability and the Ndebele state never faced the problem of a weak and indolent monarch endeavouring to operate the institutions of royal absolutism.

In so far as was possible the system was designed to eliminate principles of sectional loyalty. The Ndebele nation was socially organized on a caste basis rather than into tribal or clan divisions, and there was therefore less danger of a regional or kin combination against the central authority. 'A significant feature', writes Mr Brown, 'was the absence of any strong genealogical basis for the political structure which must have reduced the tendency otherwise usually strong in this type of "snow-ball" state to disintegrate by fission.' Gathered around their king, the Ndebele nation, composed of so many different elements, nevertheless held tightly together.

The administrative arrangements, no less than the ethos of the Ndebele system, sprang from the military life of the nation. The area of Ndebele settlement was divided into four provinces, each under its 'great chief' or senior *induna*. Each province was divided

[1] Hughes and Van Velsen, op. cit. Father Hartmann's article on the Ndebele, Aug. 1893, LO 5/2/29.

into regimental areas, grouped around large regimental kraals or towns. These towns were known only by the name of the regiment which occupied them. Each regiment was commanded by its *induna*, and the provincial senior *indunas* also commanded their own particular regiments and regimental towns. These *indunas* were the most powerful group in the Ndebele nation under the king, but their power sprang from his appointment rather than from any hereditary right to chieftainship, or from any ritual function. Already existing regiments were maintained by the recruitment of youths born and reared in the regimental towns, but some of these, together with other youths recruited from the Kalanga peoples of the Matopos or captured in raids on the Shona, were summoned to form new regiments. They underwent a rigorous period of training at the royal kraal, and after being formed into a new regiment they were regarded as being on probation until they had proved themselves in war, when they would be allowed to wear the head-ring and be permitted to marry. There was considerable rivalry among the regiments and the prestige of the crack regiments was very great; there was never any difficulty in recruiting volunteers from the lowest caste, the Lozwi or Holi, who were formed from the Shona-speaking inhabitants of the area. But command of the system was kept firmly in the hands of the superior caste, the Zansi, from whom virtually all regimental commanders and other officials were drawn. The system obviously depended upon continued military operations against the surrounding peoples in the form of the raids which we have already discussed.

The area in which this system operated was a compact one. 'The area of dense and permanent settlement', write Hughes and Van Velsen, 'was mostly confined to the flat country immediately to the north of the Zambesi–Limpopo watershed, and did not even extend very far from their original settlement at Intabas Induna. In the time of Lobengula there do not seem to have been more than a few permanent settlements more than about 30 or 40 miles from Bulawayo. It was therefore possible for nearly everyone in the kingdom . . . to have frequent and regular contact with the capital.' It was also possible for the king to pay regular visits to the regimental kraals. Within this compact area were some forty regimental towns, and an army of 15,000 to 20,000 men.[1]

[1] Hughes and Van Velsen, op. cit.

This formidable military system was not despised by the whites in the 1890s, as was Shona society, but it was bitterly hated by them, and hated as much for its self-confidence and self-sufficiency as for its brutality. The Ndebele system, though flexible enough to adapt itself to the needs of so heterogenous a society, was in many ways essentially conservative; whether in military tactics or agricultural methods it did not feel that it needed to learn from white men and it was animated by a pride in its own achievements which whites felt as an intolerable arrogance. 'I abhor the Matabele,' wrote Selous to his mother, and he was expressing the common feeling of almost all the hunters, traders and prospectors who had come into contact with the Ndebele state. Moreover this hatred was shared by the missionaries who had been working among the Ndebele in what Mr Brown has called 'a thirty years' quarantine', tolerated and sometimes exploited but isolated and totally without influence on the people. 'Their lack of success', writes Brown of the missionaries, 'made them natural, if qualified, supporters of Rhodes. Unlike their brethren in Nyasaland, they had been able to build up no vested interest to conflict with those of other Europeans.' The missionaries had come to believe that Ndebele society presented no opportunities for development towards commerce and civilization, let alone Christianity, and they saw the Ndebele as a people 'whose military system and caste tradition prevents the hope of their ever being brought, as a whole, into the circle of civilized nations'. Thus they frankly welcomed the arrival of white power in Mashonaland. 'We are very thankful for the result,' wrote Elliot and Carnegie of the London Missionary Society Matabeleland mission, congratulating Rhodes on the successful occupation of Mashonaland. 'The hateful Matabele rule is doomed. We as missionaries, with our thirty years' history behind us, have little to bind our sympathies to the Matabele people, neither can we pity the fall of their power, but we earnestly rejoice in the deliverance of the Mashona.' [1]

In what way did the missionaries expect Ndebele power to 'fall' as a result of the occupation of Mashonaland? Not at first necessarily through war. The missionaries, and others, so hated Ndebele ideas of society, and were in contrast so confident of the

[1] Selous to his mother, 30 Apr. 1890, SE 1/1/1; Elliot and Carnegie to Rhodes, 2 Dec. 1890, Rhodes House, Mss. Afr. s. 228, Vol. C. 3A.

evident superiority of European ideas, that they believed that there existed at least a potential opposition group within Matabeleland itself and that the Ndebele state would be subverted by internal dissension as the example of the European way of life began to exert its influence. Thus Carnegie argued in his *Among the Matabele* that Lobengula himself constituted 'the great obstacle to progress', and that his rule was provoking discontent both among the 'people' and among the Zansi aristocracy. Carnegie argued that the Holi caste resented their obligations to serve their superiors and wished rather to seek work in the Transvaal or Mashonaland. 'The disposition to work and be independent grows among the people.' At the same time, he asserted, the more substantial *indunas* wished to accumulate property, engage in trade, develop land, acquire European goods such as ploughs, wagons and so forth, but were prevented from moving in this progressive direction by the king's interdict on commerce, by the traditional system of land and cattle holding, and by the fear of attracting jealousy and denunciation for witchcraft as the result of too apparent prosperity. Other missionaries agreed with these assertions. J. S. Moffat, for instance, then a British official at Lobengula's court, wrote in November 1890: 'There are disintegrating forces at work here the action of which is accelerated almost month by month. There is a continuous stream of work people between here and Johannesburg and a silent revolution is going on.' The Reverend John Mackenzie argued that the opening up of the Mashonaland gold mines would accelerate this process and 'alienate the Matabele men from their warlike and cruel ways. They would get good wages and would be able to go back to their people inside Matabeleland proper when they desired to do so. . . . In the course of time it would bring on a crisis; the Chief, perhaps with a majority, but not with all the tribe, would desire to remove rather than have his military power slowly undermined. . . . But if, on the other hand, the Chief enjoyed his royalty payments, and with his headmen agreed that the gold mining was to them also a profitable thing, his power with his people as a military despot would gradually pass away, the customs of the tribe would change, and the rest of the gold mines would eventually be opened up without any huge convulsion.' [1]

[1] D. Carnegie, *Among the Matabele*; Moffat to Colquhoun, 8 Nov. 1890, CT 1/1/5; R. Brown, op. cit.

Thus it was believed that the Ndebele system might well break up as a result of pressures from within. Alternatively, after the occupation of Mashonaland it was believed with perhaps more reason that the restraints this placed on Ndebele raiding would provoke a crisis between the young warriors and the king. In 1890 and 1891 there were constant speculations about the likelihood of a civil war in Matabeleland in which the Company could profitably intervene. Neither set of expectations was realized and by 1893 the missionaries were coming to believe that the forces for progress in Ndebele society were not strong enough to develop unless the military system were overthrown from outside. 'Nothing now seems possible but to await new opportunities,' wrote Carnegie. The kind of opportunities he was awaiting are made clear in a report by Captain Lendy of the Company police after a visit to Bulawayo and conversations with Carnegie in January 1893. 'It is amusing to hear the missionaries talk,' wrote Lendy. 'Regular fire-brands, they admit that the sword alone will christianize the natives.' Carnegie and his colleagues therefore supported the invasion of Matabeleland which came later in 1893 and rejoiced in the overthrow of Lobengula. 'We expect great things,' wrote Carnegie. 'Now is the grand opportunity of Christianizing the Matabele.' [1]

The important thing to appreciate is that while the Company made use of the missionaries for its own ends, employing them to obtain a favourable press for the Matabele war, Company officials themselves shared these missionary beliefs. They too assumed after 1893, as an article of faith, that many of the Matabele welcomed the overthrow of the old system and that the way had been opened for peaceful and progressive development. In the light of what we shall have to say about Company policy in Matabeleland in a later chapter, such a belief may well appear cynical but it was certainly genuinely if somewhat carelessly held. Affected by this general optimism, the High Commissioner's representative reported to him in January 1894 that the Ndebele 'seemed greatly relieved when told that the military system of the country had been abolished and that henceforth they were freed from all liability to serve as fighting men. . . . All steps taken tended to the abolition of the Matabele military system and the substitution of the right of individuals to own land and cattle for the national

---

[1] Lendy's report, 25 Jan. 1893, LO 5/2/26; Carnegie, op. cit.

custom by virtue of which everything in the country was considered the king's property, and only lent to the inhabitants.' The Holi, it was believed, welcomed a new freedom of movement and opportunity of choice of employment; the Zansi welcomed the new security of property right and opportunity to improve their land.

Rhodes himself argued in January 1895 that there was a wide acceptance among the Ndebele of the superiority of the new system. 'From a sentimental point of view,' he told the shareholders of the Company, with a somewhat significant choice of words, 'I will say this—that I visited the territory the other day and saw nearly all the chiefs of the Matabele and I may say that they were all pleased and naturally so. In the past they have always "walked delicately" because anyone who got to any position in the country and became rich was generally "smelt out" and lost his life. You can understand,' he told the sympathetic shareholders, 'that life was not very pleasant under these conditions. In so far as the bulk of the people were concerned, they were not allowed to hold any cattle, or to possess anything of their own. Now they can hold cattle and the leaders of the people know that they do not walk daily with the fear of death over them.' And even after the rising, Colenbrander, the first Chief Native Commissioner of Matabeleland, found himself able to argue that the Ndebele had been consciously better off under Company rule. 'It is better,' he told the Bulawayo committee of inquiry in December 1896. 'Then it was dangerous to become rich. . . . Under the Chartered Company rule they have proper trial. . . . Everything belonged to the King in early days; now a native can own property and his life is safe. . . . He can go and work while before the Ama Holi race could not go where they liked, everything they brought back from the fields had to be handed over to the Matabele.' [1]

With these beliefs whites allowed themselves to be persuaded that the Ndebele had gladly submitted to their rule. 'Since the war the Matabeles have never given the least trouble,' wrote the missionary Helm in 1896. 'The people have undergone a wonderful change since Lobengula's time and were so submissive that

---

[1] Major Sawyer's report, 16 Jan. 1894, *C. 7290*, Enclosure in No. 95; Rhodes' speech to the Fourth Ordinary General Meeting, 18 Jan. 1895; Colenbrander's evidence, 3 Dec. 1896, *C. 8547*, appendix 7.

anything in the nature of a revolt seemed out of the question.' [1]

In making these estimates the Company's officers and other whites were victims of a delusion as old as British interest in African development. Rhodes might well have written of Mashonaland and Matabeleland in the 1890s what Sir Joseph Banks wrote of West Africa in 1799: 'A trading Company might be established under immediate control of the Government, who could take upon themselves the whole expense of the measure, would govern the Negros far more mildly and make them far more happy than they are now under the tyranny of their arbitrary princes, would become popular at home by converting them to the Christian religion by inculcating in their rough minds the mild morality which is engrafted on the tenets of our faith and by effecting the greatest practicable diminution of the Slavery of Mankind, upon the principles of natural justice and commercial benefit.' But the inhabitants of Southern Africa no more than those of West Africa desired to be made more happy by being freed from the tyranny of their arbitrary princes. What Sir Phillip Magnus has written of the Sudan was true of the subjects of Lobengula and other Nguni monarchs; Lobengula, like the Khalifa, might seem to the whites 'a brutal tyrant, but he effectively symbolized the nationalist aspirations of the peoples over whom he ruled. They had no desire to be liberated and showed themselves willing to die in their tens of thousands. . . . The sole argument which served to reconcile them to the acceptance of foreign rule was the overwhelming superiority of modern weapons.' [2]

A recent example of the fallacious character of these white expectations, which might have been borne in mind in the 1890s, was the failure of the British Government's Zulu policy. In 1878 the British had presented the Zulu King, Cetshwayo, with an ultimatum to the effect that he must abolish his military system, institute a proper system of trial by courts, and encourage his people in their agricultural pursuits. 'So will the King have contented subjects.' But as a recent authority on the Zulu under Cetshwayo has pointed out these demands were based on a total

---

[1] Statement by C. D. Helm, *The Times*, 2 Apr. 1896.

[2] Banks to Liverpool, 8 Sept. 1799, cited in R. Hallett, 'The European approach to the interior of Africa', *The Journal of African History*, IV, 2, 1963; P. Magnus, *Kitchener*, London, 1958.

misconception. 'No doubt it was believed that the Zulus would welcome this reform and so withdraw their support from the King. But such a belief showed an utter lack of understanding of the Zulu character, for the Zulus willingly submitted to certain hardships and disadvantages and were proud to belong to those great armies which had swept over the continent, vanquished all their enemies, and given them the reputation of being the greatest warriors among all the African races.'[1] The ultimatum was followed by war with the Zulu nation.

In exactly the same way white beliefs in the 1890s were based on 'an utter lack of understanding' of Ndebele character and of the history of the Ndebele state. Recent students of the Ndebele have agreed that so far from their system containing within itself inevitable sources of disintegration it was growing in strength until the arrival of the whites, and Mr Hughes has gone so far as to suggest that but for the colonial interruption the Ndebele and other Nguni peoples might have exercised an immense and shaping influence on the whole of southern African society. And once European pressures were experienced, these students stress, the Ndebele state proved 'highly resistant' to them. In a valuable paper Mr Brown has shown the unbroken success and prestige of the Ndebele system up to the 1890s; stressed that 'of all the conquest states resulting from the Nguni or Zulu revolution of the early nineteenth century, the Matabele state would appear to have gone furthest in solving the problem of assimilating conquered peoples'; and pointed out that prior to the 1890s the Ndebele state had successfully survived 'some serious challenges to its integrity'. Ndebele society was not broken up by the defeats it suffered at the hands of the Boers in 1837 and 1838, nor by the migrations which followed; its unity survived the death of Mzilikazi and the disputed succession of Lobengula. What the whites encountered in the Ndebele state was not merely an obstinate tyrant clinging to outmoded ways but what J. S. Moffat called a 'social system still in its aboriginal vigour' and despite the best efforts of missionaries, hunters, traders and concession seekers they failed to make much impact on Ndebele society until they were able to overthrow it. 'Matabele society was inherently unsuited to adapting easily to the incursion of European power in

[1] C. T. Binns, *The Last Zulu King*, London, 1963.

the scramble for Africa,' writes Mr Brown, 'and it neither collapsed nor was transformed, but was swept aside.' [1]

And after the defeat of 1893 the great majority of the Ndebele
castes remained loyal to a system which had enabled them to feel
pride in 'the reputation of being the greatest warriors among all
the African races'. Even if it had been true that the Company
administration guaranteed private property rights, trial by regular courts, and so on, this would have been quite beside the point.
Even the majority of the Lozwi or Holi caste continued to feel
themselves part of the Ndebele nation—'the extent of the political
achievement', writes Mr Brown, 'in constructing this powerful
and centralized state is indicated by there being today some three
quarters of a million people in Southern Rhodesia who consider
themselves to be Matabele—though, of course, having wider
affiliations—and who speak Sindebele.' So far from their complacent belief that the old Ndebele system had passed away even
from the loyalties of the people, whites in the 1890s would have
done well to ponder the warning of Major Leonard of the Company Police, who was afraid that his countrymen would once
again undervalue an enemy. 'It does not seem within the bounds
of common sense', wrote Leonard, 'to suppose that a nation of
ferocious savages . . . will allow us quietly to take possession of a
country which is virtually theirs by right of conquest without in
any way resenting it. To imagine it even is a direct insult.' And
they might have applied to the years immediately after the 1893
war the reflection which Leonard applied to the years immediately
before it: 'Talking of our old friend, the Matabele question, how
quickly and how quietly it has died a natural death!—unnatural,
I should say, or to be still more accurate, not death, but a temporary relegation to a back seat, eventually to take the stalls, or even
the boards, by storm.' [2]

---

[1] Hughes, op. cit.; Brown, op. cit.
[2] A. G. Leonard, *How we made Rhodesia*, London, 1896.

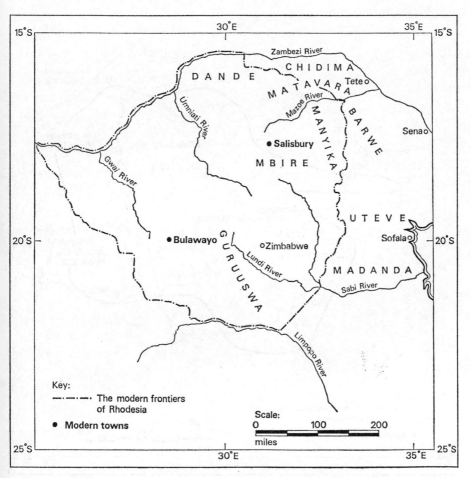

1. The Provinces of the Mwene Mutapa Confederacy at its height, *c.* 1500 A.D. (*based on a map by Donald Abraham*).

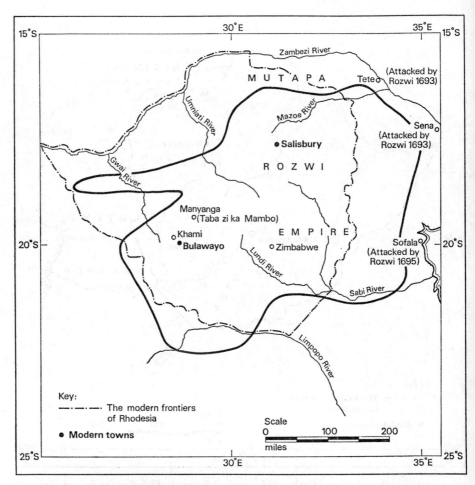

2. The Rozwi Confederacy at the height of its power, *c.* 1700 A.D.
(*based on a map by Roger Summers*).

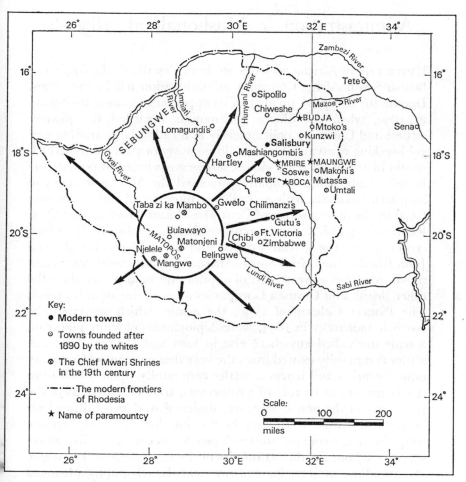

Key:
● Modern towns
⊙ Towns founded after
   1890 by the whites
⊛ The Chief Mwari Shrines
   in the 19th century
—·—·— The modern frontiers
   of Rhodesia
★ Name of paramountcy

Scale:
0   100   200

miles

3. Approximate areas of Ndebele settlement and of regular
raiding and tribute collections *c.* 1830–*c.* 1890.

CHAPTER TWO

Administration in Mashonaland, 1890–6

UPON THESE African societies we have described, the impact of British South Africa Company administration fell in the 1890s. Despite the deceptive manner of its appearance among the Shona in 1890, when the Shona paramounts regarded the pioneer settlers and Company police merely as a rather large trading and gold-seeking caravan which would go away or pass on and which would in any event not seek to exercise governmental powers, the British South Africa Company presented the African societies of Southern Rhodesia with a challenge more formidable than that faced by the other peoples of Central and East Africa at that time. Representing as it did the expansive energies of the South African economy and the private fortune and personal dreams of Cecil John Rhodes, the British South Africa Company could draw upon much greater resources both of capital and man-power than the other British and German Companies at work during this period. The Pioneer Column of 1890, the armies which shattered the Ndebele monarchy in 1893, were deployments of white power on a scale unrivalled anywhere else in East and Central Africa. A settler community existed from the very first moment of Company administration and it was a settler community upon which from the beginning in its role of prospectors, traders and farmers the prosperity of the new colony was designed to depend. Elsewhere in tropical Africa territories in the interior, relatively remote from the sea, remained undeveloped for decades, serving as reserves of labour for the economies of the coastal areas. Elsewhere the grandiose projects for railways, canals, telegraphs advanced by the young adventurers whom Professor Brunschwig has described as 'dreamers with empty hands' collapsed through the disinterest of hard-headed capital. Rhodes, however, was a dreamer with full pockets. Despite all difficulties and especially his failure to gain access to the sea, Southern Rhodesia *was* developed at a quite unusual rate. The railway arrived in Bulawayo in 1897, only four years after the occupation of

Matabeleland; it was with this vision of communications extending further and further north and ending their isolation that Rhodes tempted his missionary collaborators in the interior. Rhodes, as Milner wrote in 1897, was 'a great developer'.

It was against this background of relative strength and expansion that the white confidence which we have already described grew up. Feeling themselves strong, feeling themselves in touch with the South African colonies, whites in Rhodesia, whether settlers or administrators, did not pay that cautious respect to African military potential which characterized colonial regimes to the north. In so far as they were able to do so—and their strength was only comparative—they presented the implications of colonial rule and of a settler economy to the Africans of Southern Rhodesia with no concessions at all.

This strong white impulse met the African societies we have described, with their hidden strengths. One of the results was the outbreak of 1896 and the fierce contest between the two systems which followed. But the question remains: how far was such a contest inevitable in the face of Shona and Ndebele determination to defend their 'way of life'? Or how far was it intensified, perhaps even provoked, by maladministration or by unwise pressure?

Company and settler apologists, once they had recovered from their astonishment at the risings, argued that they had been inevitable irrespective of the character of Company administration. The Shona, grumbled Selous, would have resented a government of archangels and made a determined effort to steal their harps. More soberly Lord Grey, Administrator of Southern Rhodesia during the risings, asserted that 'universal experience in South Africa has proved that until the Kaffirs are convinced by failure that it is useless for them to try and struggle against the power of the white man, they will fret under his yoke and get rid of it if they can. . . . This being admitted, it would appear to be unnecessary to search for recondite causes of the rising in administrative mistakes'.[1]

In many ways this attitude, with its recognition of African determination to defend their 'independence', with its setting of the 1896 risings in the context of 'the history of the Eastern Province' of the Cape and of 'frontier history' generally, in the long sequence of 'Kaffir wars and rebellions during close on half

[1] Lord Grey's reply to Sir Richard Martin's report, June 1897, C. 8547.

a century', is closer to the truth than the arguments of the humanitarians of the 1890s. It was not true, for instance, as the American critic of the Company, J. E. Y. Blake, asserted, that the Ndebele and Shona were 'naturally servile and harmless' and could only have been driven to fight by atrocious ill-treatment. Nor was it true, as the Aborigines Protection Society argued, that the African peoples of Southern Rhodesia were 'submissive to the just laws of the country and were very tractable'. What was at issue in 1896 was an African repudiation of the white claim to make any laws at all.[1]

But if the philanthropists underestimated the desire of Africans for independence Company apologists undoubtedly underestimated also the important role played in the risings by the character of Company administration. After all, in other colonial situations African peoples devoted to their 'way of life' were sometimes brought to accept colonial rule through judicious concession; sometimes again the challenge to the way of life of some societies was made over so long a period of time that the power to resist was slowly sapped; and in some cases where resistance was offered it was offered only by members of the old ruling groups and did not involve the mass of the people, whose lives were often not much affected by colonial rule in its first years. The rapidity and above all the totality of African reaction in Southern Rhodesia cannot be explained merely in terms of a generalized will to resist, but must be explained also in terms of the peculiar pressure of Company rule.

In fact the British Deputy Commissioner, Sir Richard Martin, stated the relationship between administration and resistance very fairly in his report on the causes of the 1896–7 risings. The Company believed, wrote Martin, that 'all heart had been knocked out of the natives, and that they were . . . at liberty to impose what laws and place what exactions they thought fit upon them, without fear of retaliation'. Such a view defied 'common prudence' which suggested that the Company should use 'every endeavour to conciliate the natives to their rule'. In reality Africans in Southern Rhodesia were determined to regain their

---

[1] *Cape Argus*, 12 Aug. 1897; *Cape Times*, 25 Oct. 1897; evidence of John Harris, 17 Dec. 1919, CMD. 1129. B. *Southern Rhodesia: minutes of the proceedings of the Commission appointed to take account of what would have been due to the British South Africa company*, 1921.

independence. 'The only possible chance that the Government had of preventing this attempt to regain their lost position was the establishment of a strong and able Native administration and one which should have considered the conciliation and welfare of the Natives as the all important object to aim at.' [1]

We must now ask why the Company failed to establish such a Native administration and what was, in fact, the character of its native policy.

In 1893 Dr Jane Waterston, whom Rhodes' most recent biographers describe as 'one of the few women who knew him well', wrote a letter to Rhodes, expressing her hopes for the constructive use of his new power. 'You are now virtually ruler of the natives from here to Tanganyika,' she wrote, 'a position that Providence has never assigned to any man before. Your brother, Mr Herbert Rhodes, had the peculiar gift for attracting and attaching black men to himself that is sometimes given to Englishmen. I have an idea that if you were to exert it that gift is given to you. . . . Now, Sir, you have come to a point in your career where you never stood before. I plead for no sickly cant or sentiment but I do ask that you, who will shortly be known by the natives as "the Great White Chief" will treat them as men with English justice, and will find out those that are really climbing out of the old state, and give them a fair field, if no favour. Strict justice and the word of the white chief his bond is the only way to rule the native aright. . . . It is surely something to be in history not only the great Englishman who saved us Central Africa but also the great chief that ruled the many thousands of natives wisely and well. The one you have done; the other you are capable of doing. May you be delivered from being one of those to whom the grandest opportunities have been given by Providence and who have flung them away.' [2]

Something like these expectations were shared by some of Rhodes' associates. Lord Grey, for instance, expressed the view to Rhodes in December 1891 that 'objectionable German methods' must be avoided in Central Africa and that the chiefs must be persuaded that 'the Queen has spread her wing over the country

---

[1] C. 8547. British South Africa company's territories: report by Sir R. E. R. Martin on the native administration of the British South Africa Company, together with a letter from the company commenting upon that report, 1892.

[2] Jane Waterston to Rhodes, ? 1893, Rhodes House, Mss. Afr. s. 228, C. 27.

not for the purpose of crushing them but with the view of helping the chiefs in the difficult work of self protection and development. I have always hoped that when the Natives outside that part of the map which by your energy has been coloured red, compare our methods with those employed by Germany and the Congo Free State we should be able to get everything we want.' [1]

At the least, negative expectations were expressed, as in Shepstone's letter to Rhodes in May 1891. 'I always feared that the Chartered Company's territory would become the prey of white adventurers forming centres of petty independent sovereignties, amenable to nothing and guided by nothing but their own special ambitions and interests. . . . Your Company is amenable to the British Government and to British public opinion, so that whatever mistakes it may make, it cannot go radically wrong, and this is what makes me anxious for its success.' [2]

In the event all these expectations were disappointed. So far from the Ndebele and Shona having a firm impression of 'strict justice and the word of the white chief his bond', they bitterly resented what they regarded as a long history of sharp practice and arbitrary action. So far from Africans outside the Company's territories looking to them as a model, Africans within them broke out in 1896 and 1897 into desperate and savage rebellions which profoundly and adversely affected relations between black and white throughout southern Africa. So far from restraining the individual 'ambitions and interests' of white adventurers and settlers the Company allowed these a very free hand, and despite the control of the British government and British public opinion went very 'radically wrong' in the Jameson Raid and many other ways. Why was this?

Our answer must start with Cecil Rhodes himself, since he more than anyone or anything shaped the attitudes and policies of the early Rhodesian administration. It was Rhodes who enjoyed the complete trust of the London Board of the Company and was given their full power of attorney to act in Rhodesia; it was he who insisted on the appointment as Administrator there of a man 'conversant not only with the internal history of the Company and the native affairs of the North, but also one who for the last five years has had the closest personal relations with himself and

[1] Grey to Rhodes, 25 Dec. 1891, ibid., C. 3A.
[2] Shepstone to Rhodes, 8 May 1891, ibid.

is therefore imbued with his views and aims in the North'; and through Jameson, thus appointed, it was Rhodes' views and aims which prevailed. What, then, were Rhodes' views on the 'Native Question'?[1]

Rhodes' biographers have disputed as to whether he regarded Africans as children or as animals, as potential men or predestined objects. In fact the most important thing about Rhodes' views and aims was that he did not really pay much regard to Africans at all. He had, of course, to deal with Khama and Lewanika and with Lobengula before 1893 and while they were in a position to affect his 'views and aims' he devoted a good deal of time and care to persuading them or compelling them to pursue the courses he desired. But even then the exercise was an abstract one. Despite Lobengula's wish, Rhodes never met the Ndebele monarch personally and there was little opportunity to test whether Rhodes had the intuition and sympathy to understand an African point of view when he came into contact with it or whether he possessed his brother's gifts of 'attracting and attaching black men to himself' until the rising had broken out. Then, in the famous Matopos indaba, which is described below, Rhodes showed that Dr Waterston's estimate of him had not been entirely wrong; but by then it was too late. And once Rhodes had gained his point in his relations with these African monarchs he ceased to occupy his mind with consideration of their subjects. After 1893, for instance, it did not occur to Rhodes that the Ndebele were any longer a factor which had to be taken into account in adumbrating his plans for the north, and he never supposed that the Shona were. Once Mashonaland was occupied and Matabeleland conquered Rhodes felt no need to evolve any continuous native policy or to erect any regular machinery of native administration. It was typical of him that he employed a Native Commissioner in 1890 to assist in the negotiations with Mutassa of Manyika and with king Gungunhana, but that Native Commissioners in the normal sense of officers appointed to regulate and protect the Shona peoples were not appointed until the end of 1894, and even then only because some machinery was needed for the collection of the hut tax.[2]

Such a carelessness may well seem astonishing. Rhodes was

[1] Harris to London Board, 1 Dec. 1890, LO 5/2/5.
[2] See, T. O. Ranger, 'The Last Word on Rhodes?', *Past and Present*, No. 28, July 1964.

assisted in feeling it because of his willing belief in the general white illusions already described. When he thought of the subject at all he believed that the Shona and the Ndebele 'were all pleased and naturally so' by the arrival of the whites; that in the white opening up of Rhodesia the Shona had incidentally been delivered from the Ndebele and the Ndebele had incidentally been delivered from themselves. He would have defended himself against liberal attack on these lines though certainly these results were very much incidentals rather than essentials of his great designs. As for the future Rhodes believed that if Africans were capable of taking advantage of the new opportunities their society would be transformed; if not they would go to the wall. His views were a mingling of the classic doctrines of *Laisser Faire* and the Survival of the Fittest.

Rhodes' neglect of the necessity of establishing 'a strong and able Native administration and one which should have considered the conciliation and welfare of the Natives as the all important object' arose also out of his dislike for the forms of regular administration. A percipient member of the Mashonaland police noted in 1891 that Rhodes' *alter ego*, Jameson, regarded regular officers as machines 'evolved out of an amalgamation of red-tape and sealing wax', and commented: 'Jameson does not believe in excessive formality but in attaining the object by the nearest and quickest method; and it would take very little to induce either Rhodes or himself, should the occasion present itself, or the emergency arise, to ride rough-shod over forms or amenities and rules or regulations'. It was precisely for this quality in Jameson that Rhodes insisted that he be made Administrator in place of the first appointee, Colquhoun, of whom Rhodes wrote disparagingly that he would make 'an admirable official with regard to departmental details and to the organization of the Company's procedure'. With Colquhoun's departure any chance of the erection of a regular and satisfactory administrative system in Rhodesia was lost. Jameson's government of the whites was thus described by a settler lawyer in 1896: 'He may be regarded as simply a beneficent despot; he did not act on rules and regulations; he acted as each individual case led him; he did his best.' His government of the African peoples was even more haphazard.[1]

[1] Leonard, op. cit; Harris to London Board, 1 Dec. 1890, LO 5/2/5; evidence of Robert Hovell, 8 Dec. 1896, *C. 8547.*

In any case it was not with matters of 'departmental detail' that Rhodes and Jameson were concerned but with their far-ranging and ambitious aims for the north. To them Mashonaland, and later Matabeleland, were merely bases from which to launch further assaults. There was little time or money to spare for building up the base itself; all attention was given to reaching Beira and the sea, or acquiring Gazaland, or pushing north to Barotseland, or establishing rights in Bechuanaland, or overthrowing the Kruger regime in the Transvaal. 'Rhodes is a great developer,' wrote Milner in 1897, 'but he is not a good administrator.' What in fact Rhodes was above all was a great gambler—the sending in of the ill-prepared and ill-led Pioneer Column in 1890 was a gamble; the concentration on the push to the sea despite the threat of Ndebele action in the rear was a gamble; the Ndebele war of 1893 was a gamble; so supremely was the Jameson Raid of 1895. And so was Rhodes' failure to build up a Native Department to control and conciliate the African peoples of Rhodesia. It was, of course, an unsuccessful gamble for which the price was paid in 1896.[1]

Rhodes' errors in this field were both of commission and omission. As we shall see he was unscrupulous in the methods by which he destroyed the Ndebele state and unjust in the treatment of the Ndebele over land and cattle after their conquest. But above all his error was one of omission. However lightly he wore his belief that white settlement was also for the good of the Africans, Rhodes did not will or institute deliberate policies of brutality towards them. But because of his convenient conviction that all would be well without any effort on the part of the Company, because of his diversion of most of his resources and nearly all his talented men into other ventures; because of his consequent dependence upon the farmer and settler in Rhodesia itself, a situation inevitably arose in which the African peoples were not merely unconciliated but also abused and maltreated. 'The blacks have been scandalously used,' wrote Milner. 'A lot of unfit people,' he alleged, 'were allowed to exercise power, or at any rate did exercise it, especially with regard to the natives.' Rhodesia had become after all not far from 'the prey of white adventurers'. Rhodes chose to ignore this and in this respect as in many others

[1] Milner to Selborne, 2 June 1897, *The Milner Papers*, ed. C. Headlam, London, 1931, Vol. 1, pp. 105–8.

c

the judgement of history will certainly have to be that he was 'one of those to whom the grandest opportunities have been given by Providence and who have flung them away'.[1]

To give these generalizations more particularity and to show how the settler 'man on the spot' was allowed to dominate 'native affairs' we must examine administration first in Mashonaland and then in Matabeleland.

In fairness to Rhodes and to the officers of the Company it must be admitted that the task of building up an administration in Mashonaland was greatly complicated by the attitude of the British Government. That Government was prepared to recognize the right of the Company to send men into Mashonaland and to work mines there, though in defiance of the wishes of Lobengula, but it was not prepared to recognize that the Company possessed any powers of administration even over whites, let alone over the Shona. In September 1890 the Colonial Office made it plain to the London Board of the Company that 'the Company has not received from Lobengula any authority to exercise such sovereign rights as are implied by setting up courts of justice, imposing fines and penalties, declaring what acts shall constitute crimes or offences and attaching penalties to such acts'. Until such time as the Ndebele king granted specific authority to exercise such sovereign rights the Company was debarred from doing so. This was, of course, a perfectly accurate reading of the powers ceded by Lobengula in the Rudd Concession, on which the Company's claim to enter Mashonaland was based. But it was an absurdity in practical terms. It was highly unreasonable to suppose that large numbers of white men could enter Mashonaland without creating all sorts of problems of jurisdiction and if the Company were debarred from exercising authority over them, or over the Shona, it was inevitable that they would become a law unto themselves.[2]

This British refusal to approve the exercise of judicial powers was merely one of the factors which made the first Administrator,

---

[1] Milner to Chamberlain, 1 Dec. 1897; Milner to Asquith, 18 Nov. 1897, *ibid.*, pp. 139 to 146, 177.

[2] Colonial Office to London Board, 16 Sept. 1890, LO 8/3/1; for a full discussion of the legal situation in Mashonaland during the first year of Company administration see, Claire Palley, *The Constitutional History and Law of Southern Rhodesia, 1888–1965*, Oxford, 1966, chap. 3.

Colquhoun, and the commander of the police, Pennefather, so uneasy with the position in which they found themselves. Both were men temperamentally unsuited to the gamble upon which they were engaged; both desired to establish things in Mashonaland on what they regarded as a proper footing before going on with any more of Rhodes' plans. Colquhoun wanted more clerks and administrators; Pennefather wanted more police. 'Isn't it absurd?' wrote Rutherfoord Harris, the Company's Kimberley secretary, when Pennefather demanded more men to meet all his commitments in January 1891. 'He pictures us having to face (1) Loben, (2) Portuguese, (3) Boers, (4) Gungunhana, *all* simultaneously, but as I have written and told him, we *cannot* raise troops for the deluge.' The invaluable Jameson was asked 'to instil some of his strong common sense, coupled with "balls", into him.' [1]

But if Harris thought Pennefather a 'Cassandra. Troublesome officer', and quarrelled violently with Colquhoun because on matters of importance correspondence tended to be sent direct from Kimberley to Jameson rather than to the 'red-tape' minded Administrator, there was much more to be said for their view than either Harris or Rhodes were prepared to concede. Something certainly needed to be done to put Company administration in Mashonaland in order, especially with regard to 'native affairs'. On this Colquhoun and Pennefather put forward suggestions which, if followed, might have given some sort of basis of local consent and acceptance of the Company presence in Mashonaland. Impressed, as we have seen in the preceding chapter, with the evidence that Lobengula had not exercised any sort of effective jurisdiction over large areas of Mashonaland, they urged the necessity of making treaties with numbers of 'independent' Shona chiefs. Several such treaties were made, promising the central and eastern Shona paramounts an annual subsidy in return for mineral rights in their paramountcies. Moreover they urged that if the Company wished to exclude the Portuguese from eastern and central Mashonaland, it should be prepared to meet the cost of providing an alternative system of trade to replace the old commerce with Tete. 'All the natives who have been accustomed to trade with the Portuguese are protesting loudly that we have no stuff to barter with them,' wrote Pennefather to Rhodes in April

[1] Harris to Currey, 3 Jan. 1891, Rhodes House, Mss. Afr. s. 228, C. 3A.

1891, 'and that as we have driven the Portuguese out of the country they cannot now do any trade. There is no doubt that much more money must be spent if we are going to keep that country—but it would be well spent, and good returns might soon be got from it.' [1]

Neither of these suggestions met with any support from Rhodes. His view was that the Company's claim to Mashonaland rested on Lobengula's concession and on the British Government's acceptance that Lobengula's authority ran in the whole province; hence whatever the real situation the independence of Shona paramounts could not be recognized. As Harris expressed it in a letter to Colquhoun: 'You will yourself understand surely that everything included within the area assigned to the British south of the Zambesi is based on the recognition of Lobengula being supreme, and despite everything that Selous or anyone else says to the contrary, politically Lobengula and Lobengula alone has been and will be recognized, so that it is impolitic as well as useless to waste time and money on so called "independent Mashona chiefs"; an independent Mashonaland is an impossibility within the sphere assigned to the British but outside that sphere an independent Mashonaland and independent Mashona chiefs ought to commence exactly where the British sphere ends, and there it may flourish like a green bay tree.' Thus the treaties made with Makoni, Mtoko, Mangwende and the other paramounts were allowed to lapse; no subsidies were paid; and in future it was assumed that rights to minerals, and then rights to land, had been granted by the remote Ndebele monarch whose authority these chiefs had never recognized. This was one reason, certainly, for their hostility to the Company. [2]

Moreover, Rhodes had no intention of establishing a trade with the central and eastern Shona in alluvial gold; his interest was exclusively in the opening up of mining by white prospectors, which he thought would bring prospects of employment to the Shona that would more than make up for the loss of their trade with the Portuguese. Later, under Jameson, steps were taken to try to prevent the renewal of the trade with Tete, which was held to result in a drain of gold from the country. There is no doubt that this interference with a long-established and valued

[1] Pennefather to Rhodes, 20 Apr. 1891, ibid.
[2] Harris to Colquhoun, 20 Sept. 1890, CT 1/1/4.

commerce was another factor in African hostility to the new regime.

Since these suggestions were countermanded or disapproved, there was in the end virtually no native policy during Colquhoun's administration. Forbidden the exercise of judicial powers, he was too much of a stickler for form to venture on any unauthorized display of authority over black or white. The result, as Shona chiefs clashed with the prospectors and traders, was inevitably the growth of private 'justice'. One example will suffice. In March 1891 one Hudson of the Bechuanaland Exploration Company wrote to Colquhoun to report that as a result of theft from his stores in Mazoe he had raided the kraal of one of Goredema's headmen, burnt his huts, and exacted a fine of five cattle. 'It was common knowledge,' he told Colquhoun, 'that you had refused to give redress or in any way take notice of the alleged thieving on more than one occasion by a white man from white men, asserting that there was no law in this country; that you had in a similar way refused assistance when asked to recover goods and property as stolen by natives from white men and had asserted that you had no authority and could not protect white men and their property; that you had refused to give official or other sanction to the flogging of a native for theft or gross misconduct alleging that you could not.' Under these circumstances, concluded Hudson, 'I think when you come to consider the numerous thefts that have been committed in this country by the Mashonas upon white men I am sure you will agree with me that I was only doing my duty to my syndicate.' Colquhoun did not agree—'the steps taken were highly improper', he minuted—but Hudson's syndicate was managed by Major Frank Johnson, leader of the Pioneers, and nothing could be done to call him to account for taking the law into his own hands. Undoubtedly other whites were doing the same thing in other areas of Mashonaland.[1]

In July 1891 Colquhoun was replaced by Jameson. Ironically the bureaucrat left and the gambler came in just as steps were being taken to regularize the position of the Administrator and to allow him to exercise a limited jurisdiction. The need for some kind of control over the white population of Mashonaland was becoming obvious—without it, wrote the High Commissioner,

[1] Hudson to Colquhoun, 21 Mar. 1891; Colquhoun's minute, 26 Mar. 1891, CT 1/1/6.

'the place would become an Alsatia and a disgrace to civilization'. It was becoming equally obvious that Lobengula would
never make a grant of judicial powers to the Company. In May
1891, then, the British Government issued an Order in Council
declaring a Protectorate over Mashonaland and other areas. The
High Commissioner was to exercise 'all powers and jurisdiction
which Her Majesty . . . had or may have within the limits of this
Order, and particularly from time to time by proclamation to
provide for the administration of justice, the raising of revenue,
and generally for the peace, order and good government of all
persons within the limits of this Order', saving the rights of native
rulers. He was, as it soon transpired, to exercise these powers in
support of and by deputation to the Company administration.
Judicial officers were to be appointed by him on the Company's
recommendation; legislation by proclamation would only occur
when it seemed necessary to validate the Ordinances of the Company. In 1919 the Privy Council commented upon the pecu-
liarities of the legal situation thus created. Administration in
Mashonaland between June 1891 and the Ndebele War of 1893,
they wrote, rested 'on the assumption of jurisdiction by the Crown
within the territorial sovereignty of a native ruler, and yet subject
to the recognition of his rights as such'. This situation was, as the
Privy Council judicial committee remarked, 'inappropriate' to
anything but 'a nascent settlement'. But it allowed for the appointment of magistrates for Mashonaland and on June 27th 1891 such
officers were named for Fort Victoria, Fort Salisbury, Hartley
Hill and Umtali. Later in the year another apparent move to a
more regular system of government was taken. Colonel Pennefather then went the same way as Colquhoun and Jameson cut
down heavily on the numbers of police, substituting what he called
a 'civil' administration for the previous 'military' one.[1]

Neither of these events did much to improve African administration. For one thing the British Government made it clear to the
High Commissioner that he should 'confine the exercise of authority and the application of law, as far as possible, to whites,
leaving the Native Chiefs and those living under their tribal
authority almost entirely alone', since 'the extent of jurisdiction
exercisable by Her Majesty over the natives has not yet been

---

[1] In the Privy Council, Special Reference as to the ownership of the Unalienated Land
in Rhodesia, 29 July 1918; C. Palley, op. cit., chaps. 4 and 5.

accurately defined'. This instruction was forwarded to the Company by the Imperial Secretary who wrote in June 1891 that despite the new magistracies 'the natives and native chiefs should be left to follow their own laws and customs without interference from the officers of the administration'. Jameson disregarded this injunction when it suited him to do so but no doubt it coincided with his own inclinations to prevent the emergence of any regular system of native administration.[1]

For another thing there were very few magistrates and those that there were were often enough more representative of local white feeling or of one particular settler interest than they were loyal servants of the Company. The first magistrate of Umtali, Bruce, was described by his successor in a scathing letter of March 1892 as the chosen leader of the 'drunken' and 'caddish' white society of Umtali, as bitterly hostile to the Company, and as tolerant of settler sharp practice with regard to African labour. In Melsetter the first magistrate was the formidable Dunbar Moodie, leader of the Afrikaaner trek to that area. His use of his powers was later described by the Surveyor-General. 'Dunbar Moodie got himself recognized as the Company's representative and began charging incomers £7 10s., afterwards £10 18s., afterwards £15, for permission to settle and peg out. . . . Longden reports that he got altogether near £4000 in this way. . . . He squeezed the best cattle out of those who could not give money and he managed to confiscate the farms of some. . . . He fined Kaffirs for his own benefit.' He also forced Africans living on his very extensive farms to work for him. When in 1897 the Moodie family was compelled by a newly vigilant administration to surrender the land which they had illicitly acquired over and above the amount originally granted to them by the Company, Rhodes intervened in a way which characteristically demonstrated his preference for development over administration. He hoped, he wrote, that the Moodies would be treated generously, 'for they undoubtedly created the settlement of Melsetter and held the country against the Portuguese'. Rhodes' approach had been that prevailing before 1896; under Jameson's administration no one was much inclined to ask questions about the treatment of Africans from successful developers like Dunbar Moodie.[2]

[1] Imperial Secretary to Secretary, Kimberley, 5 June 1891, LO 5/2/9.
[2] Orpen to Rhodes, 10 Sept. 1897, Rhodes House, Mss. Afr. s. 228, C. 1;

As for the creation of the 'civil' regime at the end of 1891, the main effect of this was to make Jameson even more dependent upon the settlers. If the expensive police had been replaced by numbers of trained judicial officers and district commissioners the change might have inaugurated a new efficiency of administration. But there was no question of such a replacement for the main reason for the change was a desperate need of economy. On December 11th 1891, for instance, Jameson received 'a strictly private line' from the Secretary of the Company in Cape Town telling him 'that it is simply imperative that we must economize all along the line. If you can possibly do with less than 75 policemen for goodness sake do so, as they each cost nearly £300 p.a.' On December 18th he was told that 'the Bank will not advance another shilling. . . . Rhodes has got an awful sickener of the police. They are horribly expensive and do nothing but grumble. They must be reduced to a minimum. . . . Mr Rhodes would like you to sweep away entirely the military regime; give each Magistrate 10 policemen and then run the show as a civil administration pure and simple.' [1]

Jameson dutifully carried out these economies but, as he wrote in January 1892, the small forces of police retained in the main towns could not possibly cope with the problems arising out of the contact of Africans and Europeans throughout Mashonaland. 'In view of the recent disbandment of the military police,' he wrote, 'I would point out that the immediate appointment of Field Cornets is imperative, taking into account the numbers of native disputes and other slight troubles constantly occurring over a very wide area and the impossibility with our small civil police force (quite sufficient for ordinary police duties) of constantly sending out parties to inquire into these matters. These Field Cornets with the burghers in their several districts would, in the event of an emergency, be under the command of the Commandant of the burgher force . . . but will at the same time keep this office supplied with information as to all events occurring in their district.' Thus Jameson was proposing both for emergency defence and for the day to day settlement of disputes with the Shona to rely upon

---

Rhodes to Milton, 20 Sept. 1897, ibid., Mss. Afr. s. 227, Vol. 1; Graham to Caldecott, 6 Mar. 1892, J 1/7/1.

[1] Currey to Jameson, 11 Dec. and 18 Dec. 1891, A 1/2/2.

the settlers of Mashonaland. He recommended as Field Cornet of the Salisbury area one 'Marriott, an old Colonial Farmer with a large family who has about fifteen of his friends farming in the same district'. Other appointments were made on the same lines. In this way the involvement in African affairs of the local white farmer and prospector was taken into the official system and legitimized rather than restrained.[1]

There is a good deal of evidence to show us this system at work between 1891 and 1894. Matters of theft, labour desertion, etc., were sometimes dealt with on the spot by local farmers and traders acting as 'burghers' under the command of the Field Cornet. Thus we see, for instance, Marriott, a month after his appointment as Field Cornet of the Salisbury area, taking nine of his relatives and friends together with four policemen to deal with paramount chief Mashonganyika, whose people were suspected of theft, or MacDowall, the Field Cornet of the Rusape area, recovering stolen goods from a kraal in September 1893, and distributing ten goats seized from the offenders in lieu of pay to the two burghers who had assisted him. Sometimes individual whites would take action under a temporary commission. Thus the American, 'Curio' Brown, tells us that he 'was made a Special Constable by the Chief of Police for the purpose of arresting a native named Wambe, who had stolen some blankets from me'. And sometimes whites would take action without any commission at all. Thus in September 1892 a prospector in the Victoria area, one Short, set off with his workmen to arrest a certain Maseri, who was said to have assaulted one of the mine workers. The 'arrest' was resisted; Short was shot at and wounded; and in return killed his assailant with his revolver. No action was taken by the central authorities against Short; the Magistrate of Fort Victoria reported that 'the sympathies of the surrounding natives were entirely with Mr Short'; certainly his own were.[2]

But white involvement in Shona life was not restricted to these punitive occasions. As we shall see labour was pressed, and stock sometimes seized. Moreover, white farmers and traders became

[1] Jameson to Acting Secretary, Cape Town, 11 Jan. 1892, LO 5/2/17; a list of those appointed as Field Cornets is in LO 5/2/22.

[2] Hole's report, 1 Feb, 1892, LO 5/2/17; MacDowall to Hole, 9 and 15 Sept. 1893, DS 1/1/1; W. H. Brown, On the South African Frontier, New York, 1899; Chaplin to Public Prosecutor, 28 Sept. 1892, J 1/8/1.

involved in the settlement of disputes among the Shona themselves. One of the early settlers in the Victoria district tells us that
'natives who had quarrels with other natives conceived the idea
of taking their complaints to white traders or farmers and offering
to pay them if they would settle them in their favour. These disputes were usually for the recovery of cattle paid in lobola. . . .
The aggrieved party would come and present his case to the white
man and make him an offer of goats or sheep or a percentage of
the cattle he claimed, when recovered by the white man. These
tempting offers were eagerly sought by farmers and traders, the
former wishing to start cattle farming.' In default of an organized
department for African administration there was no way of preventing this.[1]

Some examples of the abuses that resulted may be given from
the Victoria area itself. In April 1892, for instance, the Victoria
Interpreter, J. S. Brabant, who was the nearest thing to an expert
on the Shona in the Company service, reported that 'while
travelling among the natives I found that they looked upon the
Europeans farming up there as sorts of magistrates from whom I
found out they got redress in minor offences. Seeing none of these
men can speak the language continual rows are bound to occur.'
Brabant discovered also that some whites were actively intervening in inter and intra tribal disputes. In April 1892 he reported
that a local farmer had assisted chief 'Gungubo' to raid chief
'Maromo', to burn his kraal and to carry off his cattle, and that
he had been given some of the captured beasts as the price of his
assistance. In July 1892 Brabant found that rival claimants to the
Goto chieftainship were being supported by local whites and that
they had raided the current paramount and seized his cattle.
Brabant was assaulted when he went to investigate the matter,
and later the unruly claimants even fired on a police patrol sent
to restore order.[2]

In this case the central administration had become involved in
an intra-tribal dispute, stimulated by local white activity. More
often the Administrator and his police were obliged to act because
a major dispute had arisen between the whites and a Shona chief
or his people, too serious to be dealt with on the spot. In their

---

[1] Weale's reminiscences, WE 3/2/6.
[2] Brabant to Magistrate, Victoria, 26 Apr. 1892, A 1/9/1; Jameson to
Harris, 15 July, 1892, CT 1/15/2.

punitive and 'judicial' activities the white farmers, traders and prospectors took extreme risks. They worked on the principle, the American adventurer, 'Curio' Brown, tells us that 'the Mashonas cannot conceive of bravery unless there is power behind it', and the experience that 'when one or two men present a bold front, these natives will often desist from violence, believing that a large force may be lying concealed in the bushes near at hand'. After a number of successful encounters with larger numbers of armed Shona, Brown came to 'fancy myself almost invulnerable'; and it was the general rule of white conduct to behave as if they were in fact invulnerable. This supreme self-confidence was the means adopted by the whites to off-set their overwhelming numerical inferiority. But inevitably occasions arose when whites proved only too vulnerable; when a kraal resisted and whites were hurt or killed. Such instances threatened, it was believed, the collapse of the whole system. What Mrs Huxley has written of a Kenya settler family was felt by all whites in Mashonaland. 'Respect was the only protection available to Europeans who lived singly, or in scattered families, among thousands of Africans accustomed to constant warfare and armed with spears and poisoned arrows. . . . This respect preserved them like an invisible coat of mail or a form of magic, and seldom failed; but it had to be very carefully guarded. The least rent or puncture might, if not immediately checked, split the whole garment asunder and expose its wearer in all his human vulnerability. Kept intact it was a thousand times stronger than all the guns and locks and metal in the world; challenged, it could be brushed aside like a spider's web.' [1]

Jameson's administration fully recognized its obligation to maintain the armour of respect, the cloak of invulnerability. Its only major activity in the field of 'native affairs' arose out of this obligation. As Rutherfoord Harris put it, somewhat under-playing the active interference of the whites with Shona society, 'I feel sure the Board will not forget the feelings of the population at Salisbury—hundreds of whom are accustomed to scatter over the country in small parties or even singly, prospecting and pegging out claims, and if it is not made evident to the few turbulent, thieving kraals that a white man's life, even if alone, is sacred, I feel sure there would be a great increase in the number of cases

[1] W. H. Brown, op. cit; E. Huxley, *The Flame Trees of Thika*, 1959.

. . . where murder of the unprotected white prospector would take place for the sake of his blankets and goods.' [1]

The need to demonstrate the sacredness of a white man's life led to the notorious police patrols of 1892, the best known incidents of Jameson's conduct of 'native affairs'. These patrols exhibited to the full the characteristic qualities of police intervention under Jameson—severity and imprecision. Entering an area of which they were ignorant, with a general mandate to impress the local Africans with a show of strength, the police were not too particular about where the impact of their action fell or how heavily. We may briefly describe two of the patrols made in support of the local white position to illustrate these generalizations.

In February 1892 a French trader was killed near Wata's Hill in the Mazoe district under circumstances which remained unknown. A patrol was sent out under Captains Graham and Lendy to apprehend the supposed murderer, chief Chirimuzimba. They found his kraal deserted, so 'having no idea as to the whereabouts of the offender', Graham decided 'to take action' against other kraals in the neighbourhood, some of which he burnt. Then, having eventually captured Chirimuzimba, he made his way back to Salisbury. On the way, however, he stopped to deal with chief Goredema, on the grounds that some of Goredema's men had guided the murdered man to Wata's Hill, and that there were a 'vast number of complaints lodged by prospectors and others against Goredema's people for theft'. This was the kind of action that Hudson had demanded but not received from Colquhoun in 1891. Goredema's kraal was surrounded and assaulted; six of his men were killed and three wounded; and the kraal was burnt. This drastic action was defended by Jameson on the grounds that 'there were numerous complaints of the impertinent and threatening attitudes of the natives in that district and in the Mazoe region but no distinct charge could be dealt with until the murder of Guerold'.[2]

The month after an even more severe taste of white power was given. This originated from an incident similar to hundreds of others. A white trader, one Bennet, believed that some of his

---

[1] Harris to Secretary, London Office, 1 June 1892, LO 5/2/19.
[2] Affidavit by Lovemore, 1 Feb. 1892; Graham's report, 12 Feb. 1892, CT 1/15/4; Jameson's report, 1 June 1892, CT 1/15/7.

goods had been stolen by men from the kraal of Ngomo, a head-man of paramount chief Mangwende. Bennet, like many others before him, went to Ngomo's kraal to recover his goods. But this was one occasion on which the white man was not invulnerable; Ngomo refused to let Bennet search his kraal and there followed 'an altercation in which Bennet and his boy were repeatedly struck by natives'. Captain Lendy was sent out from Salisbury to investigate; he found Mangwende unwilling or unable to disci-pline his headman and Ngomo still defiant. When he returned to Salisbury for further instructions, Jameson told him 'to take sum-mary measures'. Lendy did so; he returned to the area with a strong patrol of police, maxim guns and a seven pounder. They surrounded Ngomo's kraal and attacked it at dawn on March 17th. 'A well directed shot from the 7 pounder was the signal for the firing which was pretty general on both sides for some minutes. The shooting of the natives, however, was very erratic and they made but a short stand, the shells from the 7 pounder, bursting in among the huts, thoroughly demoralizing them.' 21 men were killed, including Ngomo himself, and 47 head of cattle were taken.[1]

Reactions to these displays of strength in support of the regime of burgher 'justice' varied widely. The contrast with Colquhoun's regime won the warm approval of Rhodes and of the settlers. 'I am glad to hear that you are maintaining the dignity of the law,' cabled Rhodes to Jameson on February 12th 1892. 'Curio' Brown tells us that for several months after this 'taste of the white man's power', 'the lives and property of white men travelling in distant parts of Mashonaland were more secure than in most civilized countries'.[2]

The British authorities were not so enthusiastic, however. These patrols did not sort very well with their advice that the Shona should be left to themselves as much as possible. After Graham's patrol the Imperial Secretary expressed the view that 'legally Captain Graham is as much a free-booter and murderer as the men he shot'; he also urged that kraals be not burnt and that no action be taken that involved 'the punishment of women and children, who may be presumed to be innocent'. 'I must remind you,' he wrote, 'that Mashonaland is now under a regular system

---

[1] Lendy's report, 24 Mar. 1892; Hole to Acting Secretary, Cape Town, 21 Mar. 1892, CT 1/15/7.
[2] W. H. Brown, op. cit; Rhodes to Jameson, 12 Feb. 1892, CT 1/15/4.

of law and the obligations imposed by that law are binding not
only on the citizen but also on the administrator.' Lendy's action
against Ngomo caused even stronger protests. 'The punishment
inflicted in this case, involving the loss of some twenty three lives,
appears utterly disproportionate to the original offence, which
was the theft of some goods from a Mr Bennet.' The Colonial
Office expressed itself of the opinion in May that 'Lendy acted in
this matter with recklessness and undue harshness. It appears to
his Lordship that proceedings of this character are likely to do
incalculable injury to the British South Africa Company.'

As a result of these protests what 'Curio' Brown calls 'methods
more in harmony with modern ideas of progress' were adopted in
Salisbury. But this did not involve any essential modification of
the system; the Field Cornets went on dealing with local troubles;
the police went on dealing with anything on a larger scale; but
care was taken to avoid anything as sensational as the Graham
and Lendy patrols. At the same time some attempts were made
to bring white offenders against Africans to book. On the few
occasions when these attempts were fruitful they caused much fury
among the settlers; Brown describes a case in which he himself
was involved which provoked threats of mass resignations from
the Volunteers, and he paints a vivid picture of the essential
settler, 'old Charlie Kettels', standing in the street outside the hall
in which Jameson was toasting the Volunteers and persuading
them to withdraw their resignations, shouting: 'You think the
country belongs to Dr Jameson, do you, you blank bounders?
This isn't Dr Jameson's country, nor Mr Rhodes' country, nor
none of them beggars' country. This is *our* country. We're the
pioneers of the country. Who's Rhodes? Blank him.' [1]

The voice of old Charlie Kettels was increasingly heard in the
land from early 1893 onwards as for the first time the administration, however timidly, came into conflict with the interests of the
whites. Some settler witnesses in 1896 seriously attributed the
risings to too great leniency on the part of the Company. But it is
very doubtful whether the new primness of Jameson's administration made any great difference to the general situation of the
Shona. It could hardly have done so without some system of regular local control, and the evidence is abundantly clear that most of
the old exercises of local white influence and power continued.

[1] W. H. Brown, op. cit.

And if there were no more well-publicized patrols like those of February and March 1892, the police were still available to lend their support to settler demands for labour and for respect. In March 1893, for instance, sub-inspector Bodle took a police patrol out to Amanda's kraal because the headman had replied to a message ordering him 'to send some of his boys to work' by saying that 'his men were not going to work for white men and that if Police came he would fire on them'. The headman was arrested; fined six goats and three head of cattle; and given 50 lashes 'administered in the presence of a good number of his men, besides people belonging to other kraals'.[1]

In short the old system, very little modified, continued until the creation of the Native Department late in 1894. Before describing this development we may pause to sum up the effects of four years of local white initiative, backed up by police action and imperfectly restrained by the central administration. The first days, in which both Shona and Europeans regarded each other with a half amused tolerance had long gone. Already by 1894 the contrast noted by the journalist Thomson, in his study of the Rhodesian administration, was only too apparent. 'It is not pleasant to notice,' he wrote, 'the way in which the Mashona avoid coming into contact with the settlers, and to recollect that when we first went up to Mashonaland they welcomed us gladly.' [2]

Thus Weale tells us that when he was first appointed Native Commissioner in September 1894, 'I found that I had to try and gain the confidence of the natives that they might not run away on the sight of a white man; they were very timid, especially the women. The reason for this appeared afterwards to be on account of some of the police formerly stationed there making a practice of assaulting and raping any native woman they found in the veld alone.' Edwards tells us that when he was appointed Native Commissioner in 1895, 'at first the natives, in the outlying kraals of the north and east of Mrewa, were very timid and deserted their kraals whenever they heard of our approach. We had often to wait at kraals for several days to get in touch with the people. This fear gradually died down as they found no harm was done to them.' Their memories are amply borne out by contemporary testimony.

---

[1] Bodle's report, 7 Mar. 1893; Mining Commissioner, Mazoe, to Magistrate, Salisbury, 8 Mar. and 16 Mar. 1893, DS 1/1/1.
[2] H. C. Thomson, *Rhodesia and its Government*, London, 1898.

On December 30th 1894, for instance, the new Native Commissioner at Hartley Hills wrote that he 'found that the Mashonas
were in the habit of clearing away from their villages on the
approach of any white man. This I have not yet been altogether
able to stop. . . . The chiefs have appeared to have so little
authority over their men that anyone in want of boys . . . have
had to press the first that they came across. Hence the reason of
boys clearing away from their kraals.' A similar report came from
Umtali at the end of 1894. 'Many people of Umtali have been in
the practice of going out to the neighbouring kraals and there
obtaining labour under the pretext of being Government officials;
having got the boys they bring them to Umtali and then before
their month is up so ill treat them that the boys bolt and consequently get no payment. . . . To such an extent has this been
carried on that it is *now* almost impossible to get boys from the
kraals to work in Umtali as the boys are unable to see any difference between one white man and another and say that all equally
refuse to pay them.' [1]

In 1897, during the controversy over the treatment of the
Shona, the *Cape Times* asserted that the settlers of Mashonaland
numbered 'a proportion of public school and university and army
men of a well-known English type, not saints at all, perhaps
rather tough customers, but gentlemen, not brutes, not cowards,
not liars'. The evidence does not, indeed, suggest that the typical
white settler in Mashonaland was a brute or a coward or a liar.
What it does suggest is that given the 'rather tough customers'
who settled amongst the Shona the sort of injustice and ill treatment which we have been describing was inevitable in a situation
where the central administration made so little attempt to regulate or control events. For this we must share the blame equally
between Rhodes and Jameson, who were so careless about
African reactions and African wrongs, and the British Government
which desired to have a British presence in Mashonaland but was
not prepared to face up to the implications of this desire. [2]

After the overthrow of Lobengula in the Ndebele war of 1893
the formal legal position of Mashonaland changed radically. In

[1] Weale's reminiscences, WE 3/2/5; Edwards' reminiscences, ED 6/1/1;
N.C. Hartley, to Acting Administrator, 30 Dec. 1894, A 15/1/1; Resident
Magistrate, Umtali, to Public Prosecutor, Salisbury; 23 Oct. 1894, J 1/1/1.
[2] *Cape Times*, 22 Nov. 1897.

British legal theory the Company administration no longer derived its authority there from Lobengula's grants or from the somewhat nebulous British Protectorate but enjoyed powers over both whites and blacks as the grantee of the British Crown, now sovereign of Matabeleland and Mashonaland by right of conquest. Thus for the first time there was a firm legal foundation for Company jurisdiction over the African peoples of Mashonaland which henceforth depended upon the provisions of the Matabeleland Order in Council of July 18th 1894. This change was, of course, purely a theoretical one as far as Mashonaland was concerned. Nothing had happened there to make the Shona feel any more subject to the whites; certainly they did not feel themselves to have been conquered. The notion that the downfall of the Ndebele monarch whose sovereignty many of the Shona paramounts had never accepted involved their own submission to British authority was incomprehensible to the Shona and had it been comprehended would certainly have been repudiated. But the new theory allowed the Company to move for the first time towards a more regular system of 'native administration'.[1]

To begin with, however, Jameson had no particular desire to establish such a system. The Matabeleland Order in Council did not stipulate that there should be a Native Department, in striking contrast to Milner's care over this question in 1897 and 1898. But it did allow the Company to institute a hut tax, as they had been wanting to do since 1892. Little time was wasted. In March 1894 instructions were drawn up for the collection of a hut tax at the rate of 10s. a hut per year. These instructions did not envisage any radical reorganization. Mounted police were to do the collecting; payment was to be made to the Civil Commissioners 'or the Mining Commissioner in outlying districts'; and no new responsibilities for the control of the Shona were laid down. The only innovation was the provision that 'in districts where there is no Civil Commissioner or Mining Commissioner resident, an officer will be appointed to receive the hut tax, and the Police will make known to the natives the name of the officer and where he is to be found'.[2]

These specially appointed officers, however, were not to be in any sense Native Commissioners. The Acting Administrator,

---

[1] C. Palley, op. cit., chap. 6.
[2] Instructions on the collection of hut tax, 17 Mar. 1894, A 15/1/1.

Duncan, told a correspondent who had expressed anxiety over the effect on the Shona of the levy of the tax, and argued for the creation of a proper Native Department, that 'I do not like to take the step of appointing a Native Commissioner which would involve a certain amount of expense before we get a sufficient amount of Hut Tax to justify the expenditure'. What happened was that local farmers or other Europeans were appointed as collectors for the district in which they resided. Thus, for example, Richard O'Reilly, who farmed in the Rusape district was appointed collector there, and given the power to collect the tax either in money or in labour on the roads. In the Marendellas area, the first Native Commissioner later reported, 'in their hurry to start tax collection the Company had entered into an arrangement with a local farmer to collect cattle, sheep and goats failing cash, on a share basis'. It was the last great extension of the principle of local enterprise. Not surprisingly these arrangements proved unsatisfactory. Shona resistance to the new tax was determined; and the collectors in some cases used their new powers exclusively to their own advantage. By September, for instance, Duncan was writing to O'Reilly demanding 'an explanation as to why, when you were appointed to be a Hut Tax collector, you sold goods at exorbitant prices to Makoni and demanded further payment, threatening to burn down the kraal with the assistance of the police'.[1]

But the collection of the tax by the Civil and Mining Commissioners proved little more satisfactory. These over-burdened officials either collected little tax or blundered into fierce Shona resistance. In Lomagundi, indeed, the collection of the hut tax by the Mining Commissioner provoked a major incident. Lomagundi, as we have seen, had experienced one of the rare Ndebele raids into Mashonaland after 1890; and as a result the people of paramount Lomagundi had applied to the Company for protection. By 1894 they were thoroughly disillusioned with the protection afforded to them, involving as it did virtual forced labour. The responsibility for the district was in the hands of the Mining Commissioner, an official whose methods with the Shona were direct and unsubtle. In March 1894, for instance, the Commissioner reported that he had gone with a prospector, Eyre, to

[1] Duncan to Dennison, 7 June 1894; Duncan to O'Reilly, 23 May 1894, A 2/14/1; Duncan to O'Reilly, 1 Sept. 1894, A 2/14/2.

get labourers from a kraal. 'I gave orders that all the boys in the kraal were to stop there until I had seen how many there were,' he reported, 'and one boy immediately made off and Eyre went to stop him when the boy turned on Eyre and went for him with a battle axe and assegai. Eyre repeatedly called him to stop and on his not doing so he shot him through the body. . . . Eyre's act was purely self-defence and I think the general effect on the natives will be extremely beneficial. They are a cheeky and independent lot.' [1]

It was upon this official that the responsibility for collecting the tax was now placed. Throughout 1894 he complained of the difficulty of his new task—he had only two policemen for the whole district and neither of them were mounted; the chiefs resented the new tax and would bring only derisory amounts of food or stock in settlement of it. 'If I started to force them to pay', he wrote, 'there would be lots of trouble with them and the consequence would be deserted kraals and depopulated districts.' In August 1894 a new Mining Commissioner did attempt to compel the paramount, Lomagundi, to pay his tax in full, with exactly the results that his predecessor had predicted. The new man, Pocock, was on patrol collecting labour for the mines, which was then desperately short, and demanded of the paramount that he compound for the tax due from his people by providing labour. The paramount sent too few workers; Pocock set out with two white policemen and one black to the paramount's kraal; the police were sent in 'to procure boys if possible'; and in a scuffle with the paramount one of the white Troopers was stabbed to death. [2]

Inevitably a police patrol was sent out from Salisbury; equally inevitably its punishment was both heavy and indiscriminate. On September 10th 1894 sub-inspector Hopper and his patrol arrived at the Wesleyan Mission Station in Lomagundi, situated some thirty miles south of the paramount's kraal. Hopper addressed the Shona gathered there, among them some seven chiefs or headmen, 'on the ingratitude of treacherously killing our people' who had saved them from the Ndebele; had two men, pointed out as deserters from the mines, given 'ten lashes in front of the assembly'; and departed with the seven chiefs and headmen as hostages. As

[1] Ferguson to Administrator, 29 Mar. 1894, DS 1/1/1.
[2] Reports by Mining Commissioner, Lomagundi, May, July, Aug. 1894, M 1/1/1 and CT 1/15/6.

his patrol left the Mission, some of the hostages attempted to escape; 'they were challenged to stop, but not complying, shots were fired by my men and three were killed'. This action, Hopper later reported, 'was absolutely necessary to impress upon the native mind that when the Government through its officers issues a mandate or makes a statement, such command or saying will be enforced with the utmost firmness'.

To others his action seemed the most indefensible of the acts of the old regime. The local missionary, Mr Eva, was prepared to swear on oath 'that these chiefs were entirely innocent of the policeman's death. Indeed they were at that time totally ignorant of its occurrence.' Missionary outcry was supported by the first Native Commissioner of Lomagundi on his arrival in the district. 'I greatly regret the course that was taken by the last police patrol,' he wrote, 'as the wrong natives were punished. The crime that was committed was done by Mazimagupa's people, west, and the penalty was paid by the natives in the southern part of this district, namely six chiefs shot dead and cattle and goats confiscated by the police. . . . The police *must* keep away from the kraals for the time being as I have told the natives that no-one shall interfere with them.' [1]

This Lomagundi incident, resulting in a scandal similar to those of early 1892, and resulting also in a district totally denuded of labour, finally persuaded the administration that some new arrangements were required. 'I am directed to inform you', wrote the Administrator's secretary to Pocock on September 6th, 1894, 'that Mr Duncan is getting Mr Brabant to come up to Salisbury and is appointing hut-tax collectors to deal with the natives and is particularly anxious that you should not raid the natives either for Hut Tax or labour for prospectors, as it is constantly leading the Company into troubles because once begun the thing has to be carried to a conclusion which involves shooting the natives, etc.' [2]

At long last, then, towards the end of 1894 the Mashonaland Native Department began to take shape. Even then it was very far from 'a strong and able Native administration' which 'considered the conciliation and welfare of the Natives as the all important

[1] Hopper's report, 10 Sept. 1894, CT 1/15/6; N.C., Lomagundi, to C.N.C. Salisbury, 3 Oct. 1894, N. 1/1/5.
[2] Secretary, Salisbury to Mining Commissioner, Lomagundi, 6 Sept. 1894, M 1/1/1.

object to aim at'. The new officers were appointed first and foremost to collect the hut tax; and secondly to raise labour. At first they were actually known as Hut Tax Collectors under Brabant as the Native Commissioner. The atmosphere of the new department comes over well in Native Commissioner Weale's reminiscences. 'I had half an hour's interview with the Acting Administrator,' he tells us, 'and he gave me a rough outline of what I was expected to do, consisting of establishing contact with the natives and explaining the hut tax expected of them, consisting of cattle, sheep or goats, explaining that they were now free from the dominion of the Matabele and that we intended to rule the country in future and give them good Government for which they in turn were to pay an annual tax, which they might obtain from the whites for whom they were expected to work. Any further enquiries as to procedure were invariably met with the slogan "that we were to use our own discretion". So armed with these vague commissions we went out into the blue and did our best.' [1]

The new department was also expected to deal with recalcitrant Shona without calling in the regular police. 'The white police had their stations along the main roads,' Weale tells us, 'and they were directly under the control of the Commissioner of Police and it was found inadvisable for them to be employed on Native Departmental work, which was often of a semi-political nature and not generally understood, and in case of local trouble which might be magnified and lead to panic on the part of settlers, possibly leading them to write to the home papers in which exaggerated accounts might fall into the hands of unscrupulous enemies of the Chartered Co. and result in endless enquiries from the home Govt. and possibly affect the share market adversely. All these possibilities had to be taken into account by members of the Native Dept., and led them to guard against any of their movements being known to the police or the public. It was therefore enjoined on us to observe as much secrecy as possible in matters which we could overcome with our Police boys and by ourselves without outside armed assistance, and this is the practice we invariably followed.' [2]

[1] Weale's reminiscences, WE 3/2/5.
[2] Weale, op. cit. The withdrawal of the police from active participation in 'native policy' was probably also a result of Jameson's desire to have them free for such ventures as the later Jameson Raid.

Each Native Commissioner was instructed to raise his own police and to arm them as best he could, and some motley forces were thus gathered together. 'The pay for messengers was 10s. per month and rations,' Edwards tells us; 'they had to provide their own clothing, which at first consisted of cat or monkey skins and feather head-dresses. Later at my expense I provided each of them with a second hand red infantry tunic.' These men were the main-stay of the Native Commissioner in peace as well as war; 'We were all of us very young and inexperienced', confesses Weale, 'We had to learn the language and were dependent to a great extent on our Native Police for guidance in settling disputes and to acquaint ourselves with native customs and habits, which were entirely new to us.' [1]

The new department, consisting of Chief Native Commissioner Brabant, eleven young Native Commissioners, and their locally recruited messengers and police, undoubtedly succeeded in raising large amounts of hut tax and dealing discreetly with local dis-orders. Brabant was able to claim rather smugly in February 1895 that a much greater amount of tax had been collected with far less trouble than had been the case in 1894 and to remark that where trouble was taken to explain things to natives they proved tractable, while 'where indiscriminate force has been resorted to the result has invariably proved detrimental to the object that may have been in view'. But it may be doubted whether its operations resulted in much of an improvement as far as the Shona were concerned. Obviously a greater efficiency in collecting tax was in itself going to be resented; but this resentment was magni-fied by the way in which the department was run under Brabant. [2]

Brabant, says Edwards, was 'in a way a rough diamond'. 'The Chief of the Department', writes Weale, 'was a rough and ready illiterate young man, with an aptitude to learn to speak primitive African languages. He was a great believer in corporal punish-ment and was as brave as a lion, a good rider and rifle shot, in-tensely loyal to the B.S.A. Company, quite honest, and with an 'unquenchable thirst for kaffir beer.'

The atmosphere of the Department under Brabant comes out clearly in a story which Weale tells, in no spirit of criticism, of an expedition led by the Chief Native Commissioner early in 1895 to

[1] Edwards and Weale, op. cit.
[2] Brabant to Acting Administrator, 7 Feb. 1895, A 15/1/1.

the Mtoko area, where the Budja chiefs had resisted the collection of hut tax, recaptured cattle seized for its payment, and fired on the Native Commissioner's messengers. The expedition was a formidable affair, consisting of a patrol of white police, under Brabant's orders, the messengers of the Marendellas and Salisbury districts, and some 450 Zezuru 'friendlies'; nothing less than a small army of invasion. As it approached the Native Commissioner's camp at Mtoko it was greeted by four of his messengers, 'dressed in cricket blazers, wearing second hand boots'. 'Now, if there was one thing about a native more than another that annoyed Brabant', Weale tells us, 'it was to see a raw native wearing boots.' So he had the men seized and stripped. Once he reached the Native Commissioner's camp, Brabant had these four men and all the rest of the messengers and native police flogged for their failure to collect tax and keep the district in order. He then sent out some of Weale's men to bring in chief Guripila and his headmen. Next day Guripila arrived. 'Brabant then went up to MaGuripira and started interrogating him and asked, what is the reason for this military display, now that he had come himself he found the country all armed, pointing to the surrounding hills. One of the counsellors said something to which Brabant evidently took exception and on continuing to be insolent Brabant took a jambok out of a police boy's hand and struck him with it. Immediately Guripira and his counsellors made a dash for liberty but most of them were stopped. MaGuripira then opened a box he had brought with him and displayed a helmet and breast-plate of brass together with a sword and belt and sabretash; this he offered to Brabant as a peace-offering, but Brabant spurned it with his foot and called upon everybody to go raiding the country. . . . He explained to Guripira that he could either go in person or send his counsellors to tell his people that we were going to burn and shoot and destroy everything we saw until he sent to stop us and ask for mercy, but that before we would cease he would have to fill the valley with cattle for us to pick from for hut tax and that he was also to furnish us with 200 of his picked men to go and work in the mines.'

'We then proceeded down the valley in search of something to destroy,' continues Weale. 'The police boys and messengers and camp followers scattered over the hills and burnt down all the kraals they came across until the whole atmosphere was dense with smoke of burning rapoko and other corn and grass.' The whites amused themselves meanwhile with 'a pig-sticking match on foot and horse-back'. Guripila then sent to say that he had met Brabant's conditions. 'We returned to camp to find the valley literally full of cattle, all lowing and bellowing.' Next day the hut tax was collected in cattle and goats; Guripila was fined more cattle; and 500 of his men were recruited for work in the mines.[1]

After this account of Brabant's dashing but arbitrary conduct in Mtoko it will come as little surprise that he was the particular *protégé* of Rhodes and Jameson. When Brabant was appointed head of the new Department it was noted that 'Mr Rhodes has received such excellent reports of Brabant's work that he wishes to give him this appointment and salary'; and Weale tells us that 'Jameson . . . had great confidence in Brabant's ability to deal with natives'. No doubt Jameson regarded the Mtoko patrol as a proof of the utility of the new Department, since it had been better directed, more profitable in tax and labour and less publicized than the old police patrols. But like them it was in essence a raid and bore little relation to the establishment of regular administration.[2]

It would be wrong, of course, to suggest that this operation was typical of the work of the new Department. But it was not an isolated case and there were other literal invasions of districts by Department officials at the head of 'friendly' levies. Thus Edwards tells us that later in 1895 he 'raised a force of fifty WaZizuru, armed with old muzzle loading guns' to make a patrol into the Fungwi area in the north-east of his district. Both Mtoko and the Fungwi were remote districts with few whites living in them and the authority of the administration was not fully established in either area before 1896. Despite the Brabant patrol the history of the Mtoko area in 1895 and early 1896 was one of constant refusal to pay tax, constant skirmishes between the Native Commissioner and hostile chiefs, climaxing in June 1896 with a combined attack by all the main chiefs of Mtoko on the Native Commissioner's camp. In areas like Mtoko the demand for hut tax had stimulated a resistance which the inadequately staffed Department was unable to deal with. Even in the areas closer to Salisbury and

[1] Weale, op. cit. See also, Armstrong's report on Mtoko, N 1/1/6; Armstrong to Taberer, 25 Feb. 1897, LO 5/4/2.
[2] Duncan to Spreckley, 8 June 1894, DV 1/2/1.

relatively densely populated with whites, the early history of the Department was one of clashes with protestant paramounts rather than one of the establishment of regular administration. So Weale tells us that 'on many occasions' in the Marendellas district 'the messenger boys were driven off by the natives, who refused to pay hut tax and in some cases the natives fired on them, telling them they would do the same to the white man too, and it was found necessary to arm a percentage of the messengers with Martini rifles and ball cartridges for self defence in the future'. Weale was generally able in his district to deal with these piece-meal defiances with the forces he possessed, but he comments that 'one of the effects of this policy was to lead people into the false belief that the natives were too cowardly ever to rise in open rebellion, which was disproved in 1896, causing a feeling of false security and un-preparedness, which was to prove disastrous'.[1]

Shona resistance to hut tax was, then, widespread; few Shona paramounts recognized the right of the Company administration to demand tribute from them or accepted the argument that they were under the Company's protection. Even in areas where no armed resistance was made collection of the tax during the Brabant regime was arbitrary and irregular, appearing more like the levy of a tribute than the collection of a civil tax. Almost everywhere the tax was taken in stock; 'the kraals are complaining that in some instances they are left without a single beast', wrote the Magistrate of Gwelo with reference to the activities of one of Brabant's Commissioners in his district; 'Mr Hulley got goats truly by force', wrote a Native Commissioner in Melsetter of his predecessor, 'and indeed the most loose system of work I have seen. For instance about 70 goats were taken from the Mafahuri and no exempt given.' So far had the de-stocking of some areas of Mashonaland gone under Brabant's regime that the Executive Council decided in November 1895 that the collection of the hut tax should be suspended for three months and that thereafter it should not be levied in the form of stock 'in view of the fact that at this rate there would be no cattle left to collect in a year or two'.[2]

The activity of the Department in collecting tax was undoubtedly

[1] Armstrong's report on Mtoko, N 1/1/6.
[2] Report by Magistrate, Gwelo, 8 Jan. 1895, EC 4/1/1; N.C. Meredith to Magistrate, Melsetter, 25 Feb. 1896, DM 2/9/1; Executive Council minute, 4 Nov. 1895, EC 3/1/1.

the main reason for Shona hostility to it. But it was not the only one. In theory the Department was supposed to exclude private settler initiative in the recruitment of labour, just as it was supposed to exclude police initiative in the settlement of disputes or in the 'pacification' of districts. The prevention of settler pressing of labour, which the Department on the whole achieved, should have been a great advance. But labour had to be procured somehow—indeed the Department had to demonstrate to its critics that it was actually more efficient in raising labour just as it had been more efficient in raising tax. As a result the coercion of labour continued, and probably increased, though in a different form. The coercive element was present even in the official and theoretical operation of the system. As Lord Grey told Sir Richard Martin in 1897, chiefs and headmen were 'asked' by the Commissioners to supply labour and 'expected' by them to supply it. If they did not live up to this expectation other action was taken. Thus the Native Commissioner, Hartley, having first described the private conscription of labour in his district before his appointment went on: 'I have had considerable difficulty in making the chiefs supply boys when demanded during the first quarter; they evidently not understanding the new order of things and wanting some practical experience before dropping into the way of it. . . . So many cases of boys running away from their employers have occurred that to prevent it continuing I have seized all the cattle and goats from a chief whom I consider encouraged them in it, and have told him that he will not get any back again until all the boys who have deserted have come back and been punished.' [1]

But the element of compulsion did not end there. We have already seen the extent to which the Commissioners were dependent on their Shona police and messengers. Short-staffed and under-equipped as they were the Commissioners had really no alternative but to rely on their police for collection of labour also. There is no doubt that throughout Mashonaland labour was collected in this manner by Department police and with a great deal of harshness. Thus in January 1896, yet another new Mining Commissioner in Lomagundi, now relieved of the duty of raising labour himself, was sharply critical of the way in which it was being done by the Native Department. 'A practice obtains in the Native Department', he wrote, 'of sending Native Constables to

[1] Quarterly report, Hartley, 30 Dec. 1894, A 15/1/1.

collect boys to work, unaccompanied by the Native Commissioner or an assistant, and power so placed in the hands of Native Constables is very liable to be abused, and this is just what is taking place if the reports which reach me indirectly are true. I do not attach any want of diligence to the Native Commissioner here, nor do I see how he can personally visit all kraals himself, for the district is large, the kraals scattered and many of them in the fly, and he has no one to assist him, but I think it is a matter which should receive the serious consideration of the Native Department, for any abuses of this kind give rise to a feeling of distrust and want of confidence in the justice of the white man among the natives.'

In Melsetter a new Native Commissioner, appointed by Brabant's successor, reported in February 1896 that under his predecessor 'a vast amount of injustice has been done to the natives of this district by these colonial native police. . . . These boys do as they like and in interpreting tell their own tale.' Yet despite his efforts at reform, Melsetter missionaries were still complaining in 1897 that 'much injustice has been done to the natives through the general plan adopted in the administration of native affairs. We hold that the plan of sending native constables through the country collecting the natives by armed force, compelling them to labour here and there, wherever their services happen to be required, whether they are willing or not, their wives being seized as hostages in case they attempt to escape, is unjust and government has no right thus to arrest and impress natives.' [1]

The Native Department under Brabant was not, therefore, much of an improvement over the private regime it had replaced. It was too small; too ill informed; and above all not sufficiently inspired from above with the correct attitude towards its duties. As Weale tells us, 'in those days Sir J. Frazer's "Golden Bough" was unknown to me and in any case there was scant means of obtaining books on anthropology and primitive customs. . . . None of us had been trained for administrative work or had studied law . . . and from the Administrator downwards none took much interest in the Natives except in obtaining taxes from them and the keeping of them from doing mischief.'

[1] Mining Commissioner, Lomagundi, to Registrar of Mines, Jan. 1896, ML 2/2/1; N.C. Melsetter, to Magistrate, Melsetter, 29 Feb. 1896, DM 2/9/1; Report by Chairman, American Board Mission, Mount Silinda, 18 July 1897, DM 2/7/1.

The Administrator, in fact, was still much more interested in furthering Rhodes' plans for South Africa as a whole than in building up the Rhodesian administration. In October 1895 Jameson moved the great majority of his white police to the border with the Transvaal in preparation for the planned march into the territory of the Boer republic which, it was hoped, would overthrow President Kruger and speed the day of a self-governing, English speaking South Africa. From that time onward he ceased to control the administration of Mashonaland and the defeat of his raid, his capture, imprisonment and trial effectively removed his influence from the province. In his absence steps were taken to reform the Native Department. In November 1895 Brabant was dismissed from his post by a decision of the Executive Council. The Council records give no reason for this decision but there is little doubt that 'Curio' Brown was right when he wrote of Brabant; 'This gentleman had given the tribes under him an opportunity to learn of the white man's power to rule. His regime became eventually the subject of so much criticism on account of its severity that he was dismissed from the employ of the Chartered Company.' He was replaced as Chief Native Commissioner by a very different sort of man. H. M. Taberer was a university graduate and qualified in administrative law and his appointment was clearly intended to give the Native Department a new atmosphere.

It was accompanied, as we have seen, by a general order to Native Commissioners to suspend collection of the hut tax for three months and to 'utilize their time in gaining a more thorough knowledge of their districts, in making maps and drawing up statistics'. Thus the Native Commissioners were given intimation that they were no longer to regard themselves as tax collectors first and foremost. Under Taberer 'making maps and drawing up statistics' came to bulk larger and larger in the work of the Commissioners. 'Taberer thinks I have not enough to do,' complained one of them in March 1897, 'and wires that I am required to send in a weekly summary by every mail of work done like any other policeman.' Where Brabant's instructions to Edwards had been 'for God's sake don't worry headquarters if you can avoid it', under Taberer headquarters began increasingly to worry and to control individual Native Commissioners.[1]

[1] N.C. Melsetter, to Magistrate, Melsetter, 17 Mar. 1897, DM 2/9/1.

Taberer's regime enjoyed only some six months before the outbreak of the Mashonaland rebellion and for most of that time the
combination of drought, locusts and rinderpest created emergency
conditions. It is difficult to say, therefore, what it might have
achieved. It was still under-staffed and under-supplied. But there
are indications that Taberer was hoping to build up the sort of
Native Department postulated by Sir Richard Martin. Certainly
for Melsetter, an area not involved in the rising, a series of files
survives for 1896 and 1897 which show us Taberer urging forward
his Native Commissioner to do battle against the Afrikaaner farmers and their exploitation of African labour where Brabant's
commissioners had been content to be their passive allies. There is
some evidence, even, that before the rising the new policy had
achieved a lessening in tension. Thus the Native Commissioner,
Umtali, noted that since the ban on the seizure of stock for tax
'the Natives are not in the habit of rushing their cattle to the hills
and rocks on the approach of the Native Commissioner.' But the
improvement, if improvement there was, came much too late to
affect the movement of the Shona into irreconcilable opposition to
the Company regime.[1]

In this brief account of administration in Mashonaland we have
seen how far and for what reasons the British South Africa Company government, and Jameson in particular, failed either to
control or to conciliate the Shona. We have seen, also, ample
evidence of widespread grievances which in themselves would
account for a general disposition to rebel. But what were individual
Shona reactions to the administrative and settler intrusion into
their lives? The stories of the relationship between the whites and
two of the Shona paramounts, Makoni and Kunzwi-Nyandoro,
will give some idea of the way in which the decision to challenge
the whites by co-ordinated force of arms was reached in particular
cases.

Paramount chief Makoni Mutota Cirimaunga of Maungwe was,
as Acting Administrator Vintcent wrote in 1896, 'one of the most
powerful chiefs in Mashonaland'. His kraal was still large enough
to be described by a missionary visitor as 'a real town', and his
people were widely regarded as the most war-like and formidable
of the Shona. Before the arrival of the Pioneers his career had been

[1] The Melsetter files are, DM 2/7/1, DM 2/9/1, J 1/4/1. Reply by N.C.
Umtali, to Martin's questions, C. 8547.

a characteristic one for a nineteenth-century central Shona paramount. His pre-occupations had been with the acquisition and
maintenance of his paramountcy, with his relations with the paramounts of Mbire, Nohwe, Barwe, Manyika, and the rest and with
the power of the Goanese adventurer, Gouveia. Within the tribe he
faced the incipient challenge of rival chiefly houses; his path to the
paramountcy had been an irregular one, depending upon the
exile of more senior claimants and the death by poisoning of his
elder brother; and one Ndapfunya, son of his predecessor in the
paramountcy, headed an opposition faction. Externally he followed an elaborate policy of diplomacy and war, shifting this way
and that as the one constant necessity of his feud with paramount
Mutassa of Manyika dictated. From his kraal on Gwindingwi hill,
Makoni Mutota played the necessary game of late nineteenth-
century Shona politics with shrewdness and success. It was a game
he was good at and enjoyed playing.

As far as he was concerned the arrival of the Company made
very little difference at first, except as another factor which might
be manipulated to his advantage. In October 1890 he granted a
mineral concession to Selous on the Company's behalf in exchange
for the promise of a rent of £10 a year, but two months later he was
receiving the Portuguese flag with equal complacency and promising them that 'he would eat up Mutassa' and thus nullify the
Company's claim to Manicaland. Neither the new border nor the
Company's assumption of responsibility made much difference to
Makoni's activities for the first two years of Company rule. His
orientation was still eastwards; Jameson meant less to him than
Gouveia. In January 1892, for instance, Gouveia complained that
Makoni and paramount chief Mtoko were sending men from
Rhodesia to assist paramount chief Makombe of Barwe in his
attack on the Goanese. 'Mutassa's, Matoko's and Makone's men
come across and fight me,' he protested. 'When I beat them they
run back into Company's territory.' And in June 1892 Captain
Lendy discovered that Makoni's activities were as unrestrained
within Company territory; while on patrol he passed the kraal of
chief Mbelwa who seemed 'to live in constant fear of being raided
by Makoni's people'. 'Told him', reported Lendy, 'the white
people would not allow it and he might live in peace now.' [1]

---

[1] Report of Captain Graham, Jan. 1892, A 1/9/1, CT 1/15/2; report of
Captain Lendy, 23 June 1892, CT 1/15/1.

The white people were, in fact, beginning to encroach upon Makoni. Lendy told the chiefs in Makoni's area in June 1892 that the Company would not allow 'these raids and disturbances to take place in the country we had come into but wished law and order to be established without bloodshed if possible.' Makoni had no desire for the Company to establish law and order anyway, but he was not impressed with the way it was being done. When his kraal was visited by the Anglican missionary, Frank Edwards, in 1892 he would not allow the white man to enter. 'White men were his enemies,' Edwards reported him as saying. 'They had killed some of Mangwende's people and outraged the women. After assuring him again and again that I was his friend we were admitted and then he said "If God sent the white man to teach him and his people why did God send the white men to kill and outrage the native peoples?" It was a difficult question to answer. 'You will easily see from this incident how utterly futile any mission work must be amongst the natives,' wrote Edwards to Jameson, 'if white men are allowed to kill them and outrage their women with impunity.' [1]

Soon Makoni had to deal not only with wandering white adventurers, missionaries and police patrols, but with settled farmers. Selous had reported in 1890 that 'the country between Magoni's and Mangwendi's' was 'simply magnificent for farming purposes', and had asked for a grant of land there. He was sure, he said, that he would be able to get the grant ratified by the paramount. In Shona law Makoni would not have been able to make Selous any absolute grant of land; but in any case he was not even asked to approve the grants that the Company began to make in his area. After 1892 the Company claimed that the Lippert Concession from Lobengula allowed them to dispose of land in Mashonaland and proceeded to do so. In 1919 the Privy Council found that the Lippert Concession had not given the Company authority to dispose of land anywhere, so that even in terms of legal theory their action was unfounded. More importantly it had no basis in any fact appreciated by the Shona; Makoni regarded himself as still sovereign of Maungwe and he was not prepared to recognize intruders into his area.

The records show a long history of differences between Makoni and the local farmers who accused his people of 'trespassing' on

[1] Edwards to Jameson, 17 Jan. 1892, A 1/9/1.

land which they had occupied for generations or who charged them rents. It can have done very little to persuade Makoni of the impartiality of Company justice that the Field Cornet of his area was also the leader of the neighbouring farmers with whom he had disputes over land. In January 1894 a police trooper was sent to Makoni's kraal to tell him that Mr Wood, the Field Cornet, was 'occupying that land on the authority of the Company. If he has anything to complain of he can represent the matter either to the Civil Commissioner or to the authorities in Salisbury . . . but if he allows his people constantly to trespass on the land given to Mr Wood by the Company and to kill Mr Wood's goats . . . the Company will be obliged to give Mr Wood protection and punish those who molest him.' In June 1894 another police patrol was sent to warn Makoni 'not to plough on Mr Wood's land without his permission'; in January 1895 the Executive Council debated a complaint from Makoni that one of his sub-chiefs had been compelled to pay rent to a Mr Buchanan in order to continue to remain in his old home, and decided that Buchanan was within his rights to demand such a rent. The journalist, Thomson, tells us that 'one of the greatest of Makoni's grievances was that his land should have been given away to strangers up to his very kraal'.[1]

Prevented from raiding his old enemies; prevented from taking his share of the old trade with the Portuguese; hedged in by European farms; Makoni was in a state of some resentment even before the imposition and collection of the hut tax. But the hut tax arrangements certainly increased it. O'Reilly, the local collector, used his position, as we have seen, to force goods on to Makoni at exorbitant prices and to threaten to 'burn down his kraal with the assistance of the police'; it was little wonder that when Makoni rose in 1896 his first objective was 'to seize O'Reilly's cattle and then do away with the Native Commissioner and police'. Nor was Makoni any more content to pay tax to the new Native Department. In 1896 Vintcent asserted that he had 'at no time met the Company in a proper and loyal spirit; on several occasions defying and threatening our Native Commissioners and their police'. Thomson tells us that 'Makoni always chafed under the seizure of his country and in 1894 he killed a native policeman who had been

---

[1] Duncan to Trooper Young, 14 Jan. 1894; Duncan to Chief Commissioner of Police, 2 June 1894, A 2/14/1; Minutes of the Executive Council, 5 Jan. 1895, EC 3/1/1.

misconducting himself, and in various ways showed a restive spirit'. It came as little surprise to anyone that Makoni Mutota was in the forefront of the rising in Mashonaland.[1]

The story of Kunzwi Nyandoro brings out even more clearly than that of Makoni the importance of the feeling of 'self-determination' to the central Shona paramounts since we have less evidence of specific grievances in his case. Kunzwi was a powerful figure in central Shona politics. 'Kunzwi is the only chief in this district who has any command over his people,' wrote the Native Commissioner, Salisbury, in December 1894. 'Rusiki, together with Maquendie have always been afraid to oppose Kunzwi's tribe, now numbered about 2000, and the chief kraal is the most naturally fortified position I have seen in this district. They are well armed with fire-arms and other chiefs tell me that Kunzwi was given 730 guns by Gouveia shortly before we came to the country.' We have seen above the pride with which Kunzwi regarded his position as paramount. What sort of reaction would this 'king', secure in his 'natural fortress', have to the arrival of the whites?

It is clear that his reactions to individual whites were favourable enough—provided they were content to live under his protection. The Catholic mission station at Chishawasha, for instance, established a station at Kunzwi's kraal; and Edwards, living as a young trader in the days before he became a Native Commissioner, tells of his amicable relations with Kunzwi and the manner in which the chief imposed fines or other punishments upon any of his own people, or members of other tribes, who stole from the whites or threatened them with violence. Edwards occupied the position, so he tells us, of 'Nyandoro's white man'.[2]

But Kunzwi Nyandoro was not prepared to be Dr Jameson's or Native Commissioner Campbell's black man. Too formidable to be harassed by individual whites; his relations with the missionaries and traders conducted amiably on his terms; Kunzwi's clash with the whites came with the establishment of the Native Department when for the first time he was expected to submit to the regular operation of a superior authority and to pay taxes to it. From the very beginning of Campbell's appointment as Native Commissioner for the Salisbury district he was in conflict with

[1] C.N.C. to Administrator, 17 June 1895, LO 5/6/1.
[2] Edwards, op. cit. Report by N.C. Campbell, 27 Dec. 1894, LO 5/2/40.

D

Kunzwi. In September 1894 Kunzwi's son, Panashe, killed a Zulu ox-driver after a quarrel over trespass; messengers sent to apprehend Panashe were chased away from Kunzwi's kraal and had to take refuge in Edwards' store. 'Panashe', writes Edwards, 'was never brought to trial. Nyandoro in his absence was fined twenty head of cattle. He was informed of this but made no attempt to pay and remained on guard in his hill fortress for several months and refused to have any dealings with Campbell or his messengers.'

In October 1895 Campbell tried to collect hut tax from Kunzwi for the first time; his police were fired on and driven off. This time the new Chief Native Commissioner, Taberer, was sent to tell Kunzwi 'that he had acted wrongly in firing on and pursuing Mr Campbell's police' and to exact a fine of 10 cattle. Taberer was instructed to use 'all tact and discretion' in dealing with Kunzwi. Presumably he did so, but to no long term effect. In April 1896, two months before the rebellion in the Salisbury district, Campbell reported that 'the chief Kunzwi had refused to allow the Native Police to collect hut tax in his district and had sent the police back to Mr Campbell with a threat that he would kill all police and white men in his district'. As a result of this threat a general warning was issued to all prospectors throughout Mashonaland; it was in fact the first intimation of the Shona rising.[1]

We may now sum up the character and effect of Company administration in Mashonaland. Despite its initial advantages in money and man-power the Company had devoted so little of its resources to native administration that the Shona were 'controlled' by an extremely haphazard and weak administrative machinery. It was not, however, this weakness which distinguished Southern Rhodesia from other territories in the early colonial period. The native administrations of the British and German companies in East Africa, or for that matter the early British and German administrations themselves, were equally weak and very little, if at all, more regular. The sharp distinction between Mashonaland and these other colonial situations was that in Mashonaland administrative weakness was combined with the presence and pressure of hundreds of settlers, with relatively rapid economic develop-

---

[1] Minutes of Executive Council, 4 Nov. 1895, EC 3/1/1; Instructions to C.N.C., 16 Nov. 1895, A 2/2/1; Minutes of Executive Council, 20 Apr. 1896, EC 3/1/1.

ment and with the demands of the over-confident Company itself. Generally speaking other early colonial *regimes* were aware of their weakness and ready to avoid an assault upon the total African society of the territory; moreover they could not even if they wished to do so ignore African economic systems completely and proceed at once to build up a white economy.

In Mashonaland the Company could and did see its main role as support for the extension of white economic activity. In the early years the Company presented itself to the Shona merely as an extension of settler power; its activities were confined to supporting settlers through punitive expeditions and through the compulsion of labour. It first made a more direct impact with the hut-tax demand, although both in its operation and in its intention hut tax itself was closely linked with settler economic interests. This demand for tax took place much earlier in the colonizing process in Mashonaland than elsewhere. Given the weakness of the Company administration and the fact that the Shona paramounts regarded themselves as unconquered and still possessed arms, it was bound to lead to serious disorder.

For the paramounts the tax demand came as the last in a series of grievances and led them to plan open and general armed resistance. These plans were bound to enjoy the overwhelming support of the Shona peoples. Company rule had meant for those Shona who lived in areas affected by white economic activity not only an infringement of the authority of the chiefs but a great disruption of their own lives. It had meant the loss of stock and sometimes of land; it had meant forced labour. Yet the Shona had neither been conquered by the whites nor come to terms with them in a series of treaty agreements. When there was added to all this an unprecedented sequence of natural disasters—drought, locusts and the spread of cattle disease which led to the whites shooting much of the stock that had not been taken for hut tax—the mass determination of the Shona to rid themselves of the white presence was confirmed.

Thus the Shona were 'controlled' by a native administration as weak as any in early colonial East and Central Africa but exposed to white pressures which had no parallel elsewhere unless perhaps in the enforced collective cash-crop farming areas of German East Africa which were later to be the scene of the Maji Maji rising. This white pressure created a common environment for the majority of the Shona and produced a common desire to act. What was now needed was the discovery of some effective machinery of co-ordination. And then the complacent Company administration in Mashonaland was likely to be very severely tested indeed.

CHAPTER THREE

Administration in Matabeleland, 1893 to 1896

COLONIAL ADMINISTRATION was established in Mashonaland by white infiltration into an area which was not at first equipped to comprehend what was involved nor to offer any co-ordinated resistance. Colonial administration was established in Matabeleland by the total military defeat of a resistant African state system, the leaders of which had for years been only too well aware of the implications of the white advance. The conquest of the Ndebele was followed by a considerably harsher and more intensive colonial pressure even than in Mashonaland. But it would be a mistake to suppose that such pressure was an inevitable after-effect of conquest. Many other African societies in Central and East Africa were defeated in war during the early colonial period and most of them were exposed after their conquest to significantly less pressure than the Shona, let alone the Ndebele. Once again the factor which distinguished the conquest of the Ndebele in 1893 from other early colonial conquests was the element of settler participation and the immediate expansion into Matabeleland of the economic energies of South Africa. As we shall see, just as the Company arrival in Mashonaland was signalled by the spreading out into the bush of the adventurers of the Pioneer Column so the Company victory over Lobengula was achieved largely by a white settler force determined from the beginning to exercise a free hand in post-conquest Matabeleland. And these men saw in the herds and lands of the Ndebele a richer prize than anything to be won in Mashonaland; mining prospects were thought at least as favourable; communications with South Africa were easier. Matabeleland in the three years between 1893 and 1896 witnessed a dispossession of Africans and a development of white enterprise unparalleled anywhere else in Central and East Africa. The new settlement of Bulawayo overtook Salisbury; with the railway reaching out towards it, it became the economic

capital of the Rhodesian colony. Virtually the whole of Ndebele
land and by far the greater part of Ndebele cattle passed into white
hands. Here an African economic system was taken notice of; and
having been noticed was expropriated. Profoundly involved anyway in the loss of land and cattle the Ndebele 'commoners' and the
Shona subject peoples were drawn more rapidly than the peoples
of Mashonaland into wage employment, sometimes in Matabeleland itself, sometimes in the Tati concessions, sometimes even in
the mines of South Africa.

Ndebele grievances were thus more dramatic than Shona and
their experience of the new white economy more intimate. But
these were not the only differences between the two societies. In
Mashonaland it was not the mode of arrival of the alien power,
still less a history of previously unsatisfactory relations with it, that
was resented but its steadily increasing pressure on peoples who
regarded themselves as still unconquered. In Matabeleland, on
the other hand, a long history of diplomatic relations between
the Company and the Ndebele before 1893 had already produced
a bitter Ndebele resentment even before the conquest of that year.
Moreover the manner of that conquest as well as the fact of it
added to Ndebele grievances. The Ndebele aristocracy regarded
the war of 1893 as an unjustifiable and unprovoked attack upon a
monarch who was seen as having gone to almost humiliating
lengths to avoid war with the whites. In order to understand the
atmosphere of the Ndebele rising we must explore briefly these
'national' grievances before turning to the post-conquest administration or lack of it.

It is unnecessary to describe in any detail the story of Rhodes'
negotiations with Lobengula before 1890; important as they were
to the Company's acquisition of its Charter and to the occupation
of Mashonaland and relevant though they were to Ndebele bitterness. They have often been narrated, perhaps nowhere better than
in Mr Phillip Mason's fine book, *The Birth of a Dilemma*. We need
notice here merely that the occupation of Mashonaland, theor-
etically on Lobengula's grant, was in fact carried out against his
bitter opposition and came as the climax of a series of events in
which the Ndebele aristocracy felt themselves to have been
deceived systematically by the agents of Rhodes. But it is necessary
to give some account of the movement towards the war of 1893. It
is a story which brings out clearly the unscrupulous but skilful

manipulation of men and events by Rhodes and his associates; the essential role of the white settler community; and the reasons for Ndebele bitterness after 1893.[1]

Although Rhodes had toyed in 1889 with a project for a surprise night attack on Bulawayo, and many of Lobengula's advisers had urged him to attack the Pioneer Column in 1890, between the occupation of Mashonaland and the so-called Victoria Incident of July 1893 neither Lobengula nor the Company wanted war. Lobengula almost certainly hoped to avoid war altogether for he had nothing to gain by postponing it. Rhodes and Jameson, however, planned the eventual conquest of Matabeleland—Rhodes said later that they had thought in terms of a war in 1894—but were happy to postpone the clash. They were happy because, as we have seen, it was believed that the Ndebele state was suffering from internal tensions which were progressively weakening its power to resist, and also because there were many other objects to be achieved before the Ndebele needed to be dealt with. The drastic reduction of the police at the end of 1891, which has often been put forward as a proof that Rhodes and Jameson did not plan war with the Ndebele, had in fact little to do with their intentions with regard to Matabeleland. The police had always been intended mainly to support Rhodes' attempt to push to the sea through Portuguese East Africa; they were to deal with the Portuguese rather than with the Ndebele. When Rhodes and Jameson thought of an invasion of Matabeleland they thought of it more in terms of an armed trek than of a police operation. Rhodes' Afrikaaner admirer, De Waal, has recorded a conversation between Rhodes and would-be Boer trekkers at the end of 1891 in which Rhodes promised them that they would one day be called upon to deal with the Ndebele and be given land for their assistance; while Jameson seriously discussed with the Boer trek leader, Ferreira, the outline of a dash to Bulawayo by a commando of 500 mounted Boers. Both men knew that when it came to the point of a war with the Ndebele there would be no shortage of volunteers, eager to lay their hands on Ndebele cattle and land; their main concern was to ensure that any such trek took place under their control

[1] P. Mason, *The Birth of a Dilemma*, London, 1958. The fullest treatment of the 1893 war is, S. Glass, 'The background of the Matabele War', unpublished thesis for the M.A., University of Natal, 1959. I dissent from many of the conclusions of this account.

rather than independently of the Company. And when in 1893 the invasion of Matabeleland at last took place, Jameson's triumphant column was composed in precisely this manner of white volunteer adventurers on a classic style commando raid.[1]

While bearing this consummation always in mind, Jameson was anxious so long as there was to be no war, to reduce tension, publicity and expense. He resolved to live amicably with Lobengula, and by dint of the exercise of restraint and patience on both sides found this surprisingly easy to manage. Lobengula, while not accepting that the Company enjoyed rights of jurisdiction in Mashonaland, or that their presence there put any restrictions on Ndebele raids, was in practice careful to control his regiments, so as to avoid unnecessary raiding and to avoid any clashes with the whites. On his side Jameson took a resolutely realistic view of Ndebele activities which contrasted strongly with the moral indignation later expressed. As we have seen, he dismissed the Lomagundi raid of October 1891 as 'unfortunate but in accordance with Lobengula's laws and customs'. The same attitude persisted in face of the infrequent Ndebele incursions of 1892 and early 1893—remonstrances were made to Lobengula, but there was no disposition whatever to inflate these incidents into a *casus bellum*, or to regard them as a source of serious danger to the settlers. By April 1893, in fact, Harris was writing to the London Board that 'the position of the Matabele today seems quite the reverse of what it was two years ago—*now* they fear an attack from us. Their apprehension is that the whites will enter Matabeleland and evidently they have quite abandoned any idea of offensive action but instead think they require to be on their defence. All fear of raiding into our sphere is, in our opinion, absolutely a thing of the past.'[2]

These assessments of the situation were a little too confident, however, as was demonstrated two months later when in July 1893 a large Ndebele *impi* appeared in the Fort Victoria area to punish local Shona who had been responsible for the theft of telegraph wire and for fomenting discord between Lobengula and the Company. Both Jameson and Rhodes recognized that the action of Lobengula in sending this *impi* made no essential difference to the situation. Jameson cabled that whites were in no

---

[1] De Waal, *With Rhodes in Mashonaland*, 1896; Harris to the London Board, 9 Aug. and 30 Aug. 1893, LO 5/2/28 and 29.

[2] Harris to London Board, 12 Apr. 1893, LO 5/2/26.

danger and that there was no conceivable chance of an Ndebele invasion of Mashonaland: the Victoria raid was really precisely similar to the Lomagundi raid. Jameson's first reaction was to treat it in the same way. 'Lendy's description of burning kraals and Mashonas killed on the commonage of course very harrowing,' he wired on July 11th, 'but that was at first blush and after sundown.' 'The incident, Mr Rhodes says,' cabled Harris to the London Board on July 12th, 'is greatly to be regretted' but 'it has afforded strong proof of Lobengula's determination not to come into collision with the white man'.[1]

Once Jameson arrived in Victoria, however, he changed his mind, not so much about the character of the raid as about the situation created by it. The main difference between this raid and previous ones was that it was the first to occur in an area occupied by white settlers. As Harris wrote with unusual frankness, previous raids had been 'passed over and made light of because they have not actually and seriously threatened our lives and property'. This raid did not threaten white lives either, but it did threaten property in the form of the Shona labourers who were being killed. One could no longer take the killing of the Shona so calmly when it threatened the drying up of the labour supply. 'It is simply a raid in rather large numbers,' cabled Jameson on July 17th, but 'the serious part is that every native has deserted from mines and farms. . . . The labour question is the serious one. There is no danger to the whites but unless some shooting is done I think it will be difficult to get labour even after they have all gone. There have been so many cases of Mashona labourers killed even in the presence of the white masters that the natives will not have confidence in the protection of the whites, unless we actually drive the Matabele out.' He had summoned the Ndebele *indunas*, he reported. 'I intend to treat them like dogs and order whole *impi* out of the country. Then if they do not go send Lendy out with 50 mounted men to fire into them.'[2]

For all the debate which has surrounded the events which then followed things happened exactly and simply as Jameson had said they would. The Ndebele were peremptorily ordered to go; they did not move off rapidly, and Lendy went out and fired into them.

---

[1] Jameson to Harris, 11 July 1893; Harris to London Board, 12 July 1893; LO 5/2/28.

[2] Jameson to Harris, 17 July 1893, Rhodes House, Mss. Afr. s. 228, C. 3B.

'When I arrived', cabled Jameson on the 19th after this clash, 'it was a state of siege and nothing for it but killing a few to show we were not going to negotiate for ever.' But the killing of a few Ndebele need not necessarily in itself have meant war; Jameson was sure that Lobengula did 'not want to fight but will be pleased at some of his young bloods being thrashed'. The matter might quite possibly have ended there.

Jameson was, however, as Major Leonard wrote of him, 'very much in favour of men rising to the occasion'. As he surveyed the situation on July 19th he felt that here was an occasion to rise to; there would never be a better opportunity to launch the war which was eventually to take place. 'The hare having once been started', he cabled to Harris, 'the people will not be satisfied of the security to life and property unless Loben gives in completely by paying up' the compensation to be demanded, 'or we go to Bulawayo. In fact at present they are all howling for the latter but that will pass over.' Thus Jameson dismissed the supposedly irresistible public pressure which it has often been thought forced him into the war. On the other hand this white enthusiasm could be used and Jameson thought the time had come to use it. 'Rhodes might consider the advisability of completing the thing. The cash could be found and it could be done pretty cheaply if the Macloutsie Police and the High Commissioner keep out of it. I know Ferreira's terms are for 500 mounted Boers to hand over the show, a moderate sum in cash and ammunition supplied, each man to receive a farm and his loot. . . . I suggest the Ferreira trick as we have the excuse for a row over murdered women and children now and the getting Matabeleland open would give us a tremendous lift in shares and everything else. The fact of its being shut up gives it an immense value both here and outside.' [1]

By July 22nd Jameson had come down even more firmly on the side of war—nothing would go well, he cabled, until 'some definite action is taken on our part of going into Matabeleland'. After some initial reluctance Rhodes agreed. 'Lobengula has forced this question on us. I would much rather it had been postponed for a year, but as Lobengula has brought it to a head and not we, I consider Dr Jameson has acted quite rightly in every step he has taken.' From this moment war was certain, despite the

---

[1] Jameson to Harris, 19 July 1893, ibid.

difficulties of financing it and the difficulties of escaping the High Commissioner's restraining control.[1]

It can be seen quite clearly in the Company letter books how the complex and effective propaganda machine controlled by Harris was set in motion. Ndebele aggression and their cruelty to the Shona, played down between 1890 and 1893, were now played up. The 'row over murdered women and children' was set going with a vengeance—'the question of contention between the Company and Lobengula is not one of gold or land or taxes', wrote Harris piously, 'but is the unfortunate slave or Maholi'. Details of all previous raids on the Shona, hitherto unpublicized were compiled; missionary letters calling for intervention on behalf of the Shona, hitherto ignored, were now sent to the British press. When J. S. Moffat wrote from Bulawayo to deny that Lobengula had any aggressive intention and to denounce Company preparations for war, Harris circulated privately to editors of the major British papers letters written by Moffat in 1890 in which he had predicted and welcomed just such a war.[2]

If some people remained unconvinced by this skilful propaganda, the London Board of the Company were not among them. Reassured that a forward policy would not be too expensive since Rhodes had placed £50,000 of his private fortune at Jameson's disposal 'to provide for any extra expenditure entailed by the Company at this end by the present state of affairs in Matabeleland', they only too readily supported a war to rescue the Shona and to open Matabeleland to British enterprise. There was only one difficulty, the British Government. 'Ripon sent for us the other day', wrote one of the London Board to Rhodes, 'and told us we might protect ourselves if attacked! but that we must in no case be in any way aggressive. . . . I gather it is your intention to find some way round the Governor's prohibition and settle the Matabele question this September once for all. We are in the darkness as to your plans but I have the fullest confidence in any move which you and Jameson agree in there. . . . We will support you whatever the issue.'[3]

It was indeed Rhodes' and Jameson's intention to find a way

---

[1] Jameson to Harris, 22 July 1893; Harris to London Board, 9 Aug. 1893, LO 5/2/28.
[2] Harris to London Board, 27 Sept. 1893, LO 5/2/30.
[3] Grey to Rhodes, 1 Sept. 1893, Rhodes House, Mss. Afr. s. 228, C. 3B.

round the prohibitions of the British Government. By September their troops were ready; recruited under the terms of the Victoria Agreement of August 14th, the whites of Mashonaland and adventurers from elsewhere in Southern Africa were prepared to march on Bulawayo in return for gold claims, farms, and loot. The High Commissioner, Harris thought, was convinced himself of the necessity of settling the matter but could not authorize an attack without some further pretext. But, added Harris significantly, 'I feel sure that a Matabele attack on us . . . will free his hand.' [1]

Harris therefore set about convincing the world that Lobengula was preparing to invade Mashonaland and that the Company's preparations were defensive. On September 13th, for instance, he wrote to report that Rhodes was convinced 'that within a short time Lobengula will attack us'. 'The news received today that the Mashonas are fortifying their caves and laying in supplies of water and mealies is most significant,' he continued, 'and as they are in close touch with their slave countrymen throughout Matabeleland they are thus enabled to form a very fair forecast of what Lobengula and his Nation intend to do.' 'So far we have in no way or form shewn any hostile intent . . . we have stood quietly on the defensive. Lobengula, on the other hand, has shown no sign whatever of regret or compunction but on the contrary he has shown every indication to try conclusions with us; he has doctored his roads, doctored his people, on two occasions he has sent small *impis* over the border and has moved up large bodies of men on to our borders.' On September 20th Harris was writing of 'serious hostile movements on the part of Lobengula'. Since Lobengula had neither written to ask for peace after the Victoria incident nor offered to pay compensation, it was reasonable to believe, Harris claimed, that 'he means to choose his own time and his own opportunity to re-assert his supremacy, and he is steadily moving up his men and making his internal arrangements preparatory to doing so. What is felt most in Africa is that the Colonial Office cannot see that this is the reasonable conclusion to be drawn from the events of the last two months in Mashonaland.' An Ndebele attack, wrote Harris, could be expected within the next two weeks. [2]

In fact it seems certain that what Harris himself had written

---

[1] Harris to London Board, 20 Sept, 1893, LO 5/2/29.
[2] Harris to London Board, 13 and 20 Sept. 1893, LO 5/2/29.

in April 1893 remained true and that the Ndebele had 'quite abandoned any idea of offensive action but think they require to be on their defence'. Despite the killing of members of the Victoria *impi*, Lobengula no more wanted war in September 1893 than he had ever done; he knew as well as ever what its outcome would be. When the column under Jameson actually invaded Matabeleland in October they found that the Ndebele had 'only out-posts' along the borders and that their main force was posted defensively along the Shangani. 'The western borders are more or less unprotected,' wrote Colenbrander from Bulawayo on October 11th. The 'large *impi*' whose presence near Fort Victoria had been ascertained, according to Harris, 'by their actual footpaths through the veld', had no existence save in his fertile and convenient imagination. The Ndebele were not massing along the border to attack Mashonaland. But Lobengula could not avoid the war; inevitably the necessary incidents of Ndebele firing on Company forces in the east and British forces in the south were reported; the High Commissioner gave permission for the advance; and the greatest of Jameson's gambles commenced.[1]

All military authorities had scouted Jameson's plan of a dash on Bulawayo as suicidal. But his luck was still with him and within little more than a month the Ndebele forces had been bloodily dispersed; Lobengula was in flight, and the Company's men were in Bulawayo. The details of the fighting need not concern us here, except to remark that in many ways the victory was deceptively easy. The Ndebele commanders displayed too great a military conservatism and their old tactics proved of no avail against modern firepower. 'This campaign has gone right through in the most wonderfully lucky way for our side,' wrote Selous to his mother. 'The Matabele generalship has been abominably bad. They never did what they ought to have done or took advantage of their opportunities. Had the Matabele here made a determined opposition we could never have got through and probably should have met with disaster. . . . So you see the campaign is virtually over and the fair-haired descendants of the northern pirates are in possession of the great King's kraal and the calf of the black cow has fled into the wilderness.' 'I think you will agree with me', wrote Rhodes to the High Commissioner on November 23rd, 'that

[1] Harris to London Board, 4 Oct. 1893; Colenbrander to Harris, 11 Oct. 1893; Vigers to Harris, 20 Oct. 1893, LO 5/2/30.

the matter is really over. Fancy the King in the bush in his wagon, drawn along by a few Bulawayo boys and deserted by all his royal regiments. It really is very sad.' [1]

It has often been argued that this war was both inevitable and desirable. What concerns us here is Ndebele reaction to it. Lobengula had gone to great, and in the view of many of his subjects to excessive, lengths to maintain peace. For what it was worth his position was undoubtedly the stronger in law, whether law as understood by the British or law as understood by the Ndebele. Yet he had been branded as an aggressor and war had been forced upon him. Of course the Ndebele had conquered many other peoples in their time and perhaps Selous had a valid point when he wrote that 'no one knowing their abominable history can pity them or lament their downfall. They have been paid back in their own coin.' But equally it was absurd to expect the Ndebele to see the victory of the Company in any other light than that so frankly cast by Selous himself—as the victory of the strongest set of pirates. Moreover, incidents such as the shooting of Lobengula's envoys to the High Commissioner, and the stealing of the gold with which he made his last desperate effort to buy peace, whoever was responsible for them, left the Ndebele with a lasting sense of bitterness. Against such a background Rhodes' cheerful optimism that most of the Ndebele were 'naturally' very happy to see the Company governing Matabeleland must appear fatuous to a degree. [2]

To the desire of the Ndebele to preserve institutions of which they were fiercely proud there was added, then, a deep resentment at the manner in which their state had been overthrown. And there was added, also, hatred of the system of administration actually set up by the conqueror. We must now examine the character of that administration.

The war between the Company and Lobengula was accompanied and followed by another contest, almost as sharply fought and with the same management of propaganda, between the Company and the Colonial Office. Having failed to prevent the war, the British Government were hopeful that they would be able to prevent the imposition on Matabeleland of the kind of

---

[1] Selous to his mother, 15 Nov. 1893, SE 1/1/1; Rhodes to Loch, 23 Nov. 1893, LO 5/2/31.
[2] Selous to his mother, 15 Nov. 1893, SE 1/1/1.

settlement for which the whites of Mashonaland were fighting. On October 23rd the Imperial Secretary told the Company that 'all negotiations with Lobengula are to be conducted by the High Commissioner and under his complete control'. There was an immediate and extravagant reaction. On the same day Harris wrote to tell Rhodes that there was a plot to deprive the Company of all powers in Matabeleland except the right to exploit minerals there; and Rhodes replied furiously that the 'idea as to Loch's wishing for administration at Bulawayo is so monstrous that I cannot believe it'. Within two days the press campaign was raging. The *Cape Times* of October 26th wrote of the High Commissioner seeking 'to weaken the energies of our fellow colonists by holding up some spectre of a settlement in which neither they nor Mr Rhodes shall have any controlling voice or even any concern'. The *Cape Argus* fulminated against 'Criminal Imperialism'. 'Instead of allowing its subjects in this part of the world a chance of driving monsters like Lobengula over the Zambesi', they wrote, Britain 'comes in on these wrong principles, and seems to be willing to protect a powerful Kaffir in the execution of his murders'.[1]

In their protests the Company stressed the expectations and deserts of the white volunteers who had taken Bulawayo and more than hinted that unless a settlement favourable to them was granted they would take matters into their own hands. On November 1st Harris cabled to congratulate the London Board 'on this splendid news. Seeing we beat the Matabele single-handed and we have occupied Bulawayo, surely Marquis of Ripon will not rob Mr Rhodes settlement unaided of question as our whole future will depend upon this settlement and if Marquis of Ripon refuses people of Mashonaland they will demand it.' Jameson wrote from the field of victory to say that 'there can be no question but that Matabeleland is to be treated as a portion of Mashonaland lately occupied by the Matabele. . . . Should there be any Imperial interference in the Administration of Matabeleland I am sure every member of the column would feel personally aggrieved. . . . We have all the machinery for effective civil government as in Mashonaland and if interfered with it will lead to more than discontent among the people.' The indignant *Cape Times* asked whether the High Commissioner would be able 'to impose terms

<hr/>

[1] Bower to Harris, 23 Oct. 1893; Harris to Rhodes, 23 Oct. 1893, Rhodes to Harris, 24 Oct. 1893; LO 5/2/30.

distasteful to a community which has sent two thirds of its man-
hood as volunteers to the front'. The paper darkly hinted that the
British Government might find themselves faced with the necessity
of crushing 'a new Republic, which would cause more blood and
treasure than the whole Matabele nation is worth'.[1]

The victory of Jameson and his men was in fact so complete that
the British Government felt themselves to have no alternative but
to agree to the extension of Company rule over Matabeleland.
On November 4th the Colonial Office wrote to the London
Board that 'correspondence has hitherto proceeded upon the
supposition that at the close of hostilities it would be practicable to
open negotiations with Lobengula in his capacity as King, and to
come to a settlement with him, representing the Matabele people.
But the circumstances have now, to all appearances, materially
altered owing to the success achieved by the forces of the British
South Africa Company which has apparently resulted in the
defeat of Lobengula and the destruction of his power.' Under these
circumstances the Government were prepared to allow 'terms
agreed by Mr Rhodes and High Commissioner and recommended
by High Commissioner to British Government for confirmation',
as the London Board cabled on the same day. 'Think the British
Government are anxious to meet Mr Rhodes' wish', they added,
'but fear Radical members of parliament and press.' [2]

Mr Rhodes' wish was above all for a settlement which gave a
free hand both to the Company and to the white volunteers. He
went out of his way in a speech to the volunteers in Bulawayo on
December 19th to promise an early land settlement—'It is your
right for you have conquered the country.' 'What I want you to
see,' he told them, 'is that really the mode of final settlement of the
country will not be with Her Majesty's Government, Dr Jameson
or myself, but with you the first settlers and your representatives.' [3]

The best that the High Commissioner could do was to attempt
to protect Ndebele land and cattle from wholesale expropriation.
He insisted that no final allocations of land and cattle should be
made until the British Government had decided upon the administration of Matabeleland. And in the arrangement negotiated
with Rhodes in May 1894 which became the basis of the Mata-

[1] Harris to London Board, 1 Nov. 1893; Jameson to Rhodes, 18 Nov. 1893,
LO 5/2/31.   [2] London Board to Harris, 4 Nov. 1893, LO 5/2/31.
[3] *Cape Argus*, 3 Jan. 1894.

beleland Order in Council of July 1894, provision was made for the establishment of machinery to protect Ndebele interests. This machinery was to take the form of a Land Commission, upon which the Imperial Government was to be represented, which would make provision for 'land sufficient and suitable' for Ndebele needs and for 'cattle sufficient'. Until this Commission had reported no grants of land or cattle were to be made.[1]

The history of Company administration in Matabeleland in 1894 and 1895 is largely the story of how these protective provisions of the Matabeleland Order in Council were flouted and evaded with regard both to land and to cattle. The rich agricultural and grazing land of the Ndebele home area had been one of the inducements offered to the volunteers under the Victoria Agreement, each man being given the right to peg out a farm of 3000 morgen. The overthrow of the Ndebele, indeed, led to a veritable land rush. 'There should be good immigration from the Colony and Transvaal this year,' wrote one of the victors from Bulawayo in January 1894, 'as the country has always been looked upon as a good country by all Dutchmen and the Matabele were no fools.' Quick fortunes were to be made by shrewd speculators in the days immediately following the conquest. Thus Hans Sauer tells us that his agent in Bulawayo bought up for less than £500 a number of volunteer farm pegging rights and then 'pegged and located four large blocks running into very many thousands of acres'; this land, which ran from the Bulawayo commonage to the Matopos, was sold a few months later to Rhodes himself for £20,000. The Company was generous; there seemed land and enough to spare; and no one was particular about the surveying of the blocks pegged out. A later and more careful Administrator described what happened under Jameson; 'The law has been entirely disregarded and surveyors have been employed privately to carve up the land at their discretion in accordance with the directions of their employers.' In circumstances such as these the High Commissioner's injunction against any permanent settlement of land was too frail a barrier to enterprise. Jameson merely

[1] Matabeleland Order in Council, July 1894. Mason, op. cit. has a good account of the High Commissioner's thinking on the problem of the administration of Matabeleland based on official sources. I have given here the situation as it appeared to Rhodes and Harris in order to bring out the Company approach to the problem.

replied with assurances that all his grants were provisional—'Jameson found "provisional" a blessed word', writes his biographer. 'He did all things provisionally—rewarding his followers with "provisional" farms and laying out three miles to the south of the royal kraal the "provisional" site of the "provisional" town of Bulawayo.' [1]

But the 'provisional' character of Jameson's grants did not prevent the Land Commission from being faced with a *fait accompli* which it and the British Government tamely accepted. 'The British South Africa Company has made numerous grants of land to Europeans in portions of the country where the natives formerly resided,' reported the Commission in October 1894. 'The unallotted lands between these grants are small in extent and cannot be accurately ascertained.' Therefore, they concluded, Reserves could not be established for the Ndebele in their old home land. On the other hand no grants of land had been made by the Company to the north and the north east, where few Ndebele had previously lived, and these areas, though too remote for the Commission to inspect thoroughly, they recommended as adequate and suitable Reserves. Their report was accepted by the High Commissioner, who commented merely that the smaller area of land now allocated to the Ndebele instead of their old home would certainly be sufficient for them because so many of the MaHoli caste had deserted their old masters. [2]

It is important to realize precisely what had occurred. Literally the whole of the Ndebele home area had been given away in the few months which followed the conquest. A later member of the Native Department described the situation thus created. 'The formerly dominant tribe of this territory, through whom the first titles to the territory were secured by whites . . . are, of all tribes, now in the worst position in respect of land. It is true that they were usurpers displaced by our usurpation but it is nevertheless an unfortunate fact that the premier native race whose organising power and gift for government enabled them to impose their will on the minor tribes, and whose inherent character must inevitably

---

[1] Gifford to Cawston, 14 Jan. 1894, Rhodes House, Mss. Afr. s.76; Milton to Rhodes, 8 Aug. 1898, ibid., s.228, C. 1; H. Sauer, *Ex Africa*, 1937; I. Colvin, *Life of Jameson*, London, 1912, Vol. 1.

[2] *C. 8130, Matabeleland: report of the land commission of 1894 and correspondence relating thereto*, 1896.

establish their major influences for good or bad in the future development and happiness of our natives, should suffer from an ever increasing sense of dissatisfaction with the provision made for them in this regard. Their misfortune was in the first place their national predilection for the red and black loams which co-incided with the so-called shale formation. The quartz reefs occur here and again coincide with the pasturage which their judgement informed them was the best for their cattle. Within a few months of the European occupation practically the whole of their most valued region ceased to be their patrimony and passed into the private estate of individuals and the commercial property of companies. The whole of what the term "nga pakati kew lizwe" (the midst of the land) conveyed became metamorphosed . . . into alien soil and passed out of the direct control even of the Government. . . . In the native concept Government and Ownership of land are indivisible. That land on which people live and have lived for generations can be purchased for money is a matter hard to be understood. White men of varied origin and race become in a day their landlords, their overlords, with power to dispossess and drive forth. To an aristocratic race the delegation of such power has appeared unseemly in many cases. The word "amaplazi" . . . meaning "farms" stands, it may be said, for almost all that is most distasteful in our rule. Almost it stands for helotage and servitude to a chance-made master.' [1]

Land was given out so lavishly not only to reward the volunteers but also to give important sections of English society a stake in the success of the new Colony. Jameson was surrounded by a group of aristocratic young men of the class later described by Lord Grey as filled 'with the jolly reckless spirit of adventure, which aimed at making a million in half an hour and then clearing home to Piccadilly'. The most important of these was Jameson's unofficial military adviser in the march on Bulawayo, Sir John Willoughby, who had been used by the Company since 1890 to advertise the prospects of mining and agriculture in Rhodesia. Now Willoughby and the others received a lavish reward in the shape of very extensive grants of land to the companies and syndicates which they formed. In September 1896, William Milton, who had come up to reorganize the Rhodesian administration at Rhodes' request, and who later became Administrator in his turn, commented in

[1] Superintendent of Natives, Bulawayo, to C.N.C., 1 June 1920, N 3/16/9.

amazement at the methods of Jameson. 'Everything official here is in an absolutely rotten condition,' he wrote, 'and will continue so until we can clear out the Honourable and military elements which are rampant everywhere and are evidently expecting to be rewarded with fat billets after the war. If they get them I am off. The country has been very nearly ruined by them already under the wing of Jameson, and if it is to continue the Imperial Government will be quite justified in stepping in.' 'Lady Dudley's son,' he continued, 'a youngster of the la di da class, has just been sent up here probably with an expression of Jameson's wish that half a county may be given to him. I can see that Rhodes is getting a bit sick and even Grey is beginning to see that Jameson has given nearly the whole country away to the Willoughbys, Whites and others of that class so that there is absolutely no land left which is of any value for settlement of immigrants by Government. It is perfectly sickening to see the way in which the country has been run for the sake of hob-nobbing with Lord this and the Honble that. I think Jameson must have been off his head for some time before the raid.' [1]

Indeed, once the excitement of conquest had died down, it came to be seen that Jameson had damaged the interests of the Company as well as of the Ndebele by his generosity to the various white adventurers in Matabeleland. 'Land was alienated in the most reckless manner', wrote Milner, 'to Companies and individuals. *Now* the Company—or in other words Rhodes and his principal agents—recognize this themselves. . . . They feel, what a mill stone they have tied round their necks with all these syndicates, holding thousands of square miles which they are doing nothing to develop.' 'Land is our great difficulty,' wrote Lord Grey on May 26th, 1897. 'It has all been given away. I will not give away another acre until the Native Question has been settled.' [2]

And if the homeland of the Ndebele had thus been alienated, the Reserves allocated to them were profoundly unsuitable. In 1897 the British Deputy Commissioner, Sir Richard Martin, who had not been asked to inquire into the Reserves for his report to the British Government, nevertheless raised the matter in correspondence with the High Commissioner. He reported that on

---

[1] Milton to his wife, 18 Sept. 1896, ML 1/1/2
[2] Milner to Chamberlain, 1 Dec. 1897, Headlam, op. cit., Vol. 1, pp. 139–46, Grey to Cawston, 26 May 1897, Rhodes House, Mss. Afr. s. 77.

looking into the question of the Reserves he was obliged to 'refer rather unfavourably to the Report of the Land Commission'. The areas allocated to the Ndebele were 'badly watered, sandy and unfit for settlement, therefore unsuitable for a native location'. The Land Commission, he wrote, should have recommended that land already pegged for whites be nevertheless set aside for the Ndebele. And although the Administrator, Lord Grey, fiercely contested Martin's criticisms on other points, he privately admitted the complete justice of this one. 'Unless we can provide a government farm or two in each Native Commissioner's district,' he wrote to Rhodes in May 1897, 'Martin will insist upon an independent report by some Imperial officer as to the suitability of the Guai and Shangani Reserves for natives and it would be a nasty shock for us if a report were to come out at this time condemning the Guai and Shangani Reserves as wholly unsuitable for Native Locations. . . . An inquiry into the character of the Guai and Shangani Reserves will bring out the fact that they are regarded by the natives as *cemeteries* not homes.' [1]

In fact the Ndebele almost universally refused to move into the Reserves, with the result that they found themselves living on private farms and therefore subject to rental charges, eviction, and so on. It is true that the full implications of this 'helotage and servitude to a chance-made master' were hardly grasped by 1896, since few of the white farms had been occupied and worked by the time the rising broke out. Nevertheless it was already fully appreciated that 'the white man took from the Matabili the land, as they had taken it from the Maholi and the Mashonas'. And already clashes between the new owners and the Ndebele residents were occurring. As the senior *induna*, Gambo, protested at the *indaba* of June 1897 'one cause of dissatisfaction and unrest is that after we have lived many years in a spot we are told that a white man has purchased it, and we have to go'. [2]

If the Land Commission proved totally ineffective as a protection for Ndebele land rights, it did little more to ensure justice with regard to the great herds of cattle which had belonged to the Ndebele nation in 1893. Estimates of the numbers of cattle owned by the Ndebele before the war varied widely. The missionary,

[1] Martin's Report, 12 Apr. 1897, Colonial Office, Confidential Prints. South Africa, No. 520, pp. 550 to 556; Grey to Rhodes, Rhodes House, Mss. Afr. s. 228, C. 1.   [2] *Bulawayo Chonicle*, 26 June 1897.

Carnegie, believed that there were some 280,000; the High Commissioner thought there were some 200,000; Lord Grey suggested 130,000. The highest figure was probably the most correct. Opinion also differed about the 'ownership' of the cattle. Some were said to be 'owned' by private individuals, others by the King. But there could be no disagreement about the importance of the cattle to the Ndebele nation as a whole.

Mr Philip Mason has written that the question of cattle 'was a matter which for any Bantu people lay very near that core of self respect without which a man or a people break down into degradation or desperate violence. Cattle were everywhere a prize to be captured or carried away in war as a sign of victory, but they were far more than that. Among the Mashona tribes—and many of the so-called Matabele by origin belonged to the Mashona group— cattle are often dedicated or vowed to an ancestor and regarded as held in trust for him. Among both Matabele and the Mashona . . . cattle are intimately connected with marriage and, when a woman leaves one group for another, cattle change hands and are usually distributed among her relations; cattle sustain the marriage as well as nourishing the holders with their milk; they may be handed back, or at least claimed, if there is a divorce. And among the Zulus, the Matabele and the Angoni, there was a kind of feudal network of cattle-holding; a rich man gave out his cattle to his feudal followers who used the milk but might not kill a beast without his sanction. The King's cattle were spread far and wide among his people, held in varying degrees of vassalage.'

In such a situation the debate about the 'ownership' of the Ndebele cattle was bound to be an unreal one. As Mr Mason says 'among the Matabele, the King, an ancestral spirit, a married woman, an Induna, and the man who milked her, might have said of one beast: "This is my cow." To decide who owned the cattle of the Matabele was not a tangle to unravel in a few weeks. One thing only is clear: the cattle were one of the strands that bound the Matabele people together, the way they were held contributing to the royal dominion, to the cult of the ancestors, and to the stability of marriage.' [1]

The British Government was concerned to ensure that the Ndebele retained 'enough' cattle for their needs; the Company were concerned to exploit Ndebele cattle as a source of wealth and

[1] Mason, op. cit.

patronage. Once again attempts were made to erect successful restraints; once again these attempts failed. The question was raised by the Colonial Secretary, Lord Ripon, on December 10th, 1893. Referring to reports in the press that Ndebele cattle were being rounded up by the Company's forces, Ripon wrote to the High Commissioner that he could not 'approve the continued seizure of cattle from people who have ceased to offer any organized or effective resistance'. Loch replied that he understood that only royal cattle were being seized. 'Experience in former wars,' returned Ripon, 'especially in Zululand, shows that distinction between King's cattle and people's cattle is fallacious, all cattle being in some sense King's. As I have already told you, Her Majesty's Government attach importance to securing to Matabele ample cattle for their requirements; therefore it is necessary that sufficient cattle should be held in trust, out of any that may have been seized from whatever source, to ensure attaining that object.' These interventions irked Rhodes and Jameson almost beyond endurance. In a private letter on December 25th Rhodes told Loch that Ripon's inquiries were 'really very annoying. . . . As to cattle Lord Ripon is incorrect when he states that there are no King's cattle and that the statement is a fiction; as a matter of fact there are King's cattle. All I know is that whilst I was in Bulawayo natives constantly brought in cattle of their own accord stating that they were the King's cattle; they would not be likely to do this with their own. However, we, the British South Africa Company, have been taking no cattle since I have been at Bulawayo, as we have given up patrolling for them and propose to leave King's cattle for natives to take care of. I may state that the natives readily recognize that they have in charge a large number of cattle which they consider the King's cattle; these are totally apart from those which are their own private property, but even the King's cattle we propose to leave with the natives. . . . I think Lord Ripon would be wise', concluded Rhodes, 'not to give credence to every unauthorised telegram which he reads in the English press. . . . The Transvaal party are well aware of what the conquest of Matabeleland means to them and are naturally trying to cause friction if they can between myself and Her Majesty's Government.' [1]

[1] Ripon to Loch, 10 Dec. 1893, 13 Dec. 1893, Blue Book *C. 7290*, Nos. 44 and 53; Rhodes to Loch, 25 Dec. 1893, LO 5/2/32.

On the strength of this letter and similar assurances from Jameson, the High Commissioner told Ripon on January 11th, 1894, that 'the distinction' between royal and private cattle 'is clear'; that the Company were only laying claim to the former; that these royal herds could reasonably be regarded as 'state funds'; and that in any case these cattle were being entrusted to the Ndebele kraals to keep and to milk. This state of affairs was approved by Ripon, on condition that the royal herds were regarded as a trust fund from which cattle could be drawn if it was later found that the 'private' cattle were not sufficient to Ndebele needs. A final settlement, as we have seen, was to be made by the Land Commission.

Now Rhodes' letter was extremely disingenuous, to say the least. In practice the clear distinction on which he insisted between royal and private cattle was never observed. In the weeks after the war all cattle that could be collected were rounded up and brought into Bulawayo, and later those which were distributed to the kraals about Bulawayo or left in kraals in other areas were still regarded as Company property. Edwards tells us that in March 1894 he asked the head clerk at the Magistrate's office in Bulawayo 'whether it was necessary for me to have a permit to buy cattle from the natives. He was greatly astonished at my question. "Buy cattle? What do you mean? All the cattle in the country belonged to the King and now belong to the Chartered Company." ' By the time the Land Commission reported in October the distinction had disappeared even in theory. 'It would be a most difficult if not impossible task to distinguish between "King's" and private cattle,' they reported, and this being so they recommended that all cattle in Matabeleland be regarded as belonging to the Company by right of conquest, the Company undertaking to make adequate allocation to the Ndebele.[1]

Nor was raiding for cattle long suspended. After the rains were over Jameson sent out large patrols in June 1894, one to the north, another to the south-east, and another to the west of Bulawayo, while small patrols were 'continually moving through the veld'. Of the patrol to the west Jameson reported on June 28th that it had enlisted the co-operation of the local *indunas* 'to help in the collection of the King's cattle of which a good number have been brought in'. Indeed patrols were constantly searching out cattle

[1] Edwards' reminiscences, ED 6/1/1.

from that time until the end of 1895, Native Commissioners and their police replacing the military patrols after October 1894, but the search going on.[1]

Nor were all the cattle collected put out for herding to Ndebele kraals pending a final settlement. The Victoria Agreement had laid it down that volunteers should have a share in the 'loot' taken in the conquest of Matabeleland and it was understood by everyone that the Ndebele cattle were included in that 'loot'. Thus the Company established what were called 'loot kraals' for the reception of a proportion of the cattle collected, these being managed by a 'loot committee'. From these kraals cattle were either distributed to volunteers or sold by auction, the proceeds being used for money payments instead. Little evidence survives on proceedings which were naturally not much publicized. But in the manuscript memoirs of John Meikle is to be found a story which well illustrates the manner in which the business of the Ndebele cattle was handled by the Company, at any rate immediately after the war. Meikle was in Fort Victoria with the Victoria defence force during the period of Jameson's march on Bulawayo. Soon after the capture of Bulawayo, 'news was brought into Victoria that the Mashonas were crossing over into Matabeleland and stealing the King's cattle which were not being properly herded owing to the unsettled state of the country. It was arranged that each member of the column would be entitled to peg a farm in Matabeleland of six thousand acres and that they should participate in any loot taken. The King's cattle were looked upon as loot and if this thieving continued it would mean so much less for the members of the column. Consequently a wire was sent to Mr Rhodes explaining the position to which he replied offering half the cattle brought in to those who went out to collect them. I was invited to form one of a party of twelve.' Meikle was soon in command of the patrol, the Captain of the Victoria defence force being 'reduced to the ranks' after a drunken quarrel. Under Meikle's leadership they entered Matabeleland. They came to a large kraal and sent for the headman. 'I explained to him that we had been sent by Mr Rhodes to collect the King's cattle and ordered all cattle to be brought to where we were camped. When they arrived I told them to pick out all cattle that belonged to them. This they did and out of about three hundred head they left one very old bull and one older cow,

saying those were the King's cattle. As a result of this we took the
lot knowing full well that none of the cattle really belonged to
them, that they were cattle they must have stolen and if not that
had been left in their charge.' 'These natives were disposed to be
rather nasty,' Meikle adds.

They then came to 'a flat-topped hill' on which was a large
kraal. Meikle and one other climbed up and found there the
commander and many of the members of an Ndebele regiment
which had taken part in the Shangani fight. 'After the Shangani
fight he and his men had had enough of it and taking their women
and all the cattle they could manage to drive, made for this out of
the way almost inaccessible mountain, thinking they would be
safe until things settled down again.' There were some 900 warriors there and some 600 head of cattle. 'I asked the *induna* to let us
have eighty of his men', continues Meikle, 'to assist in driving the
cattle, promising to allow them to keep their goats, of which they
had about a thousand head and to present each with a blanket on
returning to Victoria.' The *induna* agreed and Meikle set off with
80 strapping young Ndebele warriors in his train. 'They proved
invaluable as drovers and herds for the cattle.' After further ad-
ventures they returned to Victoria with some 1500 cattle. 'Each
member received as his share 72 head. . . . Although 72 head of
cattle seems a lot in actual money value it only represented about
£150. Still, it was good money for less than three weeks' work.'
And Meikle's story ends characteristically: 'A deputation came
to say the members of the expedition wished me to pick two animals
out of each one's lot and buy myself something with the proceeds.
This I refused to do so they had a ring made for me out of gold
ornaments found at the Zimbabwe Ruins and inscribed "Matabele
loot, 1893".' [1]

We may be sure that no word of this transaction reached the
High Commissioner or Colonial Secretary. How many cattle were
disposed of through the loot kraals or as rewards to patrols for
bringing them in it is impossible to say. In 1897 the Acting Administrator of Matabeleland gave the figure of 30,000 as the
number of cattle delivered to the loot committee. But we can be
certain that many more than that found their way into private
white hands. Some, indeed, were acquired by white adventurers in
spite of rather than through the Company. In the first weeks after

[1] Meikle's reminiscences, ME 1/1/1.

the overthrow of the King it was possible, as the High Commissioner reported, 'for stray Europeans to help themselves'; and undoubtedly there were a number of enterprising South Africans who managed to get 'herds into the South African Republic'. The Magistrate at Tati reported in January 1894 that he had intercepted 300 'looted Matabele oxen' being driven south but that many others had probably passed his patrols in the bush. And even when order was more or less restored the Company's doctrine that all cattle in the country belonged to them enabled unscrupulous or innocent whites to buy cattle from the Ndebele at absurdly low prices and then to smuggle them into Mashonaland. Edwards tells us frankly of his own exploits in this line. Travelling to Bulawayo he was offered and bought a number of cattle at very low prices. Discovering in Bulawayo that all were supposed to belong to the Company, he hastily got himself a brand registered, branded all the cattle with it, and drove them into Mashonaland. 'We wished to get as far away as possible from the place where "all the cattle belonged to the Chartered Company" and where the custodians, or maybe rightful owners, of the same tempted you with cattle at prices which were hard to resist.' [1]

In these various ways, together with Company requisitioning of cattle for 'police rations', large numbers of cattle had already been permanently removed from the Ndebele by the time that the Land Commission came to make its report in October 1894. Ripon's injunction that only royal cattle should be collected and that these should be held in trust until the decision of the Land Commission had certainly not been observed. In any case the Land Commission came to no decision; it could obtain no reliable figures either of the numbers of cattle still in Ndebele hands or of the numbers of Ndebele; it therefore recommended that 'the British South Africa Company without delay appoint officials entrusted with the duty of exercising supervision over the natives, ascertaining the number of natives and cattle on the Reserves, and periodically reporting to the Land Commission or Judicial Commissioner . . . the results of their inquiries, in order that the Commission, or Judicial Commissioner . . . may give such directions with regard to the delivery of cattle as may be considered

[1] Magistrate, Tati, to Imperial Secretary, 8 Jan. 1894; High Commissioner to Colonial Secretary, 16 Jan. 1894, Blue Book C. 7290, Encl. 1 in No. 92 and No. 93.

just'. After this report the commissions of the two non-judicial members were allowed to lapse and Judge Vintcent, the Judicial Commissioner, became solely responsible for the final settlement.[1]

The Commission's recommendations were the genesis of the Native Department in Matabeleland, where the Department was as essentially a cattle collecting concern as the Department in Mashonaland was essentially a tax collecting one. The Cattle Regulations of October 1894 outlined the essential duties of the new Commissioners. They were to register every kraal, noting the number of inhabitants and the number of cattle. The cattle were to be branded with the Company's brand and they were not to be sold or slaughtered without the permission of the Native Commissioner. In other words, until the final distribution, most of the remaining cattle were to be left in Ndebele hands instead of gathered up into fresh loot kraals, but they were to be clearly the property of the Company. As if to emphasize this, regular 'draughts' of cattle were made upon the kraals to meet the needs of the Company for 'police rations'. In short the activities of the Native Commissioners were conceived more in the interests of the Company than in those of compiling accurate statistics. In May 1895 for instance there was some friction between Vintcent and the Company. Vintcent, perfectly properly, began to behave as if he intended to make the final award on his own initiative; held *indabas* with the Ndebele *indunas*; and seemed inclined to be more generous to them than the Company were prepared to accept. 'Re the telegram about Vintcent and the cattle,' cabled Harris to the Acting Administrator, 'C. J. says we cannot do anything publicly to get rid of him just now, or he would. As you know "the cattle" is a very tender spot for Vintcent to touch upon and he was furious about the *indaba*. . . . I wired you that C. J.'s advice was to go on branding cattle as quickly as possible and then all we had to do in court would be to prove our brand.'[2]

In the end the settlement was agreed more harmoniously between Vintcent and the Chief Native Commissioner. The task of registration and branding was over by October 1895. It was found that there were at that time 74,500 head of cattle in African hands in Matabeleland. It was agreed that of these 40,930 should

---

[1] Report of the Land Commission, Oct. 1894.
[2] Harris to Acting Administrator, 24 May 1895, Rhodes House, Mss. Afr. s. 25.

be allocated as private property to the Ndebele; 7000 should be driven to Mashonaland for sale at 50s. a head to 'bona fide farmers'; 17,020 should be similarly sold in Matabeleland; 8850 were to be reserved for the ubiquitous Sir John Willoughby; and 700 held in the various districts for police rations. This settlement was announced to a gathering of some 200 *indunas* and headmen by the Chief Native Commissioner on November 29th, 1895. 'They expressed themselves as being highly pleased with the terms and desired Mr Taylor to convey their thanks to the Administrator.' [1]

It is hard to see what the *indunas* had to be pleased about. 40,930 cattle were left in Ndebele hands—a very considerable drop from 280,000 or even from 200,000. Where had the rest gone? The Company admitted that 30,000 had gone to the loot committee and 19,450 for police rations, in addition to the 33,570 allocated to the Company in November 1895. This amounted to a total of some 124,000. The remainder, as many again if we accept Carnegie's figures, were unaccounted for. Some went the way of the cattle acquired by Meikle; others the way of the cattle acquired by Edwards. But wherever they went it amounted to a disastrous loss for the Ndebele. Moreover, the 40,930 cattle which were actually distributed as private property were distributed in a manner which increased resentment. The Land Commission had noted that the Company were prepared to give cattle to 'the leading *indunas*'; Vintcent later said that in the final settlement 'the more deserving *indunas* and headmen' got cattle. It looks very much as if the share-out was used to reward 'loyalty' rather than to meet the needs of the Ndebele in general.

To complete the picture of what this forfeiture of cattle meant to the Ndebele we must note here that the share-out was almost immediately followed by a natural disaster which was in no way the Company's fault. No sooner had cattle been allocated than Native Commissioners were having them shot to prevent the spread of the rinderpest. A figure which will bring home more strikingly than anything else the magnitude of the disaster suffered by the Ndebele is that given by Sir William Milton in a letter of 1902. In 1893 the Ndebele alone had possessed some 200,000 cattle or more; in 1897, after the forfeitures, the rinderpest and the risings, there were only 13,983 head of cattle in African hands in the whole of Rhodesia. As Mason writes, 'Matabele society was

[1] Secretary, Bulawayo to Secretary, Cape Town, 13 Dec, 1895, LO 5/2/46.

disrupted by tearing out one of the most binding strands in the whole fabric.' [1]

This account of the handling of Ndebele land and cattle brings out the atmosphere of the Company administration of Matabeleland, and incidentally shows how ill-founded were claims that Company rule had brought to the Ndebele the benefits of secure private ownership. We must now look at 'Native administration' in more general terms. We have seen that a Native Department was set up in Matabeleland towards the end of 1894. What was the machinery for intervention in and control of Ndebele affairs before that?

For most of 1894 the administration of Matabeleland amounted to frank military despotism by Jameson's white police. We should not compare this period with 1891 in Mashonaland and with Pennefather's police activities; there, as we have seen, the commander of the police was mainly concerned with establishing legitimate treaty rights with the Shona paramounts and with initiating trade with them. Matabeleland on the other hand was a conquered country which meant that the police were deliberately attempting to break up various features of traditional life—such as the regimental kraals—in a way that never happened prior to 1896 in Mashonaland. In Mashonaland there was never any attempt before the risings to disarm the Shona; even after the Matabeleland Order in Council no one in Mashonaland was quite sure that they had the authority to do it. In Matabeleland any African seen with a gun could be shot on sight. Moreover, Matabeleland was only imperfectly conquered for most of 1894. Swift and complete though the Company's victory had been at the centre, the collapse of the Kingship had left confusion and disorder everywhere and especially in the outlying districts. As late as June 1894 Jameson and Harris were arguing that the country could 'be considered to be, in the outlying districts, more or less in a state of war. . . . Individual Matabeles, owing to the cessation of the King's rule were taking advantage of the inter-regnum and were behaving in a lawless and violent manner.' Administration in 1894, then, was administration by police patrol and if necessary with summary executions by martial law. [2]

Such methods, however, could only suppress disorder and not

[1] Milton to Rhodes, 25 Jan. 1902, Rhodes House, Mss. Afr. s. 228, C. 1.
[2] Harris to London Board, 4 July 1894, LO 5/2/36.

fill the vacuum left by the overthrow of the King. In February 1894 a percipient British officer reported to the High Commissioner that there was an urgent need for the appointment of executive and judicial officers. 'Up to the present', he wrote, 'there has been a Magistrate appointed for Bulawayo; with the increasing number of white persons in the country it will be impossible for this official alone . . . to properly attend to his office work and at the same time carry out the work that heretofore has been done by the King. The result will be that the natives, finding their little cases not attended to, will turn to their *Indunas*, thereby increasing their influence rather than lessening it. . . . I would suggest the appointment of one head native commissioner to reside at Bulawayo, who should hear and decide civil cases where natives alone are concerned, with 4 or 5 other native commissioners settled in various parts of the country.' These recommendations were not followed. A Native Commissioner was, indeed, appointed but his tasks were certainly not those of the head of a department or a civil judge. Johan Colenbrander, who had acted as the Company's agent in Bulawayo under Lobengula, now became Native Commissioner; throughout 1894 he was active accompanying police patrols, negotiating surrenders, seeking out cattle and so on. But no system of regular Native administration was set up other than Jameson's promise to leading *indunas* in June 1894 that he would establish permanent police posts at Bulawayo, Shiloh, Inyati, Gwelo, Mapondine, Fig Tree and Mangwe, through which complaints could be forwarded.[1]

Not very much evidence survives of the character of this military regime, which was actively directed by the Bulawayo Magistrate, the bitterly hated Heyman. But every now and then it came into contact with the more regular regime in Mashonaland and in the shocked reactions of the latter we can get some glimpse of the state of affairs in Matabeleland in 1894. Thus on December 10th 1894, the newly appointed Native Commissioner, Fort Victoria, reported that 5 kraals in his district had been raided by Ndebele. On investigation it proved that the Ndebele had been given arms and led on the raid by two Europeans, one a farmer 'who had some cattle stolen' and the other a Police Trooper. '30 assegais were given to the Matabele', reported the Commissioner, 'and the party proceeded to the district named and burned out 4 kraals

[1] Goold Adams to High Commissioner, 22 Feb. 1894, LO 5/2/34.

besides 1 in which the stolen cattle were found. Large quantity of
grain destroyed; 3 women taken . . . about 300 sheep and goats
were taken and 82 head cattle. Police state that kraals were
destroyed because natives had arms in their possession . . . the
natives are mostly Makalangas and have not been warned to disarm. I suggest that Police be instructed to recover what cattle,
sheep and goats they can and forward to Victoria where I could
distribute them among natives who have suffered. On my inter-
viewing the Police both at Selukwe and Iron Mine on the above
matter I was informed that they were acting under orders from
Captain Heyman and Captain White to the effect that they were
not to take any notice of myself as Hut Tax collector for the district as I had merely to collect the Hut Tax and had nothing
whatever to do with them.' This report was richly ironical considering the origins of the Ndebele war in a raid on the Karanga
of the Victoria district.[1]

Almost equally ironical was the report of the new Native Commissioner, Hartley, in December 1894 that 'the Matabele were
raiding Mashona villages along the Umfuli, Inyati and Sanyati
rivers, low down towards the Zambesi'. On investigating the
matter he found that the Ndebele raiders were collecting tribute
from the Shona and that they were in possession of certificates from
Colenbrander reading: 'The bearer is to collect tribute from the
natives on the Zambesi and Inyati according to the custom of the
country and to bring it to me.' [2]

The formation of the Native Department at the end of 1894
might have corrected the obvious faults of this military system,
replaced arbitrary private and police action with a regular system
of administrative control, and provided the machinery of contact
and communication between the Ndebele and the Company
government. It failed to do so for much the same reasons that
made the Mashonaland Native Department under Brabant so
unsatisfactory. Just as the Mashonaland Department was kept
busy until the end of 1895 collecting the hut tax so that they had no
time for studying or administering their districts, so the Matabeleland Native Commissioners were kept busy registering, branding and distributing cattle almost right up to the rising itself. Just
as the Mashonaland Department was handicapped by small num-

---

[1] N.C., Victoria, monthly report, Dec. 1894, A 15/1/1.
[2] N.C. Hartley, to C.N.C., 20 Dec. 1894, N 1/1/3.

I   The British South Africa Company arrives in Mashonaland, 1890.
The Pioneer column is shown here moving through Shona *kopje*
country. This contemporary drawing is based on a sketch by the first
Administrator of Mashonaland, Archibald Colquhoun.

II A Company view of an Ndebele raid upon the Shona. This contemporary drawing was used as part of the preparation of public opinion for the war of 1893.

bers and lack of experience so the Department in Matabeleland was similarly under-staffed and under-qualified. A correspondent to the *Bulawayo Chronicle* in January 1897 summed up the work of the Department justly enough. 'After the campaign of 1893', he wrote, 'a native policy was gradually formed by the Government. It was a lax and crude policy, and depended too much upon the individuals who were ordained to carry it out. The districts were too large and the native commissioners too few for the system to work well. They were supposed to be thoroughly acquainted with all the natives in their particular districts, which was in most cases humanly impossible. Many of them were young men, almost boys in fact, and young men are not reverenced by the native mind. Most of them had pastoral and household duties to perform which occupied no small portion of their time. The formation of two large reserves was talked about but was never carried out. The best of policies would have failed under similar conditions.' There is a good deal of evidence to suggest that working in the atmosphere of conquest and faced with these great difficulties too many of the Matabeleland Native Commissioners behaved in an overbearing and sometimes brutal way. More important still was the lack of contact or guidance. As the distinguished South African leader, Tengo Jabavu, wrote after a visit to Matabeleland in 1897 the absence of a trusted intermediary with government was a main 'cause of the last rebellion and may be the cause of others in the future. . . . There is ample ground to show that misunderstanding pure and simple of European methods of government occasioned such friction as to compel the poor, ignorant people without enlightened advisers, to surrender to despair and even wish to be exterminated.' [1]

As in Mashonaland the Native Commissioners came to depend upon their African police. But the Matabeleland force was a much more organized and formidable affair than the disparate levies of Mashonaland. The Company's first intention was to recruit Zulu police but the Natal Government 'entertained the strongest objections to Mr Rhodes' proposals' and minuted that they considered 'that the proposal would tend to keep alive the military instincts and habits which made the Zulu nation so formidable a menace in the past'. The Company, curiously unconcerned about

[1] Letter by 'Politicus', *Bulawayo Chronicle*, 23 Jan. 1897; *Cape Times*, 22 Nov. 1897.

E

keeping alive the military habits of the Ndebele, then recruited its
police from among the warriors of Lobengula's old regiments. The
Matabeleland Native Police, as described in a report of August
1895, were 'composed solely of Matabeles'. They contained 'a
great many of the Imbesu and Inoukumini Regiments, the late
Lobengula's two crack regiments'. They were drilled for a month
at Bulawayo, picking up military discipline 'wonderfully quickly'
and becoming 'fair shots', and were then sent out in June 1895 to
the Native Commissioner's stations. 'The duties of the Matabeleland Native Police', ran the report, 'are to assist Native Commissioners in the various districts in collecting labour, arresting
deserters, procuring evidence in native cases, police and detective
work generally.' Native Commissioners were enthusiastic about
their new assistants. 'Native labour is much more plentiful and
they have also been very useful in branding cattle, tracing hidden
cattle, etc.' [1]

After the rising an odd attempt was made to present the establishment of this police force as a liberal act on the Company's
part, the first stage of a sort of Home Rule policy for Matabeleland.
'The Company meant well and intended to put them in charge of
their own people?' asked the Chairman of the Bulawayo inquiry
into the risings in December 1896. 'It was a recognition by the
Government that the Matabele should have their own control?
The Company meant to make these men rulers of their own
country?' This was a gallant attempt to retrieve total disaster since
in every possible way the Matabeleland Native Police had proved
to be a mistake. Given the same sort of free hand to trace hidden
cattle and to recruit labour that the Native Messengers enjoyed in
Mashonaland, they became the tyrants of the countryside, 'more
like a brigandage' than a police force, as one witness answered the
Chairman's inquiries. There is overwhelming evidence of the
hatred with which they were regarded by the Ndebele generally.
But they were a mistake also because the training they had received had not only kept alive Ndebele military habits but had
brought them up to date, so that when many of the police deserted
to the rebels they carried effective military knowledge with
them. 'I hear some of the Matabele police deserted to their own
people,' wrote Lord Grey in March 1896. 'I cannot help liking

[1] Minute by the Prime Minister, Natal, 19 July 1894, LO 6/2/36; Report
by Col. F. Rhodes, 9 Aug. 1895, LO 5/2/44.

them for that. I should have done the same thing had I stood in their place. The fault lies with us for having employed natives to police the people in their own district. The right principle is that followed by Caesar when he kept England quiet with a legion raised from the Danube and the Danube quiet with a British legion.'[1]

These police were specially active in recruiting labour. In Matabeleland before the rising exactly the same attitudes prevailed and exactly the same methods were used as in Mashonaland though with a greater frankness and force. Before the formation of the Native Department there was private pressing of labour and police raiding for it as in Mashonaland; the patrol to the west in June 1894 brought in 500 or so workers, though Jameson insisted that all had come voluntarily. Later, as we have seen, the Matabeleland Native Police ensured that labour became 'much more plentiful'. How the system worked under the Matabeleland Native Department was described frankly by the Chief Native Commissioner, Taylor. 'The labour necessary to meet the requirement of the country generally and the mining community in particular', he wrote, 'was in the first instance procured through the *indunas* and headmen. I know of no physical force being used to compel *indunas* to procure labour. Labour was procured from the *indunas* through the police and the natives received a fair wage. "Holes" or lower class natives were used principally. The higher class native —the "Abezansi"—had a great antipathy to labour which they considered to be derogatory. The hard earned wage of the "Hole" was often taken by his former owner in the Abezansi section. Much discontent was thus caused and as the demand for labour in the mining districts increased it was deemed advisable to call upon the Abezansi to contribute their share to the labour. In many instances they refused to do so arguing that their slaves should earn money for them. This condition of semi-slavery could not be tolerated by a civilized government and in order to deal equally with all classes the young men of the Abezansi were called upon to work for two months in the year. This they refused to do on the grounds of their former argument. In some cases the Native Police had to call out some of the young men to work. They were brought before the Native Commissioner and handed over to a Master to whom they were registered for a specified term and

[1] Lord Grey to his wife, 23 Mar. 1896, GR 1/1/1.

wage. Many natives however worked voluntarily.' Forced labour, wrote the Native Commissioner, Gwelo, did exist 'to the extent that supply was not equal to the demand. The effect upon the natives, who are naturally very idle . . . was to make them shy and very difficult to be got at.'

There is evidence, also, that conditions of work were not good. Carnegie, thoroughly disillusioned by the white rule he had welcomed in 1893, wrote: 'A proud and hitherto unconquered Matabele cannot be turned in a month, or a year, into a useful servant by kicks, sjambok and blows. You cannot civilize him by quarrelling with him a few days before his pay is due, by stoning or unjustly beating him, by cursing him for not understanding an order given in English, by being too kind to him. . . . The wrong men were often chosen for handling such raw material. . . . The whole question of native policy has been left since the war in an unsettled and, therefore, most unsatisfactory condition.' [1]

Enough has now been said to show that Sir Richard Martin was undoubtedly correct to find that 'a strong and able Native administration', capable of protecting Ndebele interests, had not been established in Matabeleland, and that 'in the general excitement caused by the rush for gold, and other interests in the country, the cause of the Natives did not receive the attention from the Government that it deserved'. How, then, did the Ndebele react to this mixture of misadministration and maladministration? We are fortunate in possessing a full statement of the Ndebele case made in August 1896 by the senior *induna*, Somabulana, at the famous *indaba* with Rhodes, and recorded by the journalist Stent, who was one of the four whites present.

Like this book, Somabulana's oration began with a discussion of Ndebele history, passed on to the relations between Lobengula and the whites, and finished with the story of the Company administration in Matabeleland. All seemed to the old man to be equally relevant. After narrating the first flight and wanderings of the Ndebele, Somabulana told how they had arrived in the country of the Rozwi; how they had hoped that they had at last 'won for themselves a home where they might grow fat and prosperous and live in peace amongst their herds, their women and their children'. He described Mzilikazi's wars and raids. Then 'Lobengula, Prince "driven by the wind", came to the throne of his father. The

[1] Evidence given to Sir Richard Martin, Blue Book *c. 8547*.

Barotse were taught respect for the children of the Great House of Kumalo, and excepting for occasional expeditions to hunt or punish, all was peace in the land. But still it was not to be. The white man looked north and saw that there was gold upon the plains, which the Matabili had come to with so much blood and so many tears. Well, King Lobengula knew the power and strength of the white man, honoured the white queen, and desired no quarrel. So when there came emissaries and ambassadors, begging concessions and presents of land, and rights to mine, begging upon their knee, squatting low before the great King, Lobengula met them as a brother; killed beasts for them; extended hospitality; sent young maidens to them, and gave them half his kingdom. So the white men came with their rifles and they sat down in that half of the kingdom which had been given them to mine in, to take away the gold; and when the gold was finished to take themselves away with it. Three short years after the Mashonas gave trouble again. The Mashonas were Lobengula's subjects, and the white men had no business with the Mashonas, to protect them or shield them from the King's justice. So *impis* had to be sent to punish these Mashonas, and they had collided with the white man. And then the white man had come again with his guns that spat bullets as the heavens sometimes spit hail, and who were the naked Matabili to stand up against these guns and rifles? So the white man took from the Matabili the land as they had taken it from the Maholi and the Mashonas. And their King had been driven into exile. He had sent presents of gold, a peace offering, and the presents were taken and the peace was refused him.'

Then Somabulana turned to the time of conquest. 'He spoke of the last days of the hunted King; and then of the final settlement of the land, and the appointment of native commissioners and magistrates, and his face grew dark as he told a shameful tale. . . . The Maholi and the Mashona, he said, what are they? Dogs! Sneaking cattle thieves! Slaves! But we, the Amandabili, the sons of Kumalo, the Izulu, Children of the Stars; we are no dogs! You came, you conquered. The strongest takes the land. We accepted your rule. We lived under you. But not as dogs! If we are to be dogs it is better to be dead. You can never make the Amandebele dogs. You may wipe them out . . . but the Children of the Stars can never be dogs.' Somabulana then spoke of the treatment meted out to them; he spoke 'of the brutality of the Zulu police, who ravished their daughters and insulted their young men, who tweaked the beards of their chieftains and made lewd jokes with the elder women of the Great House, who respected none but the Native Commissioner and officers of police'; he spoke of Captain Heyman, Magistrate of Bulawayo, who had 'managed somehow to anger and insult nearly every one of the chiefs'. 'I myself once visited Bulawayo,' said Somabulana. 'I came to pay my respects to the Chief Magistrate. I brought my indunas with me, and my servants. I am a chief. I am expected to travel with attendants and advisers. I came to Bulawayo early in the morning, before the sun had dried the dew, and I sat down before the Court House, sending messages to the Chief Magistrate that I waited to pay my respects to him. And so I sat until the evening shadows were long. And then . . . I sent again to the Chief Magistrate and told him that I did not wish to hurry him in any unmannerly way; I would wait his pleasure; but my people were hungry; and when the white men visited me it was my custom to kill that they might eat. The answer from the Chief Magistrate . . . was that the town was full of stray dogs; dog to dog; we might kill those and eat them if we could catch them. So I left Bulawayo that night; and when next I tried to visit the Chief Magistrate it was with my *impis* behind me; no soft words in their mouths; but the assegai in their hands. Who blames me?' He told of how the 'tax-collectors, collecting the Company's cattle, shot four women in cold blood when there was peace, because the women would not tell them where the cattle were hidden'; of the arbitrary acts of the Native Commissioners.[1]

'Somabulana's statement was ex parte,' writes Stent. 'But we had an uneasy feeling that at any rate some part of it was true; that shocking things *had* been done; that the Native Commissioners had *not* been the friends of the people, but their unsympathetic overlords—tyrannical and unjust; that the police had been brutal.' How far the statement was true we can to some extent check against the account given in this chapter. But what is more important is that it was a statement of what the Ndebele believed to be true; an expression of their essential attitude. Stent tells us that 'the recital of their national history and what they considered

---

[1] Colenbrander, who was also present at the indaba, confirmed the story of the shooting of the four women.

to be their wrongs' stirred the Ndebele who were listening to Somabulana 'to the very core'.[1]

There are some indications to show us how the Ndebele, inspired by these feelings, moved into a determination to rebel. By an apparent paradox there was not in Matabeleland the widespread armed resistance to white administration which we have seen among the un-warlike Shona. The explanation of the paradox is, of course, a simple one. As Marshall Hole later wrote: 'The Matabeles were a fighting nation by descent and had already measured weapons with us', while the Shona were 'a race who have never been conquered, never even been warred against'. The Shona paramounts regarded themselves as still independent; the Ndebele *indunas* had had to accept the humiliations of conquest. This meant that between the 1893 war and the outbreak of the 1896 rebellion there was no instance of any Ndebele resistance by force to confiscation of cattle or compulsion of labour. But underneath the apparent acceptance there was movement to resistance.[2]

From the first the conquered Ndebele strove to protect their threatened institutions by the re-establishment of the Kingship. 'Ever since the late King's death', wrote Carnegie, 'the natives have been, as they say, "longing for a fire at which to warm themselves"; in other words, they wanted a King, with whom they could be more in touch than they found themselves with the white government. One abortive attempt was made to accomplish this, but failed; later on the Government suggested appointing a Native who should be their inter-mediary between the Natives and the Government, but their nominee was unacceptable.' Meetings held by the Ndebele *indunas* to discuss the kingship issue alarmed the administration and resulted in punitive action; in 1894 the senior *induna* Sikombo 'was punished . . . for illicitly convening a meeting of chiefs'; in 1895 Lobengula's brother, Mabele, 'was banished for holding an illegal council of indunas'. By the end of 1895 it was clear that no restoration of the Kingship could be hoped for within the framework of the Company administration and that the Ndebele 'way of life' could only be preserved by flight or resistance. Early in 1896 another of Lobengula's brothers, called by Carnegie Usipampamu, trekked with his wives and followers out of the Company's area of control northwards across the Zambesi, hoping

---

[1] De Vere Stent, *A Personal Account of Some Incidents in the Life of Cecil Rhodes*, Cape Town, 1924.   [2] Hole, Report, 29 Oct. 1896, A 1/12/26.

to find a place there to re-create the Ndebele state. Most other members of the royal family and the regimental commanders were coming rather to the conclusion that they must fight. All that was needed was an opportunity—and in January 1896 that was given. News came that Jameson, on his last and fatal gamble, had led the great majority of the white police of Rhodesia into defeat and capture in the Transvaal.[1]

From that moment it is clear that a rising was decided upon. In February meetings of *indunas* took place to prepare plans. On February 19th the Acting Administrator, Judge Vintcent, wired that reports had come in that 'several Matabele *indunas* have held meetings in the Matoppo Hills near Usher's farm and that they are massing with a view to raiding Bulawayo, stating that in consequence of capture of Dr Jameson's force the town is unprotected'. In Mashonaland friendly Shona warned whites that Ndebele emissaries had visited their kraals promising 'to give the country to them (the Mashonas) if they would help them against the Englishmen. 'These boys say that the Matabili know that there are only a few men here and no guns (maxims) . . . also that the Matabili have been waiting for an opportunity to pounce down on Salisbury and Bulawayo for months. These boys say further that there are immense numbers of Matabili ready to come down on the towns at once. These boys are absolutely reliable.' [2]

Reliable they proved to be, but little notice was taken of them. The whites were still lulled by their extraordinary sense of security. Vintcent thought the rumours of hostile meetings in the hills impossible to believe. 'I cannot credit this as reports last month, after natives knew of the Doctor's capture, were that natives quiet and pleased at our giving back to them portion of the Matabele cattle.' Most of the settlers were as complacent, though a few were affected by the palpable tension like the group of farmers who went into laager a week before the rising and were persuaded out again by their Native Commissioner. More representative of general

---

[1] Carnegie, evidence submitted to Sir Richard Martin, June 1896, *C. 8547*; *The Times*, 2 April 1896; Report by C.N.C., 19 June 1896, PO 1/2/2. Lewanika gave the royal fugitive asylum. On 25 May 1896 he replied to a demand by the A.C.N.C. that he should be returned: 'As for Sibamubamu, the king says he cannot give him over to you as he took refuge in this country and was received before they knew he had fled.' A 3/18/18/5.

[2] Vintcent to Acting Secretary, Cape Town, 13 Feb. 1896, LO 5/2/47; L. H. Gabriel to 'my dear Sir Thomas', 27 Mar. 1896, A 1/12/27.

white feeling was a man like W. A. Jarvis, one of the aristocratic adventurers connected with Sir John Willoughby's enterprises. Jarvis, whom the catalogue of the Central African Archives accurately calls 'a cast iron Tory', had been a Tory member of parliament, and had come out to Rhodesia to inspect the properties of Willoughby's Consolidated and to take part in the 'fun' in the Transvaal. Writing to his mother, Lady Jarvis of Middleton Towers, after the unexpected fiasco of the Jameson Raid, Jarvis showed a concentration upon rivalry with the Boers and a dismissal of any danger from the Ndebele which was characteristic of the circle around Jameson. As loyal as ever to Jameson—'Mother is quite right in comparing the Doctor to Gordon,' he wrote significantly. 'He seems to have just the same magnetic attraction but is not a lunatic like Gordon'—he was still determined that 'we have *got to have*' the Transvaal. 'We are *quite* ready to hold our own in *this* country,' he wrote from Bulawayo in February 1896. 'There was a rumour of a possible rising amongst some of the tribes in the Matoppo Hills but that was of course all moon-shine.' 'This is *grand* country,' he wrote less than a month before the rising, 'exceeding my most sanguine expectations. It is undoubtedly *very* rich and fertile. The natives are happy, comfortable and prosperous and its future must be magnificent . . . everything is going smoothly and well and all of us, black and white, are quite ready to "go for" the Transvaal.' Thirty years later, freed from these illusions, Jarvis realized that there had in fact been many portents of the coming storm; 'but notwithstanding all these portents, we white men pursued our daily tasks for the early development of the "promised land" without giving a moment's thought to the volcano upon which we were sitting'.[1]

'The whole population was lulled into a false sense of security,' wrote a later Rhodesian Chief of Staff. 'There was no intelligence section to sift information and all warnings given by local natives were disregarded. There was no system by which settlers could be warned of impending trouble and concentrated in places of safety. No one knew where to rally.' In all Matabeleland there were only 48 white police. Thus the whites were totally unprepared when the Ndebele abandoned soft words in March 1896 and came to Bulawayo with assegais in their hands.[2]

[1] Jarvis to Lady Jarvis, 24 and 29 Feb. 1896, JA 4/1/1; Jarvis, *Jottings from an Active Life*, London, 1928.   [2] George Parsons, Staff Study, PA 1/1/2.

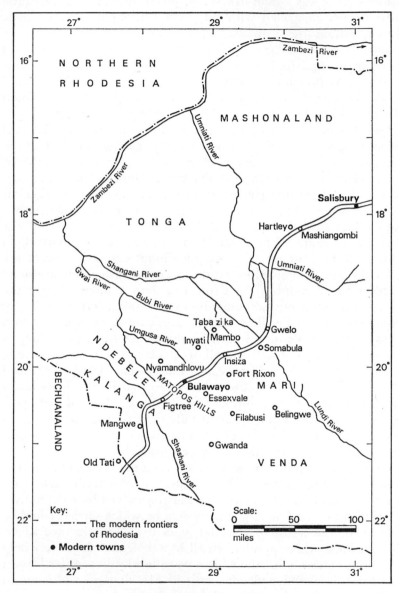

4. Matabeleland in 1896.

CHAPTER FOUR

The Outbreak and Organization of the Rebellion in Matabeleland

IN MARCH 1896 the gentle and idealistic Albert, Lord Grey, was travelling through South Africa on his way to take over the Rhodesian administration as successor to Jameson. Grey had accepted the post out of loyalty to Rhodes; it had been his hope, as we have seen, that Company rule would attract by its justice African peoples outside the borders of Rhodesia, and now he was setting out to try to achieve this in the difficult circumstances created by the Jameson Raid. It was, as he knew, an immense task. 'I have been oppressed with a feeling of dread that I may have taken up a burden I may not have strength to carry,' he confessed to Lady Grey on March 23rd, 'and that whatever I do as Administrator is sure to be wrong.' On March 24th Grey's 'new kingdom' blew up. On that day the first white was murdered in the Umzingwani district of Matabeleland. 'From the Mzingwani', ran a later account, 'the rebellion spread through the Filabusi and Insiza districts to the Shangani River and Inyati and thence to the mining camps in the neighbourhood of the Gwelo and Ingwenya Rivers.' Whites were attacked also in the Shona-speaking district of Belingwe. 'By the evening of March 30th not a white man was left alive in the outlying districts of Matabeleland whilst the survivors were confined to the laagers of Bulawayo, Gwelo, Belingwe and Tuli. Between these two dates many escaped or were brought into the laager by relief parties, but a large number, one hundred and forty five in all, were treacherously murdered.'

By the beginning of April rebel *impis* were beginning to close in on Bulawayo; 'it was found that the small patrols which issued from Bulawayo were unable to hold their ground against the rebels and were compelled after every encounter to retire'. By the middle of April Bulawayo was invested on all sides except the south-west by strong rebel forces. On April 17th the Bulawayo Staff Officer, Newman, cabled to Cape Town: 'Rebels continuing to increase in numbers and proximity round us to north and east, forming semi-circle about 3 miles on the Umgusa river, 6 miles from here, our scouts and patrols being always in touch and fighting with their advance guards.' 'The gravity of the situation is hardly realized even by the local population,' reported Newman. There was a real danger that Bulawayo might be rushed and the whites gathered there wiped out.[1]

'Poor old Albert Grey will have his work cut out for him,' wrote the irrepressible Jarvis from the Gwelo laager. 'It *is* bad luck for him.' 'My darling wife,' wrote Grey, 'this native trouble and the break-out of the cattle plague is a serious disturber of our plans. . . . The position is not a pleasant one. Bulawayo is practically a beleaguered town with barely a month's supplies, 500 miles away from its base, Mafeking.' 'All the plagues of Egypt have tumbled at once upon this unhappy country,' the new Administrator told his son. 'Drought, locusts, failure of crops, total annihilation of the cattle by rinderpest, no milk, no beef in a few days, but lots of lovely smells from dead cattle', and an all too successful native rebellion. For while the Administrator and his white subjects were bewailing this succession of disasters, the rebels were jubilant. 'It was natural for them to claim initial success,' ran a later Rhodesian staff paper, 'for they had murdered a number of the white people and raided their stores and homesteads without being punished, and driven the remainder into laager. Waverers took heart and joined the apparently winning side. . . . The counter stroke, which was so essential to success, was not forthcoming.' [2]

These remarkable events set the atmosphere of the months which followed. Bulawayo was not stormed but the whites of Matabeleland had suffered a terrible blow; a relatively high proportion of them had been killed, many others had lost their property, and all had experienced the full shock of surprise and fear. The panic in Bulawayo on the night of March 25th, when the first news of the killings reached the town and the rumour spread that the *impis* were already in the outskirts, was a thing to be remembered with shame; 'the women and children were called in from the outlying

---

[1] Grey to Lady Grey, 23 Mar. 1896, GR 1/1/1; Staff Papers on the lessons of the rising, PA 1/1/2 and PA 1/1/3; Newman to Secretary, Cape Town, 17 Apr. 1896, LO 5/2/48.

[2] Grey to Lady Grey, 11 Apr. 1896; Grey to Viscount Howick, 8 May 1896; GR 1/1/1; Jarvis to Lady Jarvis, 29 Mar. 1896, JA 4/1/1; PA 1/1/3.

parts', wrote Captain MacFarlane later; 'the gallant inhabitants lost their heads and scrambled and fought for what rifles were left in the Government Store. It was a disgraceful scene and the less said about it the better'. Moreover, the whites were filled with a genuine horror and rage at the character as well as at the fact of the murders. We must look at one of these in detail in order to understand the nature of the first days of the rising and the reasons for the violence of white reaction.[1]

By far the most illuminating account of one of these early murders was given by the Ndebele elder, Nganganyoni Mhlope, in November 1938. Mhlope had been prosecuted for murder in 1897 and had served a long prison sentence. In 1938, though with great reluctance, he was persuaded by a sympathetic white questioner to tell the story of the murder and of the first days of the rising in return for a pledge that his account 'would never be shown to anyone who might be likely to do him any harm whatsoever as a result'. Mhlope was living in 1896 in a kraal in the Inyati area. The main grievance of the Ndebele in Inyati was the pressing of labour by the police. 'When they recruited us they used to beat us. They were our own sons and they beat us. That was the cause of the rebellion. Another cause was that they left no one at the kraal. They took everybody—that is all the males. And if you had a goat at your kraal they would kill it and make you cook it for them.' Early in March 1896 a message came from the Matopos telling the people of Inyati: 'You had better fight because you are badly treated.' Mhlope and his friends thereupon 'divided off in groups to go off and kill the white people that we knew . . . we had no grievance against these people. We killed them merely because they were white people.' Mhlope and five others went to the store under the hill of Taba Zi Ka Mambo, which was kept by three whites whom he calls by their Ndebele nicknames, 'Mandevu', 'Wani' and 'Mandisi'. 'We did not show them that we were coming to fight,' Mhlope tells us. 'We found Mandevu in his hut, Wani was in the store and Mandisi was in the lands reaping mealies. . . . We divided up . . . I went into the store. When we got into the store we asked for limbo. We told Wani that we wanted to buy limbo. We were waiting to hear those people who had gone to Mandevu because we had arranged that as soon as they started on that side we would start on this side. While we were still talking to Wani and he

[1] Macfarlane, *Some Account of George Grey and his work in Africa*, 1914.

was looking at the limbo hanging up and pointing to different pieces and asking us which piece we wanted we heard a noise of something hitting boxes. We caught hold of Wani. I caught hold of Wani and we both fell down and while we were on the floor Kafuli struck him with an axe behind the head as we were struggling on the floor. The one blow killed him.'

Two of the men then went out to look for 'Mandisi' in the lands. 'When Matekenya and Ngonye reached Mandisi he did not know they were coming to kill him because he knew them. They told us that they hit him with a knobkerrie. When they got to him, he greeted them and told them that as they had come they had better help him with the reaping. They walked near him and then they hit him with a knobkerrie. Matekenya hit him. They hit him once and Ngonye then chopped his neck with an axe.' A Zulu servant was also killed 'because he was as good as a European'. 'These white people were our friends', concludes Mhlope, 'and so they did not expect that we were coming to kill them. They were our friends but since we were starting to fight they might have killed us too. It is also true that we had decided to get rid of all the white men in the country.'[1]

Mhlope's statement brings out perfectly both the rationality from their point of view of the Ndebele action and the treachery and horror of it from the point of view of the whites. 'These white people were our friends and so they did not expect that we were coming to kill them.' It leaves out one element which was very important in the white reaction, however, namely the similar murder of white women, on the effects of which Mr Mason has written perceptively. When one has added this, the strength of white desire for revenge becomes understandable enough, compounded as it was of fear, desire to recover lost prestige, and a genuine detestation of the murders. 'Were you here', wrote Carnegie from Bulawayo to a fellow missionary on April 6th, 1896, 'I could talk about things but letters and writing seem utterly unable to convey to you the strong anti-native feeling now existing in this town. . . . We are doing our best to uphold the value of human life and the honour of the Society we represent. . . . To be a missionary under these present circumstances appears to be a thankless task and to say a word on their behalf in the presence of

[1] Statement by Ngangonyi Mhlope, recorded by R. F. Windram, 20 Nov. 1938; WI 8/1/3.

some white men you are looked upon as being in league with the enemy.'[1]

Carnegie was certainly not exaggerating. Jarvis expressed the sentiments of the aristocratic element when he wrote from Gwelo on March 29th: 'I hope the natives will be pretty well exterminated. . . . Poor devils, one can't help being a bit sorry for them for they have of course been imposed upon by these wretched 'witch doctors' and the beastly missionaries have a lot to do with it, teaching the nigger that he is as good as the white man. It won't do. The nigger has got to be treated as a nigger all the world over. They only become the most brutal scoundrels if you try to turn them into Christians.' On April 20th Jarvis wrote: 'There are about 5500 niggers in this district (Gwelo) and our plan of campaign will probably be to proceed against this lot and wipe them out, then move on towards Bulawayo wiping out every nigger and every kraal we can find. . . . after these cold-blooded murders you may be sure there will be no quarter and everything black will have to die, for our men's blood is fairly up.'[2]

The general settler attitude was probably as well expressed in a piece of doggerel carried in the Salisbury paper, The Nugget, as in anything else. Entitled, The Rhodesian, it ran:

Tho' he's not been trained to fightin', 'tis a game he takes delight in,
And he's proved himself a rough and ruly chap,
For he'll trail the rebel nigger till he grasp his woolly wig,
And he'll scale the top-most kopje for a scrap.
Tho' he revels in the singing of the bullet as it's pinging
Past his ear, which makes him grin and duck his head,
'Tis primest when his lead 'un scores his gun another dead 'un,
And the nigger sinks to sleep as if in bed.
While he pots his man he'll hum 'there goes another for my chum',
But a thousand blacks won't bring the white lives back;
So he thinks 'Revenge is sweet' as he just grips his saddle seat,
And his horse bounds forward on the rebels' track.
Oh, he glories in the pig-skin as he holes another nig-skin,
He fears not deadly ambush or stray picket,

---

[1] Carnegie to Thomson, 6 Apr. 1896, L.M.S. Matabele Mission, Vol 5.
[2] Jarvis to Lady Jarvis, 29 Mar. and 20 Apr. 1896, JA 4/1/1.

For he's in the killing mood and he's got the taste of blood,
And he'll gallop through the densest bush and thicket.
Let the folk in Exeter Hall and such-like other Grundies bawl,
And rave and shout and cry that he's inhuman,
They may yell till they are hoarse for they've ne'er seen the
    ghastly corse,
Or grinning skull of some fair murdered woman.
'Tis not of blood he wants the spilling, he fights just for the
    killing,
'Venging those poor souls unburied in the veld;
The black fiends never cared so why should one of them be
    spared?
First raise up the dead; *then* ask our hearts to melt.[1]

The bishop of Mashonaland might urge that 'we must be patient and strong and just, remembering on the one hand that we have the responsibility of 19 centuries of Christianity, while the native has inherited the tendencies of at least 50 centuries of heathenism and its accompanying triple tyranny of cannibalism, polygamy and slavery', but there was little to choose between the savagery with which both sides conducted the fighting in the months after the murders of March 1896.[2]

But as well as setting the scene for a terrible struggle between the two races in Matabeleland, the events of March 1896 posed two questions which much exercised thinking whites. Firstly, why had the rising occurred? We need say nothing more about this, for it can hardly seem much of a mystery after the first three chapters of this book. Secondly, how had the rising been organized and coordinated? This second question we shall now examine.

When the first news of the murders reached England the *Standard* reported that 'African and military authorities at the House of Commons' found it 'difficult to believe that the Matabeles wretchedly armed, without leaders and still crippled by the losses they sustained when their country was first occupied will be able to hold their own against the well equipped force which can be called out to suppress them'. But, as we have seen, the rebel forces

---

[1] *The Nugget*, 22 June 1897. This issue also contains an article entitled, 'Stray Leaves from a Trooper's Notebook', which is worth reading in this context.

[2] *The Times*, 3 Apr. 1896.

more than held their own during the first month and by the middle of April were investing Bulawayo. How was this achieved?

To understand the rebel achievement we must look first at the fate of the Ndebele regimental system between 1893 and 1896. Despite the resolution of the Company to do so that system had not in fact been broken up. In 1893 by no means all the existing regiments had been engaged in the battles fought during Jameson's march on Bulawayo or the clashes with Goold-Adams' southern column. And in the case of the crack Ndebele regiments even those which had been engaged in the fighting were not thereby destroyed as military units. Goold-Adams reported to the High Commissioner in February 1894 that 'the mixed regiments after once dispersing never really came together again as a body' but that the exclusively Zansi and Enhla regiments retained their organization. 'After the defeat at the Bembesi and the dispersal of the southern *impi*', he wrote, 'the *impis* scattered in all directions to collect their wives and belongings. The old training of the Royal regiments still kept them together and although they suffered most severely the regiments still retained their separate bodies; strengthened by the Inyati regiments from the southern column they followed the king in some system.'

After the King's death the members of these regiments began to drift back to the Ndebele homeland, now occupied by whites, no longer in military formation, of course, but still with a full recognition of regimental responsibilities. Once at home they 'split up and scattered among the various kraals'. The question was whether they would come together again if summoned to do so by their old regimental commanders. 'These men have had such terrible hardships,' wrote Goold-Adams; 'first heavy losses in battle, then privations from want of food and shelter, small pox and now fever . . . that their ranks are greatly thinned and they have had such a lesson that it should be some time before they forget it, yet these are the people most likely to interfere and cause trouble by interfering, with the Police carrying out their duties.'[1]

Moreover, some of the *impis* engaged in the war did not join in the hard trek to the north after the King. Meikle, in the cattle-raiding expedition from Fort Victoria already described, found sheltering on a remote hilltop a 'head *induna*, who it turned out was in command of the young *impi* at the first Shangani battle'

[1] Goold-Adams to High Commissioner, 22 Feb. 1894, LO 5/2/34.

and 900 of his men, 'fine big strapping fellows'. 'We saw no arms,' he writes; 'these had been hidden—they did not even carry a stick.' Clearly this *impi* was not in any very terrible shape and it would not be difficult for it to recover its arms and reconstitute itself as an organized force.[1]

There was some reason from his own point of view in the feelings expressed by one of the conquerors in a letter from Bulawayo in January 1894 that the war had been won too easily. 'The young warriors still stick to the King', he wrote, 'and we shall have to kill a few more of this class to make them respect us. Privately I should like to say cut about 2000 more as we have not killed enough. I hope we shall get a chance to wipe out Wilson's score.' But that chance did not come and the war ended with a number of regiments in being; some not having been involved in the fighting at all and the rest still responsive to the calls of regimental loyalty and discipline.[2]

We have already seen how the *indunas* and the royal family moved into a position of readiness to rebel; what of the young soldiers upon whom they would have to call? All authorities agree that it was upon them that the impact of colonial rule fell most heavily. 'These are the people who will feel the change most', Goold-Adams had written in 1894. 'They have been accustomed to a life of idleness and the remainder of the Nation cringing to them. They are unaccustomed to work and they will feel the loss of their prestige and power; at present they appear to accept our rule but should any disaffection take place hereafter it will originate amongst these people.' The young warriors bitterly resented the labour policy we have seen described by the Chief Native Commissioner whereby they were forced to work by police raids. They also resented the final settlement of the cattle question whereby nearly all the cattle handed back to the Ndebele were allocated to the older men; as Carnegie wrote, the young fighting men 'who according to native law would have possessed cattle were left without their full share'. Under these circumstances the young men were only too ready to respond when called out by the regimental *indunas* in 1896 and no doubt many of them found in the rising, despite all its horrors, an opportunity for reliving a way of life which was still delightful to them. Baden-Powell has a striking passage

[1] Meikle's Reminiscences, ME 1/1/1.
[2] Gifford to Cawston, 14 Jan. 1894, Rhodes House, Mss. Afr. s. 76, Vol. 4.

in his book on the rebellions in which he describes how he watched from cover a young Ndebele warrior sunning himself in the Matopos, the very embodiment of martial virtue and youthful vigour. Baden-Powell at that moment understood why it was that such men were not prepared to accept a regime which offered them work in the mines as an alternative to the old ways.[1]

And so most of the military effectiveness of the rebellion came from a revival of the old regimental system. Intelligence reports on the rebel forces are like a roll call of the old regime. In June 1896, for example, the Chief Native Commissioner made a detailed report on the leadership of the Ndebele forces, which he estimated at some 14,000 strong. Their leaders were the sons, brothers and nephews of Lobengula; senior *indunas* like Sikombo, Dhliso, Babyaan; regimental commanders and kraal heads. In Gwanda district, for instance, 'Umsolo, who was Lieutenant of the Royal Kraal in Lobengula's time was the first to openly rebel'; in Filabusi district 'Fezela and Mahlehleni together with the police committed the murders at Filabusi store and police camp; Fezela is a brother of the late king', Mahlehleni the commander of the Godhlwayo regiment; and so the report continues. 'This is the Matabele war which did not take place three years ago,' wrote Carnegie. It had been unexpected to him to hear while on leave in England of the 'comparatively easy downfall of Lobengula in the late war of 1893'. This rising was the formidable challenge of the great majority of the Ndebele nation which he had expected then.[2]

So militarily speaking the rising in Matabeleland was largely a matter of a revived regimental system; and also an improved one in terms of tactics. The deserters from the Matabeleland Native Police carried with them improved notions of marksmanship and the lessons of the battles of 1893 had been learnt by their survivors. 'The Matabele soldier of today is a very different man to the Matabele soldier of 1893', cabled a number of experienced settlers from Bulawayo in April 1896. 'Large numbers of them are armed and they seem to have plenty of ammunition. There is no doubt that there has been a great deal of rifle practice by them for the last two years. They will not make rushes en masse but take shelter

---

[1] Goold-Adams, op. cit.; Carnegie, Evidence submitted to Sir Richard Martin, June 1896, C, 8547; Baden-Powell, *The Matabele Campaign*, 1897.

[2] Report by C.N.C., 19 June 1896, PO 1/1/2; Carnegie to Thomson, 6 Apr. 1896, L.M.S. Matabele Mission, Vol. 5.

in a good situation. . . . So far their tactics have placed our men at an utter disadvantage.'[1]

But merely to say that the main *impis* engaged in the Ndebele rising of 1896 were made up of old regiments revived is by no means to give a complete or sufficient explanation of the organization and coordination of the rebellion. There is the further problem, to begin with, of how any degree of coherence was achieved between the movements of the various regiments and regimental commanders. Before the 1893 war, as we have seen, the regiments all recognized the supreme command of the King; the institution of monarchy alone gave a directive centre to the military machine. The regimental commanders themselves had been 'to a large extent hereditary servants of the state. They had little in the way of ritual functions and depended on the King for their authority.' No single one of them, or even group of them, could substitute in any real way for the central authority of the monarch. In 1896, of course, Lobengula was dead and the efforts of the Ndebele *indunas* to restore the monarchy had failed. Lobengula's younger sons, born while he was King and thus eligible for the Kingship, had been sent to South Africa for their education. When Mzilikazi had died the inter-regnum had been bridged by a widely recognized Regent, Nombate. But in the last years of Lobengula's reign he had fallen out with and killed Nombate's son so that there was in 1896 no accepted Regent to give central direction. The senior *indunas* were much divided among themselves. There was, however, one man who symbolized the unity of the Ndebele nation and who, therefore, played an extremely significant part in the organization of the risings.[2]

The Ndebele nation recognized a senior religious officer, a 'high priest of the tribe', who was quite distinct from the witch-finders and diviners and non-Ndebele rain-makers and from the priesthood of Mwari. This officer and his family were responsible for the conduct of the Great Dance and ceremony of First Fruits, that annual demonstration of Ndebele unity. On other great national occasions the 'high priest' played a central role. The missionary, T. M. Thomas, for instance, who was present in Matabeleland when Mzilikazi died and was succeeded by Lobengula, described the part played by the 'high priest', Umtamjana, in the period of

---

[1] Rhodes to High Commissioner, enclosing cable from Selous, Colenbrander and others, 12 Apr. 1896, LO 5/2/48.   [2] Hughes, op. cit.

the inter-regnum. It was he who performed the rites of burial for Mzilikazi, sacrificing cattle and commending the dead king to his ancestors 'in the highest terms'. It was he, also, who prepared the young Lobengula 'by instructions, ceremonies and charms' for his installation as King; and it was he who on March 17th, 1870, 'in the presence of about six thousand people . . . gave the King a charge, in which he dwelt upon the laws and customs of the tribe, and the responsibilities and difficulties of the present government of the country'.[1]

Thomas' evidence gives us some idea of the role played by the 'high priest' during the crisis of the Ndebele system which followed Mzilikazi's death. In the much more profound crisis which followed the death of Lobengula the 'high priest' once again played a part of great importance. By the 1890s Umtamjana had been succeeded by Umlugulu, whom various witnesses described in 1896 as 'the head of the family who had charge of the rites'; 'the representative of the priestly family of the Matabili tribe, who during the great war dance . . . had control of the whole people and rule of the country'; 'the head dance doctor'; and the 'King Maker'. Early in 1894, just before the King's death, Lobengula sent Umlugulu a commission 'to the effect that if ever he had the power he was to re-institute the Great Dance and with it the rites of the Matabele Kingdom'. This commission and the absence of any recognized Regent made Umlugulu the central figure in the movement for the establishment of a successor to Lobengula in 1894 and 1895.[2]

During these years Umlugulu was a neighbour of F. C. Selous, then acting as manager of one of Sir John Willoughby's properties at Essexvale. Selous tells us that Umlugulu was 'a very gentle mannered savage and always courteous and polite' and the two men struck up something of a friendship. Umlugulu would complain of various aspects of the Company regime, particularly of the misbehaviour of the Matabeleland Native Police, and try to persuade Selous to protect his herds from seizure by the Company by running them with his own. But, so Selous tells us, no more was heard either of complaints or of devices to protect cattle after the

---

[1] T. M. Thomas, *Eleven Years in Central Africa*, London, 1872.
[2] Carnegie, Memorandum on the Rebellion, 29 Mar. 1896, HO 1/3/4; Carnegie, Evidence submitted to Sir Richard Martin, June 1896, *C. 8547*; Report of Acting Administrator 3 Apr. 1896, A 10/12/2.

news of the Jameson Raid had been received and Umlugulu had learnt that 'the whole of the police force of Matabeleland, together with the artillery, munitions of war, etc. . . . . had been captured by the Boers'. Umlugulu still visited Selous regularly, however, 'and always questioned me very closely as to what had actually happened in the Transvaal'.[1]

By the beginning of 1896 Umlugulu was at the centre of a group of senior *indunas*—Sikombo, Babyaan, Somabulana, etc.— who were planning an armed rising and the restoration of the King-ship. The meetings on February 1896, which have been described above, were held near Umlugulu's kraal, and the accounts we have of the organization of the rising attribute the major initiative to Umlugulu throughout. It was he, we are told, who 'induced chiefs in other districts to join in the movement'; he who was the 'chief instigator' or the 'main-spring' of the rising. However this may be, it was certainly he who was to play the main role in the ceremony which was planned to initiate the rising. It was the intention of the group of *indunas* around Umlugulu, to hold a Great Dance at full moon on the night of March 26th 'on the borders of the Filabusi mining district'. At this Dance Umlugulu was to 'go through the ceremonies', proclaim a member of the royal house, Umfezela, as the new King, 'and inaugurate, in spite of the present government, a new regime'. Thus the rising would from the start possess a directive centre and the movements of the various regiments would be controlled once again by the Ndebele King.[2]

This Dance was never held. Carnegie explained this in terms of police and military activity in the chosen area, and of the prema-ture murders of Ndebele police which set the whole movement of insurrection in motion before the new King could be proclaimed. But in view of the fact that the rebels found it impossible, once the revolt had begun, to agree upon a candidate for the Kingship and thus achieve much-needed unity, we may guess that the failure to hold the Dance had something to do with the opposition to Umfezela's candidature on the part of the 'young bloods'. Umfezela had the support of Umlugulu and the older *indunas*; the younger

---

[1] F. C. Selous, *Sunshine and Storm in Rhodesia*, 1896.
[2] Report by the C.N.C., 19 June 1896, PO 1/2/2; Acting Administrator to Secretary, Cape Town, 13 Feb. 1896, LO 5/2/47; Carnegie Memorandum, HO 1/3/4.

men, led by the militant *induna* Mpotshwana, wanted Lobengula's eldest son, Nyamanda; and the difference involved different ideas about the rising and how it should be conducted. These differences were not resolved and throughout the rising the rebel Ndebele aristocracy was divided into two rough factions.[1]

In fact, then, the various regiments stirred into action in 1896 never did act according to a plan conceived by a single Ndebele military authority, and many white observers commented with relief upon the lack of coherent central direction. 'They would have done better', wrote Selous, 'had they worked under one intelligent general.' 'It is only, even now,' wrote Baden-Powell in July 1896, 'internal jealousies among the rebel chiefs that save the whites from being blotted out. The attempt to make Nyamanda King, if ever seriously intended, fell through abortively; each of the great chiefs desires that honour for himself; and thus the different *impis* do not amalgamate to crush us.'[2]

More than this; some of the most senior Ndebele *indunas* held aloof from the plans for a rising altogether, and refused to come into it once it had begun. Gambo, Mjaan, Faku—all remained 'loyal', and carried many of their followers with them. Nevertheless we should not underestimate the contribution made by Umlugulu to the effectiveness of the rising. Before the March outbreak whites had been confident that the Ndebele were so divided amongst themselves that they would never be able to coordinate resistance; and even after the outbreak many believed that 'the Matabele *impis* are far from unanimous in their determination to fight' and that it would be possible 'to cause such a split amongst them that dog will eat dog and take a lot of trouble off our hands'. Umlugulu's influence was one major reason why these expectations were confounded; he was certainly at the centre of the planning which preceded the rising and after its outbreak he was a focus of loyalty for one of the two broad factions into which the rebels were divided. 'Umlugulu lives at Essexvale', noted the Staff Diary for 5 June 1896, 'and is the most powerful man in the country; Nyamanda, Lobengula's son, heads the eastern faction, mostly young men.' Thus the rising was not merely a chaos of independent action by totally distinct regiments; those engaged in it did group themselves around the contrasting principals of Ndebele

---

[1] Carnegie, Evidence submitted to Sir Richard Martin, *C. 8547*.
[2] Selous, op. cit; Baden-Powell, op. cit.

unity represented by Umlugulu, the 'high priest', and Nyamanda, the eldest son of Lobengula.[1]

But a discussion of the attempt to coordinate the action of the Ndebele regiments and the limited extent to which it was successful by no means brings to an end the inquiry into the organization of the rising in Matabeleland. So far, after all, we have been talking only about the Ndebele aristocracy and although these played a leading role they were by no means alone involved. To mobilize and bring into action the Ndebele nation meant calling the Holi caste into action as well; and to make the rising really effective and general meant persuading the ex-tributary Shona peoples to join it.

And here lies precisely one of the main differences between the 1893 war and the Matabeleland rising of 1896. In 1893 there is good evidence to suggest that the Holi regiments did not fight very vigorously; and it is clear that the tributary Shona made no sort of attempt to come to the aid of their Ndebele over-lords. Shona from the eastern areas of Matabeleland in fact joined the invading white column as 'friendlies', while the Kalanga peoples of the south-west and of the Matopos area remained studiously neutral. 'The Makalakas', wrote Goold-Adams in February 1894, 'never answered the call to turn out and fight the whites but remained in their fastnesses . . . and sent representatives to the whites to ask for peace. At the present the whole of the Makalakas are at their own homes, they never having left them, and I think welcome the turn of events.'[2]

Yet in 1896 it was at once strikingly apparent that over and above the Ndebele Zansi and Enhla regiments large numbers of the Holi were also engaged in the revolt and that the Shona peoples of the east, north-east and north of Matabeleland were thoroughly committed to it. So much was this so that early press comment on the rising tended to regard it as largely the work of the old subject peoples. Thus *The Times* reported on March 28 that 'the natives who are making the disturbances are not the true Matabeles but the AmaHoli and the Mashonas'; and on the same day the *Pall Mall Gazette* reported that the rebels were 'not Matabele but their enfranchized subjects'. These reports were

---

[1] Staff Diary, June 1896, C.O., C.P., S.A., No. 520, pp. 243–5; *Bulawayo Sketch*, 18 Apr. 1896.

[2] Goold-Adams to High Commissioner, 22 Feb. 1894, LO 5/2/34.

soon corrected as the commitment of 'the true Matabele' became obvious but they may serve to remind us of the important part played in the rebellion by these other groups.

Why was there this difference between 1893 and 1896? It was certainly not because of the continuance or the revival of the authority of the regimental indunas or of Umlugulu, Umfezela or Nyamanda. As Umlugulu himself complained, 'the MaHoli do not recognize us any longer; they say, "We belong to the white men as well as you".' As for the Kalanga, Karanga and other Shona peoples they were no more responsive in 1896 than they had been in 1893 to the appeals of the Ndebele aristocracy. Selous tells us, for instance, that Umfezela sent his own son to the Kalanga of the Fig Tree area, calling upon them in the name of racial solidarity to make common cause against the whites who were 'killing all the black men they can catch'. The Kalanga chief merely replied that the 'people don't wish to fight; they wish to sit still'. And sit still they did.[1]

But if the Shona peoples of Matabeleland had not changed their attitude to the Ndebele since 1893 they had certainly changed their attitude to the whites. They may have welcomed 'the turn of events' in 1893 but they were almost as heavily affected by Company rule as the Ndebele themselves. They did not lose their land in the same wholesale way and they did not suffer the same collapse of aristocratic self-esteem; but they, too, were disarmed; they, too, were forced to work; their cattle were also siezed. By 1896 they had every reason to hope for the overthrow of the new regime; indeed some of them were already resisting it in the same sort of way that it had been resisted in Mashonaland through the piecemeal opposition of individual chiefs before the actual outbreak of the rising. Thus the first shots fired by Africans in Matabeleland after the end of the 1893 war were fired not by the Ndebele but by the Shona peoples of eastern Belingwe. Infuriated by siezures of cattle and the pressing of labour a band of Belingwe Shona ambushed a police patrol early in March 1896. 'This is the second patrol of native police which has been fired on by Mashonas on the Belingwe Victoria boundary', wrote the Acting Chief Native Commissioner. He sought permission 'to hunt out these troublesome natives', to 'shoot any natives bearing arms in that district on sight', and to nip any trouble in the bud. Before any action could

[1] *The Bulawayo Chronicle*, 26 June 1897; Selous, op. cit.

be taken these disorders were dwarfed by the outbreak of the rising. But clearly there is no need to postulate any Ndebele coercion or persuasion to explain the involvement of the Belingwe Shona in the rising; they were only too ready to throw off Company rule. And the same was true of the Shona peoples of the north and north-east.[1]

However, there still is need of an explanation of how any degree of coordination was established between these Shona groups and the Ndebele rebels, for such coordination existed. The answer seems to lie largely in the role of the Mwari-Mlimo cult officers as allies of the Ndebele aristocracy on the one hand and as authorities amongst the ex-tributary Shona on the other. We have seen something of the history of the Mwari cult in Chapter One. The time has now come for a more detailed examination of its fortunes after the collapse of the Rozwi confederation; its relations with the Ndebele state and its influence in 1896.

It has been claimed by some authorities that even before the death of the last Mambo there had been a breach between the Rozwi kings and the Mwari priesthood, and that the latter had moved from the cult centre at Zimbabwe to the shrines in the Matopos hills which from then on became the nuclear area of the cult. However this may be, the cult certainly survived the overthrow of the Rozwi state with which it had been so closely associated. The overthrow itself was explained, indeed, in terms of the displeasure of Mwari. At first, moreover, it looked as if the new Ndebele rulers might come to the same sort of working arrangement with the cult which the Rozwi themselves had so successfully established. 'On arriving in their land, about forty years ago', T. M. Thomas wrote in 1872, 'Umzilikazi found several Ama-Kalanga doctors and wizards there, and for a time, on account of their influence over the chiefs of their own tribes, and knowledge of the country, they were of much use to him as news-mongers and leaders of his troops on their raids into different parts of the interior.'[2]

---

[1] Acting C.N.C. to Acting Administrator, 10 Mar. 1896, A 1/12/27; for the effect of Company administration on the south-western Kalanga, see Cullen Reed to Sir Richard Martin, 2 July 1896, Blue Book C. 8547.

[2] Thomas, op. cit. For a full version of oral tradition concerning the displeasure of Mwari with the Mambos, see N. G., 'Magango Hutari', NADA, 1933.

But the Ndebele state was built on different principles from the Rozwi confederacy. Within the highly concentrated and centralized Ndebele state proper there was little need for the Mwari priesthood as a coordinating agency. Thus Thomas tells us that once the priests 'failed to discover any more Ama-Kalanga or AmaSwina cattle they were dispatched'. The word dispatched, however, gives altogether too dramatic an idea of the fate of the Mwari priesthood. They were certainly not exterminated; it was merely that the cult was no longer used for continuous central political purposes and that it was closely controlled and watched. Its chief officials, no longer based at the capital of the monarch, were allowed to preside over the various shrines in the Matopos. After all, the Ndebele felt the need which Father Devlin tells us was common to all conquerors of Rhodesia before the white man to be at 'peace with the land', and Mwari was pre-eminently the god of fertility and harvest. It seems that at all times under the Ndebele kingship the dispatch of gifts to the chief Mwari shrines was permitted and that it was a recognized responsibility of the Ndebele king to send such gifts on behalf of the nation. If Hughes is right, the Mwari priesthood were even formally represented each year in a special compound at the Great Dance and the Feast of the First Fruits.[1]

But at the same time there was a feeling, as Thomas puts it, that the 'fame and influence' of the cult 'were inconsistent with those of the Ndebele king'. Thus our evidence suggests that it was only at times when the power of the Ndebele monarchy was for some reason or another at an ebb that the cult was able to manifest its old vigour and its emissaries able to travel freely through the whole area of its influence. Thomas tells us, for instance, that Mwari messengers did not begin to go round the military kraals 'until Mzilikazi had become old and feeble'; that they then rapidly built up a great influence, becoming in each town they entered 'the real lord of the place'; that the cult centre was even consulted after the death of Mzilikazi on the choice of his successor; but that almost immediately after the succession of the new king 'this underground mysterious being was denounced and his representatives roughly handled.'[2]

In the same way after Lobengula's death there was a similar

[1] Hughes, *The Re-construction of the Ndebele state under European control.*
[2] Thomas, op. cit.

expansion of the cult's activities. The priesthood emphatically dissociated itself from the dying monarchy in 1893 and did nothing to persuade the tributary Shona peoples to support the Ndebele against the whites. 'In 1893, when the Salisbury-Victoria columns were steadily coming into the country', ran a press report in July 1896, 'the Matoppo prophet saw that the white man would come and sit in Bulawayo.' 'Look!' the voice of Mwari was later believed among the Ndebele to have told Lobengula, 'You who are so busy killing people. You are a little man. Climb on top of a high hill and see these people who are coming up. See their dust rising in the South. My white sons whose ears shine in the sun are coming here.' Mwari's white sons, having come, paid little attention to his priesthood, but while they did not come to terms with them as former conquerors had done, no more did they control them. Released from Lobengula's restrictions the Mwari officials greatly extended their activities between 1893 and 1896. 'The Wosana were rain bringers', Nyanganyoni Mhlope tells us in his account of the outbreak of the rising: 'They used to come in a group and say that they were sent by the Mlimo to make rain. They would dance at the kraal and the people would give them presents. In the time of Lobengula they were not allowed to go round the kraals and dance. Lobengula used to send a few men to Njelele with black oxen and they would find Wosana there and the Wosana would dance to make rain. When the white people came into the country then the Wosana started to go round from kraal to kraal.' And Mhlope tells also of the new prestige of the Mwari officers. In the Inyati area in this period, he says, the chief Mwari messenger was one Mkwati. 'He was just like an Nkosi (King). He was not an Nkosi but we took him as an Nkosi because he had been sent by the Mlimo.'[1]

Clearly the Mwari officers, with their increased activity and prestige, and their continuing 'influence over the chiefs of their own tribes and knowledge of the country', could be of great assistance to the Ndebele leaders. The cult still offered considerable possibilities of coordination. It is important to ask at this point what precisely those possibilities were.

In July 1896 General Carrington, commander of the British forces operating against the Ndebele, gave his view of the Mwari cult. 'The Mlimo is a Makalaka institution,' he wrote, 'which has

[1] *Cape Times*, 10 July 1896; Richards, 'The Mlimo-Belief and Practice of the Kalanga', *NADA*, 1942; Mhlope, op. cit.

been adopted with great fervour by the Matabele. . . . For special occasions the people appear to travel enormous distances in order to consult the Mlimo and his orders fly about from one end of the country to another with great rapidity.' This account, with its emphasis upon a single 'Mlimo' or high priest of Mwari and its notion of orders from this single authority being carried and obeyed everywhere, fairly represents the general white view in 1896. But it certainly overestimates both the centralization and the authoritarianism of the cult. Whatever may have been the case under the Rozwi Mambos in 1896 there was no single cult centre which was generally accepted as senior to all others, and certainly no single cult officer who could command the obedience of all adherents of the cult. There were, rather, some four cult centres of major importance, and a large number of subsidiary shrines scattered about the area of the cult's activities.[1]

The location of the four important shrines in the nineteenth century is given in a valuable account of Ndebele and Shona religious belief written from Hope Fountain Mission by Joseph Cockin in 1872. 'They have great faith in certain deified men. Amongst the Amaswena are numbers of men who claim to be Gods. To the East amongst the Amatoppo Mountains there is a town named Ematjetjeni [Matonjeni], to the South is another named Enjeleli [Njelele] and to the South West is a third, named Umkombo. These belong to a man named Ungwali, a god in whom the Matabili have great faith. They say he is not a man but a spirit, that you cannot see him nor feel him. He dwells in a cave or series of caves. . . . Not very far from Emhlangeni (Inyati Mission Station) there dwells another God named Ujugwa.'[2]

These four shrines were still operative in 1896, though many observers counted the two Matopos shrines as one. Thus Baden-Powell wrote: 'The Mlimo is an invisible god who has three priests about the country, one in the north east beyond Inyati, one in the south in the Matopo hills and one south west near Mangwe.' In addition to these major cult centres there was another important shrine outside the borders of Rhodesia in the Transvaal, and there were local oracular caves in the various districts of Matabeleland and western Mashonaland.[3]

[1] Carrington to Goodenough, 25 July 1896, BA 2/1/1.
[2] Cockin to Mullins, May 1879, LO 6/1/4. I owe this reference to Mr Richard Brown. [3] Baden-Powell, op. cit.

These shrines stood in no simple relationship to each other. Moreover, as Bullock writes, 'Mwari is not a fetish god bound to some stick or stone. He may not only move from cave to cave, but if so disposed can pass like a shooting star over the breadth of the land, manifesting his presence, perhaps, on Mount Rungai, a hundred miles away from the caves.' Even at cult centres there was no one cave sacred to the god; a Mwari messenger from Chibi district who made annual visits to the Matonjeni shrine testified in 1932 that 'during his period of service' he had 'visited ten different caves there'.[1]

Yet despite all this there was still a high degree of centralization in the cult which was of major significance in 1896. For one thing each of the four chief cult centres appears to have possessed a particular area of influence, though no doubt there was overlapping. The evidence suggests a situation in which the shrine at Njelele exercised an influence particularly in the Matopos themselves and in the country south and west of Bulawayo; the shrine at Matonjeni exercised an influence particularly between Essexvale and western areas of Mashonaland; the south-western shrine, situated outside the Matopos near Mangwe fort, exercised an influence over the Kalanga peoples of south-west Matabeleland, northern Bechuanaland and the Tati concession; and the north-eastern shrine of the god 'Ujugwa'—which is merely another name for a child of Mwari—exercised an influence particularly over the people to the north and north-east of Bulawayo, extending to the Gwelo and Selukwe areas and perhaps beyond. For another thing there is good evidence of close links between the major cult centres and between the families who supplied their officials. The full commitment of the Mwari cult to any course of action would require rather the consultation and agreement of a number of senior officials than the orders of one high priest, but such consultation and agreement was by no means impossible to achieve. And such a full commitment to the rebellion would give the rebel leaders if not one centre, then at any rate four major centres of intelligence, information and influence.[2]

---

[1] C. Bullock, *The Mashona and the Matabele*, 1950; Franklin, 'Manyusa', *NADA*, 1932.

[2] For the meaning of Ujugwa or Ujukwa see N. C. Belingwe, Report for Oct. 1899, LO 5/7/1; in 1910 the clerk to the N.C., Insiza, wrote that 'Majukwa' was 'a name given to the first appearers in starting a rebellion'. A 3/18/2.

There is ample evidence to suggest that in the early months of 1896 the Ndebele leaders, and especially Umlugulu and Mpotshwana, were in contact with these leading priestly families. Moreover the circumstances of those months made a popular appeal to the Mwari cult for guidance almost inevitable. The cult was, after all, especially concerned with fertility, particularly on the 'national' scale. In early 1896 rinderpest, drought, locusts, all added up to a most formidable threat to fertility—and one which the whites seemed to be doing nothing about. The situation was well described by 'Matabele' Wilson in his unpublished reminiscences of the period of the rebellions. 'It is strange but true', he wrote, 'that since the white men have come into the country that the years 1894-5-6-7 have been years of drought. Practically speaking we have only had about half the rainfall (as most of the older men can vouch for); some of the streams that are now without water, they never remember to have seen them stop running before. They say the white men cannot make rain. What do the white men know about collecting clouds in the sky? They can live quite well without rain, why should they go to the trouble to make it, all the food-stuffs they want to eat come up in waggons and trains, they have water as they can go into a shop (meaning a hotel) and buy a drink and they have not sufficient interest in the natives to care whether they want food or not. When the rinderpest broke out in the country and swept over the land and wiped out all their cattle and herds, it drove them mad to think such a thing should happen. They reasoned thus, if such a thing had happened in the days of Lobengula, he would have sent people to the borders of his country and sprinkled medicine, and drove in posts and it would have prevented the disease from crossing into their country, but the whites are fools, they did not know anything about medicine of that description, and the cattle that the whites had in their possession had not cost them anything, and the whites had not tried in any way to stop the disease, they had even shot the cattle that they had remaining to them. . . . They said that the sickness and the bullet will soon deprive us of every living thing that we possess.' [1]

In short, alone among the conquerors of Rhodesia the whites had, in African eyes, neglected the necessity of making peace with the land; no accommodation had been made with Mwari; and

[1] Reminiscences of 'Matabele' Wilson, WI 6/2/1.

Mwari in his wrath was punishing all. As the people turned to Mwari's officers for advice in early 1896, and as they consulted with the Ndebele leaders and with each other, most of the senior Mwari priests came to the conclusion that the whites must be driven out. Only then could the rain fall, the cattle recover, the locusts pass on. Their mood was similar in essentials to that of the leaders of the Boxer rebellion which broke out in China four years later. 'The Catholic and Protestant religions being insolent to the gods', ran a Boxer proclamation, 'and extinguishing sanctity . . . the rain clouds no longer visit us; but eight million spirit soldiers will descend from Heaven and sweep the Empire clean of all foreigners. Then will the gentle showers once more water our lands.' So in early 1896 supplicants to Mwari were told in the God's name: 'These white men are your enemies. They killed your fathers, sent the locusts, this disease among the cattle, and bewitched the clouds so that we have no rain. Now you go and kill these white people and drive them out of our fathers' land and I will take away the cattle disease and the locusts and send you rain.'[1]

In this way most of the leading officers of the Mwari cult lent both their moral support and their organizational apparatus to the preparations for the rebellion. Three out of the four main shrines advocated a rising and it was in the areas where those shrines were influential that the rising broke out. One shrine refused to commit itself to the rebellion and the area of its influence remained 'loyal' throughout. The dissentient shrine was that in the south-west near Mangwe. The chief officers there advised the Kalanga peoples to stay out of the movement; the priests themselves took a leading part in warning whites, including missionaries, of their danger; under their influence the peoples of Plumtree and the south-west continued to 'sit still'; and the baffling fact that the road south to Bechuanaland from Bulawayo was left open by the rebels is partly to be explained by the strict neutrality maintained by the south-western cult officers and their followers.

The other three cult centres, however, were fully committed to the rising and it is interesting to trace their role in it. Curiously enough there is least evidence about the Njelele shrine, which all

[1] Fleming, *The Siege of Peking*, London, 1959, p. 35; Carnegie, Memorandum, 29 Mar. 1896, HO 1/3/4.

III*a* The British South Africa Company arrives in Matabeleland, 1893; a contemporary drawing of the repulse of an Ndebele attack on a white laager during the march on Bulawayo.

III*b* The Headquarters staff during the defence of Bulawayo, 1896.

Left to Right, Top Row: Capt. R. Macfarlane, late 5th Lancers, Intelligence Officer; Capt. H. Brown, late King's Royal Rifles, Staff Officer; Capt. Nicholson, 7th Hussars, Military Secretary; Capt. G. Grey, Grey's Scouts; Gen. D. Willoughby, Chief of Staff; Capt. Newman, Staff Officer; Capt. Carden, Adjutant, Bulawayo Field Force. *Bottom Row:* Col. W. Napier, Commanding Troops in Matabeleland; Mr A. H. Duncan, Acting Administrator; Col. J. Spreckley, Commanding Officer, Bulawayo Field Force.

IV A contemporary impression, based on the reports of Burnham
and Armstrong of their alleged pursuit by an Ndebele *impi* after the
'shooting of the Mlimo', June 1896.

authorities agreed to be the senior and most influential. It had been to Njelele that Lobengula sent cattle and other presents to the God, and as Mr Hughes tells us the shrine still enjoyed extensive prestige into the 1950s. 'The Umlimo shrine at Injelele was regularly visited by agents of the cult . . . resident in distant parts of the country, both in the Ndebele area and from beyond the Ndebele borders,' he writes. 'At the present time some of these visitors come from extreme distances, even from Portuguese territory beyond the eastern borders of Southern Rhodesia. Mojajai, the "rain queen" of the Lovedhu . . . is known to have sent gifts of black cattle to Injelele.' We may reasonably assume, therefore, that Njelele was influential in the same way in 1896 also and that the general assertions of its participation in the rising imply the exercise of its influence over a wide area. But while we can construct a list of the chief cult officers at Matonjeni from 1896 to the 1930s there is no record of the names of any of the Njelele priests. 'I have been told the name of the priest at Njelele', wrote Native Commissioner Jackson in 1896, 'but have forgotten it.' [1]

The role of the Matonjeni shrine emerges much more clearly. The chief officer there in 1896 was a man variously described as Mwabani, Mwabane or Mtabane; he may possibly have been identical with the Umtuwani whom Rhodes described as the 'Mlimo's mouthpiece' in the Matopos in September 1896. At any rate his shrine at Matonjeni was situated very close to Umlugulu's kraal on the Umzingwani river and there seems little doubt that he was the cult representative with whom Umlugulu worked most closely. Matonjeni's influence, to judge by later evidence, was particularly strong in the Belingwe, Chibi, Gutu and Ndanga areas of eastern Matabeleland and western Mashonaland. There are many references in Native Department files to the post-rebellion activities of Mwari messengers from Matonjeni in those areas, including Mwabani's alleged involvement in a plot to bring Belingwe out in rebellion in 1900, and the supposed circulation of seditious messages 'believed to have emanated Ematojeni' which necessitated a police patrol through the Victoria circle in 1913. [2]

[1] Jackson, Memorandum on the Mwari cult, 1896, JA 5/4/3; Hughes, op. cit.
[2] Rhodes to Grey, 21 Sept. 1896, LO 5/6/4; files N 3/31/1; N 3/33/12; N 3/14/5; N 3/32/1.

F

The allegations by an African spy in the Belingwe area of Mwabani's supposed insurrectionary role in 1900 are particularly interesting, since it is a recurrent feature of the Native Department files that what actually did happen in 1896 continued for years to form the basis of rumours of new plots. According to the spy, Mwabani was the leading figure in a plot to restore the Ndebele monarchy and to take advantage of the Boer war to oust the whites; he was allied to Umlugulu, Sikombo and other Ndebele *indunas*; and had sent messengers who 'had appeared at some place close to Belingwe and ordered the people that this year they were to kill the white people'. It seems very improbable that anything of this sort happened in 1900 but not at all improbable that something like it had happened in 1896. At any rate the Belingwe district rose *en masse* at the end of March, and it is clear that direct Ndebele influence had very little to do with this. As the Chief Native Commissioner noted in June 1896 when listing the areas affected by the outbreak and their Ndebele commanders, 'no Matabele live in the Belingwe district which is peopled by tribes of the Mashona type'. There is little doubt, on the other hand, that Mwabani's influence was effective in the area and was used to stimulate rebellion.[1]

The character of this influence in Belingwe and adjoining districts, and the close contact between the Matonjeni priesthood and local Mwari officers, comes out very clearly in a valuable description of the cult organization by the Native Commissioner, Chibi. His account refers to the 1920s but it is not unreasonable to suppose that it describes a situation substantially similar to that existing thirty years earlier. In the Belingwe, Chibi, and Victoria districts, so he tells us, there were families of *Manyusa*, or Mwari messengers. These messengers visited the Matonjeni shrine twice a year; on the first occasion carrying gifts from the chiefs and people in supplication for rain; on the second occasion on 'a visit of thanksgiving'. 'A Nyusa must not go to Mwari on his own accord—he must have the authority of his Chief'; in Belingwe and Chibi the practice was for the local paramount chief to call together all his headmen and inform them 'the number of cattle each is expected to supply' towards the gift for Mwari; the *Nyusa* then carried a communal gift on behalf of the chief and people.

[1] LO 5/7/1, 2, 3, 4, 5; LO 5/5/3, 4, 5, 8, 15; C.O., C.P., S.A., No. 656; C.N.C.'s report, 19 June 1896, PO 1/1/1.

'When a Chief dies Mwari must be informed of the fact, also of the appointment of his successor. A Nyusa will be sent with four yards of black limbo as a present. This is handed to one of the priests. The cause of death is very strictly inquired into. The Nyusa is then conducted to one of the caves, where Mwari lives. There he sits down. The priest than says: "Your children have come to tell you that Nyakuti (so and so) who was a Chief cannot be found." (The real words are: "Their hill has been burst asunder.") A voice replies from a large stone: "I thank you, my children. Go back, do not forget to tell me who will succeed in his place." '

On their normal bi-annual visits to Matonjeni in the 1920s the *Manyusa* of the various districts usually travelled together in a party. They would go to the kraal of Matiza, the younger son of Mwabani; Matiza would send his mother 'to discover whether it is agreeable for Mwari to receive the deputation'. Then Matiza would take the *Manyusa* to the cave and present their gifts. 'Mwari thanks the giver and then predicts when rain will fall, what he shall say to his Chief on return, and the number of cattle to be slaughtered.' 'The deputation then retires to Matiza's Kraal, where they are supplied with food and drink. . . . The affairs of the people of the several Manyusa are discussed. Matiza is conversant with several languages and can carry on a conversation with any Native.'

The *Manyusa* then returned home. 'On his return home, the Nyusa announces his return to his Chief, after which a day is decided on for a gathering of the people to hear Mwari's prediction.' On that day cattle were sacrificed; the *Manyusa* met together so that those who had not gone on the mission could be informed of Mwari's message. 'Afterwards the Chief is given the message and he declares it to his people.' [1]

This, then, is what we may imagine as having happened in Belingwe in 1896; the *Manyusa* sent to seek an end of the drought, the locusts and the rinderpest; the meeting and exchange of information at Mwabani's kraal; the return and formal announcement of Mwari's advice; an effective mechanism of stimulation and coordination. But we should note that the peoples of Chibi and Ndanga did not come into the rebellion despite the messages from Matonjeni. In the Chibi district the local senior spirit medium, Mazarire, 'had a great deal to do with holding the Chibi

[1] Franklin, 'Manyusa', *NADA*, 1932.

tribe back from committing any overt act during the 1896 rebellion'; in Ndanga the local Mwari officers themselves seem to
have restrained the people from rebellion. At any rate in 1910 a
remarkable ceremony took place at the Matonjeni shrine, where
a Ndanga Mwari representative imposed a fine on the manifestation of the god-head there 'because he had incited the Matabele
to rebel in 1896. . . . The fine was demanded and paid for (the)
wrongful act in inciting the 1896 rebellion.' It was in Belingwe,
where as we have seen, the people were beginning to resist police
patrols even before the outbreak of the rising, that disposition to
rebel and the influence of the Matonjeni shrine came together in
effective combination.[1]

We know most of all about the role of the leading officer at the
north-eastern shrine which in 1896 was situated at Taba Zi Ka
Mambo, the hill on which the last Rozwi Mambo had died. The
name by which this officer was known was Mkwati; he was a Leya
in origin, and had been captured by a Ndebele slaving party
near the Zambesi. Before 1893 he had lived in the great regimental
kraal at Zingeni or Jingen and had been sent with gifts to Njelele
as a *Nyusa*; after 1893 he moved to Taba Zi Ka Mambo, where he
established an oracular cave and rapidly built up an extensive and
formidable reputation. Though the evidence suggests that before
the downfall of Lobengula Mkwati was a relatively junior member
of the Mwari hierarchy, that hierarchy had never been so institutionalized as to prevent the rise of men of remarkable prophetic
talent or supernatural gifts. Jackson, who tells us that he only
heard of Mkwati after the rebellion had broken out and that 'the
cave in Ntaba Zi Ka Mambo I never heard of before the rebellion',
also tells us that 'there is no regular head priest of the Mlimo. One
man at a time comes to the front and is believed in. Then for some
reason his influence wanes and some new man springs up and
ousts him.' There is no doubt that between 1893 and 1896
Mkwati's prestige grew very greatly indeed.[2]

He was helped by his association with two remarkable allies.
One of these was the woman, Tenkela, known to the Shona-
speaking peoples as the Mother or Wife of Mwari, and to the
Ndebele as Usalugazana. 'After the white people came',

---

[1] N.C., Insiza, to Superintendent, Gwelo, 28 Sept. 1910, A 3/18/2. The
officer of the Matonjeni shrine in 1910 was Mwabani's son, Khuliza.

[2] Jackson, Memorandum, 1896, JA 5/4/3; Mhlope, op. cit.

Mhlope tells us, 'Mkwati came back from Njelele with a woman—a tall woman with a light complexion; her name was Tengela. And he told the people that she was the Inkosikazi of the Mlimo.' 'The Mlimo has one wife', an African prisoner testified in August 1896, 'and three children. Umkwati is the father of these children.' Now, this figure, the Mother or Wife of Mwari, certainly plays an important if mysterious part in the cult. In 1913, for instance, when messages from Matonjeni were being carried to the Chibi district one of them was an injunction to observe a certain rest day 'to propitiate the Mwali's Mother, who is the imbuya or grandmother of all the natives'.[1]

And if, as our evidence suggests, Tenkela is also to be associated with the Ndebele belief in Usalugazana there is additional reason to regard her as an important figure. Cockin, in his 1879 letter, referred to this personage as well as to the Mwari shrines. 'To the north are a God and also a Goddess. The name of the Goddess is Salugazani.' Hughes and Van Velsen, writing on Ndebele religious belief, tell us that worship of Salugazana amounts almost to 'a parallel cult'. It is not surprising, then, that Tenkela should have been consulted by Ndebele leaders as well as Mkwati. 'It has been reported to me', wrote Father Prestage in April 1896, 'that Umpotshana . . . went at the beginning of the last hoping to consult Usalukazana (mother of Mlimo). She advised that the Amandebele should kill the white man in the country outside Bulawayo, undertaking to send a bolt of fire to destroy Bulawayo with its inhabitants at the time of rain.'[2]

Mkwati's other ally was Siginyamatshe, the 'stone-swallower', whose real name was Siminya. Siginyamatshe, a prominent Mwari messenger, lived at the Ntembeni kraal in the neighbourhood of Bulawayo. He had a considerable reputation as a wonder worker. At his trial in 1898 one witness testified, according to the obviously hostile and slanted report in the magazine, *Rhodesia*, that Siginyamatshe 'would go down on his hands and knees and imitate animals. On one occasion he butted with his head a big stone on which they ground their corn and broke the stone in halves. The people on that occasion were quite convinced he was supernatural and went forth to murder the whites with cheerful

---

[1] Mhlope, op. cit., Malema's statement, August 1896, LO 5/6/2; N.C. Chibi to Superintendent of Natives, Victoria, N 3/33/12.
[2] Prestage to C.N.C., 24 Apr. 1896, A 10/1/2.

ardour.' Siginyamatshe worked particularly with the Taba Zi Ka Mambo shrine. In 1898 also one of the subordinate officers of that shrine, Matafeni, was reported as saying that 'messengers were sent round to the people to come and see the prisoner, who was described as the wonderful child of the Mlimo. When a number of them arrived, the prisoner would be found talking to Mkwati. Mkwati would then mysteriously disappear. As a matter of fact, he would slink round the hill and get into a cave and between the two of them they would deceive the people and induce them to murder the whites.' [1]

Our sources agree that Mkwati and these formidable allies exercised a powerful influence on the Shona peoples of north and north-east Matabeleland. By basing himself at Taba Zi Ka Mambo, the site of the last Zimbabwe of the Mambos, Mkwati was appealing to memories of the old confederacy. Some of his most militant supporters, the men who formed his personal body-guard and were remarkable for the fanaticism with which they upheld the cause of the rebellion, were Rozwis of the Inyati area. And, as we shall see, Mkwati had close connections with the cult officers of the Hartley and Charter districts of western Mashona-land which were to be of the greatest importance in linking the Shona with the Ndebele rising.

How Mkwati acted as a link between the Ndebele commanders and the Shona peoples of the north and north-east is shown by the case of the Rozwi chief Uwini. Uwini was one of the most in-fluential chiefs of the Gwelo district. According to the *Bulawayo Sketch* he 'was a chief well known from the Limpopo to the Zam-besi. By his possession of a stronghold, which is a natural fortress pierced by caves running in all directions and well supplied with water from subterranean springs running through them, he suc-cessfully defied Lobengula and his impis for years and was after-wards left severely alone.' His hostility to the Ndebele is well attested from other sources. Yet in March 1896 Uwini was the 'instigator' of rebellion among the Shona peoples of the Gwelo area, despatching his men 'to kill white people near the Gwelo river'. Thereafter he remained an obdurate leader of the rebellion and 'withstood all endeavours to be brought peacefully into sub-jection'.

Uwini and Mkwati were closely allied. Mkwati had married

[1] 'How the rebellion was worked', *Rhodesia*, 7 May 1898.

one of the Rozwi chief's daughters. In his turn Uwini was regarded as particularly responsible to Mwari and his priesthood. In October 1896 he was described by a Native Commissioner as 'an Induna appointed by the Mlimo to compel the allegiance of the Maholi to his cause'; Baden-Powell wrote that 'Uwini was one of the chief leaders of the rebellion and was supposed by his people to be one of the chiefs appointed by the Mlimo and therefore immortal'. As far as the Shona of the Gwelo area were concerned the rising was a matter of the old alliance between Rozwi secular authority and the Mwari cult rather than a matter of response to Ndebele overlordship.[1]

We have now shown how the Mwari cult could be—and was— used to help bring the Holi of the old Ndebele home area, the Karanga of Belingwe, the Rozwi and other Shona groups of Gwelo and Selukwe into the rising in March 1896. But there remains a good deal more to say of the role of the Mwari cult in 1896. Important though it was in mobilizing men who were not responsive to the influence of the Ndebele royal family or regimental commanders, this was by no means its only importance.

By 1896 many of the Zansi and the Enhla castes of the Ndebele themselves extended respect and even devotion to the leading officers of the Mwari cult and there is no doubt that men like Mkwati and Siginyamatshe played an important part not only in bringing out the Shona but in directing the first murders of whites by Ndebele and in bringing the Ndebele regiments together around Bulawayo. Just before news came into Bulawayo of the first murders, for instance, Acting Administrator Duncan received a letter of warning from a settler who was in touch with 'our old guide, Munisi—the man who led the Salisbury and Victoria columns into this country' in 1893. Munisi reported on the activities of the Mwari messengers among both the Shona and the Ndebele. 'He stated the God—Mulima—was amongst the MaHolis . . . and had called the natives in to do homage to him.' It seems highly probable that Mkwati was being referred to in this passage and those that follow. 'He informed them to go and put handles on their assegais—those who had hidden their arms

[1] *Bulawayo Sketch*, 24 Oct. 1896; R. S. Baden-Powell, *The Campaign in Rhodesia*, Dublin, March 1897; Fynn to Baden-Powell, 1 Oct. 1896; Gielgud to Baden-Powell, 1 Oct. 1896; proceedings of the court martial of Uwini, 13 Sept. 1896; PO 1/1/1.

when the country was taken to take them from their hiding places
and clean them as he was going to kill all the white people after
the corn was reaped. . . . One of the messengers sent by Mulima
. . . told one of Munisi's boys that the God had sent him to tell
all the Matabeles to arm at once. The God also stated that he had
an army of his own coming but would not bring it in before the
corn was reaped. The whites had destroyed his power—now he
intended to destroy them. . . . Your police (native) must have all
this information but do not tell you of it—they are not faithful to
you.' The settler author of this remarkable warning added that
'the Mulima had sent several days before I got to Shangani to
call all natives from the Inxla, Halolodhlo and Insiza districts in
to him'. [1]

The warning was too late, being written as the first murders
were being committed. There is no doubt that Mkwati was
deeply involved in those committed in the Inyati area at least.
The Ndebele warrior, Nganganyoni Mhlope, tells us that 'the
first place where we started to fight was Inyati. . . . We had news
from the Matopos that the Mlimo was going to help us. . . . We
were going to kill all white people because we had news that the
Mlimo was going to help us. . . . Mkwati brought back the message from the Mlimo. . . . We did not touch anything at the
store' at Taba Zi Ka Mambo 'because we had been told that we
were not to touch anything belonging to the white people. We
were told that the Mlimo would come and take them. There was
a man who was delivering the message. His name was Mkwati and
he came round collecting all the things. . . . When we killed the
white people it took some time and Mkwati came and stayed at
the store and told us all to bring everything there. He was just like
an Nkosi.' [2]

While Mkwati was bringing out the north-east into rebellion,
Siginyamatshe was playing the same part in the kraals immediately to the south of Bulawayo. 'Umgalu, induna of the Elibeni
kraal,' runs a report of Siginyamatshe's trial, 'said that the
accused came to his kraal just before the fighting. He came with a
lot of girls in front, who were jumping and dancing and clapping
their hands; he said he came from the Mlimo. He said, "You must
close up the road and if any white men come you must kill them."
They covered the road as they were told.' One is reminded here

[1] Napier to Duncan, 24 Mar. 1896, A 10/1/1.   [2] Mhlope, op. cit.

of Thomas' account of the entry of the Mwari officers into the Ndebele kraals in the last months of Mzilikazi's reign. 'One of these young men, covered all over with ornaments, which consisted of buttons, beads, bangles, shells and various kinds of charms, entering into a village or town so overawes and allures the inhabitants that they are soon entirely in his power. That his favour may be secured, presents are heaped upon him, while he in turn, finding that he has become the real lord of the place, does as he likes—commands, orders, sends, or calls whomsoever he pleases.' 'Had it not been for the accused', commented the judge at Siginyamatshe's trial, 'many of the natives around Bulawayo would not have arisen.' [1]

It is also clear that the Mwari officers continued to play an important part in maintaining Ndebele morale in the first months of the rising. The military command of the campaign, which remained in the hands of the regimental *indunas*, was less important in many ways than the moral command, which as we shall see was exercised by Mkwati and his fellows. The main thing was to get the *impis* to the Bulawayo area and then to persuade them to stay there after their defeats; there was little enough of military tactics once they were there. 'All through they behaved in an incomprehensible manner,' wrote Selous, who expected Ndebele regiments to behave like coordinated armies, as in 1893, 'their leaders apparently never having arranged any settled plan of campaign, the consequence being that there has never been any understanding or community of action between the various hordes into which the nation is now divided. All through there appears to have been a general belief amongst them that they would receive supernatural aid from Umlimo or God, but . . . they would have done far better had they worked together under one intelligent general.' Yet as we have seen there was no single commander acceptable to all the Ndebele rebels, and Baden-Powell's estimate of the contribution of the Mwari cult to the rebel military offensive was probably a juster one. 'They were fanatics,' he told a Dublin audience in 1897, describing the Ndebele rebels. 'They believed everything Mlimo told them and this really accounted for much of their courage.' [2]

[1] Thomas, op. cit., *Rhodesia*, 9 July 1898.

[2] Selous, *Sunshine and Storm in Rhodesia*, 1896; R. S. Baden-Powell, *The Campaign in Rhodesia*, 1897.

Thus the senior Mwari officers were most intimately involved with the Ndebele leadership. Indeed, the division among the Ndebele was to some extent reflected in the Mwari cult as well. Umlugulu and the senior *indunas* worked mostly with Mwabani of Matonjeni and with the Njelele officers; Mpotshwana and the younger men worked rather with Mkwati and Siginyamatshe. The character of the alliance between the Ndebele leaders and the Mwari priests has been variously described. Selous held that the cult had 'only been an instrument employed by the actual leaders of the insurrection to work upon the superstitions of the people', and more recently Blake-Thompson and Summers have told us that 'the subservience of the cult to the Matabele was made abundantly clear in 1896'. But these estimates are almost certainly wrong.[1]

The evidence already cited suggests that merely to say that 'the Umlimo was made use of for the purpose of the present rebellion by Umlugulu' is not an adequate account of what happened in 1896. As we have seen there was a clear distinction between the interests of the cult and those of Lobengula in 1893 and subsequently the cult appears to have achieved increasing influence over the Ndebele rather than becoming more subservient to them. In 1896 both Umlugulu and most of the Mwari priesthood favoured rebellion; there was community of interest on that point. But Mkwati and his fellows were, after all, appealing to groups whose interests were very different from those of the Ndebele; groups which responded to the appeal not because the Mwari officers were allies of Umlugulu or Mpotshwana but because they spoke to their memories of the pre-Ndebele past.

Let us take the example of Mkwati and the Rozwi groups of the north-east. These groups certainly had no reason to love the Ndebele state. Writing in 1893 the missionary, Elliott, told how the Rozwi of the Inyati area complained; ' "How can we pray now that the Ma Tebele have conquered us. We are afraid to go pa dzimbabwe (to the graves) but offer our little offerings in our villages and houses. Our oppressors have taken all we had." Sometimes they, too, mourn over the departed glories of their race.' The hostility of Mkwati's father-in-law, Uwini, to the Ndebele was obvious enough to provoke a remarkable account by the Native Commissioner, Inyati, of a Rozwi plot against the Ndebele!

---

[1] Selous, op. cit; Blake-Thompson and Summers, op. cit.

'Uwinya was a chieftain of the AbaLozwi tribe, tributary to Lobengula, and lived at the Madwaleni mouth of the Shangani,' wrote Fynn in October 1896. 'He consulted with Umkwati . . . and these two having laid their heads together and having in common a bitter personal and tribal feeling against the Matabele and having probably been approached by the Chiefs of the latter with a request for aid in the rebellion they were fomenting against the White man, made a deep scheme for the destruction and complete humiliation of their hereditary foes, the Matabele. This scheme was as follows: Umkwati was to concede the requests of the Chiefs and prophecy the extinction of the whites and the success of the rebels, thus strengthening the hands of the Chiefs, as without the divine aid of the Mlimo the common people could not have been persuaded to rise. The far-seeing Umkwati had no doubt that the ultimate success would be with the whites, and then Uwinya would play his part. The part of the country occupied by him is one which would from its position be naturally used as a place to flee to, and there the Matabele went upon their forces being broken up by the whites in the southern parts of the country. There also went Umkwati, who had allied himself to Uwinya by marrying his daughter. Uwinya then laid himself out to discourage by every means in his power the surrender of the Matabele and for that purpose he established a force which he called "Police", whose work was to kill all natives who showed any intention of surrendering, and they did their work thoroughly. The Natives who remained would become a prey to famine and the young women and girls would become wives to Uwinya's people, whereby he would be able to make his own tribe more powerful.' Fynn thought that this scheme had worked well and that in this way Mkwati and Uwini had taken their revenge on the Ndebele for the overthrow of the Rozwi confederacy. The idea that Mkwati plotted the downfall of the Ndebele from the beginning is, of course, absurdly improbable, but Fynn's account could only have been given in the context of a bitter divergence between Mkwati and his Ndebele allies. How this difference arose we shall see later but it should be stressed here that it was implicit from the beginning. The Shona peoples to whom Mkwati and the other priests appealed joined in the rising to safeguard *their* interests and their 'way of life', not to restore the Ndebele monarchy. They had at no time any intention of being the tools of the Ndebele and, as we shall see, their rebellion continued even after the Ndebele aristocracy had made a peace which preserved something of their authority but which was irrelevant to the concerns of their Shona allies.[1]

The rising in Matabeleland, then, was a coalition of different, and even hostile, groups combined in the common interest of over-throwing the whites. That these groups were able to launch an attack on outlying whites which was roughly synchronized and to put into the field a force to invest Bulawayo was partly due to the continued authority and efficiency of Ndebele institutions and partly due to the existence of a widely influential religious or-ganization which was at one and the same time in touch with the Ndebele leadership and with men of influence and decision in the tributary Shona areas. In some of these areas—the Kalanga country of the south-west, for example—the men of authority combined with senior Mwari officers to keep their people out of the rising; in other areas—Ndanga and Chibi, for instance—men of authority kept their people out of the rising despite the contrary advice of the Mwari priesthood. But in most parts of Matabele-land the Shona men of authority joined with the Mwari priests to bring out their people in an alliance of convenience with the Ndebele. By so doing they made the rising much more formidable, not so much because they provided additional fighting men for the *impis* ringing Bulawayo, but because they forced whites almost everywhere else in Matabeleland onto the defensive and threatened to disrupt communications between Bulawayo and the outside world.

We have seen how and to what extent the Ndebele leadership succeeded in spreading the rising within Matabeleland. We shall see later in what way the rebellion spread to Mashonaland. Here we can mention the repercussions of the rising outside Southern Rhodesia. When the news of the rising reached South Africa many feared that it would be the signal for a general challenge to white rule by blacks. It did, indeed, have far-reaching effects on race relations and it probably sparked off the Southern Tswana rising of 1897. But there was no general rallying to the Ndebele cause.

The Ndebele state had been bitterly unpopular with its African neighbours. Khama of Bechuanaland, who could have cut the road to the south and doomed Bulawayo had he and his people

[1] Fynn to Baden-Powell, 1 Oct. 1896, PO 1/1/1.

joined the rising, had no sympathy with the rebels. Despite his growing dislike of the Company he stood by his traditional policy of support for them against the Ndebele. He had sent runners ahead of the Pioneer Column in 1890 advising the Shona chiefs to submit; he had sent numbers of his fighting men with Goold Adams' southern column in 1893; now he was prepared to allow the recruitment of 'friendlies' from among his people and gave all facilities for transport through his country.

Lewanika of Barotseland was less strategically placed, and could hardly have affected the struggle much had he supported the rebels. The significance of his hostility to them was more that the northern escape route, which they might otherwise have taken after their defeat outside Bulawayo, was cut off. 'The King is sending orders to his son Litia to stop any Matabele who henceforth would seek refuge in his country,' ran a letter from Lewanika to the Acting Chief Native Commissioner in May 1896. 'The King is very anxious in hearing of the Matabele rebellion and hopes the Government will soon beat them a second time.' Lewanika gave refuge to traders and missionaries in northern Matabeleland who were threatened by Mpotshwana, and arrested and held prisoner members of the Ndebele royal family later in the year when they were trying to escape across the Zambesi.[1]

Thus although in some ways the March rising in Matabeleland displayed a surprising ability to coordinate and cooperate, in other ways it showed the characteristic weaknesses and divisions of nineteenth-century African revolts. Neither within nor without Matabeleland was there a common rallying to an anti-white cause. Inside Matabeleland important Ndebele groups under Gambo, Mjaan and Faku remained 'loyal' throughout the rising and the south-western Kalanga also refused to participate. Outside Matabeleland Khama and Lewanika remained faithful to their chosen policy of cooperation with the whites. And even in the ranks of the rebels themselves there were serious divisions—between Umlugulu's 'party' and Mpotshwana's 'party'; between the Ndebele and the Shona tributary peoples—which were to have their effect upon the course of the rising after the first unanimous triumphant days.

[1] Lewanika to Acting C.N.C., 25 May 1896; petition by Cook, 21 June 1921; A 3/18/18/5.

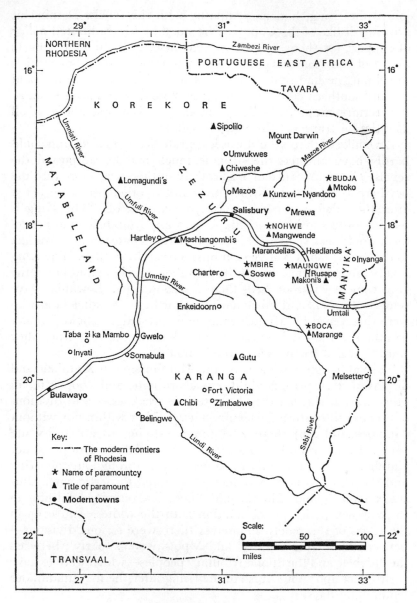

5. Mashonaland in 1896–7.

CHAPTER FIVE

The Relief of Bulawayo
and the 'Shooting of the Mlimo'

WHEN LATER leaders of African opposition to white control in Southern Rhodesia looked back to nineteenth-century resistance movements it was this lack of unity which struck them most forcibly. Thus in 1929, when the Bulawayo branch of the Industrial and Commercial Workers' Union was endeavouring to bring radical politics to the African workers of Southern Rhodesia, their speakers hammered away at the need for unity if any impression was to be made upon the whites. 'If Lobengula had wanted to,' said one speaker, 'he would have called every nation to help him. He did not. That is why he was conquered. In Somaliland they are still fighting. That is because they are united. Let us be united.' 'You see you cannot conquer the white people,' said another, 'because they are united. If you fight one white man the whole group will come upon you. Do not say "I am a Blantyrer or a Sindebele". Then we shall obtain our country.' [1]

This was certainly a reasonable lesson to draw from African experience but it considerably over-estimated past white solidarity. In the crisis of 1896 Rhodesian whites also found themselves almost cripplingly divided. Settlers were divided from the Company administration and both from the Imperial Government. The white governments of Southern Africa were unable to give combined support to their fellows in Rhodesia because of the divisions between Boer and Briton. These divisions affected white response to the Ndebele rising as much as African divisions affected its conduct.

The old alliance between the settlers and the Company on which the occupation of Mashonaland and the defeat of the Ndebele in 1893 had been based broke down in the face of the rising in Matabeleland. With every reason the white population of Bulawayo blamed the Company for the withdrawal of the

[1] Speeches by John Mphamba and Peter Mfulu, C.I.D. report, 29 June 1929, S 84/A/300.

Police for the Jameson Raid; with less reason they blamed it for what they regarded as a soft Native Policy. In late March and early April feeling in the beleaguered city ran very high against the Company and its administration. This feeling was intensified by the Company's initial absurd complacency. 'Reuters agency is informed upon inquiry at the offices of the British South Africa Company', reported the British press on March 28th, 'that the directors of that Company do not attach any great importance to the native rising in Matabeleland. The trouble . . . is not in the least likely to extend. The people of Rhodesia were never better prepared to meet an outbreak on the part of the natives, and the volunteer force entitled the Rhodesian Horse is regarded as fully capable of dealing with the rebels.' [1]

The whites of Bulawayo finding themselves extremely ill prepared to meet an outbreak were concerned that a more accurate version of events should reach the outside world. 'We have reason to believe', wrote the missionary, Cullen Reed, from Bulawayo on April 10th, 'that the Govt. here is stopping all letters and telegrams to people at home in order to conceal the very serious state of affairs here. Not only do the Matabele hold the whole country but there is a very considerable danger of famine here owing to the impossibility of reaping the crops and since all the oxen are dead. . . . Over a hundred whites have been massacred. Two columns sent out recently; one 200 strong has been driven back with loss of commanding officers . . . one 100 strong has with great difficulty cut its way back into town today, 6 killed, 19 wounded. Populace speak of lynching Acting Administrator, believed to be bribed by the Company to conceal the true seriousness of the situation.' Acting Administrator Duncan escaped this fate but Lord Grey found the hostility still bitter when he arrived a month later in Bulawayo. 'Shortly after my arrival here', he wrote wryly to his son, 'they held a public meeting in the Square and passed a resolution unanimously to the effect that the gaol should be cleared of all its occupants and the Administrator and other members of the Government take their place.' [2]

[1] *The Globe*, 28 Mar. 1896; this and many other press cuttings are preserved in a series of files compiled by the Company's London Office, now catalogued as files S 142/4/1–6.

[2] Reed to Thompson, 10 Apr. 1896, L.M.S., Matabele Mission, Vol. 5, No. 97; Grey to Charles Grey, 15 June 1896, GR 1/1/1.

Nor did the whites in Matabeleland feel any more kindly towards the Imperial Government. As a result of the Jameson Raid the Imperial Government had imposed tight controls on military or police activity in Rhodesia. No military mobilization could take place without the sanction of the High Commissioner and all ammunition and arms in Bulawayo were placed under the control of an Imperial officer, Captain Nicholson. There is no doubt that these cumbrous arrangements did delay an immediately effective reaction to the first news of the rising. Thus on March 24th, when news of the killing of whites in the Filabusi district reached Bulawayo, and patrols were raised to 'relieve the white men in the Inceza district and then to take the necessary measures to settle the district', there was a twenty-four hour delay while the High Commissioner's permission was sought for the despatch of the patrols and the issue of ammunition. It was not until the 25th that the Imperial Secretary replied that ammunition could be issued to 'not more than 100 volunteers' since the raising of a larger force than that would exacerbate feeling in the Transvaal![1]

It became an article of settler belief that if the Company had been guilty of causing the rising or allowing it to happen the Imperial Government had been guilty of preventing its rapid suppression. In December 1896 one P. D. Crewe, giving evidence to a Bulawayo committee of inquiry, expressed the general opinion. 'When the news came of murder outside it was decided to send out a number of men, but the difficulty was that at the time the ammunition was in the hands of the Imperial Government . . . the patrol was stopped at the Umgusa for quite a day. . . . It was common report in the town that they could not get ammunition. I consider that had the rebellion been dealt with promptly it could never have attained its ultimate dimensions and had the patrol got away at once it might have put an end to the outbreak.' And the point was made more sharply by the Chairman of the inquiry—'The rebellion could have been quelled at the outset had the Imperial Government not stepped in and stopped it.' [2]

Nor, finally, could the sore-pressed whites of Rhodesia look for help to their nearest white neighbours. Suspicion between Briton and Boer was running so high at that time, indeed, that the

[1] Duncan to Secretary, Cape Town, 24 Mar. 1896; Imperial Secretary to Secretary, Cape Town, 25 Mar. 1896; LO 5/2/47; CT 1/19/3.
[2] Evidence of P. D. Crewe, 3 Dec. 1896, Appendix 7, *Blue Book C. 8547.*

settlers of Matabeleland were inclined to believe that their Afrikaaner neighbours in the Transvaal were behind the whole rising! A Rhodesian settler, writing in the *Pall Mall Gazette* on April 17th, remarked that 'the Chartered Company in accordance with our English policy has always favoured Boer immigration within their territories. There are in consequence a number of Boers in Matabeleland, all of whom are agents—in some cases paid agents—of the South African Republic. These Boers who are as a body more in touch with the natives than the British settlers, have undoubtedly spread abroad exaggerated reports of the defeat of Dr Jameson's expedition and the collapse of the Jo'burg insurrection and have led the natives to believe that their conquerors are not as formidable as they imagined. There can be no doubt also that the Boers have bought cattle largely from the natives . . . and that the cattle so purchased . . . have been paid for by the surreptitious sale of guns. . . . Had it not been for the action of the Boers the native rising against the authority of the Chartered Co. would never have assumed serious proportions even supposing it had taken place.' Speculations even more improbable were made. 'It is an open secret', wrote the *Morning Post* on March 28th, 'that the Boers have long had their agents in Matabeleland, and it is not at all impossible that the witch doctor considered that the moment was a convenient one to remind the natives of the increasing power of President Kruger.' It was a far cry from the days of 1893 when Jameson could suggest that a Boer commando be used to help deal with Lobengula.[1]

In this crisis, distrustful of the Company, of the Imperial Government and of the Transvaal, the settlers of Matabeleland determined that in future they would achieve the power to protect themselves. 'There is full determination in the minds of the people', wrote the *Bulawayo Sketch* on April 18th 1896, 'that our future welfare shall be no more at the mercy of deputies or clerks or sacrificed to the exigencies of the Company's interests.' This determination was to play a significant part in the making of the settlement after the rising was suppressed.

[1] It should perhaps be added that as late as October 1897 Rhodes wrote to the new Administrator, Milton: 'I should certainly let the world know that from evidence in your possession you believe the Transvaal did assist the Matabele with arms.' Rhodes to Milton, 7 Oct. 1897, Rhodes House Mss. Afr. s. 227, Vol. 12.

Meanwhile there was a crisis also for the officers of the Company. For here was a situation which could no longer be dealt with by giving full scope to the initiative of the men on the spot. Early in April the facts of the situation were spelt out by a distinguished group of 'old hands' in Bulawayo. Colenbrander, Selous, Frank Rhodes and others waited on Acting Administrator Duncan to give him their opinion that the rising was a much more formidable military proposition than the 1893 war. It could not be dealt with by the Rhodesia Horse and so far from the settlers being in a good position to meet the outbreak, 'there was a great deal of dissatisfaction in the community and a general feeling that the Chartered Company by supineness has caused this present difficulty, and we doubt whether at a serious juncture the present enrolled troops can be depended upon to maintain order and discipline'.[1]

With gloomy relish the 'old hands' set out the unpalatable necessities. 'You want men enrolled for the special purpose of a war and not merely volunteers who are enrolled for the defence of their own homes. For these reasons we consider that you would not subjugate the Matabele within the next five months with less than 1300. The expense attached to the commissariat department for this force will be enormous owing to the cattle disease but otherwise we think you will be carrying on a desultory warfare for a year or more and meantime the whole of the outside districts will remain depopulated and all mining operations will be stopped.' Gradually and reluctantly the Company came to terms with the need to meet an 'enormous' expense and to raise special forces.

But the very raising of such forces was itself complicated by the tensions between Boer and Briton in South Africa and by the suspicious watchfulness which the Imperial Government now exercised over the Company's activities. Thus, in the dire emergency of the first days of the rising and faced with the prospect of the total severance of his communications with the south, Acting Administrator Duncan suggested that the Company should at once recruit and arm 500 men and send them by the quickest route—through the Transvaal—to effect a junction with him south of Bulawayo. But on representations from Rhodes he at once withdrew what would in other circumstances have been an

[1] Rhodes to High Commissioner, 12 Apr. 1896, LO 5/2/48.

eminently sensible suggestion, and when his proposal reached the attention of the London Board of the Company it was stigmatized as 'preposterous'. Even when the necessity to bring troops up by the longer route through Bechuanaland had been accepted there were further difficulties over the raising of the 500 men. At the end of March Duncan had issued orders to Rutherfoord Harris at Kimberley to enrol 'a very hard active force which would have to operate on foot if necessary', suggesting that the core of it might be members of Jameson's raiding party, now released and desirous of returning to Rhodesia. But it was hardly likely that the Imperial Government would allow the reconstitution of the Company force which had raided the Transvaal. On April 1st Harris was informed by the Cape Town office of the Company that 'the High Commissioner has received instructions from the Secretary of State . . . that the force raised is to be under the command of Imperial officers. 200 men are already on their way from England. An Imperial officer, Colonel Plumer, proceeds to Kimberley by tomorrow night's train to enrol the remainder. . . . Under these circumstances the High Commissioner cannot sanction the raising of any force by you on your own initiative.' [1]

The Company did its best to reduce both the expense and the extent of Imperial intervention which these arrangements involved. Lord Grey was appalled at the difficulty and cost of transporting and supplying such a force. 'The transport problem still appears to me to be very much more formidable than the native,' he wrote on April 11th. 'Under the most favourable circumstances transport wagons take a good deal over a month from Mafeking to Bulawayo when the roads are at their best, with oxen instead of mules and without any fear of native attacks. As the roads are still off and we shall have to rely on mules . . . and we shall have to take certain precautions as to possible native surprises the task of moving supplies and ammunition into Bulawayo will not be an easy one.' Accordingly Grey attempted to persuade the Imperial authorities to bear part of the cost. The Company did not need, he protested, 'so large a force of white men as it would appear Colonel Plumer has been authorized to raise and his Lordship concludes that the force is also partly required for the protection of the Bechuanaland Protectorate in the event of a native disturbance occurring there and that the Imperial Government will

[1] Secretary, Cape Town, to Harris, 1 Apr. 1896, CT 1/19/3.

be willing to defray a portion of the expenses.' As for the employment of British officers on full pay, the Company assumed that they would have 'the option of terminating this arrangement without notice when the services of Imperial Officers are no longer required'.[1]

But events were in fact pushing the Company into a position where it had to accept both more expense and further Imperial control. The tone of English press comment, at first optimistic, began to change as reports from Bulawayo came in. In the first week of April the press began to demand that the British Government take adequate steps to deal with the situation and not leave it to the Company's 'half trained and badly disciplined levies to cope with a rising which may rapidly extend until it covers the whole vast territory between the Limpopo and the Zambesi'. In the light of press comments such as this, the Colonial Secretary, Joseph Chamberlain, wired to the High Commissioner on April 9th: 'It is evident that the Matabele insurrection is a very serious matter and that its importance has hitherto been underestimated. Are you absolutely certain that the precautions you are taking will furnish force amply sufficient to put it down? The history of war with South African natives contains several disasters both to Colonial and Imperial troops. A disaster to the force attacking the Matopo Hills would probably entail loss of life to very many of the white inhabitants of Matabeleland and Mashonaland and this would entail the sending out of an expeditionary force from this country. Public opinion would be certain to fix responsibility for such a disaster upon Her Majesty's Government and upon yourself.' [2]

The High Commissioner at first replied that Grey seemed to feel that 500 men were more than enough to deal with the situation. But a few days later the mounting tension in Bulawayo had its effect. On April 12th the deputation of 'old hands' waited on Duncan with the advice already cited; he at once wired to the High Commissioner asking for at least another 500 men. Rhodes also cabled from the Gwelo laager in support of this request. The High Commissioner responded immediately and offered Grey 500

[1] Acting Secretary, Cape Town, to Imperial Secretary, 10 Apr. 1896, CT 1/19/3; Grey to his wife, 11 Apr. 1896, GR 1/1/1.
[2] Colonial Secretary to High Commissioner, 9 Apr. 1896, C.O., C.P., S.A., No. 520, p. 16.

troops of the Imperial forces then stationed in Natal. Grey pondered the offer in much agony of mind. He had been out of telegraphic communication with Rhodesia and knew nothing of the opinions expressed by Duncan and Rhodes. He realized the full implications of accepting the services of Imperial troops and accepting the direction of the campaign by Imperial officers. This had been avoided in 1890 and in 1893; if at all possible it should surely be avoided now. There was the enormous expense to consider also. In short by accepting the offer Grey knew that he was endangering the position of the Company; that the financial burden might prove too heavy to bear; that the exercise of British authority once begun might not be withdrawn. On the other hand a military disaster in Rhodesia would bring a more rapid end to the Company's ambitions. So Grey accepted. 'Had one sleepless night after I had accepted the High Commissioner's offer,' he confided to his wife. 'I was satisfied that the critical character of the situation made this necessary and so accepted the offer on my own responsibility without consulting anyone. The wires were closed . . . so I could not consult Rhodes. I was afraid that he and the Board might think I had acted with unnecessary precipitation in accepting Imperial troops . . . and it was a great relief to me when I got a wire from Rhodes two days afterwards advising me to accept the High Commissioner's offer at once.' [1]

The implications of the commitment of Imperial troops to Rhodesia were rapidly apparent. The High Commissioner insisted that the Company should meet all costs—'I am afraid the expense is going to be enormous', Grey told Rhodes on April 17th. At the same time the British Government demanded control of both the military and political aspects of operations in Matabeleland. On April 13th Chamberlain noted 'with some surprise' in a despatch to the High Commissioner 'that whereas one day Lord Grey . . . objects to the numbers of your proposed relief column as excessive, two days later he presses urgently for 750 more men. In these circumstances Her Majesty's Government feel that they cannot absolutely rely on the opinions expressed by the representatives of the Company.' Four days later he announced decisions which removed the conduct of the war and the making of the subsequent settlement from the hands of these unreliable representatives. Command of all forces in Rhodesia—the Rhodesia

[1] Grey to his wife, 18 Apr. 1896, GR 1/1/1.

Horse and other settler units, the 500 specially raised men under Plumer, and the 500 Imperial troops from Natal—was to be given to 'a military officer on full pay'. Sir Frederick Carrington had been nominated by the War Office for this position. The political aspects of suppressing the rebellion were to be the sole responsibility of Sir Richard Martin, Imperial Deputy Commissioner, who was to decide 'to what extent punitive measures are necessary'.[1]

On April 25th Chamberlain spelt out to Carrington the division of power between him and Martin. Carrington was to have supreme command of all operations, remembering the need to allow 'much latitude . . . to men commanding temporary levies of settlers and working from isolated centres for the common cause'. As for Martin, once the military defeat of the rising was assured, he would 'practically control your operations against the remnant of the rebellion, for it will devolve on him to judge what punitive measures are necessary and permissible and as to accepting the submission of the rebels and other measures connected with the pacification of the country and the future of the natives'.[2]

Divisions among the whites, then, did not in the end result in failure to provide a force strong enough to deal with the rising. But the force when raised was controlled by a variety of authorities which rivalled the divisions among the Ndebele rebels between Umfezela and Nyamanda, Umlugulu and Mkwati. 'I should like to know how you find the system of government to work,' wrote Acting High Commissioner Goodenough to Carrington in July 1896. 'There is a sort of Triumverate and I think none but Englishmen, who give and take, could make it work.'[3]

Even among Englishmen the system did not work very well. The different assumptions, responsibilities and interests of the members of the Triumverate—Carrington, Martin and Grey— were bound to produce friction. On personal grounds Carrington was in fact very acceptable to Rhodesians generally. An astute Rhodesian police officer had thus described him on an earlier visit to the Colony. 'When fighting or sport of any kind is going

[1] Notes of telephone conversations between Grey, Duncan and Rhodes, 14 and 17 Apr. 1896, LO 5/2/48; Chamberlain to Robinson, 13 Apr. 1896, C.O., C.P., S.A., No. 520, p. 21.

[2] Chamberlain to Carrington, 25 Apr. 1896, ibid., No. 517, pp. 105–7.

[3] Goodenough to Carrington, 8 July 1896, BA 2/1/1.

on he is in his element, and the more the danger the greater the element. To see him ride or shoot is to understand how, in his younger days, he raised colonial corps and commanded them by sheer force of strength and skill of fisticuffs; and to see him stand on his own strong legs, or bestriding a horse, he is a splendid specimen of a man and a soldier—tall, active and daring.' It was true that this observer went on to qualify his praise. 'But it is in his physical accomplishments that Carrington principally shines and in comparison to them his mental development is very small. And while there is no danger that he would not face, he has not the head-piece to get a force out of a self-imposed predicament.' This limitation, however, was overlooked by most Rhodesians until, perhaps, the stalemate in the Matopos reminded them uncomfortably of Carrington's lack of imagination. For most whites in Matabeleland, Jarvis' view that 'Carrington is a clinker' summed up the General well enough.[1]

But despite his popularity and despite the fact that he shared most white Rhodesian assumptions, allowing himself for instance to advocate the extermination or deportation of the Ndebele at a public banquet, Carrington came to have profound reservations about the men he was working with. He was a man of simple loyalties and strong personality. The attitude of both settlers and Company to the Imperial authority he represented was sufficiently equivocal to prevent any permanently cordial relationships with them. When he left Rhodesia at the end of 1896 Carrington summed up his views in a confidential report. 'The officials of the Company both in Rhodesia and in England have—probably with a view to re-assuring the stock-market—systematically endeavoured to make the least of the dangerous aspects of the rebellion; and possibly from a fear of the Imperial Government obtaining too strong a claim upon the country they have steadily opposed the bringing in of Imperial troops and have belittled or ignored the work done by those troops when brought in.' As for the settlers, 'the local forces, though possessed of individual courage, hardihood and aptitude for veld life, were difficult to work with. They were very independent, would not willingly do fort duty, long patrols or unpleasantly dangerous work. Their discipline, reconnaissance and shooting were poor.'[2]

[1] Leonard, *How We Made Rhodesia*, 1896.
[2] Carrington to High Commissioner, 4 Jan. 1897, PO 1/2/2.

Sir Richard Martin's responsibilities were such that he was even more likely to fall out with the Company's representatives, and in his case the relationship was made more difficult by incompatibilities of personality. Martin was the very embodiment of the stickler for routine whom Rhodes and his followers despised, but who was so much needed in Rhodesia. The first impressions of William Jarvis, writing in his new capacity as personal secretary to Lord Grey, were about the most charitable words ever penned on Martin by a Company supporter. 'Sir Richard Martin is a nice man but a great deal too much the stereotyped official. We don't want anything but rough and ready men for this sort of job.' Before long Martin was figuring in Jarvis' letters as 'that consummate ass' or 'that silly old woman'. But however much the precisian, Martin was a man of forceful personality, determined to make his authority felt. As we shall see, a series of clashes on a heroic scale arose between him and the Company representatives.[1]

The chief of these and third member of the Triumvirate was Lord Grey, undoubtedly the mildest and most self-doubting of the three. Milner, when High Commissioner, characterized him as a 'reasonable and conciliatory creature' and we have already seen instances of the diffidence with which he approached his task. It is true that he found that he was almost coming to enjoy it— 'I don't think I have made a mistake so far', he wrote to his son in June—but he never emerges from the correspondence of his subordinates as a strong man. Milton, his successor as Administrator, found him in September 1896 'very genial and pleasant but a little off hand and sketchy'. Grey's mildness and sketchiness, however, did not unbalance the Triumvirate or leave the Company in the weakest position. For behind Grey loomed the most forceful figure of all. 'The Government is, as you suggest,' Carrington told Goodenough, 'rather a difficult one, especially with the additional factor of the strongest mind among them occupying no recognized position.'[2]

Behind Grey stood Rhodes. 'Grey is Rhodes' clerk', wrote Milton unkindly, 'and does what he is told.' Rhodes, in disgrace,

[1] Jarvis to his mother, 27 June, 12 July, 27 Aug. 1896, JA 4/1/1.
[2] Milner to Selborne, 15 June 1897, Headlam, op. cit., Vol. 1, pp. 109–11; Milton to his wife, 2 Sept. 1896, ML 1/1/2; Carrington to Goodenough, 25 July 1896, BA 2/1/1.

with no formal status whatever, having resigned his place on the Board of Directors, no longer possessing the Company's power of attorney, and with no military or civil rank, was nevertheless a key figure in Rhodesia in 1896. One way of putting it would be to say that he played on the white side, at least as far as the settlers were concerned, the role that Mkwati and his fellows played for the rebels; he was the great inspirer of enthusiasm and morale. Able as always to attract to himself enlarging legendary stories, he came to represent for many whites their own situation on a heroic scale. Like them all his work was in ruins; like them he was fighting back—and fighting back with a conspicuous energy, resilience, ferocity. In what many of his biographers have agreed to call his 'finest hour', Rhodes was highly unlikely to tolerate the prosecution of war or the making of peace in a manner of which he disapproved.[1]

Now that we have seen something of the organization of the rebellion and the organization of white resistance to it, and identified the leading figures on both sides, it is time to turn to the military operations themselves.

At the beginning of April 1896 the forces of both the rebels and the whites were scattered over a large area of Matabeleland, the whites in laager in Bulawayo, Mangwe, Gwelo and Belingwe, the rebels holding the greater part of the countryside. The key area was clearly Bulawayo and both the rebels and the whites attempted to concentrate forces there. This the rebels were able to do more rapidly but in the end much less completely than the whites. By the end of May the great majority of white fighting men, not only from the Matabeleland laagers but also from Mashonaland, had been brought successfully into Bulawayo, while the majority of the rebels in arms remained scattered throughout the province during the whole of the fighting. Nevertheless, though white organization proved in the end predictably more effective in this respect, during the month of April the African high command showed an ability, remarkable under the circumstances, to concentrate the most effective fighting units on the rebel side, and as late as June they were still able to bring together in one force the picked men of a dozen different *impis*.

[1] Milton to 'my dear child', 11 Sept. 1896, ML 1/1/2.

These concentrations of rebel power were brought together in the vicinity of Bulawayo and the key engagements of the first phase of the rebellion were fought there.

This concentration a few miles north-west of Bulawayo, on the far bank of the river Umgusa, was very much the work of the Mkwati-Nyamanda faction. Throughout April and May the *impis* led by Umlugulu and his faction took up their position much further from the town; they were, moreover, much more dispersed than the concentrated force of the north-eastern faction. On May 1st, for instance, the Chief Native Commissioner reported that the total fighting strength of the rebels amounted to some 10,000 men, divided into five main *impis*. The largest of these was the force which based itself on the Umgusa, and which was commanded militarily by Mtini (*induna* of the Ngnoba regiment, leader of the first attacks on whites in the Inyati area, and close associate of Mkwati), and spiritually by Siginyamatshe. Nyamanda, eldest son of Lobengula and the northern faction's candidate for the kingship was also with this force; so was Mpotshwana, induna of the Nyamandhlovu regiment and the main leader of the rising in the area around Bulawayo itself. Many members of the Ndebele royal family were also present. As for the fighting members of this impressive force they were drawn from the regiments of the Inyati area—the Jingen regiment among whom Mkwati had lived under their induna, Nkomo, for example; the regiments of the Bulawayo area—the Elibeni whom Siginyamatshe had brought out for example; and some men at least from the area of the Matopos. In all the force amounted to some 4000 men.

Umlugulu and Sikombo were out with an *impi* of some 2000 men 25 miles south-east of Bulawayo, blocking the Tuli road; Babyaan and Dhliso, other members of the Umlugulu faction, were out with an *impi* some 800 strong on the Khami river, 14 miles south of Bulawayo. The other *impis*, each 2000 strong, were in the Inyoka and Shangani districts, relatively remote from Bulawayo. It is hard to say whether there was a combined strategy jointly devised between the various rebel factions; probably there was not. There was, however, plenty of contact between them during this period, and constant movement of people from one area to another.[1]

[1] Report by C.N.C. Taylor, 1 May 1896, LO 5/6/1; report of events, 21 Apr. 1896, A 10/12/2.

In the later defensive stage of the rising from mid-June to September 1896 it was the forces of Umlugulu, Sikombo, Dhliso, Babyaan, and the rest of that faction, by then concentrated in the Matopos, which played the key role. But in the earlier period of offensive against Bulawayo the north-eastern faction made all the running. The force which they had brought together on the Umgusa experienced the most concentrated fighting of the rebellion; there were no less than five battles there in April, and when in early June the forces of the north-eastern faction returned for a final offensive throw it was to the Umgusa that they came. The banks of the little river, undramatic though they appear to a visitor, witnessed the decisive encounters of the Ndebele–European struggle; it was there that the rebel attack was broken and there also that Ndebele determination showed to most advantage.

When the fighting was over the Umgusa battlefield still bore silent witness to the intensity of the struggle. 'All the ant-bear holes are filled with the corpses of niggers,' wrote Lady Victoria Grey after a visit to the site in August; 'they are only skeletons now. In several places we came across skeletons lying in the bush with the shield and assegai and sandals lying beside them.' [1]

The only evidence we have about the intentions of the leaders of this force comes from testimony later given in the trial of Siginyamatshe. We have seen already how the Mwari messenger roused the men of the Elibeni kraal and brought them into the rising in March 1896. Thereafter, according to the testimony of the *induna* Umgalu, he led them 'to the Umgusa and said they must look sharply out for the Mlimo. Accused was giving orders. He told them that the Mlimo had said that this *impi* was to watch the town of Bulawayo and kill anyone who came out of it. Accused told them that when the white men crossed the river their bullets would turn to water and the maxim could not fire any longer as there were no bullets left. He had a horn which he was blowing.' [2]

We may reasonably give some stress to Siginymatshe's orders. The evidence suggests that there was very close cooperation between the Mwari officers and the military leaders of the north-eastern faction. Mtini, commander of the Umgusa force, regularly reported back to Mkwati, who in turn received specifically military advice from Mtini himself and from Mpotshwana.

[1] Diary of Lady Victoria Grey, 30 Aug. 1896, GR 4/2/1.
[2] Evidence of Umgalu, *Rhodesia*, Vol. 2, 9 July 1897.

Siginyamatshe, Mwari representative on the battlefield, was very well known to Mtini, in whose regimental kraal he had lived before becoming prominent in the cult. We may perhaps assume that military policy was the result of agreement between the two groups of leaders. If we do take Siginyamatshe's orders to the Elibeni regiment as a guide it would seem that the Umgusa position was chosen as a place near enough to Bulawayo to allow the rebels to watch the town closely and to take decisive action at any sign of evacuation, while at the same time offering good defensive potentialities should the white garrison attempt an attack. In 1893 the two great battles between the Ndebele regiments and the white columns both took place on the banks of rivers, and the continued promises of the Mwari priesthood that the whites would not be able to force the crossing of the Umgusa would seem to demonstrate the significance paid to this in rebel military planning. As a matter of fact, the position did prove a strong one. In the encounters of April 16th, April 19th, April 20th and April 22nd, on all of which days the Umgusa force was attacked by white patrols of varying strength, the Ndebele held their ground despite the presence of maxim and hotchkiss guns.

Siginyamatshe's horn sounded throughout these early engagements. Shemheli of the Elibeni kraal later 'remembered him at the Umgusa fight, where he had a horn and an assegai; the former he was blowing. . . . When everyone heard it they said, "That is Siginyamatshe's horn". ' Clearly his spiritual prestige and that of Mkwati was heavily committed to the Umgusa strategy; equally clearly the discipline and faith in their own strength which the strategy called for from the Ndebele fighting men could hardly have been achieved without the addition of the charismatic Mwari leadership to the authority of the regimental *indunas* and the members of the Ndebele royal family. But on April 25th the wisdom of the Umgusa strategy, the probable success of the rising, and the prestige of the Mwari leadership were all called into doubt.[1]

On that day Captain MacFarlane with a force of 115 mounted settlers, 70 African friendlies from the Cape, 100 local friendlies, one hotchkiss and one maxim, succeeded in pressing home an attack on the Umgusa position. The fighting was fierce and at one moment there was a possibility that the white patrol would be overrun, but in the end the rebels were forced to retreat with

[1] Evidence of Shemheli and Lukaso, *Rhodesia*, Vol. 2, 9 July 1897.

heavy losses. 'The natives had a good loss on Saturday last,' wrote Grey. 'Best authorities think they will attack us no more but remain on the defensive and wait to be attacked. Our fear is that they may on rumours of reinforcements coming retire further into the bush where it will be difficult and dangerous to follow them. This will be a great calamity as all are agreed that if we do not punish the Matabele now with sufficient severity the country will be liable to annual raids and consequently made unsafe for the outlying whites.' [1]

It was a moment in which decisive action on the white side might have brought the rising to a rapid end. Umlugulu and his allies had so far shown no very offensive spirit; and the defeat of April 25th had broken up and disheartened the Umgusa force. Intelligence reports described how many of its members had returned to the Matopos hills and how the remainder, allegedly disillusioned with the promises of the Mwari officers, was waiting for some explanation of the defeat to be sent from Taba Zi Ka Mambo. But paradoxically the victory revealed the essential weakness of the white position. Grey might boast that Bulawayo was now as 'safe as London' and publicly regret that uncalled for panic had led to the invitation to Imperial troops, but the Company and settler forces were quite incapable of 'punishing the Matabele now with sufficient severity'. They could defend the laagers and defeat Ndebele *impis* in pitched battles, though both with difficulty, but they could not pursue the African forces rapidly and vigorously or clear the country outside the towns.

Years later a Rhodesian Staff Officer analysed the problems which faced the whites. 'In the 1893 Matabele War', he wrote, 'the objective was the capture of Bulawayo and of Lobengula, and the advance on the former compelled the latter to assemble his regiments and give battle at the Shangani and Bembesi rivers. When there is no great king to overthrow the selection of an objective is not so easy. . . . In the 1896 rebellion there was no king or country to overthrow so the object then was the destruction of kraals and the capture of supplies and cattle, and then to hunt the rebels relentlessly into their strongholds and caves.' The requirements for successfully undertaking such a course of action he defined as follows. 'The question of the seizure of the initiative does not exist in this class of warfare,' he wrote with a lofty

[1] Grey to Lady Grey, 2 May 1896, GR 1/1/1.

disregard for the shock and fear of the settlers in 1896. 'Under ordinary circumstances, the native may make the first move but the massacre of a few residents does not constitute the seizure of the initiative in the military sense. The campaign only commences when troops are set in motion to put the disturbance down by force. The native will by then have retired to his strongholds from whence he will have to be ejected and punished. The initiative will then rest with the attacking forces. Promptitude in opening hostilities is essential, but the great point to aim at is not delay in getting into motion so much as that when once in motion there shall be no check. The initiative must be maintained. Natives are impressionable and are greatly influenced by a resolute bearing and a determined course of action. Delays must not occur; they cause an enemy to pluck up courage; every pause is interpreted as a sign of weakness and every halt gives new life. That being so the campaign should not be started till there are sufficient troops on the spot to prosecute the work with vigour, and sufficient supplies and transport available to maintain them in the field.' [1]

Grey certainly wanted to follow up MacFarlane's victory with promptitude but he had neither sufficient troops to prosecute the work with vigour nor sufficient supplies to maintain them. In the very difficult situation created by the rinderpest epidemic organization of supply was an especial weakness of the settler forces; it was not until Carrington arrived that a really effective supply system was built up. Finally, both the Colonial Secretary and the High Commissioner were urging caution upon the Company administration. They had had too many lessons in Company rashness and now demanded that no major offensive should be undertaken until Carrington had arrived to assume command. As a result the month of May was a month of consolidation on both the white and the African side. During the month there was only one significant engagement when a patrol ran into the old Umgusa force, or the bulk of it, at Thabas Induna and there was a brisk fight.

On the other hand the concentration of the white forces was successfully achieved. By the end of May Grey's strength had been much increased by the arrival of Plumer and his 500 men, of the men from the Gwelo laager, Rhodes among them, and of the Salisbury column. On June 3rd Carrington arrived and at once

[1] Study of the lessons of 1896, George Parsons, PA 1/1/3.

began to plan a system of adequately supported and supplied patrols.

Meanwhile the north-eastern rebel faction, of whose intentions the whites remained ignorant, had also consolidated. After the Umgusa defeat Grey had confidently informed the Company office in Cape Town that 'the back of the rebellion is already broken. The defeat of April 25th having caused rebels round Bulawayo to realize the worthlessness of the Mlimo's pretensions and the hopelessness of the struggle against us. The rebels will continue fighting but will act on the defensive and wait to be attacked, retiring into the hills and thick bush.' These were certainly not the intentions of Mkwati and Mtini, however, who were determined that the offensive should be resumed. And the delay in following up the Umgusa defeat meant that the confidence of their followers had been very largely restored.

We are fortunate in having a statement made in August 1896 by a prisoner, one Malima, who had acted as a messenger and go-between for Mkwati with the force on the Umgusa. It deserves extensive quotation. According to Malima, Siginyamatshe himself had gone to Taba Zi Ka Mambo to report back to Mkwati after the defeat of April 25th. It was then evidently decided that the force should be kept together and reinforced. After the encounter at Thabas Induna in May, the leading *indunas* sent Malima, together with two *indunas* of the Elibeni kraal, to report to Mkwati and to seek the advice of Mwari. 'When I got to Taba Zi Ka Mambo', Malima testified, 'I saw the people of the Mlimo, to wit, Umkwati of the Zingeni, Zenkele, Undabambi and others who I do not know. The names of those I have mentioned are the principal men of the Mlimo. We came to the approach of the cave which was curtained with grass. . . . I told the Mlimo the message I had been given by the indunas and told him the whites had gone on towards the Shangani. The Mlimo who, invisible to me, spoke from the cave told me to return to the impi and tell them to follow the white man as far as the Shangani river and on the Shangani river being crossed by the white men the impi was to return. We went with the impi and followed the white man as far as the stony ridges of the Enxa district. There a fight took place and then the white men re-directed their course towards Bulawayo. We . . . were then sent by the indunas to the Mlimo to whom we reported the course taken by the forces of the white men.

As before the Mlimo told me to return and to tell them to go again to the Umgusa. They did so.' [1]

Mkwati's determination that the attack on the whites should be kept up emerges clearly from this account. Other evidence suggests that he and Siginyamatshe were working in May 1896 to pull a new striking force together much as they had worked in February and March to bring about the rising. Meanwhile, as we have seen, the whites in Bulawayo totally discounted the possibility of another rebel offensive. 'Our difficulty now', cabled Rhodes, 'is that the natives have disappeared.' On June 4th and on June 5th two large patrols set out from Bulawayo to try to establish contact with rebel *impis*; on June 6th a small patrol on a routine journey north of Bulawayo suddenly ran into a large rebel force in the least expected place—the old battlefield of the Umgusa. [2]

The engagement which rapidly developed was in many ways the decisive test of strength of 1896. On the white side striking power and efficiency had been greatly increased; on the African side the force on the Umgusa represented the pick of the rebel fighting men. 'The rebel forces consisted of carefully selected, picked men from eight different *impis*, who had been chosen to take part in this venture, the success of which had been guaranteed by the Mlimo.' But it was overwhelmingly defeated. 'The rebels probably lost more heavily on this occasion than at any other action during the campaign. . . . After this engagement the rebels could never be persuaded to fight until they were by pressure compelled to do so.' [3]

'The other day a strong force suddenly appeared within 6 miles of Bulawayo', Grey wrote to his son on June 15th, 'on the other side of a little stream called the Umgusa; they were told by their prophet (Mlimo) that the white man's horses would not be able to cross the river, but would fall down dead if they attempted to cross to the other side. We thoroughly cured them of that little superstition and I only wish the other *impis*—of which there are several—would be similarly advised by their spiritual guides and give us an opportunity of knocking them out.' [4]

---

[1] Malima's statement, 1 Aug. 1896, LO 5/6/2.
[2] Rhodes to Secretary, Cape Town, 22 May 1896, LO 5/2/48.
[3] *Report on the Native Disturbances in Rhodesia, 1896–7*, 1898.
[4] Grey to his son, 15 June 1896, GR 1/1/1.

G

The 'spiritual guides', however, now accepted the inevitability of a withdrawal. Siginyamatshe, together with Mpotshwana, Mtini, the men of the Inyati area and the men of the kraals round Bulawayo, withdrew to Mkwati's stronghold of Taba Zi Ka Mambo. Umlugulu and his faction withdrew into the Matopos. Contact was maintained between the two areas but from June 1896 there were effectively two distinct centres of Ndebele resistance, whose attitudes grew wider and wider apart.

By mid-June 1896, then, a new stage of the rebellion was beginning which posed serious problems for both sides. The rebels had failed to drive out the white man or to sustain an offensive; they now faced the prospect of a long defensive struggle with little prospect of final victory. On the other hand the whites were at last, now that all their strength had been mobilized, and after the battle of June 6th, face to face with the problem of storming the Ndebele strongholds. It was not a prospect to which anyone looked forward with pleasure or confidence. Both Taba Zi Ka Mambo and the Matopos were extremely difficult country of granite hills, honeycombed with caves and crevices. 'A ghastly country for fighting,' wrote Jarvis, whose earlier zeal for stand-up fights with the rebels was sobered by the prospect of the Matopos. 'Huge granite kopjes full of caves (like the other place, Taba sa Mambo, but of course more of them). Many of the coves who know tell me that it is just about the most difficult country in the world—worse than Afghanistan or Chitral. I should say that it would not be easy to find a more beastly place to fight in and these niggers are so nippy.' [1]

Both sides, then, needed some dramatic moral reinforcement in June 1896. Both were given it. On the rebel side there was the great boost of the outbreak of the rising in Mashonaland, which is described in the next chapter. And on the side of the whites there was the sensational claim that the chief leader of the rebellion, the man upon whom its continuance chiefly depended, had been identified, tracked down and shot. The story of this 'shooting of the Mlimo' is a strange episode in the confrontation of the African religious authorities and the white administration which is one of our dominant themes.

As the whites faced up to the prospect of the Matopos the desire to identify a central rebel leadership which might provide

[1] Jarvis to his mother, July 1896, JA 4/1/1.

the kind of target for action that had existed in the 1893 war naturally grew stronger. The evidence that was beginning to come in, pieced together by Baden-Powell's intelligence unit from the statements of prisoners and spies, seemed to point to the Mwari or Mlimo cult as the mainspring of the rising. The full story of its involvement was at the time known to no one; the character of the cult was also misunderstood. As a result white attention began to focus upon 'the Mlimo' himself, by which was understood a man, claiming to be a god, who exercised dictatorial control over the rebels and was the focus of the rising. It began to be argued that if 'the Mlimo' could be identified and killed the rising would collapse—the analogy most often drawn was between the Mlimo and the Mahdi. In this atmosphere old hands racked their memories for scraps of information which might lead to 'the Mlimo'. Among them was the Native Commissioner of Mangwe, Armstrong, who recalled that in 1894 a police patrol had discovered a Mwari cult centre and dispersed its officers.

In the last week of June 1896 the news spread that Armstrong and the American Scout, Burnham, had followed up this clue; had found 'the Mlimo' and shot him dead; that their report had been accepted by Lord Grey, who was proposing to reward the heroic participants in the deed. The story as Grey accepted it, a story which became a classic tale of Imperial daring-do, cannot be better told than it was by its chief actor, Burnham.

'One day in June', so it begins, 'a young man came through the lines and knocked on the door of the small brick house. . . . He asked for the Chief of Scouts as he had something to tell me. On seeing my wife inside he said shortly, "I prefer not to talk before women". . . . Then he told me his name was Armstrong and that he was Native Commissioner stationed at Mangwe, in the pass through the Matoppo mountains. He said that a certain Zulu who had a Matabele wife had betrayed to him the location of the Mlimo's cave in the Matoppos. . . . Armstrong had come to propose to me that we go together, find this cave, kill the Mlimo and put an end to the source of all our troubles with the natives.'

Burnham welcomed the suggestion with alacrity, so the tale continues, and the two men took the project to Grey and Carrington and secured their consent to the risky adventure. They scouted for the cave and at length found it; but noticing the huts built at the base of the hill in which it was set and 'the ceremonial dancing floor . . . wide enough to accommodate a thousand natives at one time', they despaired of reaching the cave unseen. That night, however, Armstrong discovered from the Zulu— 'Armstrong could extract more information from a native than any man I ever knew'—information which made it essential that they should reach the cave on the following day. The Zulu told them that an Ndebele regiment was coming to be 'doctored' and that its *indunas* were going to the cave to witness a special ceremony to be conducted by 'the Mlimo' himself and to receive instructions. Armstrong and Burnham rose at dawn on June 23rd, then, and managed to reach the cave without being seen. They concealed themselves within it and after a while saw a number of men coming up the path towards it. 'I saw with surprise', Burnham tells us, 'that a man striding in advance of the others was not a Matabele at all, but a pure Makalaka, one of the ancient people of the country. He separated from the Ring Kops [*indunas*] and kept on alone, moving higher and higher up the path to the cave; pausing at certain points along his ascent to make cabbalistic signs and utter prayers, as if he were a high priest preparing to meet the god supposed to dwell inside the cave and for whom the great Mlimo acted as a mouthpiece.' As the man reached and entered the cave they became convinced that he *was* the 'great Mlimo'; taking in his 'forceful, hard, cruel' face and simple clothing, the two men prepared for action.

'Here was the author of all our woes. Because of him my little daughter was dead and the bones of hundreds of brave men and good women were scattered on the veld by hyenas. Carrington's command, "Capture him if you can; kill him if you must", rang in my ears. The moment had come for action; but after all, it was young Armstrong's skill that had located our arch enemy, and I knew Armstrong never intended to ride back to Bulawayo until the Mlimo was dead. I whispered "Armstrong, this is your work. When he enters the cave you kill him." "No," he replied, "you do it." So, as the Mlimo came in, I made a slight sound and gave him his last chance to turn the white man's bullet to water. I put the bullet under his heart.'

The two men then ran from the cave to the spot where their horses were hidden. The *indunas*, terrified by the unexpected reverberation of the shot from the cave, took to their heels, and Burnham and Armstrong were able to reach their horses unmolested. But as they galloped off, having first fired the ceremonial huts at the base of the hill, the Ndebele regiment came up with them. 'For two hours we were hotly pursued and had a long hard ride and a running fight over hard ground until we were nearly exhausted, but the savages abandoned the chase after we had crossed the Shashani river.'

Thus Burnham recollected his great exploit in tranquillity some forty years later in his book, *Scouting on Two Continents*. The story had lost none of its dramatic quality in the intervening years; but it had gained little either. In essence it was still the story told by Burnham and Armstrong in their report to Grey on June 26th 1896 and taken up with such delight by the British press at that time.[1]

After the shooting the two men took steps to substantiate their claim that the dead man was indeed 'the Mlimo'. They picked up and sent into Bulawayo as prisoners the family and assistants of the dead chief priest. (These men were still in prison in September when Grey's daughter, Lady Victoria, wrote to her sister that she had visited Bulawayo Jail to see 'a few rebel priests and men who call themselves Mlimos there. They have things like handcuffs round their ankles attached to one another by a light chain about fifteen inches long so they could not possibly walk fast and escape.') They obtained from the *indunas* of the Mangwe area affidavits that the dead man, Jobani or Habangana, had been the High Priest of Mwari and the chief instigator of the rebellion. They recruited the support of old Matabeleland hands, like Alfred Taylor who affirmed that the Mangwe Africans described Jobani as 'the head of the Mlimos who told the kaffirs that they were to fight with the white men and that our bullets would turn to water'. Burnham himself was in no doubt about the matter. 'I heard the ceremonies with my own ears', he wrote on June 26th, 'and saw the preparation for the indaba myself. I am convinced that all the information given was absolutely correct and that this was the principal Mlimo of the Nation.'[2]

Presented with these assurances the authorities accepted Burnham's claim. 'Mlimo is dead,' Grey told Vintcent jubilantly

---

[1] F. R. Burnham, *Scouting on Two Continents*, Los Angeles, 1934; report by Burnham and Armstrong, 26 June 1896, LO 5/6/1, p. 296.

[2] Taylor to Burnham, 27 June 1896, LO 5/6/2; *Bulawayo Sketch*, 4 July 1896; Victoria Grey to Evelyn Grey, 1 Sept. 1896, GR 1/1/1.

over the telephone to Salisbury on June 25th. Next month Grey's secretary wrote to the London Board of the Company enclosing full reports of 'a very brave act on the part of Native Commissioner Armstrong and Mr Burnham . . . who at the risk of their own lives killed the principal Mlimo in his cave in the Matoppos, which is the head centre of the witch-craft and superstition which has had such a fatal influence upon the Natives of Matabeleland in their rising against the Government.' [1]

Expectations of the devastating effect that the shooting would have on rebel morale were widely expressed. 'Another wire', wrote the Anglican missionary, Douglas Pelly, 'gives the report (which we much hope is true) of the shooting of the Mlimo, the great witch-doctor of the Matabele. If he really is dead the back-bone of the Matabele rising will soon be broken.' And that is precisely what Burnham later claimed; Armstrong and he had done 'Rhodesia stupendous service by exploding the myth of the cave and destroying the Mlimo's power'. [2]

What, then, had really happened? Had Armstrong and Burn-ham penetrated to Njelele or Matonjeni and killed the chief cult officer at one of these undoubted centres of rebel activity? Had they even stumbled upon Mkwati himself paying a visit to Njelele to coordinate action after the Umgusa defeat? Many people pointed out at the time that it was strictly speaking im-possible to shoot the Mlimo, and for this reason challenged Burnham's claim to have delivered a severe blow to the rebellion. The objection was, of course, a perfectly valid one; but at the same time there is no doubt that the shooting of Mkwati, say, under the dramatic circumstances described by Burnham would have had a very great effect on rebel morale. Fortunately we can reconstruct what really happened because doubts of Burnham's story rose so persistently among contemporaries that a confidential inquiry was held by government. And although the report of that inquiry is lost there is plenty of evidence to suggest what was in it.

Where, first of all, was the cave? It is clear even from the story told by Armstrong and Burnham themselves that the cave to which they penetrated was certainly not either Njelele or Maton-jeni; indeed that it was not in the Matopos at all. According to

[1] Grey to Vintcent, notes of a telephone conversation, 25 June 1896, LO 5/6/1; Inskipp to London Board, 24 July 1896, LO 5/6/2.
[2] Pelly diary, entry for 24 June 1896, PE 3/1/2.

Marshall Hole who went through all the evidence it was in fact situated very near Mangwe, 'near Banko's kraal, close to the Shashi river and within about 30 miles of the Matopo Hills'. This in itself gave rise to some justified scepticism at the time. 'I never could understand', wrote Acting High Commissioner Goodenough on July 8th, 'how the big Mlimo could have been found so near Mangwe as Burnham with his shot located him.' [1]

As doubts began to rise about Burnham and Armstrong's story it was often alleged that the two men had not shot a Mwari official at all, but had merely ridden out of the Mangwe laager, picked on the first old African to hand and shot him. This was not true. They did indeed shoot a high priest of Mwari but it was the high priest of the south-western shrine. This emerges clearly from Baden-Powell's sympathetic account which nevertheless differs significantly from Burnham's in many ways; and it is supported by oral evidence. In 1961 the American scholar R. Werbner was working among the Kalanga of the Plum Tree area; he was told by them that their high priest had been shot at Mangwe in 1896 by a fellow American. The name of the dead man's successor in the south-west, moreover, is given in Kalanga tradition as Njenjema, and a man of this name was amongst the prisoners held in Bulawayo jail as associates of the high priest. There can be little doubt that the man killed and called in official documents Jobani or Tshobani was the high priest of Mwari for the south-west, remembered by the Kalanga today under the name Habangana.[2]

Given then, that the shooting took place many miles from the Matopos and in a 'friendly' or at least neutral area, what are we to make of the story of the running fight with the Ndebele regiment? There seems no doubt that the whole tale was invented by Burnham and assented to by Armstrong. This was certainly the conclusion reached by the official commissioner of inquiry. A contemporary diarist tells us of that commissioner's summary of his findings—'the whole thing was a "fake" and a lie of self-glorification of young Armstrong and Burnham. The Mlimo was an old native working in a kaffir garden.' Marshall Hole, who had

---

[1] Goodenough to Carrington, 8 July 1896, BA 2/1/1; Burnham and Armstrong's report, 26 June 1896, LO 5/6/1.

[2] Baden Powell, *The Matabele Campaign*, 1896; information supplied by Mr R. Werbner; interview between the author and Mr Masola Kumile, 6 Sept. 1962.

read the now lost report and the evidence upon which it was based, has left a full account of the affair. Armstrong, he tells us, heard 'that there was a certain cave where the Makalanga used to offer up sacrifice to the ancestral spirit known as the Mlimo. He concocted a story in connection with the cave, and the rites that were carried on there, which completely deceived Earl Grey and General Sir Frederick Carrington. He made it appear that he knew of the whereabouts of the Mlimo himself, who had, he said, influenced the Matabele to rise in rebellion. . . . The two men proceeded forthwith to Mangwe and set out for the cave in company with a native confederate called Kutji. On arriving at the cave Kutji pointed out a native named Dshobani in the fields. Armstrong sent for him and ordered him to walk towards the caves. When at the mouth of the cave he was deliberately shot from behind. The party then returned to Mangwe where Armstrong called the principal natives of the district; informed them that he had "killed the Mlimo" and told them to spread the news through the country.' Years later Armstrong himself confided to a close friend that 'neither going nor returning did they contact any male natives and that the statements that they were chased by natives, etc., were absolutely untrue'.[1]

The famous late Victorian adventure story begins to look a little shabby; gone are the incantations and the firing of the huts and the hard fight and ride; what was left, in the opinion of some contemporaries, was 'a cold-blooded murder of an innocent and unresisting old Negro'. But the final irony of this odd story remains to be told. It may be remembered that the south-western shrine officials had *refused* to come into the rebellion in March 1896; by shooting the head priest of the shrine and arresting the other cult officers there Armstrong and Burnham were removing the one influential centre which had been *opposed* to the rising. Indeed, the indications are that the Mangwe shrine saw itself as the repository of the true and original Mwari tradition, now being revolutionized and distorted by Mkwati and his allies. In April 1896, for instance, Cullen Reed, a missionary stationed among the Kalanga, wrote to the Acting Administrator to say that the Kalanga headmen around Mangwe had warned him of the approach of an Ndebele *impi* sent to kill him. 'Unless com-

[1] Bertodano diary, entry for 13 Sept. 1896, BE 3/2; Notes by Marshall Hole, HO 1/4/6.

pelled by fear of the Matabele,' he wrote, 'I have very little doubt that the Makalanga in the west will remain perfectly quiet. In connection with the influence of the Mlimo in this struggle I may say that the eldest son of the man representing the Mlimo in the west was the first to warn me, on behalf of his father, of my danger.' 'The Makalanga, whose tutelary deity and special property this Mlimo is,' wrote Native Commissioner Thomas in October 1896, 'did not as a tribe join in the rebellion.' [1]

The fact of Kalanga neutrality was so well known that even Burnham was obliged to make some reference to it in his second report to Grey on July 8th. 'The family of the Mlimo claim to be friendly to the whites and it is doubtless true that they have never killed a white man in this district. They also claim to have brought to Mangwe news of the movements of the hostiles and various information—a little grain, a few goats, and many promises of loyalty. This, I believe, is true. I went into the district believing these Kaffirs to be loyal, knowing they took no visible part in the first war.' Burnham went on, naturally enough, to claim that this loyalty was feigned. 'I know that these Friendlies mix up and are in daily contact with the hostiles. . . . I am quite sure every move of the whites is constantly conveyed to the hostiles.' But this was a far cry from the claims of his first report and his later book. [2]

This white master-stroke, then, was far from being a serious blow to the rebels. The rebels in the Matopos and the north-cast repudiated the influence of the Mangwe cult centre; when Jobani's son was released from prison and used as an emissary to the rebels in August 1896 it became obvious that he enjoyed no special prestige among them at all. 'It was ascertained', so Hole tells us, 'that the so-called Mlimo—the man that is who was generally known by that name—was still at large, being in fact the native . . . Mgwati. The natives denied all knowledge of Dshobani.' [3]

The only effect of the shooting on the rising was that it nearly brought the south-western Kalanga in after all. The decision of their cult officers to stay out of the rebellion had been rewarded with death for the chief priest and imprisonment in chains for the

[1] *The St James Gazette*, July 1897; Cullen Reed to Duncan, 4 Apr. 1896, A 10/1/1; *Report on the Native Disturbances in Rhodesia, 1896–7*, Schedule H.
[2] Burnham to Grey, 8 July 1896, LO 5/6/2.
[3] Thomas to Grey, 18 Aug. 1896, LO 5/6/3; Notes by Hole, HO 1/4/6.

remainder; no wonder there was resentment and discontent. In July 1896 there were serious alarms in the Tati Concession and in Bechuanaland that the Kalanga would rise and at last block the road to Bulawayo. 'I have outside information,' wrote the Financial Manager, Tati, on July 2nd, 'that Makalakas are greatly disturbed by killing of their Mlimo'; he thought that a rising was a serious possibility. In the end the agitation subsided but it was an ironic consequence of an attempt to break the back of the rising by shooting 'the great Mlimo'.[1]

Mkwati's counter-stroke, on the other hand, was very much more effective. The Shona rising, in the planning of which he was deeply involved, was at once a dreadful blow to the hard pressed settler community and an indication that the Mwari network still had much more life in it than could be extinguished by Burnham's bullet.

[1] Financial Manager, Tati, to Imperial Secretary, Cape Town, 2 July 1896; Assistant Commissioner, Palapye, to Acting High Commissioner, Cape Town, 6 July 1896, Colonial Office, Confidential Prints, Southern Africa, No. 520, pp. 294–7. The subsequent fate of the participants in this drama was as follows. The family of Jobani were released on 17 Oct. 1896 by Grey's order; one of them, Ntshentshema or Njenjema, became Mwari priest in his turn, operating at the Hongwe Habalume cave in the south west. Burnham went on to gain further publicity by his exploits in the Boer War, becoming a Major and winning the D.S.O. Armstrong's career, on the other hand, was ruined by the episode and he eventually resigned from the administrative service.

CHAPTER SIX

The Outbreak and Organization of the Rebellion in Mashonaland

THE OUTBREAK of the Shona rising in the third week of June 1896 is one of the great dramas of white Rhodesian history. Its total unexpectedness; its appalling impact upon a community most of whose fighting men were away in Matabeleland; the terror and courage of the isolated groups of settlers; all this gives a quality of true excitement and even grandeur to the many reminiscences which survive.

We may perhaps appropriately see the outbreak of the rising through the eyes of Native Commissioner 'Wiri' Edwards, whom we have met several times before in this book—as the young adventurer illicitly buying cattle in the Matabeland of 1894; as 'Nyandoro's white man' with his store in chief Kunzwi's district; as the rough and ready administrator of the Mrewa area under Brabant's regime—and whose account sets it in a wider perspective than most.

At the beginning of 1896 things were going on in the Mrewa district much the same as they had done since Edwards took over as Native Commissioner there. Perhaps there were a few more skirmishes with headmen and chiefs refusing tax or resenting the operations of 'justice', but Edwards wrote them off as 'old die-hards who objected to interference with some of their time-honoured practices'. He did not believe that the young men or the mass of the people were hostile; 'on the whole', he found, 'the Mashona natives gave very little cause for worry in the work of the district'. Yet, as it transpired later, it was in this very period of apparent calm that preparations for revolt were being made, especially by the young men, with paramount chief Mangwende's son, Mchemwa, at their head. Looking back ruefully Edwards admitted that he had understood very little about his Shona charges—their history, their language, their attachment to their religious authorities. 'We had under-rated the Mashona native', he wrote, 'They were certainly not a warrior race like the Zulu but they were steeped in superstition, and were cunning and clever, far more so than their late over-lords, the Matabele. . . . We were sitting on a smouldering fire and didn't know it.'

At the time, however, Edward's confidence was universally shared. Soon after the outbreak of the rising in Matabeleland Rhodes came through from the coast and stopped at Marendellas for a talk with Edwards; the two men sat on the wall outside the Marendellas hotel 'and discussed the natives'. Rhodes 'was very worried about the position in Matabeleland, but like many more of us he did not suspect that the Mashona would follow the lead given by the Matabele'. Even when in early June Edwards heard that his fellow Native Commissioner, Ruping, was having serious difficulty with the Budja people of Mtoko, to the extreme north-east of Native Department territory, he did not attribute any general significance to it. 'I hadn't the faintest idea that within a week the country would be in a blaze of rebellion.'

There were, he realized later, some signs of strangeness in the last days before the rising. 'Warnings we did get but we did not understand them. There was talk amongst the people in my camp about a little bird from Mwari arriving. They themselves did not know what this meant; it was just talk from the kraals. On Monday morning, the 15th, a pair of native sandals were found at my door but who put them there no one knew. Some well-wisher, but we did not read the meaning they were intended to convey.'

Then on June 17th Edwards received a letter from the Chief Native Commissioner, Taberer. Paramount chief Makoni of Maungwe to the south-east of Mrewa was playing up and the Chief Native Commissioner proposed to visit him to nip any trouble in the bud; he wanted Edwards and four or five of his men as reinforcements. This meant that both to the north-east and the south-east of Edwards' area there was discontent, but when he left Marendellas for Headlands, where Taberer was based, everything was quiet. At Headlands on June 19th, however, the two men received appalling news over the wire: a rising had broken out in the Hartley area and was rapidly spreading through Western Mashonaland. The trouble in Mtoko and Makoni's recalcitrance at once began to fall into a more sinister perspective. That same night, back in Marendellas, Edwards' men in camp saw 'fires on the tops of mountains in different parts of the district'. Mchemwa and the other rebel leaders were calling out their men.

On June 20th the rebels of paramount chief Mangwende's people, under Mchemwa's leadership, attacked Edwards' camp near Marendellas, looted it, and surrounded the store where most of the local whites had taken refuge. Edwards, meanwhile, knowing nothing of this, had volunteered to ride back along the road from Headlands in order to secure the ammunition stores in Marendellas. As he rode towards the besieged store so he saw the signal fires moving towards him, springing up on the hilltops to the north and south of the road; 'they were the sign that had been arranged for the killing of the whites'. Within days of the rising in Western Mashonaland the whole of Central Mashonaland was also coming out in arms.

Edwards managed to join the rest of the whites in the store by crawling through the bush at the back of it. 'We were surrounded by a horde of savages out for our blood. They kept shouting out what they would do with us when daylight came. It was the first time I heard the rebellion war-cry "Murenga We".' Next day they saw that the road to Salisbury was completely blocked by the rebels; they managed, however, to make a break in their wagons in the other direction and to reach Taberer's group at Headlands. That night Headlands was attacked also, by a combined force of Mangwende and Makoni rebels. On June 22nd the Headlands post was also abandoned and the whites set out for Umtali. They reached there just as the false news of the shooting of the Mlimo was being broadcast; the rest of the news did little to cheer them. The whole vital stretch of the road between Salisbury and Umtali, upon which Salisbury had been dependent for supplies since the outbreak of the rebellion in Matabeleland, was now in rebel hands; so also was the greater part of the Mashonaland stretch of the road between Salisbury and Bulawayo. The far north was not in revolt; nor the south and south-east; otherwise virtually the whole of Mashonaland was up. Once again outlying settlers had suffered frightful casualties; an administration had collapsed; native commissioners and other officials had been killed.[1]

To Grey in Bulawayo the Shona rising came as a shattering blow. On June 15th he had been writing cheerfully to his son,

[1] Reminiscences of 'Wiri' Edwards, ED 6/1/1.

describing the last Umgusa fight and the patrols that were now
being sent out in all directions; 'until we catch them and thoroughly convince them that this country is to be the country of
the white, and not the black, man we must go on hammering and
hunting them'. On July 3rd he wrote despondently: 'We were just
getting abreast of our Matabeleland troubles when this buffet
came from Mashonaland. It is most provoking; it throws everything back and will cost the Company more money than it is
pleasant to spend not to speak of the many poor fellows that have
been killed.' 'It was as you can imagine a profound disappoint-
ment', he wrote to his wife, 'this Mashonaland rising. We were
nearing the end here and I was looking forward so much to meeting you . . . at Salisbury. No one who knew the Mashonas ever
expected them to rise and even if they did they thought that
50 men would be able to march through the country and put
things down.' Yet here were the Shona fighting, so the white
patrols reported, as fiercely as the Ndebele themselves, and
Salisbury cut off from the sea until an Imperial column could be
landed at Beira to clear the road.[1]

The outbreak of the Shona rising was, indeed, one of the great
dramas of black Rhodesian history as well as of white. White
astonishment at it was not unreasonable; its achievement was
only possible through a successful solution being found to the
problem of Shona disunity, and such a solution appeared very
improbable. Yet such a solution had been found. It is a story
which has not been fully told; there is no literature of reminis-
cence from the African side as there is from the white. It seems
worth-while, therefore, to devote the rest of this chapter to examining how the Shona rising was organized in much the same way as
we examined the organization of the rising in Matabeleland.

The chief white explanation, once the shock had worn off a
little was that the Shona had been intimidated into rising by the
desperate Ndebele. As we have seen, whites believed that neither
the secular nor religious authorities of the Shona commanded
any significant power, and though the Native Commissioner who
had expressed the view that the Hartley chiefs were completely
powerless now lay dead near paramount chief Mashiangombi's
kraal there was a considerable reluctance initially to abandon these

[1] Grey to Charles Grey, 15 June and 3 July, to Lady Grey, 3 July 1896,
GR 1/1/1.

beliefs. 'This Mashonaland rising is rather the devil,' wrote the irrepressible Jarvis from Bulawayo on June 27th. 'Of course it is nothing to be compared to this job, for the Mashonas are a *wretched* lot, but still there it is and has got to be smashed and of course *will* be smashed. They have murdered a lot of good fellows there and I am quite sure that the Matabele have instigated the whole thing. In fact I think a great deal of it is caused by the Matabele being defeated here and bolting off to Mashonaland to have a "cut in" there, thinking we have left that country defenceless.'[1]

To begin with Judge Vintcent, the Acting Administrator in Salisbury, held the same view. There had been reports for some time—most of them discounted—of Ndebele overtures to the Shona. As early as March 27th, for instance, a Salisbury resident had warned the administration that Shona kraals near the town 'have lately been visited by Matabili who promised to give the country to them (the Mashonas) if they would help them against the Englishmen. These boys say that the Matabili know there are only a few men here and no guns (maxims) . . . also that the Matabili have been waiting for an opportunity to pounce down on Salisbury and Bulawayo for months. These boys say further that there are immense numbers of Matabili ready to come down on the towns at once. These boys are absolutely reliable.' Chief Native Commissioner Taberer 'after the most careful inquiry' failed to find substantiation for this report in March, but the possibility of some such bargain between Ndebele and Shona remained in the minds of the administration.[2]

Then, after the Shona rising had broken out, there were many reports, some true and some false, of Ndebele participation and leadership in the initial outbreaks all over Mashonaland. There were undeniably Ndebele warriors in Western Mashonaland, where an *impi* later based itself on Mashiangombi's kraal; and it was reported also that white settlers and patrols in the Salisbury area had identified Ndebele among their attackers. 'During the evening', ran one such report to Vintcent, 'some of the Mashonas were very much disheartened and wanted to go home. We could hear the Matabele leaders haranguing them and scolding them for not fighting better. Also we could distinguish the voices of

[1] Jarvis to his mother, 27 June 1896, JA 4/1/1.
[2] Leon. H. Gabriel to 'my dear Sir Thomas', 27 Mar. 1896, A 1/12/27.

Cape boys in the debate. I with others had no fear previously of a rising amongst the Mashona and was much surprised thereat and still more surprised at the amount of courage and diplomacy displayed by them.'[1]

These Mazoe Ndebeles were almost certainly imaginary, though the courage and diplomacy of the Shona in that area were not. Gradually it became clear that there had been little direct Ndebele influence in the greater part of Mashonaland. Marshall Hole, summing up the information available in October 1896, confessed that the Shona 'have shown themselves capable of concerted action' and admitted that this was certainly not the work of the Ndebele. 'The rebellion here is of a very different nature to that in Matabeleland', he wrote. 'Here we have a race who have never been conquered, never even been warred against: the Matabeles were a fighting nation by descent and had already measured weapons with us. That the outbreak of the latter gave the opportunity to the former no one can doubt, but the causes of the rebellion in the two parts of the country are widely different.'[2]

How, then, did the rising come about? We have already demonstrated how false many white beliefs about the Shona were; have shown how long Shona history had been and how keen a sense they preserved of it; have shown how resilient their way of life had proved over centuries of white pressure and how determined they were to defend it. For these reasons, and because of the specific grievances of white administration, it can be little surprise to us that the Shona rose in arms in 1896. But the problem still remains; in 1896 they showed 'themselves capable of concerted action'.

Contemporary white observers felt that two aspects of this concerted action required explanation. In the first place action *within* the Shona paramountcy units was much more coherent than had been expected; in the second place cooperation *between* the Shona paramountcies was much more effective.

A great deal of the white criticism of the weaknesses of the Shona chiefly system proved justified during the rebellion. The customary rotation of the chieftainship among a number of chiefly lines sometimes meant that a rebel paramount would find himself opposed by a rival claimant to the chiefly title leading a 'loyalist' faction. This happened, for instance, in the case of

---

[1] J. Folliott Darling to Vintcent, 26 June 1896, A 1/12/25.
[2] Marshall Hole's report, 29 Oct. 1896, A 1/12/26.

paramount chief Makoni of Maungwe, where the rebel paramount was opposed by a 'loyalist' faction under the command of Ndapfunya, son of a former chief and claimant of the paramountcy. The past history of Shona paramountcies, as well as supplying plenty of material for this sort of family feud, also often produced situations in which influential sub-chiefs or headmen could remember a time of political independence and resented their relatively recent subordination to the paramount. This was the case once again in Maungwe, where sub-chief Chipunza attempted to take advantage of Makoni's commitment to the rebellion to gain his independence. Moreover, in some cases the old rivalries between paramounts meant that one paramount would stay out of the rising because another had entered it. Once again this was the case with the rising in Maungwe; because Makoni was leading the men of his paramountcy into rebellion his old enemy, Mutassa of Manyika, remained 'loyal', lent support to Ndapfunya, and sent men to assist the white attack on Makoni's kraal at Gwindingwi kraal. Finally, the Shona paramounts were usually middle-aged and sometimes old men; even where they committed themselves to the rising they often found others more radically committed than themselves—young men who had not yet had a chance to prove themselves in war, often their own sons. Potential challenges to the leadership of the paramount thus existed in Nohwe, where paramount Mangwede's son, Mchemwa, emerged from the beginning as the more radical leader, in Maungwe, where Makoni's son, Miripiri, played much the same role, and even in Manyika, where Mutassa's decision to stay out of the rising was opposed by his eldest son.

None of these weaknesses, however, prevented the Shona paramountcies from demonstrating formidable capacities for leadership in 1896 and 1897. All rebel paramounts were supported by substantial majorities of their people and the whites often found that the extent to which 'loyal' dissident sections could be effectively employed against them was greatly limited by the respect in which the paramount was held—none of Ndapfunya's men, for example, were prepared to lay hands on the Makoni. Mutassa's decision to stay out of the rising because of old rivalries was not followed by the majority of the central Shona paramounts who showed a surprising capacity to sink their old differences. And however much friction might arise between a paramount and his militant sons there was no case in which a son carried the people of a paramountcy into rebellion—or out of it—against the will of the paramount himself. Makoni, despite all the weaknesses recorded above, was rightly regarded by the administration as 'one of the most powerful chiefs in Mashonaland' who 'had his people under control'.[1]

We may illustrate the way in which the administration came to realize the real authority of the paramounts by looking for a moment at one area—the Salisbury Native Commissioner's district, under Native Commissioner Campbell. Before the rising Campbell had been as convinced of the paramounts' weakness as anyone. He was lucky, indeed, not to share the fate of his colleague in Hartley. On June 20th he visited paramount Mashanganyika's kraal, where his main camp was situated and where his brother, George Campbell, operated as a trader. He talked to Mashanganyika about the rebellion 'and what he meant to do. He said: "The white men are my fathers, I will stand by them".' Almost immediately after the Native Commissioner had ridden on, however, an *impi* led by paramount chief Chiquaqua and his head fighting man, Zhanta, approached Mashanganyika's kraal. As George Campbell stood watching its approach he was killed by Mashanganyika's men; when Chiquaqua entered the kraal Mashanganyika shouted to his fellow paramount, 'We have killed George but there is the policeman. Kill him.' 'Chiquaqua shouted, "How many have you killed?"; Mashanganyika replied, "Only one". Then I heard Chikwakwa say', so testified a witness later, 'let us make a ring around George's brother and kill him too.' And, indeed, when the unsuspecting Native Commissioner returned to Mashanganyika's kraal and his own camp he was fired on by a force of some 500 Africans and managed only narrowly to escape. The two paramounts then sent out their men to bring in and to kill the whites of the neighbourhood. 'I was told by the old man—by Mashanganyika—to go out and bring in prisoners,' testified one warrior later. 'As I came back I was told . . . all white men were to be killed.' 'Mashanganyika did not join the *impi*,' testified another. 'He sent us to Chiquaqua who took command and told us to kill the white men.'[2]

---

[1] Vintcent to Carrington, 23 Oct. 1896, BA 2/3/1.
[2] Regina versus Zhanta; Regina versus Rusere and Wampi and Chiquaqua; Regina versus Mashanganyika, Gonto and others; HC/M, Nos. 213, 255, 300.

It was small wonder that after these experiences Native Commissioner Campbell reported that the chief instigators of the rising in his district had been the paramounts. And as the rising continued he became increasingly impressed with the evidence of their power. In May 1897 he gave eloquent evidence of this. 'The people south of the Ufumasi river in my district would willingly give in if the example were set them by Kunswi and Mashanganyika. The power that this latter chief has acquired since the beginning of the rebellion is enormous. . . . It is absolutely useless to expect the smaller chiefs to give in before the paramounts no matter how anxious they may be for peace; if the paramounts held no power before the rebellion they certainly have a great influence now.'[1]

At the level of the paramountcy, then, co-ordination was achieved through the paramount himself or his family. We have seen that in the Ndebele rising the military strength of the rebels depended upon the surviving institutions of the Ndebele military system, even if Mwari officers appear to have exercised a remarkable influence over the regiments. In the same way the military strength of the Shona rising—which was very different in nature from that of the rebel Ndebele—depended upon the mobilization of the fighting men of the tribes by the paramounts and their sons. In neither case was there an attempt to create a new military system, even if in both cases the emergency conditions gave scope for the emergence as war leaders of 'new men', not of traditionally leading families, whose abilities to handle modern weapons brought them to the fore. Thus the rebellion in each province could not rise above the limitations of the old military system and in Mashonaland this meant that it was not possible to put effective armies into the field, even when co-operation between various paramounts was achieved. The sort of discipline and regimental tradition which enabled the raising of the Umgusa force and the laying siege to Bulawayo could not be called upon in Mashonaland; Salisbury was not besieged in the same way, nor were there a series of pitched stand-up fights on the banks of any Shona river. The most that could be achieved was an exchange of intelligence; the offering of refuge by one paramount to another forced to flee from his home area; combined raids or ambushes by the forces of two or more paramounts, and so on. The epic fights of the Shona

[1] N.C. Campbell to C.N.C., 15 May 1897, N 1/1/9 and LO 5/4/3.

rebellion were all essentially defensive ones, fights to defend the kraal of the paramount. The equivalent to the five battles on the Umgusa as far as the Shona rising was concerned was the series of white assaults on Mashiangombi's kraal.

But if dependence upon the military resources of the paramountcies involved these limitations, nevertheless observers were astonished by the degree of coordination that was achieved between the paramountcy units. There was, of course, the coordination which lay behind the almost simultaneous outbreak of the rising itself; later there was certainly coordination of the response made to white peace overtures; and there was constant coordination of military matters in the limited senses described above. This supra-paramountcy coordination was not achieved through the paramounts alone, however willing they might show themselves to cooperate. There was no machinery for a central council of paramounts or anything like it. We have to look once again to the traditional religious authorities of the Shona to understand the coordination of the rising above the paramountcy level—and also to understand the commitment of people to the rising at the paramountcy level, a commitment so complete and even fanatical that it cannot be explained simply in terms of loyalty to the paramount chief.

We have already seen how two distinct but inter-related systems of approach to the divine evolved among the Shona peoples— the Mwari cult, of which we have already said so much, and the hierarchy of the spirit mediums. Both systems were deeply involved in the Shona rising.

We may begin with the role of the Mwari cult. During the discussion of the organization of the rising in Matabeleland the point was made that the influence of the Mwari cult centres stretched outside that province. Evidence was cited to show that the influence of Njelele, at any rate at certain periods, was felt even in Portuguese East Africa; that the Matonjeni cult centre was especially influential in the Shona areas of Belingwe, Chibi, Gutu and Ndanga; and that Mkwati, with his base at the old Rozwi centre of Taba Zi Ka Mambo, was able to appeal to memories of the Shona past not only in north eastern Matabeleland but also in the western districts of Mashonaland. It is important to make a distinction at this stage between areas in which the prestige of the Mwari cult was high but in which the formal organization of recognized *Wosana* or *Manyusa* and local oracular caves did not exist, and areas where the full system was established. In the latter category fell large parts of Western Mashonaland. There is no doubt from evidence compiled in the years after the risings that there were Mwari messengers, a regular system of gifts to the main shrines, local caves, etc., in the Charter, Chibi, Gutu, Hartley, Ndanga and Victoria districts of Mashonaland; a great crescent lying immediately to the east of the Matabeleland border in which in 1896 the Mwari cult was in full operation and in constant contact with its Matabeleland centres.[1]

Outside this area I have come across no references to organized cult activity in Mashonaland. But the prestige of the cult, inextricably bound up with the surviving prestige of the Rozwi, extended much further afield. Thus the Native Commissioner, Salisbury, reported in January 1896 that the Shona peoples of his area believed that 'every MaRaswi is supposed to have a familiar spirit' which 'answers all questions asked of by its owner ... from the sky, the tops of trees or out in the veld'. Thus the Native Commissioner, Makoni, reported in December 1894 that in Maungwe they spoke 'of the WaRosi ... as God's chosen people and have great respect for them, the VaRosi being looked upon as priests'. Even in Umtali, on the eastern border of Mashonaland, a reasonably full account of the Mwari cult was collected by the Native Commissioner in 1896. 'The natives of Manicaland', he reported, 'worship a supreme being known as Morimo, Mali or Murunga. They believe he is omni-present but that he speaks to them only from one place, viz. Matjamahopli near Bulawayo, and then he will speak only to a chosen few. . . . The generality of the people don't presume to pray to the Morimo personally but address Muzimo, the spirits of their ancestors and ask them to intercede for them. . . . Before the Matabele came the whole of the country was tributary to the BaRozi. Then they used to build huts in which to pray to the spirits, but this is seldom done now. They say the BaRozi are more holy than they and Morimo always listens to them.' If the existence of the cult in fully organized form in western Mashonaland gave Mkwati an opportunity to link up discontent there with the rising in Matabeleland, the continuing

[1] Evidence relating to the Mwari cult in Western Mashonaland after the rebellion may be found in the following files: A 3/18/2; A 11/2/12/11; N 3/14/5; N 3/31/3; N 3/33/12; N 3/32/1; LO 5/7/1 to 5; LO 5/5/5 to 33.

prestige of the Mwari cult and of the Rozwi over this much wider
area was also a factor of some importance in coordinating the
rebellion in Mashonaland as a whole.[1]

Let us look first at the activities of the Mwari representatives in
western Mashonaland. The existence of a fully operative Mwari
system in an area did not automatically mean that it came out in
rebellion. The Kalanga of south western Matabeleland did not
rise and the districts of Ndanga and Chibi also resisted the influence of Mwabani of Matonjeni and stayed out of the rising.
But there is no doubt of the significance of Mkwati's influence in
the other districts of western Mashonaland.

His key ally in those districts was a Mwari representative named
Bonda, who worked so closely with him that Marshall Hole was
later convinced that they were one and the same man! Bonda was
a Rozwi headman, living under chief Musarurwa in the Range-
Charter district, 'the nursery of the Mashona rebellion', as the
official report on the disturbances later described it. Some time in
April 1896 Mkwati sent a Rozwi Child of Mwari, Tshiwa, to
summon Bonda and other representatives from the western
Mashonaland area to his head-quarters at Taba Zi Ka Mambo.
Bonda went there in May and with him went representatives of
paramount chief Mashiangombi of the Hartley district. 'I hear
from one of my spies', wrote the Native Commissioner, Hartley, on
May 24th, 'that Mashayingombi himself is in communication with
some-one in Matabeleland and has lately sent some young men
down. I taxed Mashayingombi with this but he informed me that
he had only sent to the Matabele Umlimo for some medicines to
prevent the locusts from eating his crops next year. This spy also
told me that it had been proposed by the Matabele and Maholi
inhabitants to rise and first kill all my police . . . and then try
Hartley. . . . I attach no importance whatsoever to the above,'
concluded this tragically complacent officer. 'I find the natives
very quiet and civil when I go to their kraals to collect tax.
But I am just complying with your instructions to report all I
hear.'[2]

Within two weeks the Native Commissioner was dead, killed
near Mashiangombi's kraal in the first outbreak of rebellion in

[1] N.C. Campbell's report, Jan. 1896, N 1/1/9; N.C. Meredith's report, Dec.
1894, A 15/1/1; Native Commissioner Nesbitt's report, 1896, N 1/1/11.
[2] N.C. Hartley, to C.N.C., 24 May 1896, N 1/1/3.

Mashonaland. This outbreak was stimulated by the return from Taba Zi Ka Mambo early in June of Tshiwa, Bonda and Mashiangombi's emissaries, bringing with them 'the Mangoba regiment ... to incite the Mashonas into rebellion'. Most of the Ndebele *impi* remained at Mashiangombi's kraal, which became the centre of the rebellion in western Mashonaland. Tshiwa and Bonda went on to carry the rising further afield. We get a glimpse of Tshiwa at work in the vivid reminiscences of Native Commissioner Weale. 'I sent messengers out into Ndema's country to spy out the land,' he tells us of the period just after the outbreak of the rising, 'and the police boys brought back word to say that the whole of the country ahead was disaffected and that a Mondoro of the Mlimo, a MaRozwi named "Tshiwa" was doctoring the rivers so that the whiteman and his horse's feet would burn up when they stepped into the water, and stated that he had arranged it that our bullets would be as harmless as water, but what was more to the point was that they had distributed among them some Matabele braves to help and urge them on to fight. There does not seem to be the slightest doubt but that the Mashona rebels did believe that "Tshiwa" could perform miracles. Even some of Chilimanzi's people did and to show that he had more faith in the white man than in these rumours he went with a party of white men and police boys, taking his own men too, and stepped into the river dividing Banga's country from his own, and no doubt he felt very relieved to find his feet still normal after he had crossed. He then told his son to trust the whites as he had done and to follow them while he returned to his kraal to brag to his wives and to tell them what a brave man he was in spite of his old age.' But Chilimanzi was very much the exception; his rival Banga and many other chiefs answered Tshiwa's call and joined the rebellion.[1]

Bonda had equal success in his home area. 'Mkwati ... the high priest of the Mlimo had ... despatched agents to Mashonaland', the Company Report of 1898 tells us, 'to work up a rebellion there, by playing on the credulity of the people and leaguing themselves to the local witch-doctors. These emissaries spread false reports of the annihilation of the white impis in Matabeleland and the fall of Bulawayo, and had little difficulty in urging

[1] Tshiwa's statement, 10 Jan. 1897, LO 5/4/1; Weale's reminiscences, WE 3/2/6.

Maromo, Umtigeza and other chiefs in the Charter district to fall in with their suggestions.' In July 1896 Colonel Beal collected evidence in the Charter district which showed what happened in some detail. According to his informants, Bonda had returned to his own kraal, accompanied by six Ndebele. He had then sent out the men of his kraal, as messengers of Mwari, to carry instructions to the smaller kraals in the neighbourhood, while he himself went to the kraals of chiefs Umtigesa, Meromo and Msango. 'From there they went to Meromo's,' deposed one witness; 'when they came there they said they were sent by Umlimo and they were the Umlimo's people. Meromo said he also was one of Umlimo's people; he joined hands with them.' The other chiefs in the district reacted in the same way and soon the local whites were being attacked and killed.[1]

We may legitimately draw on some later evidence to demonstrate the sort of prestige that men like Tshiwa and Bonda enjoyed in western Mashonaland and the way in which the cult could be used for the transmission of messages. In 1904 one Manyanga, a representative of the south-western Mwari shrine, travelled through Chilimanzi, Gutu and Ndema and eventually came to the kraal of the Njanja paramount, Gambiza, in the Hartley district. He 'told Gambiza to give him meat and shelter . . . then told Gambiza to send for all his people. Gambiza did so and on their assembling told them that the prisoner had come from GwaMari, i.e. the Gods.' Gambiza, though paramount, gave up his own hut to the messenger of Mwari; he and his headmen squatted on the floor in an adjacent hut, speaking with Manyanga through an intermediary because he 'represented himself to be a big man and would not speak directly to us'. Manyanga was then escorted about the surrounding kraals by the paramount's messenger, announcing that he 'lived on beer, milk and meat and not on the ordinary food of natives and that if he got plenty of the former he would drive the white man from the land'. The only chief who refused to receive him was the cautious Gwenda, who testified significantly that Manyanga appeared to be 'a big man . . . and was going about all the land. I concluded that this was a similar affair to that which happened before the last rebellion and would have nothing to do with it. What alarmed me about the accused coming to the kraal in the manner he did

[1] Evidence taken by Colonel Beal, July 1896, A 1/12/11.

was that a man came in a similar manner just before the last rebellion and I compared him with that man.' [1]

Considerably later, in 1915, Mwari messages were being passed from kraal to kraal in Gutu, Selukwe, Chilimanzi, Charter, Victoria and Ndanga. In Charter, for instance, 'six young men and five young women wearing fantastic head-dresses made of limbo and drawing people around them by their talk, singing and tom-tom playing . . . were telling the people that they were sent by Mwari to convey his tidings to the people and to sing and play to them.' In the Gutu area the messages were being passed on from village to village, chain-letter fashion. 'They all say they got the message from adjoining kraals; people came singing and dancing and saying that they had received a message from Mwari that they were to visit six kraals, dance and sing and demand a fowl', and to tell the people of those six kraals to do the same. The Native Police in Charter thought 'that the movement is a mischievous one and similar to that which took place prior to the rebellion of 1896'. [2]

In this sort of way we may imagine the message of rebellion being sent out in western Mashonaland in 1896. In some places Tshiwa or Bonda or some other important Child of Mwari carrying the message himself and being greeted with instant respect; elsewhere the message being passed on from kraal to kraal until it had spread through the whole area. Nor did the importance of men like Bonda end when the rising had begun. We catch constant glimpses of him in the next few months, carrying messages from Mashiangombi's kraal to the south and east, leading *impis* on raids on loyalists, and generally playing a most significant role in keeping western Mashonaland mobilized behind the rising. [3]

This then was the role of the Mwari cult in western Mashonaland; to help to link the rising there to the Ndebele rising, to help coordinate the rising within the area itself, and to maintain morale once the rising had begun. The links established between the western Mashonaland rising and Matabeleland were very much with Mkwati's north-eastern faction. The Ndebele warriors who were sent to assist Mashiangombi and the other chiefs were members of the young man's group which supported Mpotshwana

[1] Preliminary examination on Manyanga, A 11/2/12/11.
[2] Reports on Mwari messages, 1915, N 3/14/5.   [3] See especially N 1/1/3.

and Nyamanda; reports of events in western Mashonaland flowed back as regularly to Taba Zi Ka Mambo as they had done from the banks of the Umgusa; and as we shall see when Mkwati was forced to flee from Matabeleland it was to Mashiangombi's kraal that he chose to go. And if the western Shona were brought into the rising by Mkwati it was certainly not in the narrow interests of any Ndebele faction. The outbreak in Mashonaland indeed, made Mkwati's 'connection' at least as much a Shona as an Ndebele one; and recalcitrant Ndebele received short shrift at the hands of the western Mashonaland cult officers. In May 1897, for instance, Bonda was sent from Mashiangombi's to bring into the rising an Ndebele *induna* named Simbobora, who had taken refuge in the Hartley district after the 1893 war. By that time the rising in Matabeleland was over and the main body of the Ndebele aristocracy had made their peace. Simbobora refused to rise and instead handed Bonda over to the police. The latter escaped during the night and returned with a punitive *impi*, killing many of the Ndebele and capturing more. Ironically, when Mashiangombi's stronghold was finally stormed the besiegers saw a number of Ndebele escaping from it and shot them on the spot, supposing that they were punishing the men who had incited the Shona to rebel. They turned out to have been some of the unfortunate 'loyalist' Ndebele taken prisoner in Bonda's raid. The incident was a nice commentary on the supposed and the real organization of the western Mashonaland rebellion.[1]

But what of the rebellion in central Mashonaland, in areas where the Mwari cult only enjoyed a generalized prestige? There is evidence that Bonda was sent on missions in central Mashonaland also, but this was long after the outbreak of the rising and those missions were directed to scattered Rozwi groups who might be expected to be especially receptive to a summons to action from the Mwari priesthood. To understand the coordination of the central Shona rising and to complete our understanding of the western Shona rising we need to turn to look at the hierarchy of the spirit mediums.

Here we must at once make one important point. When the leading student of the ritual and structure of the spirit medium system, Professor Gelfand, first set down his conclusions about it he postulated a clear spirit hierarchy operative all over Mashona-

---

[1] N.C. Hartley, to C.N.C., 12 Sept. 1897, N 1/1/3.

land, in which the mediums of the less important ancestor figures were junior to those of the more important, and these junior to the spirits of dead kings, and all subordinate to the spirit of Chaminuka, so that the recognized Chaminuka medium at any one time would be at the apex of the whole system. When he came to study the system as it operated in north eastern Mashonaland, however, he became convinced that this picture would not do; one had to postulate at least two distinct hierarchies, if not more—the Chaminuka-Nehanda hierarchy of central and western Mashonaland, and the Mutota-Dzivaguru hierarchy of the north-east and east. As we shall see this picture in itself is probably an over-simplification but we must note here that whatever other modifications have to be made the division between these two areas, between the Chaminuka-Nehanda hierarchy and the Mutota-Dzivaguru hierarchy, does seem to be of particular significance. It derives, no doubt, from the past history of Mashonaland and in particular from the fact that the north-east and east was the nuclear area of the Mwene Mutapa confederacy. In 1896 the western and central areas of Mashonaland were generally involved in the rebellion and the Korekore and Tavara of the north-east were not. This can be explained partly in terms of the much lighter impact of Company administration in the Kore-Kore and Tavara areas, to which Native Department control and tax collection had hardly been extended by 1896, partly in terms of the resentment of the Korekore and Tavara at the raids into their areas which were a substitute for routine administration and which appeared to them rather as Zezuru invasions than anything else. It has also been explained by Father Devlin in terms of the religious division. However this may be, it is true that in our account of the 1896–7 rising we have to deal with the Mwari cult and with the mediums of the Chaminuka-Nehanda hierarchy but not with the mediums of the Mutota-Dzivaguru network. The mediums of this network were also capable of inspiring resistance and coordinating rebellion and they did so in the so-called Mapondera rebellion of 1900. But they did not use their influence in favour of rebellion in 1896.[1]

We must next turn to examine the idea of a Chaminuka-Nehanda hierarchy in more detail. How far did the mediums of

[1] M. Gelfand, *Shona Ritual*, 1959; *Shona Religion*, 1962; Devlin, 'The Mashona and the Portuguese', *The Shield*, May 1961.

central and western Mashonaland form a regular and effective hierarchy, in constant communication with each other? How far could they provide an effective principle of centralization? The answer is that the system of the spirit mediums was even more complex than that of the Mwari cult and the relations of the mediums to each other even less susceptible of definition. No one senior medium enjoyed a determining influence over the whole area of the Shona rising nor did the mediums as a whole unanimously agree to support it. (Thus Mr Abraham's distinction between the mediums operative at the tribal and those at the supra-tribal level can be seen at work in the case of paramount Kunzwi-Nyandoro, whose tribal medium, Ganyere, advised against the rising, but who chose rather to follow the advice of the Nehanda medium.) Nevertheless, when these qualifications are made it remains true that the influence of the senior mediums was even in normal times more extensive than that of any secular authority and could bring together for ritual purposes rival, and even warring, paramounts. Once again we have later evidence which we can use to demonstrate the range of influence of an accepted Chaminuka or Nehanda medium. In 1903 a new Chaminuka medium emerged in the Hartley area and the following chiefs either sent gifts or went in person to pay their respects, despite the dangers of administration suspicion and despite the fact that paramounts in office after the rebellion were mostly new appointments made on grounds of 'loyalty'—paramounts Mashiangombi, Mashaba, and Tumbare of Hartley district; paramounts Mashanganyika, Chinamora, Kunzwi-Nyandoro, Seki, Makumbi, Chiota, Mangwende and Zwimba of central Mashonaland. It was the combination that made the rebellion in miniature. They heard the medium pronounce—or so it was alleged; 'I am Chamenuka. I know everything. I am all powerful. I caused the downfall of the Ba-Rozwi and the Matabele and I will cause the white man to leave the country.' In 1906 a Nehanda medium arose, the first since the execution of the rebel Nehanda medium in 1898. Claiming to have come 'to take care of all the Mashonas again', she was visited by paramounts Wata, Chiweshe, Chinamora, Seki, Chikwakwa, Masembura and Gutu.[1]

The chiefs shown in these lists as acknowledging the influence

[1] Correspondence on the Chaminuka medium, 1903, A 11/2/12/11; correspondence on the Nehanda medium, 1906, 1915, N 3/31/4 and N 3/14/5.

of the mediums of Chaminuka and Nehanda were the successors of men who had been locked in bitter rivalries in the early 1890s but who had come together in the rising of 1896. That they were able to come together then was partly due to the principle of unity embodied in the senior mediums and in them alone.

Let us look at the part played by one of these senior mediums— the medium of Nehanda. Before the rising it was believed in official circles that her influence was no longer significant. 'Great belief was also formerly placed in the Mandoras or Lion Gods, and especially in one called Nianda,' wrote the Native Commissioner, Salisbury, in June 1896, 'but as Mr Selous puts it "since the arrival of the white man the Mashonas have lost belief in their Mandoras and the Mandoras have lost belief in themselves".' Two years later the same official was writing in very different vein. 'Nianda has been constantly spoken of in my hearing ever since I came to Mashonaland in 1890 by the Mashonas. At the present moment Nianda is the most powerful wizard in Mashonaland and has the power of ordering all the people who rose lately and her orders would in every case be obeyed.' Behind this change of opinion lay two years of activity on the part of the Nehanda medium in mobilizing and sustaining the rising in central Mashonaland.[1]

She was directly responsible for the death of Pollard, the Native Commissioner of the Mazoe area, at the outbreak of the rising. 'I was a native messenger,' testified one Gutsa in January 1898. 'I went with Pollard to the M'Kori Kori. While there we heard of the God. Then we went to Chipadza'; there they fired at us. We then went to Jeta and there they fired at us. Pollard gave us money to buy sweet potatoes and as we returned a lot of boys came with us. Gwazi was told to catch hold of Pollard. I was told to hold his hands so that he should not hurt us with his gun. So they took him to Nianda . . . She said, "Bring him here." Then she came and knelt down and spoke with Pollard, but we constables were surrounded in the middle. I heard Nianda say to Wata, "Kill Pollard but take him some way off to the river or he will stink", so they took him off. We were there still surrounded close to him. Wata said, "Nianda sent me." Then he took his axe and chopped him behind the head.'[2]

[1] N.C. Campbell's report, Jan. 1896, N 1/1/9; N.C. Salisbury, to C.N.C., 3 Mar. 1893, N 1/1/9.　　[2] Gutsa's evidence, 12 Jan. 1898, HC/M, No. 252.

Her influence was dominant on the rising in the Mazoe area generally. 'Nehanda is responsible for rain and sometimes fighting,' we are told by an old man living in the Chiweshe Reserve. 'She was behind the rebellion right from the start. Her great injunction was that the African people should touch nothing that belonged to the white man. The defeat of the Africans was the result of the violation of this great order. During the rebellion the power of the spirits rendered the white bullets useless and ineffective. Not many Africans were killed in the actual fighting.' Encouraged by such promises of immunity the people of Mazoe and Chiweshe rose against the whites, and obeying the orders of the medium they carried the goods captured to Nehanda's kraal, just as in Matabeleland such goods were carried to Mkwati's cave in Taba Zi Ka Mambo. 'She received a very large share of the loot obtained by the natives', reported the Chief Native Commissioner in March 1898. 'Among other things obtained from Nianda's kraal have been numerous rifles and over £140 in gold. I know that she still has concealed some £700, but because of the spirit she possesses the natives are afraid of giving any information thereon.'[1]

In this way the Nehanda medium and many others helped to bring central Mashonaland into the rising in June 1896, just at the moment that Bonda and Tshiwa and the rest were raising western Mashonaland. How was this coordination established? One answer to this is that the mediums of central Mashonaland were in touch with the mediums of the Hartley and Charter districts and that the latter were working in an area in which the Mwari cult also existed in an organized form. This overlapping of the two systems was one of the main reasons why the Hartley and Charter districts became the 'nursery' of the Shona rising. Thus we have seen how the Children of Mwari carried the message to the chiefs in those districts, how Mashiangombi was in touch with Mkwati and how his kraal later became the main Mwari centre in Mashonaland. But at the same time, and with no sense of incongruity, the chiefs consulted the spirit mediums of the area. Mashiangombi had his own tribal medium, his half-brother Dekwende, who appears in the sources as helping to raise the country in June 1896, and the other chiefs, or some of them, had similar mediums at the tribal level. But over and above this

[1] Interview between Mr S. Nengubo and Mr Bob Nyatsinga, Nyachuru, Howard, 20 Jan. 1893; C.N.C.'s report, 4 Mar. 1898, LO 5/4/8.

the Hartley area had been the home of the great mediums of Chaminuka, round whom the Shona had rallied in the nineteenth century when under heavy Ndebele pressure. The ruined kraal at Chitungwiza, destroyed by the Ndebele raiders instructed by Lobengula to break the power of the great mediums, remained one of the sacred places of Shona religious feeling. An active Chaminuka medium would, indeed, be the easiest way of accounting for the coordination of the Shona rising; we have already seen the scope of the influence of such a medium when one appeared in 1903; and the old links between the idea of Chaminuka and the Mwari cult were strong.

In fact it does not seem that a recognized Chaminuka medium was active in 1896. No reference is made to one in the written sources and oral information holds that 'there were several mediums here who claimed that at the time of the fighting they carried Chaminuka's spirit but they were lying'. Oral tradition now envisages the role of the great Chaminuka spirit in a more metaphysical and disembodied way: 'After his death he had no particular medium', says one informant, 'and was everywhere. The influence of Chaminuka was considerable during the rebellion and he would appear here and there. He was capable of inspiring masses of people and inciting them.'[1]

Other supra-tribal mediums of the Chaminuka hierarchy were, however, active in western Mashonaland in 1896. Two who emerge particularly clearly from the evidence as having been deeply involved in the rising are the medium of the Goronga spirit and the medium of the VaChikare spirit. The Goronga medium lived in the Lomagundi district, where his influence on the rising seems to have been decisive; the Vachikare medium lived in Hartley district, but fled in the later stages of the rising to join 'Goronga' in Lomagundi. According to Bullock, in his very interesting treatment of Shona religion, these two spirits were very closely connected with Chaminuka in western Shona theology and ritual. He tells us, for instance, that after the death of Bute, one of the famous nineteenth-century Chaminuka mediums, the new medium was sent by the representative of Vachikare to present himself to 'Goronga' in Lomagundi; and he tells us also that the medium of the Gwenzi ancestor spirit, who acts as tribal

[1] Interviews between Mr Solomon Nengubo and Mr Maponga and Mr Nyatsinga, 18 and 20 Jan. 1963.

medium for chief Chiveru of the Hartley area, recognizes his inferiority to the supra-tribal mediums of Chaminuka, VaChikare and Goronga; that he goes every year to commune with the Goronga spirit in Lomagundi, 'at whose home his coming is heralded by magic fire'. The involvement of the VaChikare and Goronga mediums in 1896–7, then, clearly implies the commitment of the Chaminuka hierarchy to the rising. It also indicates one way in which the western Shona were linked with the central Shona; Bullock tells us that the great spirits of Chaminuka, Vachikare, Goronga, Nehanda, and the rest were members of 'a spiritual brotherhood'; Gelfand tells us that one can discern a Chaminuka-Nehanda system; and we may very reasonably imagine that the Nehanda spirit, whose activities we have already seen, was in communication with her 'spritual brothers' in Hartley and Lomagundi. Moreover, these great mediums of the Chaminuka circle, so Bullock tells us, not only over-lapped with the Mwari cult territorially but were connected to it in a variety of ways; Bullock himself believes that the supra-tribal mediums were originally manifestations of the Mwari god-head who were then absorbed into the Shona system of ancestor spirits and mediumship. Thus we might reasonably account for the coordination between north-eastern Matabeleland, western Mashonaland and central Mashonaland in terms of a working alliance between the Mwari officers, the mediums of the Chaminuka circle and the mediums of the Nehanda circle. This, in fact, is precisely how it was explained by the man whom the authorities themselves came to regard as primarily responsible for the rising—Gumporeshumba, medium of the Kagubi spirit. Facing trial in 1897 for instigating the risings, Gumporeshumba exclaimed, 'I want Nehanda, Goronga and Wamponga brought in. They started the rebellion.'[1]

There was still more to the story than that, however, and the authorities were right to suppose that the Kagubi medium was of central importance. In the remarkable emergence and dominance of this man we reach the final part of our explanation.

Before describing his career we need to make the point that although the Mwari cult and the system of the spirit mediums

---

[1] Gumporeshumba's evidence, 29 Oct. 1897, HC/M, No. 253; C. Bullock, *The Mashona and the Matabele*, 1950, chap. XI; for VaChikare, see, *Rhodesia Herald*, 12 Jan. 1898; for Goronga, see, *Rhodesia Herald*, 2 Feb. 1898; quarterly report, Lomagundi, 4 Apr. 1898, LO 5/4/11.

Va   A Shona attack on the communications system; the Mail Coach
from Gwelo is ambushed by rebels on the Salisbury road, 1896.

Vb   An eye-witness impression of the Mangwe *indaba* of June 29th, 1896,
at which Native Commissioner Armstrong and Captain Van Rooyen
announced to the Kalanga that the 'Mlimo' was dead.

VI The storming of Mkwati's stronghold at Taba Zi Ka Mambo, 5th July, 1896. This contemporary drawing illustrates the important part played in this, as in other engagements, by African troops from the Cape, the so-called 'Cape Boys'.

were long established and associated with the great political systems of the past; although both were hierarchical to a greater or lesser extent; although the normal influence of both can be described as 'conservative' in the sense that they called people back to the norms of the past; both of them nevertheless gave plenty of scope for the emergence of figures with special supernatural gifts and with new injunctions and commands. We have so far written of the involvement of these systems as the involvement of 'traditional' religious officers and structures; an elaborate and aged machinery lying to hand which was made use of in the rebellion of 1896. Such a view has a certain truth but we should not forget two things. One is that the systems as they existed in 1896 were the products of countless changes, some of which have already been indicated; they were not static or fixed, nor were the relationships between the various priests and mediums. The other is that however much these systems were linked up with supra-tribal or tribal political systems—with the institutional 'establishments' of Shona history—they still retained their essential charismatic character. From out of the Mwari cult and from out of the hierarchies of the spirit mediums there could emerge—and no doubt there often had in the past emerged— charismatic prophet figures, whose spiritual power or power of personality was capable of throwing relationships within the cults into a new pattern, and who were able to break away from the established inter-relationship with political authority. One might speculate, indeed, that a constant theme of Shona political history has been the rise and fall of figures of this kind, sometimes offering a challenge to established political power, sometimes acting as a rallying point in a period of political breakdown, as the great Chaminuka mediums did in the middle decades of the nineteenth century.

The situation in 1896–7 was particularly propitious to the emergence of such charismatic prophet figures. It was in a true sense a revolutionary situation, revolutionary in the sense that what was needed was the total overthrow of existing white control, in the sense that what was needed was a revolutionary fervour and commitment on the part of the rebels, and in the sense also that something was required over and above the fragmented remnants of pre-European political systems, both in order to organize a rising and to provide a vision of society when

H

the rising had been successful. The rising could not be organized merely by making use of surviving political institutions; nor could the aims of the rising be merely to return to a state of impotent fragmentation.

What one can call 'traditional' religious systems could help to provide, as we have seen, co-ordination and inspiration. But perhaps a new element was required even in the field of belief. The 'traditional' systems offered many advantages—an area of normal influence larger than that of any secular authority; the ability to command the support of both Ndebele and Shona; the ability to appeal to a glorious past. Full use was made of all these advantages. But at the same time there emerged a leadership able to transform the appeal of the religious systems into something more radical and revolutionary; a prophetic leadership operating over and above all the restrictions implied by hierarchic order and links with the past. This was the sort of leadership offered by Mkwati in Matabeleland. As we have seen, he had no claim before the rising to be the senior Mwari cult representative; at that time Mhlope tells us, he was merely a messenger of Mwari, and as a Leya ex-slave not a member of the inner-circle of the Rozwi. It was just before and especially during the rising that he emerged as 'the great Mlimo', to use European terminology. When he did so it was with a revolutionary message and with a revolutionary set of instructions. His followers were promised invulnerability and even immortality; they entered a new society which transcended the old, no matter how effective at the same time were his appeals to the memory of both the Ndebele and the Rozwi empires. As we shall see, when the rising became really desperate, the authority of Mkwati and the other cult officers who had chosen the same path was elevated above that of 'traditional' political authorities; *indunas* and chiefs were deposed. For however brief a period Mkwati was seeking not merely to co-ordinate but to create a 'new order'. He was opposed, as we have seen, by those who believed themselves to be guarding the true traditions of the Mwari cult—the officers of the south-western shrine— as well as by those whose interests were vested in the old political order.

The Kagubi medium seems to fit into the same pattern. As we grow to learn more about the spirit mediums—and investigation of the Kagubi spirit is one of the most important tasks for

African scholars of the rebellion—it may be that we shall discover that the Kagubi spirit has always held an important place in Shona theology. There is little evidence to suggest this at the moment. The Kagubi spirit does not appear as part of Professor Gelfand's Chaminuka-Nehanda hierarchy; Bullock tells us that the claims of the medium in 1896 were novel and were eventually repudiated by the Shona themselves as fraudulent so that no medium of the Kagubi spirit re-appeared after his death. I am unaware of any documentary reference to the Kagubi spirit or its medium prior to 1896, while there are many such references to Nehanda and Chaminuka. And both contemporary European and African oral evidence suggest that the Kagubi medium's commanding influence developed only in association with the movement towards rebellion.

The Native Department, summing up their knowledge of the causes of the Mashonaland rising in 1898, were decisive in their view that the Kagubi medium had not been an important figure before the rising; and equally decisive in their view that during it he had been by far the most important figure. 'Previous to the late rebellion', wrote Native Commissioner Campbell, in whose areas 'Kagubi' had lived, 'Kagubi was of no more importance than any other common or barn door Mondoro. . . . He was only a common mondoro, scores of which can be found in every district.' 'Prior to the rebellion', wrote the Chief Native Commissioner, 'Kagubi was a common Mondoro (one who purports and is believed to be possessed of a spirit). He resided in the Salisbury district, and was believed by the natives to be possessed of the supernatural power of locating and enabling people to capture game. . . . Immediately previous to the present rebellion Kagubi betook himself to the Hartley Hills and immediately became the most prominent Mondoro in connection with the rebellion. . . . As Kagubi was, previous to the rebellion, only a common Mondoro, and as his great scheme (the rebellion) failed, I do not think anyone will arise purporting to have received his supernatural powers. With Nianda it is different. Previous to the rebellion she was by far the most important wizard in Mashonaland and was in the habit of receiving tribute from all the chiefs who took part in the rebellion.'

And yet, the Chief Native Commissioner continued, 'during the recent rebellion Nianda appears to have greatly respected

Kagubi and his cause and to have sent tribute to him and assisted him in every manner. The natives around the Mazoe district communicated with Kagubi through Nianda.' This reversal of roles understandably puzzled the Native Department. But once the rising was over, they were convinced, the normal hierarchical relationship would be restored. 'There is no doubt that now the rebellion is over Nianda would be far more dangerous to the peace of the country than even Kagubi would be.'[1]

The African oral evidence presented by Joshua Chidziwa, in his collection of Shawasha tradition, really amounts to a 'mythical' account of how the Shawasha people of the Salisbury district moved out of the era of inter-tribal conflict and reliance on group loyalty and sanctions and into the period of attempted African collaboration against the whites. It is an account which hinges around the Kagubi medium and which brings out his significance in this context; it is an account, also, which shows his authority before 1896 as potential rather than actual; repudiated by the Shawasha rather than accepted. The story, which is worth telling briefly, runs as follows. After the death at the hands of the Ndebele of the great medium of the Chaminuka spirit, Pasipamire, the Shawasha people sent out a party to seize the herds of the dead man. This action was followed by famine. 'In Chishawasha there was a man called Kaguvi of the tribe of Rwize and he was the brother of Pasipamire. Kaguvi explained to the people of Chishawasha and to the people of Seke saying, "This starvation which has come to your countries was brought by Chaminuka whose treasures you have taken. I have heard the voice of God coming from a rock saying. 'You must pay back the cattle of Chaminuka'." When the VaShawasha heard this they refused because among them there was no medium of mhondoro. Kaguvi told them to give two cattle to Nehanda but they refused. There came much starvation to Chishawasha and the people went to other countries to buy food.' During the course of this famine the Shawasha suffered an even worse disaster; they lost the powerful war medicine which had made them invincible through all their nineteenth-century wanderings. Thus when in 1896 the Kagubi medium told them: 'I have heard a voice from trees and rocks saying, "Kill all the white men but do not take their things," ' the Shawasha

---

[1] N.C. Campbell to C.N.C., 3 Mar. 1898, N 1/1/9; report by C.N.C., Mashonaland, 4 Mar. 1898, LO 5/4/8.

hastened to obey. In this new struggle the Shawasha were linked with 'Makoni, Svosve, Mashayamombe, Nyandoro and all the chiefs of the vaZezuru'; in place of their own war medicine which in the past had sustained them against these new allies they trusted in the pledge of 'Kagubi' and 'Nehanda'; 'They will not kill you because if they try to shoot you with their guns, Mwari will turn their bullets into water.'[1]

It is doubtful whether a complete account of how the Kagubi medium came to assume this central role will ever be possible. But certain things can be said. Like the Mwari cult the system of the spirit mediums readily allowed for reversals of influence and for the emergence of new men of power. Spirit mediums were respected partly because they stood in a long line of mediums of powerful spirits, partly because of their own evident spiritual gifts. New manifestations of the divine, moreover, had been fitted into the system regularly over the centuries. The 'Kagubi' medium clearly possessed striking gifts of personality and prophecy; he also gained great prestige through his close association with the Mwari cult, and may, as we shall see, have been regarded in addition as the vehicle of a new manifestation of the god-head; at any rate he emerged in 1896 as the Mashonaland equivalent to Mkwati; the layer down of the new law; the guarantor of invulnerability; the bringer, almost, of a new dispensation. Over and above the paramounts effective in their own area; over and above the complex inter-relations of the Nehanda with the Chaminuka hierarchy and both with the Mwari cult; the figure of the Kagubi medium provided coherence to the Shona rising.[2]

---

[1] Joshua Chidziwa, 'History of the Vashawasha', *NADA*, Vol. IX, No. 1, 1964.

[2] It should be said that there are two interesting references in a diary kept during the 1896 rebellion, which if genuine would seem to indicate that 'Kagubi' was well known to old timers and expected by them to play a leading role in the rising. The entry for June 17th 1896 in the diary kept by a young resident of Bulawayo, F. R. De Bertodano, runs: 'Selous says witchdoctor Kagubi and witch Inyanga are the chief ones to start the Mashona trouble'. The entry for June 19th runs: 'Johann Colenbrander told us at the club this evening that the Mashona rising had been caused by a Mlimo named Kagubi and Nyanda a witch-doctor,' I find these entries hard to accept as contemporary—Bertodano's diary is deposited in the Salisbury Archives in type-script and it is not possible to check with the original. I can find no similar references

No doubt it was because of his supernatural gifts partly that the Kagubi medium was first summoned to assume this position, called out of the Shawasha area in April 1896 by paramount chief Mashiangombi when there was need for a man to link the planned rising in the west with the paramounts of central Mashonaland. But there were other reasons also. If Shawasha tradition is correct the Kagubi medium was related to the heroic figure of Pasipamire. Certainly he was well known to Mashiangombi himself; he had been born in the Hartley area and was a member of the family of chief Chiveru, whose own medium's place in the Chaminuka circle we saw above. Moreover 'Kagubi' was well known to the central Shona paramounts also. He operated in the years before the rising in paramount chief Chiquaqua's area, was son-in-law of paramount chief Mashanganyika, and was consulted by paramount chief Kunzwi Nyandoro. He was an excellent choice for liaison purposes.

Events appear to have followed this course. In April 1896 Mashiangombi received messages from Mkwati, offering assistance to a rising in Mashonaland if one could be organized. Mashiangombi then sent for the Kagubi medium, and when the paramount's messengers accompanied Tshiwa and Bonda back to Taba Zi Ka Mambo some of 'Kagubi's' people went with them. According to the Native Commissioner, Mazoe, reconstructing from the evidence of prisoners in 1897, 'Umquarti told them that he himself was a God and could kill all the whites and was doing so at that time in Matabeleland and that Kargubi would be given the same power as he, Umquarti, had and was to start killing the whites in Mashonaland. Immediately on receipt of these messages Mashiangombi started killing the whites and Kargubi then sent orders to all the paramounts and people of influence to start killing the whites and that he would help them as he was a God.' There is some reason to suppose that after his contact with Mkwati the Kagubi medium was claiming to represent the manifestation of Mwari which was designated by the title 'Mulenga' or 'Murenga' in Shona theology, but however we interpret the evidence there is no doubt that he did base himself on Mashiangombi's kraal from April 1896 to the end of

---

to 'Kagubi' in any of Selous' or Colenbrander's papers or publications nor in any official correspondence until the end of 1896.

the year and that he did send out from there messengers to central Mashonaland who played the same part in mobilizing the country there that Tshiwa and Bonda were playing in the west.[1]

We can follow this process in some detail from the record of scores of preliminary examinations into charges of murder of whites held in Mashonaland in 1897 and 1898. It appears from these that at the end of May or the beginning of June 1896 the Kagubi medium summoned representatives of the central Shona paramounts to his new headquarters, using the same pretext as

[1] N.C. Mazoe, to C.N.C., 20 Oct. 1897, N 1/1/6.
There seems no doubt that the Kagubi medium became widely known during 1896 and 1897 under the title 'Mulenga' or 'Murenga'. The problem is what that title meant. The name is a common one in Central Africa—it is used for a figure in the Bemba spiritual hierarchy, for example. According to the missionary scholar, Von Sicard, Mulenga was the title of one of the manifestations of the Shona trinity; a trinity consisting of Mwari, the father; the mother or wife of Mwari; and the son, Mulenga. According to Francois Coillard, recording a visit in 1874 by Basuto evangelists to Shona chiefs, amongst them Mashiangombi, the Shona were impressed by the resemblance of the gospel story to 'one of their ancient traditions—namely that the son of one of their great chiefs had disappeared mysteriously and that every tenth day ought to be observed among them in his memory until he should come back. They also shaved their heads at the new moon in his honour'. It is tempting in this context to see the collaboration of Mkwati, Tenkela-Wamponga and 'Kagubi' as an embodiment of this trinitarian notion, and the new power of the 'Kagubi' medium as the result of his acceptance as the returned Mulenga. There is even evidence of a sort which could be held to justify such an interpretation. At a preliminary inquiry in 1898, for instance, a witness described how at the gatherings at Mashiangombi's the Kagubi medium would rush "into the centre of the people, who were sitting in a circle, shouting out 'I am the Son of God'." At another examination a man charged with the killing of a white near Mashiangombi's kraal testified that he was called to join the attack upon the Europeans with the words 'M'Lenga has risen'. To the Shona the rising came to be known as Chi-Murenga. On the other hand the evidence is not very strong; African evidence in preliminary inquiries was often mis-translated; most Shona today explain the meaning of Chi-Murenga as a time of violent upheaval, without reference to a Mulenga divinity. The theory remains unproven, therefore, but it would be extremely interesting to see it followed up if more oral evidence about the Kagubi medium and his role in 1896–7 is forthcoming (see Report on preliminary examination in Dekwende's case, Rhodesia, 4 June 1898; preliminary examination in the case of Regina versus Rusere, HC/M, No. 246. Von Sicard's views on the trinity are cited in, Hilda Kuper, A. J. B. Hughes, J. Van Velsen, The Shona and Ndebele of Southern Rhodesia, 1954. The account of the Basuto evangelists is given in, F. Coillard, On the Threshold of Central Africa, London, 1902, p. xxv).

Mashiangombi had advanced for sending his messengers to Mkwati. 'I remember the recent rebellion,' testified a witness in 1898. 'I was then living near Mashiangombi's kraal. I remember the people assembling at Mashiangombi's kraal to get medicine for the locusts.' It was a distinguished assembly, or rather series of assemblies. The central Shona chiefs sent trusted headmen or close relatives, in many cases their sons. Chief Chiquaqua, for instance, sent Zhanta, his best warrior and commander of his *impis* before 1890 and again after the outbreak of the rising; chief Zwimba sent his son; chief M'Sonthi sent his younger brother; chief Garamombe sent his son. These we know to have been there; others, in view of their later close collaboration with Kagubi we may guess to have been there: men like Panashe, bandit son of chief Kunzwi-Nyandoro, or Mchemwa, or the turbulent sons of Makoni.[1]

At these meetings news of the progress of the Ndebele rising was given; at this time, it will be remembered, Mkwati was bringing his picked *impi* back to the Umgusa. Assurances of the support of Mkwati and his Ndebele allies were also given and the Kagubi medium urged the central Shona peoples to join the west in a movement against the whites. Plans for an outbreak as simultaneous as possible were laid; it was to wait until the arrival at Mashiangombi's of Bonda and Tshiwa with the Ndebele warriors; and once it had begun the news was to be carried to central Mashonaland by messengers and passed from hill to hill there by the signal fires which Edwards saw on his way to Marendellas. The leading role of 'Kagubi' emerges quite clearly from the evidence. We possess a report of him, assisted by Mashiangombi's medium, Dekwende, addressing the assembled representatives of the central Shona chiefs while in a state of trance, 'pretending', as the hostile account has it, 'to be possessed by the Mulenga', and in that condition giving 'order for the destruction of anybody obnoxious to him. . . . These orders were believed by the natives to be inspired by their God'. 'What can I say?' asked Zawara, son of chief Garamombe, when facing trial for murder in November 1897. 'All this occurred through Kagubi. He said all whites must die this year. . . . He gathered us to his kraal and said I am the God.'[2]

---

[1] Evidence of Marowa, 7 Dec. 1898, HC/M, No. 391.

[2] *Rhodesia*, 4 June 1898; evidence of Zawusa, 23 Nov. 1897, HC/M, Nos. 213 and 215.

From these gatherings word was swiftly carried back to central Mashonaland. We can see the process at work in the Salisbury district in which the role of the paramounts has already been examined—and so add an essential element in the story of the outbreak of the rising in paramount chiefs Chiquaqua and Mashanganyika's areas. It will be remembered that 'Kagubi' had lived in Chiquaqua's paramountcy and was well known to the chief and to men like Zhanta, and that he was connected to Mashanganyika through marriage. It might be expected, then, that his influence would be strongly felt in the area, and strongly felt it certainly was.

We have seen that Zhanta, the war-leader, was sent as represenentative of the area to the meetings at Kagubi's kraal. 'Kagubi sent two messengers to Mashanganyika's,' testified the old warrior in October 1897. 'They went to Gonta's and told the people they were to come to Kagubi's at once. I went with them. I thought he would give us something to kill the locusts. When I got there he ordered me to kill the white men. He said he had orders from the gods.' Zhanta's return from the meeting is vividly described by other witnesses. "Zhanta was Kagubi's postman. He brought a message that day that the Mashonas must kill all whites. I heard him deliver a message to Chiquaqua.' After the message was delivered, Chiquaqua's *impi* set out for Mashanganyika's kraal; seeing George Campbell being attacked, so witnesses testified, 'Zhanta shouted,"Kill him, Kill him. Kagubi says so." ' 'I was living at my kraal,' testified Chiquaqua. 'Mr Campbell came there the day the God said kill all the white people. I killed no one. My people murdered the white men. . . . I lived all right in my kraal with Mr Campbell but Kagubi said all the white men must be killed. That's all.'[1]

Evidence of this sort, testifying to an implicit obedience to Kagubi's commands, comes not only from his old home area, but from all over central and western Mashonaland. 'It was said by Kagubi that the whites must be killed so Nuja my father told his people that it was the order'; 'The M'Lenga said all the white men must be killed so I gathered all my people and went to White's farm'; 'The God came and said "Kill all the white men". So we said we had better go and kill'; 'I was at the kraal and

[1] Regina versus Zhanta; Regina versus Mashanganyika, Gonto and others; Regina versus Wampi, Chiquaqua, and Rusere; HC/M, Nos. 213, 248, 300.

heard all the whites were being killed. They said it was Kagubi's orders'; 'The murders were committed by order of Kagubi. I heard his messengers give the order. . . . Zwimba's son brought us the message Kagubi sent to Zwimba'; 'I am not guilty. It is the law which was given by the God'; 'They said it was Kagubi's order to hit the white man so I did'; 'I was sent by God to go and kill George. Kagubi sent his *impi* to my kraal and said all the white men must be killed'; 'We should not have gone to kill Eyre without M'Sonthi's orders. Kalunga brought the order from Kagubi to M'Sonti. We should not have killed him without orders'; 'I was working for Eyre when the word came from Kagubi that all the white men were to be killed and a lot of men came to my master's place. I was told to get hold of his legs so I threw him on the ground and the others hit him on the face'; 'It was Kagubi's fault'. These testimonies came from the Hartley, Marendellas, Lomagundi, Mazoe, Umvukwes and Gutu districts—a spread covering virtually the whole area of the Shona rebellion. Their spirit is perhaps best summed up in the evidence of Chinende, house-maid to White of Marendellas. She testified that four men from Chizengeni's kraal entered her master's house, and that she heard them cry out, 'The will of God.' 'That is why I looked inside. I expected to find the white man dead, that is Kagubi's law.'[1]

The impression given by this evidence that the mere orders of the 'Kagubi' medium could transform loyal servants and peaceful neighbours into ferocious adversaries of the whites is no doubt in many ways a misleading one. It clearly overstates the importance of the 'Kagubi' medium as distinct from other influences—those of the other senior spirit mediums, for instance. We should perhaps rather imagine a general response to his initiative in which the Nehanda and the Goronga and other senior mediums also played a significant part. 'Whilst referring to the Mondoros',

---

[1] Evidence of Mutuma, 4 Feb. 1898, HC/M, No. 241; evidence of Chizengeni, 26 Jan. 1898, HC/M, No. 243; evidence of Chiriseri, 30 Dec. 1897, HC/M, No. 244; evidence of Zidemo, 3 Feb. 1898, HC/M, No. 247; evidence of Tinani, 4 Jan. 1898, HC/M, No. 256; evidence of Mabidza, 30 Dec. 1897, HC/M, No. 258; evidence of Masenda, 8 Feb. 1898, HC/M, No. 261; evidence of Chizanga, 24 June 1898, HC/M, No. 333; evidence of N'Dawere, 27 June. 1898, HC/M, No. 341; evidence of Kakobongo, 25 Aug. 1898, HC/M, No. 378; evidence of Gutu, 15 June 1898, HC/M, No. 342; evidence of Chinende, Jan. 1898, HC/M, No. 243.

wrote a Native Commissioner after the rising, 'in the event of a
rising it will be to them that all blame must be attached, as there
is without doubt a certain secrecy among the Mondoros which
has yet to be found out. As we all know in our last rebellion there
were, so to say, two heads to the Mondoro following, viz. Kagubi
and Nehanda, to whom pretty well all other petty Mondoros
were continually communicating. . . . The importance of such
people is so great, that I have no hesitation in stating that no
matter what other influence was in vogue could they be captured
at any time previous to a contemplated rebellion the whole
conspiracy would collapse.'[1]

Moreover we should remember that the call to revolt came into
a situation of general grievance; a situation in which powerful
paramounts had already been moving into intransigent defiance
of the law and in which their subjects increasingly resented tax
and forced labour. The great missionary, John White, then at the
beginning of his long career in Mashonaland, wrote to the press
in January 1897; 'As is their custom these Mashonas when they
need advice resort to these mediums of their gods. The witch-
doctors then inquire from the Murenga—the Great Spirit. "If
you want to get rid of all your troubles," they replied, "kill all the
white men." That the advice was atrociously cruel and fearfully
indiscriminate we will all admit. But think for a moment. These
people are utterly savage and reason accordingly. They believed
they had grievances; they ignorantly thought we had brought the
plague amongst them; they knew nothing of venting their grievances in a constitutional manner. According to their notions the
best way to rid themselves of an evil is to destroy its cause. Hence
they listened to the advice of their prophets. . . . These witch-
doctors through their coming much into contact with men are
naturally shrewd and cunning. They took good care to give their
advice when it was likely to be acted upon.'[2] We must remember,
after all, that there were areas which defied the call both of the
Mwari officers and the mediums and refused to enter the rising.

Nevertheless when these qualifications have been made, and
when we have borne in mind also the very natural tendency of
men on trial for their lives to find someone else upon whom to
place the blame, it is clear that the Kagubi medium not only

[1] N.C. Kenny, 1 May 1904, N 3/14/7.
[2] John White's letter in *The Methodist Times*, Jan. 1897.

played a very important role in coordinating the rising at a supra-tribal level, but also that as the prophetic leader of a revolutionary rebellion he exercised a much more authoritarian command than anthropologists have found to be the case with spirit mediums in 'normal' situations. The spirit medium is said to be an expresser of the consensus rather than a commander; but though the Kagubi medium could also be described as the articulator of the consensus that the time had come to rebel he was clearly more than that. After the rising had broken out he continued to play an authoritarian role. He not only stimulated the first killings but also in some senses directed them, making sure that goods taken from the whites were sent to him and taking particular care over the distribution of firearms. Thus a witness who was describing the killing of whites in the Mazoe area—the famous attack on the Norton farm on June 17th 1896—told how after the fighting, 'we went home and feasted and were driving off the cattle when Kagubi sent and stopped us and took them himself'. Another witness, describing a killing in the Hartley area, told how a gun was taken from the dead white and how 'Kagubi's people took the gun away that day but they sent it back afterwards to the prisoner because he had killed a white man'. Another described how after the killing of a Cape African in Hartley the dead man's gun was taken 'to Kagubi who took it and kept it. Then we stripped the place and took everything to Kagubi.' Chief Gutu was said by witnesses in 1898 to have sent the live-stock of whites murdered in his area to the Kagubi medium's headquarters.[1]

The Kagubi medium also received reports on the progress of fighting and issued advice in much the same way as Mkwati had done in Matabeleland. One illustration out of many that might be quoted will suffice. In July 1896 two spies reported that they had been out to Norton's farm in Mazoe, now occupied by rebels. The rebels were drumming in the hills and when asked what was happening answered that they had sent a messenger to Mashiangombi's and 'were anxious to know when the messenger to the "Lion God" would be back, as they wanted orders'. And, as we shall see, the Kagubi medium exercised a most profound

<hr />

[1] Evidence of Vellem and Tonga, 3 and 7 Feb. 1898, HC/M, No. 242; evidence of Sarurgwa, 19 Jan. 1898, HC/M, No. 257; evidence of Chimana, 24 June 1898, HC/M, No. 333; Regina versus Gutu, HC/M, No. 342.

influence over the conduct of the paramounts when the first white peace overtures were made to them at the end of 1896.[1]

All this serves to emphasize the point that has already been made. The Kagubi medium was more than a senior spirit medium. He brought thousands of Shona into membership of a new society, the true-believers in the M'lenga, with their own distinguishing symbols and obligations and their own promises of divine favour. This loyalty to a supra-tribal society and this belief in the millenarian transformation of colonial society helps to account for the fervour of the Shona rising. 'They promised to give charms to all who would fight,' wrote Marshall Hole of the Kagubi medium and his allies in 1897, 'to render them proof against the bullets of the white man which would turn to water or drop harmless from the mouths of those they struck. . . . In almost every kraal the natives, even the women and children, put on the black beads, which were the badge of the Mondoro, while their fighting men, with Kaffir cunning, waited quietly for the signal to strike down the whites at one blow. So cleverly was their secret kept, and so well laid the plans of the witch-doctors, that when the time came the rising was almost simultaneous and in five days over one hundred white men, women and children were massacred in the outlying districts of Mashonaland.'[2]

Here this chapter has returned to the theme of its opening—the sudden attack upon the settlers of Mashonaland, which, as Mr Gann has recently reminded us, cost them 'something like ten per cent of their total number, a staggeringly high figure, infinitely greater than the proportion of casualties suffered by white colonists in the Algerian national rising or the Mau Mau war in Kenya in the twentieth century'. As we began with the memories of one white of those days of astonishment and terror let us end by seeing the outbreak of the rising through the eyes of an African participant.

The story told by Gonye, resident of Marawera's kraal, near Mashiangombi's, of the killing of the trader Mooney on June 20th, 1896, is in its way a parable of the relations between black and white in Mashonaland in the year of the rising. 'Finangundu said

[1] Intelligence report by Captain Judson, Salisbury laager, 6 July 1896, A 1/12/27.

[2] H. M. Marshall Hole, 'Witch-craft in Rhodesia', The African Review, 6 Nov. 1897.

"M'lenga has risen", and I heard the guns firing as the white man was on horseback. Then Chiramangu fired and the whiteman rode on and then he jumped off and tied up his horse. . . . I heard Rusere say, "The white man is up in the kopje", and as we came he fired, so we lay down, and the second shot hit Chiweshe. And as we came closer the white man said, "Come here all you boys ", and then Chiweshe fired and then Rusere and Maromo fired and there were no more shots from the white man and Rusere said, "If you hear another shot then I am not Rusere for I have hit him in the forehead and killed him." ' In this way began the bitter struggle which was to shake both white prestige and Shona society to their foundations.[1]

[1] Evidence of Gonye, 3 Feb. 1898, HC/M, No. 246.

CHAPTER SEVEN

War and Peace in Matabeleland, June to December 1896

THE IMPACT of the Shona rising upon the situation in Matabeleland was not primarily a military one. The Mashonaland settler forces were, of course, rushed back to their own province but it was decided not to divert the main body of the imperial troops away from their task of breaking Ndebele resistance and storming Taba Zi Ka Mambo and the Matopos strongholds. A new force was to be landed at Bcira, whose main task would be to clear the road between Salisbury and the sea and then to attack the main centres of the rising in Mashonaland. Save for a delay of a week or so while the implications of the Shona rising were digested and these arrangements agreed to, military operations in Matabeleland were not much affected by the new rebellion.

Nevertheless, the fact of the Shona rising did have a most profound impact upon the situation in Matabeleland more generally and provided the context in which the events of the second half of 1896 must be understood. This was because the Shona rising greatly weakened the position of the British South Africa Company administration. Already financially strained by the Ndebele rising itself the Company now faced in Mashonaland the expenditure of much more money—to meet the costs of the new imperial force; to compensate the Mashonaland settlers; to keep Salisbury supplied. Unless the rebellion in the two provinces could be brought to an end in 1896 the Company faced bankruptcy; the maintenance of forces through the wet season and campaigning on perhaps a more extended scale in 1897 could well force a surrender of the Charter and of administrative responsibility.

In any case this administrative responsibility was threatened. During 1896, of course, the inquiry into the Jameson Raid was taking place; the outbreak of the rising in Matabeleland had provided more ammunition for the Company's critics and allowed an imperial foothold in Rhodesia; the outbreak in Mashonaland, so unexpected, weakened the moral position of the Company still more. It increased the bitterness of the settlers against an administration which had been unable to protect them, intensified the suspicion that the native policy of the Company must be oppressive, and involved the despatch of further imperial forces. Two comments made in June 1896 will sufficiently demonstrate the dangers to Company control brought about by the sequence of disasters which had culminated in the Shona rising.

One comment was made by the missionary, Douglas Pelly, who had worked in Makoni's area, then gone to Matabeleland with the Salisbury column, and was now hastening back to see if his colleagues and property in Maungwe were safe. (They were not; the mission property had been destroyed by Miripiri's men, and Bernard Mzeki, his South African catechist, had been killed.) 'Things are serious,' he wrote on June 28th, 'and the rising in Mashonaland is general and is now reported to have spread into the Portuguese country. Everyone out here seems to think that the Charter is doomed and Jameson is pretty freely execrated as the chief cause of all our troubles. I hope the Charter will go; it would be a real blessing to get rid of financial men as rulers. They always have far too many interests to serve, their own private ones being by no means the least of these.' [1]

A day later another, an even more threatening, comment was made by the Acting High Commissioner, General Goodenough. In a memorandum entitled 'The future military occupation of Rhodesia', Goodenough reviewed the situation created by the Shona outbreak. 'The numbers and attitude of the Mashona and Matabele make it probable that the maintenance of a large force in the country will be necessary for a considerable time. The settlers can with difficulty furnish this force, and are wanted to continue the work of development; any strong police would be extremely expensive.' The answer, thought Goodenough, was to retain a strong imperial garrison under the command of an officer responsible to Sir Richard Martin. 'On very many grounds', he concluded, 'the having a substantial Imperial force in Rhodesia would be satisfactory. . . . The South African Republic Government have asked the Imperial to take over Charterland and for once we might agree with them so far.' [2]

[1] Entry for 28 June, Pelly diary, PE 3/1/2.
[2] Goodenough to Robinson, 29 June 1896, C.O., C.P., S.A., No. 520, p. 265; BA 2/1/1.

In comments like these Rhodes saw a greater threat to his plans for Rhodesia than that presented by the rebels themselves. At all costs the Company must prove itself capable of bringing the risings to a rapid end; the settlers must be won over to continued Company administration; the imperial troops must be got out of the country before their presence there turned gradually but inevitably into imperial control of the administration.

Meanwhile the task of tackling the Ndebele strongholds remained to be attempted. We have seen that after the final Umgusa defeat and the arrival of the imperial troops the rebel forces fell back into two very strong defensive positions—Taba Zi Ka Mambo and the Matopos hills. The new ability of the whites to send out strong patrols into the open country had brought about the concentration of the rebel forces in these two areas, the Umlugulu faction in the Matopos, the north-eastern faction gathered around Mkwati at Taba Zi Ka Mambo. In the last days of June forts were established close to each rebel concentration and preparations were made to assault them.

Taba Zi Ka Mambo was chosen as the first target. There, after the Umgusa fight, were gathered together Mkwati, Tenkela and Siginyamatshe, with the many minor officers and messengers of the Mwari cult centre; Mpotshwana and his Nyamandhlovu regiment, Mtini and his Ngnoba regiment, Nkomo and his Jingen or Zingeni force, together with other Ndebele fighting men from the Bulawayo area and elsewhere. Nyamanda and many other members of the royal family were there also. And there were large numbers of Shona fighting men, drawn from the tributary peoples of the north-east; a group of them, under the command of Makumbi, who had led the killings of the whites at Taba Zi Ka Mambo, now formed the special bodyguard of Mkwati. There also was the Rozwi messenger, Tshiwa, returned from western Mashonaland after his part in bringing about the rising there. Taba Zi Ka Mambo thus represented a still formidable concentration of the various elements in the risings. Nor was its offensive spirit broken. At the beginning of July Mtini, who still served as overall military commander, and Siginyamatshe were planning to attack the new fort at Inyati and to wipe out its garrison.[1]

[1] This picture of the grouping at Taba Zi Ka Mambo is built up out of scattered references in files BA 2/9/1 and BA 2/9/2, and files LO 5/6/1 and LO 5/6/2.

The attack on them, entrusted to Plumer, was delivered first. Plumer's assault was perhaps the most successful single action of the white forces during the fighting of 1896 and 1897. Plumer and his force left Bulawayo on June 30th and reached Inyati on July 3rd. On the 4th the scout, John Grootboom, was sent out; he reported that rebel pickets were out during the day watching the approaches to Taba Zi Ka Mambo and that they were aware of the arrival of Plumer's force. That afternoon, indeed, in the Taba Zi Ka Mambo stronghold, preparations were being made for a defence against the white attack, which was expected to be delivered the next day; the great herds of cattle and sheep which had been collected there and the mass of property taken from the whites killed in March were gathered together to be despatched northwards on July 5th. Plumer, however, decided that nothing effective could be done unless the defenders were taken by surprise and therefore ordered a night march, so timed that the assault on Taba Zi Ka Mambo would be delivered at dawn on July 5th. He also ordered a series of flanking movements, so that the main attack would be delivered from the north and so that the flight of the defenders in that direction and to the west would be intercepted; fugitives from Taba Zi Ka Mambo were to be driven south or east into open country.[1]

A number of accounts of the fighting at Taba Zi Ka Mambo exist. Almost everyone who could manage it accompanied Plumer's force—Rhodes himself, Jarvis, Stent, the recently arrived correspondent of *The Times*, Baden-Powell—and most of them wrote about it. Stent's account is by all odds the most vivid. 'All through the night we rode—a stealthy band of khaki grey intruders . . . on towards the mountain looming indistinct before us. Then the picket fires of the rebels lifted through the cumber of the night. Men gripped their rifles, loosened a round or two in the bandoliers, and peered grimly out into the murk. Now the column broke —some to outflank the position, others to move into the heart of the enemy's fastness. . . . Grey dawn found us standing to our horses. In front of us a crop of isolated granite kopjes which formed the object of Plumer's attack. Clear upon the cool wind of the morning, the wind that wakes, came the crack! crack! of the Martinis, answering the dull heavy explosions of the old elephant guns which the Matabili carried. . . . Out of the hills the retreating

[1] Plumer's diary of the Taba Zi Ka Mambo action, July 1896, BA 2/9/1.

Mashonas—Mashonas invariably led the retreat—came streaming across our front. The machine-guns spat viciously at them as they ran. Among the hills the musketry began to babble incessantly. The dawn glowed red. The Matabili were making a stand in a central kopje—a nasty one to tackle. Suddenly just in front of us a few men that looked like a picket fired on us and bolted. The squadron trailed after them in pursuit. One man drew out ahead, in spite of warnings and expostulations. I spurred on to see. It was Rhodes himself, riding unarmed, a switch in hand, leading the hunt.' [1]

Stent was with the flanking cavalry; meanwhile a stiff fight was going on in the central fastness of Taba Zi Ka Mambo. Plumer later described it 'as a confused mass of kopjes with grassy hollows scattered among them; all these kopjes are full of caves and shelters formed among the interstices of the boulders and capable of containing many thousand people. . . . The whole position is one of vast natural strength and capable of protracted defence.' Nevertheless it was stormed, as Plumer laconically recorded. 'The fighting resolved itself into a series of independent actions among the kopjes and these lasted from 6 a.m. till 12 noon. The rebels fought determinedly in the kopjes but were finally driven out. Their loss is estimated at about 100.' [2]

Once in possession the triumphant whites examined their prize. There was the Mwari cave to investigate; the cave from which the Umgusa force had received its orders. 'An examination of the caves in the gorge behind West's store pointed to one in particular as being probably the residence of the Mlimo, being arranged so that the oracle could speak through a crevice in the rocks to the indunas assembled in the cave. Large quantities of loot from various localities were found there. . . . One party of women evinced the greatest reluctance to passing near the cave supposed to be the Mlimo's.' There was the old hill of the Mambo itself, where once before an African leadership had made a stand against invaders—a kopje on the eastern side of the entrance to the valley, the passage to which 'is not more than 70 yards wide and is completely dominated by precipitous rocks on either side'. Some of the

[1] De Vere Stent, *A Personal Record of Some Incidents in the Life of Cecil Rhodes*, Cape Town, 1924.
[2] Note on Taba Zi Ka Mambo by Plumer, July 1896; Plumer to Chief Staff Officer, Bulawayo, 5 July 1896, BA 2/9/1.

stiffest fighting of the engagement had taken place there. And there were crowds of women and children and herds of cattle. Stent describes the triumphant return from Taba Zi Ka Mambo, so different from the stealthy approach. 'An extraordinary spectacle. First the screen of scouts, riding in careless mood . . . then a great mob of cattle—ten thousand head, they said; they seemed to cover the veld for miles. They suggested gigantic locusts and were not in a hurry. . . . Then, tramping in rough formation, the prisoners and the women and children . . . then our ambulances, such as they were, and the main body.' [1]

The attack on Taba Zi Ka Mambo had been a spectacular success, even though the calibre of African resistance had been disconcerting—'this Matabele rising is a tough nut to crack', wrote the *Bulawayo Sketch* on July 11th, as the white casualty lists came in. Plumer's tactics had resulted in the breaking up of the force which had been together since the first Umgusa fights of April. The hundreds of fighting men who escaped from Taba Zi Ka Mambo on July 5th made mainly southwards; 'the tracks leading from Tabas I Mamba show that a considerable number of the rebels fled in a south-easterly direction towards the Matopos'. These men joined the forces of Umlugulu, Sikombo, Dhliso and the rest in the defence of the Matopos strongholds. But the leadership of the north-eastern faction went in other directions, and thus lost from July 5th onwards, a large proportion of their followers. [2]

The intriguing confrontation of the two inspirers of white and black morale—Rhodes with his riding switch and Mkwati with the staff which Baden-Powell later acquired and used as a blackboard pointer during his lectures on the campaign—did not materialize on July 5th. By the time the white attack was delivered Mkwati had already gone. 'When the white forces were advancing on Ntaba Zi Ka Mambo the Mlimo said he was going to examine and inspect the land in the Somabula forest,' Malima tells us, 'and on the night before the fight Umkwati followed him.' Mkwati was not alone, however, and his flight was not the panic affair depicted in the white press. Mtini, Nkomo and Makumbi and their men went with him; so, of course, did Tshiwa and the officers of the Taba Zi Ka Mambo shrine; so did a number of members of the royal family. Siginyamatshe was left behind with the remaining

[1] Plumer to C.S.O., 8 July 1896, BA 2/9/1; Stent, op. cit.
[2] Plumer to C.S.O., 8 July 1896, BA 2/9/1.

force; from all indications it seems that he was intended to evacuate the stronghold on the following day and to bring the remaining fighting men, the cattle, and the women and children on after Mkwati.[1]

This plan was, as we have seen, frustrated; most of the defenders of Taba Zi Ka Mambo, Siginyamatshe among them, fled south instead. Contact was never again resumed between Siginyamatshe and Mkwati. Moreover, there was soon a division even amongst those who had left Taba Zi Ka Mambo before the attack. Mpotshwana, *induna* of the Nyamandhlovu, hitherto a close associate of Mkwati and Mtini, now decided to break with them and to pursue his own line. He determined, as Selous put it, 'to establish an independent nation' in the north; his mind turned to the classic Ndebele expedient of the trek away into new territory. On July 27th it was reported that 'Mpotshwana with a number of men is at junction of Gwai and Shangani rivers', far in the north-western corner of Matabeleland, 'arranging for boats to take them across the Zambesi. The Nyamandhlovu regiment started for the Zambesi but sickness having broken out among them, they have returned to the Bembesi river.' [2]

Mkwati had no intention of following a trek across the Zambesi or participating in an attempt to refound the Ndebele state somewhere in north-western Rhodesia. The Mwari cult, universal though its divinity was, was also rooted in the past of Southern Rhodesia; Mkwati was moving closer to his Shona allies and the fundamental divergence of interest between him and the men whose main aim was a return to the system of Mzilikazi was beginning to show. After the fall of Taba Zi Ka Mambo, Mkwati fell back along a line between Inyati and the main centres of the western Mashonaland rising, moving out of the area of the Ndebele rising proper and into the area of the Shona subject peoples. In late July he and his followers, Mtini, Nkomo and Makumbi still among them, were in the Somabula forest, close to the country of his father-in-law, Uwini, from which he planned to draw provisions.

Carrington was fully justified, then, in his claim that the action at Taba Zi Ka Mambo had broken up 'such cohesion as remained

[1] Malima's statement, 1 Aug. 1896, LO 5/6/2.
[2] Staff Diary entry for 27 July 1896; Secretary, Administrator, to Cape Town Office, 31 July 1896, LO 5/6/2.

among the rebels threatening the country round Bulawayo'. The remarkable achievement of the north-eastern faction, which had combined so many divergent interests into so effective a force, was now falling apart.[1]

And yet the fighting at Taba Zi Ka Mambo had one other important result—successful as it was it still helped to turn Rhodes' mind towards the idea of a negotiated peace with the rebels. Stent tells us of Rhodes' reaction. Dramatic, even melodramatic, as Rhodes' part in the attack had been—'Rhodes is very like Napoleon', wrote Jarvis admiringly. 'He quite thinks that he was not intended to be killed by a d . . . d nigger!'—the impression he carried away was not one of triumph. Nine whites had been killed in the fighting; they were buried on the spot, wrapped in the hides of some of the captured cattle which had been shot for food. 'There had been a good many natives killed, too,' Stent tells us. 'But the death of the rebels who had murdered white women and children did not come home to us as the death of these of our own kind and colour. It cut Rhodes to the heart. . . . Soldiers of fortune, if you will; having their faults, not too overburdened with humane considerations; they asked for no quarter; they probably would have given none. But they were the men that Rhodesia wanted to smooth her rugged ways; to break her in. They were the price of victory and the price was heavy. . . . This rough and hurried burial of the men who had given their lives for Rhodesia brought home to him, as nothing else could have done, the meaning of war—the cruel bloodiness of war.' That night, as Rhodes brooded over the camp fires, 'there came to him the idea of meeting the Matabili themselves, learning what they fought for, and trying to bring about Peace'.[2]

Though other considerations were certainly also in Rhodes' mind there seems no doubt that the resistance put up at Taba Zi Ka Mambo did turn his thoughts in this direction. Rhodes' party— Jarvis and the rest—had been as loud as anyone in their demands for a total and unconditional victory; for the trial and execution of all instigators of the rebellions; for a final smashing lesson that Rhodesia was white man's country. But Rhodes knew of the dangers to the Company of allowing the rising to drag on; it must be ended in 1896; and the experience of Taba Zi Ka Mambo made

---

[1] Carrington to High Commissioner, 8 July 1896, BA 2/9/1.
[2] Jarvis to his mother, 19 Aug. 1896, JA 4/1/1; Stent, op. cit.

him doubt whether it could be ended by fighting. The Matopos presented a much greater problem for an attacking force and they were held by rebel *impis* still fresh and confident. If the rising could not be ended in 1896 by force it must be ended in some other way. After Taba Zi Ka Mambo Rhodes was determined to seize the first chance of negotiation, or to manufacture a chance if none arose.

First, however, as Stent puts it, the small group in favour of negotiations had 'to let the troops blood themselves a little'. This they certainly did in the fighting in the Matopos which followed. The Matopos area was much too extensive to allow the sort of flanking tactic which Plumer used successfully at Taba Zi Ka Mambo. Its kopjes had to be stormed one by one in an often vain attempt to force their defenders to a stand-up fight. The area was now occupied by the experienced senior *indunas* of the Umlugulu faction. 'Under Lobengula there were two factions,' wrote the missionary Carnegie in July; 'one representing the old warriors and the other the "young bloods". From all I can gather today these two parties still exist in the land; the one in the Matopo hills and the other in the bush country in the north. . . . The nation as such, in my opinion, is divided into two factions, the one under Umlugulu and Umfesela among the Matopo hills and the other under Umtini, Buqwele and others in the bushy country. The final stand will most likely be made among the Matopo hills.' Strengthened by the refugees from the Taba Zi Ka Mambo garrison, 'the old warriors' and their young followers prepared to resist Carrington's attack. 'They are aware of General Carrington's preparations and intend to fight', it was reported on July 20th, 'but will not make a stand in one place.' [1]

Despite these difficulties a momentary optimism possessed settlers and soldiers as Carrington's forces moved off to the Matopos. 'Rebels to be attacked all sides Monday,' ran one cable despatched from Bulawayo, 'Natives flying northwards in large numbers. Rebellion will be crushed in three weeks. Settlers now hopeful. Position of whites strong all over.' There followed an agonizing series of engagements in the Matopos; Babyaan's stronghold was attacked; Sikombo's stronghold was attacked; Dhliso's stronghold was attacked. In each case the rebels were compelled to evacuate

[1] Carnegie to Sir Richard Martin, July 1896, *C. 8547*; *The Times*, 20 July 1896.

the kopjes which they had been defending, but in each case they moved to a similar area, as easy to defend; rebel losses in these engagements were relatively low, white losses relatively high. 'The Matopos, as you know by now,' wrote Lady Grey to her children, 'extend a very long distance and fighting in them is practically throwing away valuable lives for no adequate gain. The men are simply shot at from behind rocks without ever really a chance of an open fight and if they do drive the enemy back a kopje or two and kill a certain number of them very little is gained for they simply retire on other kopjes and after a time come back and re-occupy the old positions when the white force has moved somewhere else.' 'Our poor men are quite helpless,' wrote her daughter, Victoria, 'for they can only hear the bullets whizzing and they never see the niggers who fire out of these hidden caves.' [1]

As the pattern of the Matopos fighting emerged so settler optimism sharply receded. 'If things don't look up', wrote the *Bulawayo Sketch* on July 25th, 'it will be our backbone that will be broken not that of the rebels.' 'Captain Laing's and Captain Nicholson's engagements with the Matabele crack regiments are described as "drawn battles",' commented the *Westminster Gazette* on July 27th, 'but when the officers in charge have to sound "cease firing" and the troops fall back "without making any impression on the enemy", can we be wrong in supposing that the Matabele themselves would regard both events as victories?' 'Press correspondents here complain of the action of the authorities in suppressing details of recent engagements,' reported *The Times* on July 28th. 'Arrivals from the front confirm previous reports as to the extreme confidence and arrogant bearing of the rebels who jeer at the whites and call them cowards. They also state that in the last engagement the enemy sustained no loss . . . there is a growing fear that the troops are insufficient to put down the rebellion effectively.'

This was a conclusion that many were coming to. At the end of July Jarvis, for instance, was still demanding the annihilation of the rebels. 'The witch-doctors have a great power over the rascals,' he wrote on July 30th, 'and the fanaticism is extraordinary—they are told and believe all sorts of things, poor devils. The only thing to be said is that wherever the mission station is there are the biggest blackguards, so the best thing to do is to wipe

[1] Lady Grey to her children, 27 Aug. 1896; Victoria Grey to Charles Grey, 14 Sept. 1896; GR 1/1/1.

them all out as far as one can—everything black. It would do some of these wretched Exeter Hall crowd a power of good to go through a job like this—I don't think we should have such a lot of cant and hypocrisy and false sentimentalism in the Old Country if they could be sent out in batches and put through a healthy course of kaffir fighting.' But Jarvis' own course of kaffir fighting was compelling him to realize how difficult it would be to punish the Ndebele in the way that he desired. 'It would take an army of ten thousand men', he wrote in the same letter, 'to thoroughly sweep the place and even then there would be great loss of life and you would have to calculate how many men you could afford to lose in order to gain each position.' General Carrington, irked and baffled by a military situation which did not respond to his customary direct methods, had also become convinced that the Matopos campaign was going to be a long job which needed many more men. 'They are now attacking the Matopo hills,' wrote Carnegie on July 24th, 'but Sir Frederick Carrington who has been out with Col. Plumer in one of these engagements is reported to have stated that until he gets 3000 men these hills can't be cleared of rebels. There has been some severe fighting this week and at least over 20 white men have been killed and twice that amount wounded. . . . My own opinion is that if it is not over in six weeks it won't be in six months . . . if the *indunas* refuse the war may drag on all through the rainy season which will soon be upon us.' Carrington's own view, expressed some six weeks later, was that if the rebels in the Matopos were to be dealt with by fighting 'we shall probably have to blockade and harass them until the next dry season and then get up a larger force with recognized transport.' For the campaign of 1897, he wrote, he would ask for a further 2500 white infantry, a detachment of engineers for blasting operations, two to four mountain guns, and 2000 carriers.[1]

This was exactly the sort of thinking that Rhodes dreaded and could not allow to develop. By the end of July he had resolved to make contact with the Ndebele leaders and to offer a negotiated settlement. Despite the rebel successes there were, in fact, some indications that the senior *indunas* would welcome such overtures. While the fighting at Taba Zi Ka Mambo and in the Matopos had

[1] Jarvis to his mother, 30 July 1896, JA 4/1/1; Carnegie to Thompson, 24 July 1896, L.M.S., Matabele Mission, Vol. 5; Carrington to Rosmead, 11 Sept. 1896, C.O., C.P., 520, p. 543.

been going on, white patrols had been destroying crops and burning kraals in the open country; in July there was already a great shortage of food in the hills; and continued resistance through the wet season would mean that no new crops could be grown and the nation would face starvation. Scraps of information came to hand which indicated that there was a growing dispute between the intransigents, headed by the Mwari officers, and these who were inclined to a settlement or perhaps even a surrender. On July 14th, for instance, it was reported that the Mwari officers had 'deprived' Dhliso 'of his indunaship'; Dhliso had been one of the last to enter the rising and was suspected by the radicals. 'Such was the belief they had in this Mlimo', wrote the Chief Native Commissioner later, 'that any headman or induna who showed the slightest sign of wavering in not joining in with the instigators of the rebellion was immediately removed from his indunaship and his cattle and other possessions were at once handed over to the Mlimo's lieutenants. This I learn and am convinced was the case with the *induna* Dhliso. . . . Other cases where certain *indunas* have lost their titles by order of the Mlimo have also been brought to my notice.' It was hardly surprising that friction grew up between the Mwari officers and the Ndebele leaders generally; the same divergence of interests between the two parties was developing both in the north and in the Matopos. In the Matopos, however, the Mwari officers did not possess a personal body-guard of devoted Shona adherents, nor were the Ndebele leaders in a minority among a Shona population, as was the case in the Somabula. The Matopos cult leaders were able to retain the loyalty of many of the young men, but they could not prevent Umlugulu and the older *indunas* from re-asserting their separate authority. By the beginning of August, so the whites learnt from a captured member of the Ndebele royal family, Umlugulu, Sikombo and other senior *indunas* had quarrelled with the Mwari priests, who were threatening to leave the Matopos. 'Mlimo now has nothing to do with the revolt. He does not like the Matabele and talks of clearing out of the Matopos. . . . Before they had determined to surrender the Mlimo had ordered them on no account to leave the hills. The Matabele are now fighting in self-defence. If chance had been left to them of coming in, they would have done so.' [1]

[1] Staff Diary, 14 July and 9 August 1896; C.N.C. to Grey, 2 Sept. 1896; LO 5/6/2, LO 5/6/3 and LO 5/6/4.

It was Rhodes' plan to play upon these divisions in the Ndebele ranks and to appeal to the senior *indunas*. At the same time as his attempts to make contact with them, there was also an imperial peace endeavour on foot, though on a very different basis from Rhodes'. On July 4th the Acting High Commissioner, Goodenough, had issued a Proclamation of Amnesty. This defined the area formally regarded as being in rebellion; notified the penalties for remaining in arms in those areas; described a method of submission; and promised amnesty and security of life and property to all those who laid down their arms by August 10th, 1896. In a schedule attached to the proclamation were listed the names of the ring-leaders excluded from the amnesty offer, which included the names of Umlugulu, Sikombo, Babyaan, Somabulana, Nyamanda and the rest of the Ndebele leadership. The intention of the imperial authorities was to give a chance for the ordinary man to make his peace and to ensure that ordinary prisoners taken in the fighting would receive proper treatment. In the last weeks of July most of the prisoners taken were disarmed and then sent back with copies of the proclamation to spread the news of it among the rebels.[1]

At the time the issue of the proclamation was very severely criticized by the white settler press. 'It offers pardon to those who are revelling in their past successes', wrote the *Bulawayo Sketch* savagely on July 18th, 'and still feel themselves secure in their fortresses. It sentences by edict those leaders who are now living in savage pomp, surrounded by a host of zealous followers and still think themselves irresistible. It threatens before it has the power to perform and hawks clemency to those that will have none of it.' Though it was the idea of offering an amnesty at all which aroused settler wrath, the real weakness of the proclamation was rather its proscription of the only men who had the power to decide upon a surrender. As Grey wrote, 'To insist upon a surrender under terms of the Proclamation will be accepted by the rebels as an invitation to the Chiefs to come out of the hills and be hung and this they will not do.' As far as Rhodes was concerned the imperial attempt at conciliation was an obstacle rather than an assistance.[2]

His intention was to ignore the rank and file and appeal to the

[1] Correspondence relating to the issue of the proclamation is printed in C.O., C.P., S.A., No. 520, pp. 188, 214, 216, 239.

[2] Grey to Goodenough, 28 Aug. 1896, ibid., p. 495.

leadership. It was an intention born of necessity but perhaps there was also a philosophical difference between his approach and that of Goodenough. Goodenough regarded the Ndebele leadership as the real criminals, who had led their followers into error. Rhodes admired strong leadership and had little time for weak followers. Stent describes his attitude at that time in a revealing way. 'One class did the fighting and the other the murdering. The Matabili faced the rifles and the machine-guns; the Maholi and the Mashona killed the women and children.' Rhodes, so Stent assures us, felt a proper contempt and hatred for the Shona and the Holi but had great sympathy 'with that fine upstanding fighting man, the Matabili, with his Zulu blood and his clean military antecedents', now suffering 'as all must for the sins of their associates'. As history it was grotesque but as an emotion it seems to have enabled men like Jarvis to make his transition from total war to conditional peace.[1]

Because the military and settlers were hostile to any idea of negotiations and because of the disparity between his approach and that of Goodenough and Martin, Rhodes had to begin his attempts to make contact with the rebel leaders in some secrecy. He tried a variety of methods. Late in July, for instance, he approached a brother of Lobengula who had remained 'loyal' and was living in Bulawayo, asking him to carry a message to the rebel commanders in the hills; the loyalist flatly refused. Attempts were then made to contact Sikombo by sending in two 'friendlies' with two of Sikombo's men specially released from jail for the purpose. The men were never seen again. So far Rhodes had not been particularly successful, but after the bloody stalemate of the attack on Sikombo's of August 5th, a feeling in favour of negotiations began to spread among the military themselves, and Rhodes was able to work much more openly.[2]

Legend sees the story of the famous *indaba* to which these tentatives led up as the achievement of Rhodes alone. In fact there were many people involved, some of whom risked their lives earlier and more often than Rhodes did. But his was the moral courage of the idea of making peace; their physical courage was a commoner commodity. The chief associate of Rhodes was Johan Colenbrander, ex-Chief Native Commissioner of Matabeleland,

[1] Stent, op. cit.
[2] Hans Sauer, *Ex Africa*, 1937, chap. XIV.

and a man well known to all the Ndebele leaders. Colenbrander's lawyers were probably not much over-stating his role when they wrote to claim a much larger reward for his work than the 1000 guineas which the Company in fact paid him. 'It was mainly through the medium of Mr Colenbrander that your costly Matabele war was brought to an end. . . . When the crucial point arrived and Mr Colenbrander consented to go at peril of his life to initiate the "surrender" negotiations . . . it would have been wiser of him if he had simply said: "This is a very responsible and dangerous business—will you please give me a cheque for £10,000 for my wife and £10,000 for my company. Being a servant of the latter I have no business to risk my life at the request of Mr Cecil Rhodes for the benefit of the Chartered Company." Mr Rhodes himself at that time consulted of course his own interests in running all the risks of life, etc., he did. . . . Mr Colenbrander did all the work and was the primary cause of the success of that meeting.' [1]

Other important associates were the young Native Commissioners of the area, especially Richardson, Native Commissioner, Matopos. He was instructed on August 10th to 'use every endeavour in your power to obtain the surrender of the rebels in the Matopo Hills and in connection therewith the Company will give you a free hand in the matter'. Thereafter Richardson devoted himself to the task of establishing contact. Nor should we forget the Africans involved, the most important of whom was the scout, John Grootboom. [2]

But with all these associates success still eluded Rhodes in the first days of August. Thus on August 18th Chief Native Commissioner Thomas had to report another failure. 'Last week two of Colenbrander's boys accompanied by a boy named Dick (taken out of gaol for the set purpose) and a son of Jobani (the priest shot by Burnham) arrived at Faku's kraal where they sent Dick and Jobani's son to the rebels with a message. The messengers entered the Matopos and saw the following *indunas*—Nkonkobela, Hole, Matisa, Godhlo—and delivered their message which they report to the effect that the rebels would come in and surrender their arms and themselves to the whites. These *indunas* sent the following reply: "Yesterday was yesterday, today is today. Why should we

[1] Witt to Canning, 8 May 1897, Rhodes House, Mss. Afr. s. 228, Vol. 4.
[2] Secretary, Administrator, to Native Commissioner, Matopos, 10 Aug. 1896, AM 1/8/1.

surrender? We have held our own and driven the whites back each time they have attacked us here. . . . If the whites are tired of fighting they can come and surrender to us here." ' The messengers had had the misfortune to encounter a group of *indunas* who still supported the Mwari priesthood and its intransigent refusal to contemplate negotiation; Matisa especially was noted for his loyalty to the Mwari representatives.[1]

It was beginning to look as though Rhodes' plan had failed and fighting would have to continue for the period and on the scale foreseen by Carrington. And then one of the peace overtures succeeded. 'Some little time previously', wrote Lady Grey in what is the most accurate and fresh account, 'they had discovered in a deserted kraal in the Matopos where they were fighting a little old woman left behind all alone with her cows and chickens in one of those natural sorts of fortresses. They carried her down to the camp in a skin, notwithstanding her furious indignation, and there discovered that she was a widow of Moselikatse . . . and the mother of one of the principal chiefs now in the Matopos, Inyanda.' The old lady was in fact captured on August 9th; it was she who gave the news of the tension between the Mwari officers and the senior *indunas*; and Rhodes at once saw that she might prove a valuable contact. In the instructions to Richardson of August 10th it was noted that 'Mr Rhodes thinks that some use might be made of the old lady who claims to be mother of Inyanda. She is, Mr Rhodes is aware, too old to move but a message might be taken for her by the other women in the camp.' [2]

Richardson went one better; the old lady had been carried from her kraal, she should be carried back there. Accordingly on August 11th or 12th he took her back with an escort of friendlies and flying a white flag, informing a party of rebels with whom he made contact that she had a message for them. 'Hearing from her that many of the rebels would like the war to cease,' wrote Lady Grey, 'they told her that she was to be taken back to where they had found her and that they would give her a white flag and that when her people came to visit her . . . she was to give them the flag and say that if they wanted to negotiate for peace they were to stick up the white flag as a sign. The old lady was carried back to her fastness and soon after both she and the white flag disappeared.

[1] C.N.C. to Grey, 18 Aug. 1896, LO 5/6/3.
[2] Lady Grey to her children, 27 Aug. 1896, GR 1/1/1.

In 2 or 3 days the white flag reappeared, and upon this Mr Rhodes and Mr Colenbrander began to devise how to contrive communications.' On August 14th the two men themselves went out to the Matopos and established their camp some distance away from Plumer's column. 'Mr Rhodes' party having arrived . . . they decided on seeing the white flag returned to send messengers to the rebels to find out if they wished to treat and surrender. They therefore called for volunteers to act as envoys and eventually 4 black men volunteered to go. They were each promised £25 by Mr Rhodes and he and his little party went up the kopje with them . . . and started them off from the white flag. When once they had disappeared from view I don't think our people had much hope of ever seeing them again for it was thought very likely that they would all be killed, but lo and behold about 6 o'clock they all turned up again. I forgot to say that 2 rebel prisoners were also sent with them, one of them being an old man and the other a young one who was a follower of Sikombo, one of the principal rebels. They all came in and sat down in a row by the fire looking very miserable and melancholy. Not a word was said for 5 minutes or so. They had to possess their souls in patience without being able to ask questions, for natives must never be hurried or you will get nothing out of them. After about five minutes' silence Mr Colenbrander said they might be addressed and then began a long palaver. They said that they had found the rebels just over the second ridge in great numbers all sitting watching and waiting; that the hills were black with them. They sent on Sikombo's boy in advance and he was taken straight to the chiefs and told them what they had come for. The boy saw messages despatched at once to the other chiefs who were some distance off and who would have to be consulted and he was told that these chiefs would have to have a voice in the matter so that they must have some days in which to think things over and consult each other, that they were sick of fighting and would like to come in. . . . Sikombo's boy was the one who saw the principal chiefs, the others only seeing lesser dignitaries. They said they had been well treated and had not been threatened by the young warriors so their melancholy appearance on arriving had quite belied them . . . Mr Rhodes and the rest were rather inspirited by this first attempt and waited to see what would follow.' This meeting of Rhodes' emissaries, led by John Grootboom, with the rebel leaders took place on August 16th.

'Over a thousand met our envoys,' cabled Carrington on August
18th, 'including Sekombo and Nyanda, and heard our conditions
of surrender. They promised reply today.' [1]

On August 18th two emissaries from the rebels came in to
Rhodes' camp and, as Lady Grey tells us, 'another long talk began
over the camp fire. The whole gist of it was that they were anxious
to leave fighting but they must consult each other and that they
wasted time and that they were afraid of coming in while the big
impi was so near; that a great deal of the trouble had been caused
by the Matabele native police who had misused their authority
and been unjust often, etc. etc., and that they must have time. Mr
Rhodes gave them three days for consultation and said that they
must make up their minds in that time whether it was to be peace
or war. Then they departed and another period of waiting began.' [2]

The waiting ended on August 21st when Rhodes' messengers
returned to tell him that the rebel chiefs were ready to meet him
and a few companions. Umlugulu, Sikombo, Babyaan, Somabulana, Dhliso, Nyanda, together with some 36 other *indunas*, had
assembled in the hills to discuss peace. Colenbrander told Rhodes
that only four white men could go; 'and that they must all four
close up and ride together even . . . for fear of the rebels imagining
that there might be small parties of 2 following each other'.
Rhodes went of course; Colenbrander also. The other two invited
were Dr Hans Sauer, an old business associate of Rhodes' and the
correspondent of *The Times*, De Vere Stent.

'It was a lovely winter's day,' wrote Stent later, 'the sun just
beginning to western; comfortably hot; the grasses, bronze and
golden, swaying in the slight wind; the hills ahead of us blurred in
the quivering image of the early afternoon. The track debouched
into a tiny basin, rimmed by kopjes and floored by fallow. In the
centre of the fallow lay some tree stumps and the remnants of a
big ant heap.' They dismounted, Stent and Sauer with some trep-
idation, and waited for the Ndebele to show the white flag and to
appear at the rendezvous. 'A second or so later they did. The folds
of the great stretch of calico showed dead white against the ever-
green shrubs that fringed the granite kopjes . . . at the same time a

---

[1] Lady Grey, ibid; *Daily News,* 13 Aug. 1896; *The Times,* 15 Aug. 1896;
Jarvis to his mother, 13 Aug. 1896, JA 4/1/1; Carrington to Goodenough, 18
Aug. 1896, C.O., C.P., S.A., No. 520, p. 464.
[2] C.S.O. to High Commissioner, 19 Aug. 1896, ibid., p. 465.

VII Two contemporary impressions of the white attack on African food supplies after the relief of Bulawayo. The first (*above*) shows Spreckley's column joining Colonel Napier's *laager* on the Shangani with captured cattle; the second (*below*) shows the demolition and looting of a *kopje* kraal by the Mounted Infantry.

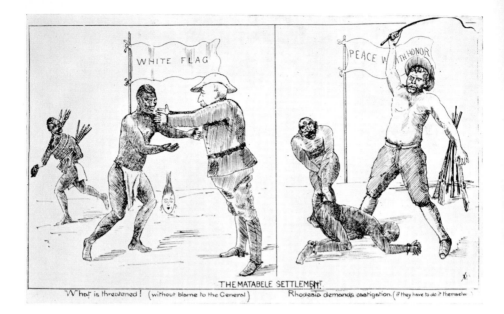

THE MATABELE SETTLEMENT

What is threatened! (without blame to the General)   Rhodesia demands castigation. (if they have to do it themselve

VIII   White Rhodesian reactions to Rhodes' negotiations with the Ndebele are shown in these cartoons from the *Bulawayo Sketch* of August 22nd and September 12th, 1896. In the first (*above*) General Carrington is seen embracing an Ndebele murderer in contrast to the castigation demanded by Rhodesians. In the second (*below*) Rhodes' *indaba* with the Ndebele is contrasted with the arrest and shooting of Makoni in Mashonaland.

A CONTRAST.

number of dark forms could be seen gathering around it. Slowly a little procession formed, headed by the flag, and came towards us. The wonderful smile broke out on Rhodes' face as he said, "Yes, Yes, there they are. This is one of those moments in life that make it worth living. Here they come!" . . . The tableau was as unique as it was impressive. The four white men, seated upon the remains of the ant-heap, dominated the foreground. Rhodes—the central figure. To his left, Colenbrander, interpreting and advising. To his right, Sauer and myself, spectators, silent. Below us the demilune of natives, in the centre of which sat the high chiefs—the commoners squatted on their haunches. Most of them were mat bearers and attendants upon the five or six important *indunas* who took part in the discussion.' 'Is it peace?' asked Rhodes. 'It is peace, my father,' answered Somabulana, 'but we would speak with you.' The *indaba* had begun.

In his enthusiastic report to Grey later that day Hans Sauer claimed that the *indunas* had offered Rhodes 'practically unconditional surrender'. This was certainly not the case. From the beginning—with Somabulana's 'but'—the *indaba* took the form of negotiation rather than submission. The Ndebele leaders seized the opportunity to recite the wrongs of the nation, Somabulana in the great oration already cited, Sikombo and Babyaan dominating the long first part of the discussions. Rhodes heard of the misdeeds of the Native Commissioner, the Ndebele Police, the first Magistrate of Bulawayo, Heyman; heard how cattle and land had been seized, how the *indunas* had been treated like 'dogs', how women and children, even, had been shot. 'The natives', wrote Stent, 'seemed to be having it a little too much their own way. Somabulana, clever advocate that he was, was putting us in the wrong. We were not accepting a surrender. It began to look very much as if we were making terms.'

We have seen that the defects of Company administration of which the *indunas* now so bitterly complained were in fact very much due to Rhodes himself, to his sense of priorities, to his choice of men, to his tolerance of the rough and ready method. But now, as he at long last did what Dr Waterston had urged him to do and tried to enter imaginatively into the Ndebele situation, he was able to demonstrate, and even to feel, surprised shock at the particular allegations made. He had not, after all, willed that these things should happen; he had merely not considered African opinion worth bothering about after 1893. Now the Ndebele had shown, in the rebellion and in their defence of the Matopos, that they were very much worth bothering about. Alert to them for the first time Rhodes began to feel out how he could 'square' the senior *indunas*.

At this first *indaba*, even while insisting that the matter to be discussed was peace and not grievances, he made some significant concessions. There was the explicit promise to disband the Ndebele Police; there was the clearly implied promise to reform adminis-tration and the pledge that he himself would stay on in Rhodesia to do it. The abuses they complained of, said Rhodes, were 'past and done with. Such things will not happen again.' And Stent makes it clear, in his account of the Ndebele reaction, that these promises were taken as such. 'Rhodes was on their side. He was not going to defend the cattle collectors. There was to be a fresh start.' Most importantly of all, however, Rhodes also pledged the personal security of the senior *indunas*, proscribed though they were under the terms of the Proclamation. Nearly a year later Rhodes, who had hitherto maintained that the future of the *indunas* had not been discussed, gave an account of the guarantee given 'at my first meeting with the Matabele'. 'I myself considered', he wrote, 'that any Chief who ordered any *individual* murder was equally guilty with the man who actually committed the crime and would not be exempted from punishment'; however 'proof of a *general* instruction to wipe out the whites must not render the chiefs liable to be tried for murder'. The distinction was an important one for the Ndebele leaders in the Matopos, none of whom were in the event put on trial.[1]

These leaders felt at the end of the first *indaba* that enough had been gained to justify continuing negotiations; they assured Rhodes of their desire to surrender; and asked for time to consult the leaders of other sections of the nation. Rhodes and his party rode home elated. 'I have been sitting with the rebel chiefs in the hills for about four hours,' wrote Rhodes to Grey, 'and the war is over as far as this part is concerned.' As for Sauer and Stent they rushed off to wire instructions to their agents 'to buy Chartered'.[2]

It will be seen that Rhodes was being somewhat disingenuous

[1] Rhodes to Secretary, B.S.A.C., Cape Town, 24 June 1897; Grey to Milner, 2 July 1897, C.O., C.P., S.A., No. 522, enclosures No. 4 and 8 in No. 61.
[2] Rhodes to Grey, 21 Aug. 1896, AM 1/2/1.

when he assured Sir Richard Martin a few days later that 'trans-
actions with rebel chiefs are taking the form of nothing more than
preliminary negotiations. He is confident that they will ultimately
submit in terms of the Proclamation. He has given no undertaking or promise to the chiefs of any kind. In his first interview
Mr Rhodes did not deal with the question of the chiefs' personal
treatment in case of surrender.' And as the negotiations continued
so more undertakings and promises were given. Individual *indunas*
who came into Rhodes' camp after August 21st—and there were a
stream of them—were given individual assurances. And at the
second *indaba* on August 28th Rhodes found himself forced to give
further general pledges.[1]

This *indaba* was, indeed, a much stormier affair than the first and
more famous meeting. It was attended not only by the senior *indunas* but also by representatives of the party that wanted to continue fighting—'the Mlimo's headmen' and the younger warriors.
'It was remarked by one who was present at both *indabas*', recorded
the *Morning Post* on October 12th, 'that he felt much more nervous
and uncomfortable through the second of these than at the first.
Indeed, had it not been for the personal influence of Dhliso there
might have been trouble. The rebels could be seen on the neighbouring kopjes in considerable numbers and all seemed to carry
rifles while many had well filled bandoliers. . . . In one of the lulls
in the conversation an old induna exclaimed, "the happiest man
in the country is the man who is dead for at least he died fighting
for his country".'

Dhliso and Babyaan began as spokesmen, once again enumer-
ating the grievances of the nation as at the first *indaba*. This time,
however, they 'were continually interrupted by the younger
men'. The younger element found a spokesman in Lobengula's
secretary, Karl Kumalo, who had been arrested in Bulawayo at
the beginning of the rising; convicted of intent to rebel on no other
ground, he maintained, than that he was 'an educated native';
shot through the head 'while attempting to escape' and left for
dead. Kumalo's 'resurrection', as the white press called it, was
decidedly inconvenient; not only was he animated by bitter personal grievance but he also showed disconcerting knowledge of the
political situation among the whites and of Sir Richard Martin's

[1] Martin to Goodenough, 27 Aug. 1896, C.O., C.P., S.A., No. 520, p. 493;
The Times, 9 Sept. 1896.

intention to hold an inquiry into the past administration of Rhodesia. Kumalo, however, was a less typical spokesman of the intransigents than the young *induna* whose exchanges with Rhodes are recorded by Stent. 'There was a movement among the natives and a young chief who might best be described as insolent to the elders of his own tribe and particularly so to the white men put in a pertinent question. "Where are we to live when it is over?" he said. "The white man claims all the land." Rhodes replied at once, "We will give you settlements. We will set apart locations for you; we will give you land." The young chief shouted angrily, "You will give us land in our own country! That's good of you!" '

Rhodes then objected to talking to the young chief while he still had his rifle in his hand; the young chief said, 'You will have to talk to me with my rifle in my hand. I find if I talk with my rifle in my hand the white man pays more attention to what I say. Once I put my rifle down I am nothing. I am just a dog to be kicked.'

Rhodes rose to the challenge to his negotiating skill. 'Rhodes actually left the European side of the *indaba* and, crossing over to the rebels, as it were, sat with them, seeming to speak for them.' Some of the demands expressed clearly had to be rejected out of hand. 'One *induna* made a virulent attack on the friendly chief, Faku, and demanded his removal from the country. Mr Rhodes refused to comply with this demand and went on to defend Faku's conduct. His remarks occasioned an angry demonstration among the young Matabele, but Dhliso succeeded in calming them.' But other demands could be met. Kumalo, so Stent tells us, was 'squared' by 'a dip into the wonderful leather bag in which it was the habit of . . . [Rhodes' secretary] . . . to carry a considerable sum in hard cash'. On the key land issue Rhodes promised, as we have seen, to make an adequate land settlement; later he went further. In September the senior *indunas* followed up the question raised by the young firebrand. 'The Chiefs said the Matabele wanted to come out of the hills but the question of where they were to settle presented a difficulty. Somabulana, Secombo and Dhliso . . . wanted to settle on the gardens occupied by them in Lobengula's time. Mr Rhodes replied that it could be arranged.'

As this example shows the senior *indunas* of the Umlugulu faction were shrewd negotiators themselves. Though they used their influence to calm down the young men it was much in their interests for the whites to be aware that there was a continued readiness to fight among the Ndebele and they presented themselves to Rhodes and Colenbrander as the indispensable intermediaries through whom alone peace could be achieved. Moreover they were quick to follow up any advantage won by the more intransigent party in debate. Thus Babyaan, at this second *indaba*, 'after inveighing for some time against the treatment of the Matabele', picked up Karl Kumalo's point. 'He had heard that an induna from the white queen had come into the country to conduct an inquiry. The news had made him glad because he was sure the truth would now be heard.' He and the other leaders now demanded that the 'queen's induna' should attend the next *indaba*. An accommodation between Rhodes and Babyaan and his colleagues, it was being subtly suggested, was necessary not only to achieve peace but also to avert the worst consequences of an imperial inquiry into Company administration. It is interesting to note that the hint was taken; in October 1896 the senior *indunas* were so satisfied with the terms that they had achieved that Colenbrander was able to inform the Colonial Office that he was prepared to bring a delegation of them over to London to testify to their support of the new system of native administration and of continuing Company rule.[1]

Meanwhile, outside the small circle of the negotiators, there was almost universal white dismay. Members of Rhodes' personal faction were able to take the sudden change from war to peace in their stride—'Rhodes is a marvellous man', wrote Jarvis on August 25th, 'and brought off this *Indaba* with the Chiefs splendidly. It was an extraordinarily plucky thing for him to do'—but settlers and soldiers were disconcerted and suspicious. 'The authorities refuse to give particulars of the conditions arranged with the Matopo rebels', it was reported late in August, 'and all sorts of rumours are in circulation'; it was said that the loyalist chief Gambo and the scout John Grootboom had both warned that the rebels were insincere in the negotiations. 'Rhodesia demands a little more than peace,' cried the *Bulawayo Sketch*; 'they demand justice. . . . Let it not be said that all this noble blood has been spilt without meeting the reward that has been the great incentive to volunteering—punishment for the dastardly crimes committed. Imagine the disgust of a man who has jeopardized his life daily for

[1] For this account of the second *indaba* I have drawn upon Stent, op. cit; *The Times*, 31 Aug. and 19 Sept; Colenbrander to Colonial Office, 30 Oct. 1896, CO., CP., S.A., No. 517, pp. 330–1.

a purpose, seen his friends fall around him, and then learnt that the foe he was bent on punishing had been petted and encouraged. . . . They deserve no consideration as patriots . . . their grievances bear no comparison with the cowardly un-Zulu-like outrages they have committed. As is surmised, rinderpest had little to do with it; the Rising was the execution of a deeply laid scheme planned by the leaders such as Umlugulu and Sekombo and the murders a deliberate determination to fiendish cruelty.' [1]

Nor did the published defences of the negotiations do much to pacify this indignation since they all admitted that the Ndebele had not been fully defeated. 'It is easy to imagine how hard a task it must have been for Mr Rhodes to treat for peace with armed and unsubdued rebels,' wrote John X. Merriman to the *South African Telegraph* on August 28th. 'By so doing he has, at the cost of his own natural feelings, averted the chance of a great disaster to South Africa. Few recognize how critical the position in Matabeleland has become, with the handful of white men in a vast country, with rinderpest and famine all around, and with the rainy season drawing near. Time in these matters is on the side of civilization and the white man and it is just this precious gain that has been secured by Mr Rhodes' negotiations. I would take leave to remind his critics that . . . [it is not] . . . the first time that an inconclusive native war has terminated by a peace, but in the long run the white man has gone forward.'

Even less palatable to settlers was De Vere Stent's advocacy of the negotiations. 'It would perhaps have been more dramatic to have made Somabulana degrade and abase himself as did King Prempeh,' he wrote to the *Cape Times* in October, 'but it would have cost hundreds of lives, both white and black. Then, again, we have not all the right on our side. The native administration in Matabeleland has been rotten and corrupt to the core. . . . A few weeks more fighting would have turned these men into banditti whose hand would have been turned against every white man and Rhodesia would have known no peace for years to come.'

Nor was discontent limited to the whites of Rhodesia. It was fully shared by the representatives of that very imperial government which in 1893 had been so suspicious of the alliance between Rhodes and the settlers and so anxious to negotiate itself with the

[1] *The Times*, 20 Aug. 1896; *Bulawayo Sketch*, 22 Aug. and 29 Aug. 1896; Jarvis to his mother, 25 Aug. 1896, JA 4/1/1.

Ndebele leaders. Circumstances had now changed greatly; the only constant was that once again the imperial authorities found themselves presented by Rhodes with a *fait accompli*.

The most important of those who found Rhodes' proceedings difficult to stomach in 1896 was Sir Richard Martin, imperial Deputy-Commissioner. This was partly because he had been entrusted with the duty of making peace and imposing surrender conditions and yet had not been informed of Rhodes' intentions to meet the rebels on August 21st. But he had more solid reasons which are best set out in an elaborate protest recorded by him after the second *indaba*. He desired just administration *after* complete conquest and aimed to balance the essential interests of black and white 'small men'. He feared that in the *indabas* the 'big men' were coming to terms at the expense of their followers and that neither severity nor justice would be assured. 'On August 22nd Mr Rhodes reported a most successful meeting with the rebels in the Matopos', he wrote, 'and declared the war over as far as that part was concerned. However, at a subsequent meeting on August 28th, judging from the report of Mr Stent . . . I conclude that the attitude of the Chiefs was by no means one of decided submission but took the form rather of self defence. On August 31st Mr Rhodes sent me a message saying he did not think it would be wise just at present to send to the rebels to come to another meeting; they would interpret a kind of weakness. From this I gather Mr Rhodes was not satisfied that the Chiefs and people had shown that spirit of submission which, having a view to permanent tranquillity in the future, it is essential that a defeated native race should show to their white conquerors; that negotiations appear to me from information received to have been rather of a conciliating than dictating character and though this policy may appear expedient to the Government of the country for the time being, it can only have one effect on the native mind, namely, to exaggerate their strength and our weakness.' Martin declared himself 'entirely opposed to the manner in which the present negotiations were being conducted'; denouncing them as inconsistent with the terms of the Proclamation, as unworthy of the dignity of the Queen's Government—'native customs demand that the lesser chief should come to meet the greater', and as likely to produce constant trouble in the future. Martin's own view was that 'none of the principal Chiefs in the Matopos should be allowed to escape trial, as their strength and influence is acknowledged by all, and they appear to have been either instigators in rebellion or implicated in murders'.[1]

Martin, backed by Acting High Commissioner Goodenough, proposed to assume control of the negotiations; to present the Ndebele *indunas* with a formal warning that they would be put on trial but might thereafter be pardoned; and to demand an unconditional surrender and giving up of arms within a few days. 'The message I propose to send to the Chiefs', he wrote, 'amounts to an ultimatum and from what Mr Rhodes says will, I think, stop his further negotiations.' 'That consummate ass, Sir Richard Martin,' wrote Jarvis, 'will try his best to upset everything and prolong hostilities.' [2] Prospects of stopping Rhodes from further negotiations—even 'provisional' ones—seemed much better than in 1893.

Martin at this moment enjoyed the support of the great majority of whites in Southern Rhodesia; his formal position was unassailable under the terms of the instructions issued to him by the Colonial Secretary; he was possessed with a conviction that Rhodes was out to save the Chartered Company's skin no matter what happened thereafter to the settlers—or to the Africans for that matter. But even in his strange alliance with the settlers he was no match for Rhodes. Rhodes had a keen sense of the likely reactions of Joseph Chamberlain, the Colonial Secretary. He did not respect him—'Chamberlain has been too weak for words', wrote Jarvis from Inyati on the march to Taba Zi Ka Mambo. 'As Rhodes truly says, "I thought he was a strong man but after all you cannot expect much out of Birmingham workshops." He has allowed himself to be scared off at every point when he had the ball at his feet.' But he knew that Chamberlain was in a difficult position between the philanthropists on the one hand and the fact of Rhodes' knowledge of the extent of his involvement in the events that led up to the Jameson Raid on the other. Rhodes knew that Chamberlain was prepared to let the Company maintain its jurisdiction in Rhodesia if it was at all possible in return for silence about the ramifications of the Jameson Raid. He knew also that the Colonial Secretary would find it difficult, if not impossible,

---

[1] Martin to Goodenough, 1 Sept. 1896, C.O., C.P., S.A., No. 520, pp. 520–1.
[2] Martin to Goodenough, 27 Aug. 1896, ibid., p. 493; Jarvis to his mother, 27 Aug. 1896, JA 4/1/1.

to over-rule his negotiations because of objections that they were too merciful to the Ndebele. It was for this reason that he had chosen Stent to accompany the party to the first *indaba*; in addition to his vivid gifts as a journalist Stent had a reputation as a humanitarian, had criticized the treatment of the Ndebele in 1893 and was now prepared to make amends by defending the negotiations on humanitarian and progressive grounds.[1]

These calculations turned out to be correct. 'If as I gather', Chamberlain cabled to Goodenough on August 26th, 'Grey and Rhodes lean to clemency Martin and Carrington should work cordially with former. . . . Martin's powers, you will understand, were given to him in order to enable him to restrain tendency to harshness.' 'There would be great difficulty', he cabled on the 27th, 'in defending an attitude of less leniency than that advocated by representatives of the British South Africa Company.' And on September 4th he cut through Martin's continued objections. 'I am in favour of accepting the views of Lord Grey with regard to exercising clemency towards rebel chiefs in making terms with them,' he cabled. 'I am prepared to agree to ring-leaders, mentioned in the Proclamation being promised their lives, and, if necessary, exempted from trial should the negotiations require it. Even in the case of those implicated in murders I should be willing to adopt the same course if it is considered to be required.'[2]

Since Chamberlain also expressed the view that there was no reason why Rhodes should not continue to conduct negotiations, with Martin's advice, and that the opinions of Lord Grey should be given great weight, Martin found himself obliged to abandon his plan for an ultimatum. Indeed, he found himself agreeing to appear with Rhodes and Grey at a third *indaba* at which formal royal approval of the previous negotiations would be expressed. Once again we owe our most vivid record of the third *indaba*, held on September 9th, to Lady Grey. 'Yesterday was a very interesting and rather an exciting day,' she wrote on September 10th, 'for we went to a real *indaba* with the rebels about 5 or 6 miles off in the Matopos Hills, where they were to have clearly explained to them the terms on which their surrender would be accepted if they truly wish for the end of the war and peace, i.e. that they must give up

[1] Jarvis to his mother, July 1896, ibid.
[2] Chamberlain to Goodenough, 26 Aug., 27 Aug., and 4 Sept. 1896, C.O., C.P., S.A., No. 520, p. 402, p. 403, p. 427.

their arms and come out of the Matopos and go to their kraals and dig and sow as usual and then those that have taken part in the rebellion without any connection with murder committed in cold blood shall be freely pardoned, while those who did take part in the murders must stand their trial and receive punishment. . . . We had brought some of the camp chairs with us so that we might sit with the more dignity and had the honour at the *indaba* of sitting in the posh row. . . . His Honour the Administrator in the middle, to his right Sir Richard Martin, and to his left Mr Rhodes . . . the rebel chiefs squatted on the ground immediately in front, a compact little body; there were 44 of them not counting a few friendlies who had come too. We had to wait some time after we arrived and took up position before they appeared and meanwhile we all ate our luncheon. Then with glasses we saw them descending a kopje about a mile away in front of us. They were being brought to us by a Mr Armstrong and a Mr Fynn, 2 young Native Commissioners, who had gone in to fetch them.' After some difficulty, created by the sight of Martin's cavalry escort and the Union Jack standard which he had erected, the *indunas* were persuaded to approach and the *indaba* began.[1]

Rhodes began the proceedings by introducing Grey and Martin to the *indunas*, amongst whom were Umlugulu, Babyaan, Sikombo, Dhliso, Somabulana. Grey then told the Ndebele that 'Her Majesty approves words already spoken to them at two previous *indabas*', and continued to spell out the demand for the surrender of arms and the surrender of murderers. Martin then spoke, doing his best to give a new tone to the proceedings. 'I expressed regret at seeing Chiefs and people before me under present conditions. I said when I left England Her Majesty the Queen was under the impression natives and whites were living together in harmony. I pointed out how they had burnt houses and killed women and children without mercy and could not understand how they had dared to commit such acts if they realized government of the country was under Her Majesty the Queen. Government surprised at such a man as Babyaan, who had been to England and seen power of Queen, not realizing the hopelessness of such a war, and imagining for a moment that the Queen would allow such acts to go unpunished. However, the Queen, in her mercy, will even now pardon those who have killed her people in fair fight,

[1] Lady Grey to her children, 10 Sept. 1896, GR 1/1/1.

and even the Chiefs who led *impis* in fight; but she, in her justice, says those who have committed murder must suffer. It is not the time to discuss grievances, but to make known the terms on which the rebels can surrender.' [1]

Rhodes must have been glad when this meeting, so different from the two earlier *indabas*, was safely over. The *indunas* had had no chance to recite the grievances of the nation but had had to sit and listen to Martin lecture them with as good a grace as they could manage. Still, all previous promises had been confirmed— even if Martin had very little idea what those were. Above all the promise of personal amnesty had been repeated and as Lady Grey wrote, 'there was no great fear for this lot in the thought of surrender for you see they have been promised a pardon for their rebellion provided none of them individually took part in or instigated any of the real murders, and as none of them in this district did commit any murders, as long as they put over their guns they have nothing to fear if they can only be convinced of this'. Grey himself thought that the meeting had been very successful. Martin remained totally unconvinced. 'I cannot say I considered the tone of the meeting satisfactory. The Chiefs did not salute and at times showed a decidedly impertinent air, and spoke as though they had as much right to demand the withdrawal of troops which they complained were in their gardens, as we had to call them to lay down their arms. I am still of the opinion that this is a cunning device on the part of the rebels and if the troops were withdrawn I think they would still remain in the hills and be still less inclined to give up their arms.' [2]

Nothing now remained to complete Rhodes' design and to complete the discomfiture of Martin save the actual surrenders and the bringing in of guns. There followed a period of agonizing suspense. 'The surrender is a very ticklish business,' wrote Lady Victoria Grey on September 14th. 'Of course they have not yet really done so. At each fresh *indaba* the chiefs say they must have time to collect their people before they come out of the hills and as long as they remain in the Matopos and do not deliver up their arms the imperial military authorities will not pay any attention to these

---

[1] Martin to Rosmead, 10 Sept. 1896, C.O., C.P., S.A., No. 520, p. 446.
[2] Lady Grey to her children, op. cit; Martin to Goodenough, 13 Sept. 1896, C.O., C.P., S.A., No. 520, pp. 574-5; verbatim account of the *indaba* of 9 Sept, 1896, ibid., pp. 575-7.

negotiations but carry on their own tactics as if no surrender was being contemplated and as if they were going to fight on all through the wet season. This annoys Daddy very much as *the* important thing now is to give the natives confidence and not to frighten them by any more attacks. . . . They said at the *indaba*, "If you remove the white *impis* we will come out and go to our gardens." The general, on the other hand, says, "Until they have come out and gone to their gardens and delivered up their arms my men shall not budge an inch." So proceedings are rather at a standstill at present.' Carrington sat down to make a list of the additional men and equipment he would need when fighting began again in 1897; Martin gave interviews to the press in which he admitted with gloomy relish that the rebels 'had shown no sign of any intention' to give up arms and that 'he could not say what steps would be taken in the event of their persisting in their refusal'. Rhodes, waiting in his camp in the Matopos, feared that the Mwari representatives had won the upper hand after all; he remembered that on September 9th the 'Mlimo's mouthpiece' had turned up to the *indaba* arrogantly wearing the coat of a murdered white.[1]

We get a picture of the tensions of September from the first reports home of William Henry Milton, the man recruited by Rhodes to reform the Rhodesian administrative service. On September 18th Milton wrote: 'Things here are very mixed and until today no one knew what would result—Peace or War. Earl Grey however came in this morning and told me at once that the news is distinctly good. The 2 principal rebels in the Matopos have sent to C. J. Rhodes to say they are surrendering to him today and it is certain that their followers will come out so I hope that matter is settled. Rhodes, Grey, Carrington and a few titled under-strappers are all talking at once in the next room . . . Rhodes is in town today for the first time since beginning of August and is trying to induce Carrington to clear out with his troops.' With this idea Milton was in full sympathy, adding the dislike of the born civil servant for military display and extravagance to the other Company motives for getting the imperial forces out of Rhodesia. 'Everything official here', he wrote, 'is in an absolutely rotten condition and will continue so until we can clear out the Honourable

---

[1] Victoria Grey to Charles Grey, 14 Sept. 1896, GR 1/1/1; *The Times*, 17 Sept. 1896.

and military elements which are rampant everywhere. . . . If we can only induce the natives to surrender and disarm and get rid of Carrington everything will go ahead.' [1]

The tension was beginning to tell on Rhodes and Grey; to their pleas for an immediate reduction of the imperial forces on grounds of approaching famine, the answer came stolidly back that nothing could be done until the African surrender had been made a reality. On September 18th Grey reported that Rhodes had at last taken the step urged earlier by Martin and delivered an ultimatum; through Babyaan and Dhliso he had informed 'the minor *indunas*' that unless they surrendered quickly fighting would begin. Whether because of this or whether because the senior *indunas* had learnt of the Company's intentions to institute a new structure of African administration in which as salaried and recognized officials they were to have a part, the long African deliberations drew suddenly to an end. On September 21st Rhodes wrote jubilantly from his camp: 'Things are looking really bright. Babyaan is still with me. Dhliso went to Plumer this morning and from there to fetch his wives. Finally the man we considered would fight to the last, namely Unthwani, the man who wore Fynn's coat at the last *indaba*, is here and sleeps here tonight. You must remember that Unthwani is the Mlimo's mouthpiece and it speaks volumes that he should have come out. . . . We may say the matter is over as far as these hills are concerned; but I shall not move until Babyaan and Dhliso are at their kraals for fear of some misunderstanding.' Shortly after reports came in that Sikombo and Somabulana were at Colenbrander's camp. Peace had become a reality. [2]

Rhodes and Grey moved quickly to cement their good relations with the senior *indunas*. On October 13th the fourth *indaba* was held, attended by all the rebel leaders and also by the most important of the loyalists. 'They were asked to state their grievances,' wrote Grey, 'assurances being given to them that they would be carefully considered and if proved to be well founded would be removed. Their chief grievance was that they were as sheep without a herd and had no one to whom they could go for advice and guidance. They were informed that it is the intention of the government to make those indunas who can satisfy the government that they are worthy of trust salaried headmen.' The loyalists Gambo,

[1] Milton to his wife, 18 Sept. 1896, ML 1/1/2.
[2] Rhodes to Grey, 21 Sept. 1896, BA 2/1/1; *The Times*, 23 Sept. 1896.

Faku and Mjaan were at once made salaried *indunas*; the rebels
Sikombo, Somabulana and Dhliso were given horses to enable
them to collect their people together and told that if they proved
trustworthy they would also be recognized as official heads of one
of the twelve districts into which Matabeleland was now to be
divided.[1]

As might have been expected, these conversions of proscribed
rebels into rewarded and recognized authorities was received with
fury by the whites of Bulawayo. 'Sekombo has licked the ground
and the promise of horses has been received with acclamation but
these little civilities, however interesting as illustrating high life in
the Matopos, is not yet consummation of peace and does not necessarily mean pacification,' thundered the *Bulawayo Sketch* on October 17th. 'The iron hand must now be felt beneath its glove covering.' On October 24th it greeted the recent visit of the rebel
leaders to Bulawayo with ferocious irony. 'Among the fashionable
arrivals of this week we have the honour to record that of the
Rebel Chiefs, looking none the worse for wear after their arduous
labours in the Matopos. At an interview kindly vouchsafed by
them they report with becoming modesty that they consider good
work has been done. Sekombo, who looks fit for anything (and
doesn't belie his looks) reckons that they have done more to settle
the native question in a few months than the Government would
have done in five years. He intends taking a little rest after his
labours and with his friends spend a short vacation in the plains.
Horses and topboots have been supplied to them by their ad-
mirers so that they can get about a little quicker and without fear
of hurting their feet which have become slightly chafed from climbing over and under the rugged boulders of the late scene of their
labours.' In this way was the work of Rhodes, which later generations have agreed to accept as his crowning achievement, received
initially by the settlers of Rhodesia.

Yet in the irony of the *Sketch* there was an element of truth.
Looked at in one light the Ndebele rebellion and the negotiations
which ended it *had* done more 'to settle the native question' than
the preceding years of Company rule. After 1893 the Ndebele
leaders had become 'non-persons'; they were never consulted
about their people; the institutions of the Ndebele state were

[1] Grey to Rosmead, 13 Oct. 1896, C.O., C.P., S.A., p. 640; verbatim report
of the *indaba*, ibid., pp. 692–3.

either destroyed or ignored. The new era initiated by the series of *indabas* of 1896—which were followed by an even more elaborate wooing of the *indunas* in 1897—was very different. Grey described the new policy as 'restoring as far as we can to the *indunas* the authority which they had in Lobengula's time and which since his overthrow they have lacked'. What were to be the full implications of this policy—slightly re-worded by the *Pall Mall Gazette* to, 'the *indunas* are to get back all of their authority of Lobengula's time that is compatible with white supremacy'—remained to be seen. But at the end of 1896 it might have been claimed that the rebellion had been far from futile. The Ndebele nation had come into official existence once more; promises had been received about the redress of grievances; many of the Ndebele were back at their old homes for the first time since 1893.[1]

This view of the peace negotiations was no more taken by the intransigents of the north-east than it was by the settlers of Bulawayo. Mkwati, Mtini, Mpotshwana and other leaders of the old north-east faction totally rejected all surrender overtures and took stringent steps to see that their followers did not respond to them either. After his flight from Taba Zi Ka Mambo, Mkwati gathered his followers around him in the Somabula forest which now became the country of the new order. 'The Mlimo is in the Somabula forest', testified Malima, 'and has told the natives that the Shangani river is the boundary between the whites and him, a boundary which the whites will not cross and that they can live there without fear.' The pause in military operations which followed the beginning of the Matopos negotiations appeared to justify this promise; the whites waited for Mkwati's following to surrender but very few surrenders came.[2]

Gradually a very interesting picture emerged from the reports of prisoners and spies. While the leaders of the old Ndebele nation in the Matopos were seeking the best terms for it through negotiation Mkwati was using his Shona support to prevent Ndebele surrenders in the Somabula area. On August 3rd, for instance, Native Commissioner Gielgud wrote to say that the hard core of Mkwati's force consisted of the Jingen regiment under Nkomo, Mtini's people, and the followers of the Shona commander,

[1] Grey to Hawksley, 16 Oct. 1896, C.O., C.P., S.A., No. 517, pp. 300–4; *Pall Mall Gazette*, 28 Nov. 1896.

[2] Malima's evidence, 1 Aug. 1896, LO 5/6/2.

Makumbi. The local MaHoli were also 'armed and declared they will fight for the Mlimo'. 'My informant further says that the Mlimo has instituted a "police force" of his own and is doing his utmost to prevent the Matabele coming to in surrender. Any messenger found with a pass unless he goes straight to the Mlimo with it is killed; any people speaking of the Mlimo as a fraud are dealt with in like manner. I have here an umfaan who managed to escape when his people were killed by an *impi* acting under the orders of Incomo because the head-man, named Somapunga, talked of going in to surrender. In other cases people who are suspected of disloyalty to the Mlimo are surprised by the "Police" and disarmed, their guns, etc., being given to the Maholi who have declared heart and soul for the Mlimo.' On August 6th he wrote again: 'The Mlimo has instructed the Maholes to kill all Matabele they may find returning to the white people or carrying messages calling on the people to surrender.' On the 10th Native Commissioner Fynn reported the same situation from his district. 'From what I can gather from the natives that the Makalakas are the strongest today in that district and prevent the Matabeles from coming to surrender.' In his view once the news of the surrender negotiations reached them the Ndebele would 'break away from this band of Makalakas'.[1]

This determined struggle against any attempt to 'betray the revolution' continued for several months, though increasingly as a desperate rear-guard action. On September 14th *The Times* reported that an ex-teacher from the Inyati mission had managed to escape from the Shangani district. 'He says that the rebels cannot retire northwards even if they wished to do so. They are entirely under the influence of Mkwati, the Mlimo's prophet, who has posted pickets of his staunchest followers around the district, between the Umvungo and Shashi rivers, so as to completely hem the natives in. The country is difficult, being densely wooded. Matombo adds that many of the rebels long for the advent of a strong power to counteract Mkwati's influence.' As late as November Ndebele messengers came in to warn the Native Commissioner of Gwelo 'that Mkwati, one of Mlimo's prophets, intends sending an *impi* to murder those who have surrendered'.[2]

[1] Gielgud to C.N.C., 6 Aug. 1896, LO 5/6/2; Gielgud to C.N.C., 3 Aug. 1896; Fynn to C.N.C., 10 Aug. 1896, BA 2/9/2.
[2] *The Daily Telegraph*, 28 Nov. 1896.

As far as the Ndebele were concerned Mkwati's attempt to keep the rebellion alive was doomed to failure. News began to come through of the Matopos negotiations and increasingly they seemed to hold out some promise of advantage to the Ndebele, though none to the Shona. Surrender in the Matopos meant that the whites were free to turn their full strength on to the north-east—at the end of August and in September the white attack on the Somabula and Shangani area was opened and Baden-Powell's patrol harried the rebels in the forest. Uwini, Mkwati's father-in-law, after a desperate defence of his stronghold was captured, court-martialled, and shot on the spot. Mtini and Mkwati kept only one move ahead of the white patrols. These events were followed by large-scale surrenders of Ndebele. 'I asked the natives now on Battlefield Block what was their opinion of the death of Uwinya,' wrote Fynn, 'and they replied that they were glad; that "the Government had now opened the way for the surrender of the Matabele". Since then many natives from that district have come in to surrender to mc.' On September 23rd Baden-Powell, though disappointed that he had not captured Mkwati or Makumbi or Mtini, reported to Carrington that his patrols 'have had a great effect on the rebels generally. Mkombi's "preventive" posts having been broken up, natives are coming in to the Native Commissioner in numbers'. After September the trickle of surrenders became a flood; some of the leading figures of the old north-east faction came in to take advantage of the new amnesty conditions, Nyamanda among them. Mkwati's leadership was coming to appear as a Rozwi conspiracy against Ndebele interests and in late September a number of members of the Ndebele royal family told Native Commissioner Fynn the story of Mkwati and Uwini's plot for 'the destruction and complete humiliation of their hereditary foes, the Matabele', which has been cited in Chapter Four.[1]

Nor was Mpotshwana's different form of intransigence any more successful. His idea of trekking north and crossing the Zambesi ran into a number of serious difficulties. One was that drought had made the northern areas virtually impossible for large numbers of men to move through; there was no food to be had. Another was that the Lozi were guarding the fords across the Zambesi and that

[1] Fynn to Baden-Powell, 1 Oct. 1896; Baden-Powell to Carrington, 23 Sept. 1896, PO 1/1/1. See also BA 2/9/2.

those members of the royal family and other senior Ndebele who managed to reach them were arrested and put under custody by King Lewanika's son, Litia; some of them committed suicide rather than be returned as prisoners to the whites. It soon became clear, in short, that the time had passed for the preservation of the Ndebele ideal by means of the trek north; if anything was to be saved, so it seemed, it would have to be saved in Umlugulu and Sikombo's way, through hard negotiation with Rhodes.

Yet irrational as the appeal of the intransigents seemed in the last months of 1896 it is possible now to see that from some points of view their instinct was the sound one. We have already seen what dangers the events of 1896 presented to continued Company rule in Southern Rhodesia. Elsewhere in Africa African resistance and rebellion forced the withdrawal of Company administrations and compelled the imperial powers, however reluctantly, to commit themselves directly. This happened both in British and in German East Africa, for instance, and no-one can doubt that the history of Kenya would have been very different had Company rule persisted there until 1923 as was the case in Southern Rhodesia. Martin's insensitive handling of the surrender issue might not have held out much hope for the management of African affairs under direct imperial administration, but it was not long before the growing sophistication of African politics in Rhodesia brought home the advantages of imperial over local control. Nyamanda, the eldest son of Lobengula, proscribed leader of the rising, the young man's candidate for King in 1896, who surrendered under the terms of the Matopos agreement and became a salaried *induna* under the new administrative regime, was also the chief signatory of a petition in 1919, demanding on behalf of the whole Ndebele nation direct imperial control of African affairs. Company rule, especially Company rule preserved as it was preserved in 1896 partly through a series of concessions to the indignant settlers, implied an inevitable movement towards settler self-government.[1]

Even after the *indaba* of September 9th there was still resistance to Rhodes' and Grey's desire to get the imperial troops out of Rhodesia before the end of the year; Martin for a long time refused

---

[1] For Nyamanda's later political career see, T. O. Ranger, 'Traditional Authorities and the Rise of Modern Politics in Southern Rhodesia', *The Zambesian Past*, eds. E. T. Stokes and R. Brown, Manchester, 1966.

to accept the surrenders as 'satisfactory' and demanded the retention of a considerable force. Chamberlain, in the end conceding Grey's reiterated demands, did so with the rider that Grey must assume full responsibility for the future; another rising and the Charter could not be saved. It is plain that in this situation the readiness of the Ndebele leaders to come to terms—even if they were good terms—was a main element in the preservation of the Company's control of Rhodesia and hence in the later movement to settler rule. Because of the increasing evidence of their submission all imperial troops were in fact removed from Matabeleland before the end of the year, save for 200 Hussars kept to reassure the timid citizens of Bulawayo, and these were soon despatched to Mashonaland. Ndebele acceptance of and satisfaction with the new administrative arrangements could be—and was—used as an argument against any change of government. Thus Colenbrander was able to write on October 30th, 1896, to emphasize that the whole settlement with the Ndebele depended solely upon their trust in Rhodes. 'They do not know, or dread, Imperial officers. I consider the situation so grave in the event of the Parliamentary Committee recommending a change which would be likely to shake the native confidence in Mr Rhodes and the native policy he has succeeded in establishing that I have felt it my duty to write this letter.' He was fully prepared, he concluded, to bring the Ndebele chiefs over to England to express there their loyalty and their faith 'in the present system of administration as it has been explained to them by Mr Rhodes'. The irony of the contrast between Nyamanda's situation in 1896—prepared to testify in England on behalf of Company rule—and his situation in 1919 —petitioning the English Government for an assumption of direct responsibility—is one to be savoured; in it lies one of the essential themes of the political history of Southern Rhodesian Africans.[1]

But these are considerations which, however important in retrospect, were remote from African thinking in 1896. What most concerned the Africans of Matabeleland as that terrible year drew to a close was the devastated condition of the province and the fate of those individuals who had played a leading role in the rising. The rising left Matabeleland devastated. It was not so much the loss of life during the fighting but the destruction of crops which struck

[1] Colenbrander to Colonial Office, 30 Oct. 1896, C.O., C.P., S.A., No. 517, pp. 330–1.

African society hardest. 'The people are starving,' wrote Carnegie in October. 'A man said to me last week, "Teacher, I would have been to see you long ago but was afraid of dying from hunger when I got half way to your house." They eat ox-skins, rinderpest ones, boiled in water; roots and berries in the veld. It's the most hungry season I have known in the country. The poor bairns look thin, pale and starving and the old folk haggard and miserable. It's among such people I live now, who come in crowds clamouring for a few peas of corn to eat. The cry of the children strikes me hard. I have already assisted 50 families but many more require immediate help and there is no food to give them. How can you preach to a starving people? I can't.'

'Rinderpest, war and famine had left the natives in a truly exhausted state,' wrote a later memorialist. 'In the whole of Matabeleland there remained not more than 5000 head of cattle . . . milk was practically unobtainable for the sustenance of Native child-life. Women travelled miles to beg sufficient cow dung for preservation of their hut floors. Old residents of Bulawayo will remember the hordes of men, women and children, in all stages of emaciation, seeking a dole of three pounds of mealies at the Native Department office. An incredible number of deaths from starvation occurred.' The miseries which had impelled the Ndebele and their subject peoples to rebel were less acute than those which they now endured. Dependent upon the help of the very administration they had been fighting—one of Grey's arguments for the evacuation of the imperial troops was that 'the food needed for the troops might have kept 6000 natives alive for six months'—there was possibly little inclination among the majority of the people to worry much about the relationship of the rising and its ending to their political future.[1]

The leaders of the various rebel factions, however, were most personally concerned with the aftermath of the rising and with the way white attitudes towards it had developed. There was, as might have been expected, a sharp contrast between the lot of those who had led the surrenders in the Matopos and those who had headed the intransigents of the north-east. For a time little could be too good for the senior *indunas* who had made the peace— a correspondent who suggested, in no satirical spirit, early in 1897

[1] Carnegie to Thompson, 12 Oct. 1896, L.M.S., Matabele Mission, Vol. 5, No. 102; A statement of Native Policy, no date, S 82/A/260.

that each *induna* might be presented with a musical box was told by the Acting Administrator that the suggestion was an excellent one but 'that we have to expend a large amount on more tangible presents (and) I am afraid that at present we cannot carry your suggestion into effect'. On January 5th, 1897, a fifth *indaba* began, the most comprehensive of all, this time in Bulawayo itself. The Acting Administrator, Lawley, explained the new system to the chiefs, and the final appointments to the administrative districts were made. Of the 10 appointments announced during the *indaba* six went to ex-leaders of the rising. Nyamanda became head *induna* of the Bulawayo district; Nkomo head *induna* of the Inyati district; Somabulana head *induna* of Upper Insiza district; Sikombo head *induna* of Umzingwani district; Umlugulu head *induna* of Gwanda district; and Dhliso head *induna* of Matoppo district. The most surprising of these appointments, perhaps, was that of Umlugulu, who was regarded by many whites as the chief instigator of the rising, and who had not been in a position of secular authority during Lobengula's reign. 'Mlugulu though never an induna during Lobengula's reign', wrote the Chief Native Commissioner, 'had a considerable influence with the King and was one of his principal war doctors and also held the position of king maker. It was deemed advisable from a political point of view to make him a salaried induna.' [1]

The fate of others who had been associated with Umlugulu in the outbreak of the rising was very different. Siginyamatshe, for instance, was captured in the Filabusi district by Assistant Native Commissioner Wilson, in October 1897. 'On Sunday evening the Mlimo was secured to the wagon and had also gyves at his ankles,' reported the *Bulawayo Chronicle* on October 7th. 'A few hours after retiring the party was awakened by the barking of a dog, and hastily rising found the Mlimo had escaped. . . . After about half an hour, the night having a bright moon, Sgt-Major Ottey saw, on coming up to a spruit, the Mlimo up to his shoulders in water and brought him out, finding that his ankles were still secured. He was resecured and lodged in jail about 7 o'clock yesterday morning.' Siginyamatshe was charged with sedition and sentenced in June 1898 to 12 years with hard labour which he served 'on the break-water at Cape-Town'. In 1922 Siginyamatshe was one of three Mwari messengers active in Belingwe; now an old man who had

[1] *Chief Native Commissioner's Report for Matabeleland, year ending 31 Mar. 1898.*

survived into a new age, his efforts 'to recover some of his former prestige' were noted with tolerance by the Native Department.[1]

Makumbi, the commander of Mkwati's bodyguard, was sentenced to death for murder on August 19th, 1897, and hanged on November 15th of that year. Mtini was captured early in May 1897. 'Mtini, the Inyati induna, who headed the murder of Mr Native Commissioner Graham's party,' reported the *Chronicle* on May 1st, 'only appeared to realize that he was a prisoner when he was taken to the gaol on Monday. On being taken into the gaol Mtini suddenly whipped out a knife and tried to cut his throat. He, however, only succeeded in inflicting a slight gash before being secured.' 'Why Mtini, the murderers' chief from Inyati, should have been hindered on Monday last from committing suicide in the gaol where he had been placed is one of those questions where civilization over-rules the mark,' commented the *Sketch*. 'It would have saved a lot of trouble had the brute been allowed to give himself his own quietus.' Mtini was hanged later in the year. It was Mpotshwana who gave the most trouble. Hunted by patrols in the north he managed to elude them until captured by Gielgud in July 1897 'within a few miles of the Zambesi'. His death was thus recorded by the *Bulawayo Chronicle* on October 21st, 1897, 'Mpotchwana, the famous rebel chief, has died in gaol. His record was a singularly black one, even for a rebel chief. When he first appeared in the dock his expression was fearless and half amused. To the ordinary observer there was nothing in his appearance denoting a lust for bloodshed. As time after time he was remanded his confident bearing disappeared; suspense and confinement were evidently doing their work on the child of the desert. Before his demise enough evidence to convict him of murder ten times over had been adduced.' [2]

What, finally, of Mkwati, that remarkable man who had been responsible for so many of the crises of 1896? Mkwati was the most persistent and resilient of the rebel leaders. Driven out of the Somabula forest by Baden-Powell and at bitter odds with the Ndebele, he made for western Mashonaland. On the way 'the Matabele followers, who had suffered very much from hunger and

---

[1] Regina versus Siginyamatshe, HC/M, No. 329; N.C. Belingwe, to Superintendent of Natives, Bulawayo, 13 Apr. 1922, S/N/Byo. to C.N.C., Apr. 1922 and C.N.C. to Secretary, Administrator, 28 Apr. 1922, N 3/31/1.

[2] Regina versus Makumbi, HC/M, No. 177/63.

sickness, began to lose faith in the Mlimo's high priest, saying that they were being humbugged, and made a plot to kill him . . . but Matafen gave the priest, Mukwati, the tip and both Mukwati and Matafen cleared that night and the Matabeles being disgusted began to trek back. When they had gone Mukwati and Matafen returned and Mashiangombi sent over and his people carried the Mlimo's loot and placed it in his kraal and we all went and lived there.' So the Rozwi Child of Mwari, Tshiwa, described the arrival of Mkwati and the Taba Zi Ka Mambo cult representatives at Mashiangombi's kraal in October 1896. Deserted by the last of his Ndebele followers, Mkwati was as determined as ever that the fight should continue. The message given to Mashiangombi's people from Mkwati's oracular hut was still the same message that Mkwati had given to the Ndebele in March and to the western Shona in April and May: 'The Mlimo will kill all natives who made peace and we are going to fight again.' [1]

[1] Tshiwa's statement, 10 Jan. 1897, LO 5/4/1.

CHAPTER EIGHT

The Suppression of the Shona Rising

MEANWHILE a desperate struggle had been going on in Mashonaland. When the rising broke out there in June the whites were
taken at an even greater disadvantage than had been the case in
Matabeleland; on the news of the first killings in Hartley the
Salisbury administration had issued a warning to prospectors,
traders and farmers in which it had been compelled to spell out
that it was in no position to offer them protection or assistance.
'If the Makalakas and Mashonas were as clever and brave as they
are ignorant and feeble,' wrote *The Globe* on June 24th, in an un-
conscious testimony to the efficiency of the organization of the
rising, 'they could not have managed better or more boldly for
themselves.'

Salisbury seemed much more vulnerable to rebel attack than
Bulawayo had been and even although, as we have seen, the military organization of the Shona rising was unable to bring an
attacking force against the town, the first weeks in the Salisbury
laager were very nervous ones. Shona servants and labourers were
rounded up, and when they tried to escape, court-martialled and
shot: 'This is a time', said the Acting Administrator in Mashonaland, Judge Vintcent, 'for arbitrary power in the interests of the
general public.' He could only hold the whites of Salisbury loyal
to the charter by meeting their clamour for stern measures. The
clamour was, of course, a loud one. 'The last news from Mashonaland is still depressing,' wrote the *Bulawayo Sketch* on July 11th,
'and the Mashona are coming out in their true colours, fine beaut-
ies to be made pets of. If we are to hold this land a terrible example
must be made amongst the murderous insurgents. Punishment
first and kindness (if any Colonist can experience kindness to such
fiends) afterwards. The Mashonas have less excuse for such crimes,
inasmuch as they are not fighting for their independence; they
never possessed it in the past, and have experienced infinitely
better times than they ever had before the occupation. There is no
palliation to their crimes; punishment condign, if slow, must be
wreaked, and the Imperial Government should undertake it at

their own cost, as this is distinctly a colony for Englishmen, and the most true and loyal Colony Britain possesses.'[1]

Punishment condign if slow was an accurate prophecy; in the end the Shona paid heavily for the rising but it took a long time for this payment to be exacted. Contrary to all expectation the Shona rising, which broke out only two months before negotiations began with the Ndebele, long outlasted the rebellion in Matabeleland; it was not until the end of 1897 that it was crushed.

The offensive phase of the rising, its equivalent to the Umgusa phase in Matabeleland, lasted from June until the end of August; it took the form of an attack upon the communications system of white Mashonaland. On June 24th Vintcent cabled that the roads between Salisbury and Umtali and between Salisbury and Hartley were in rebel hands; 'the rebels are apparently cleverly sticking to the schantzes on hills and kopjes and lining all available roads'. It was impossible to clear the road to Umtali until the imperial force arrived, and that force would have to carry with it its own provisions and possess mountain guns; as for the Hartley road the commander of a patrol sent out along it had met 'the natives in a very large force strongly schantzed on the numerous kopjes lining the road. He had to fight his way through under heavy fire.'[2]

As we have seen it was decided to clear the roads by a double move towards Salisbury. The Mashonaland column, with some reinforcement, was sent under Colonel Beal to march from Bulawayo to Salisbury and thus to relieve the Salisbury laager and clear the Hartley road. Meanwhile arrangements were made for an imperial force to land at Beira in Portuguese East Africa and to move from there to Salisbury, clearing the vital road to the sea and attacking rebel positions as it went. Until such time as these relieving forces arrived in their area the rebels of Mashonaland were left very much to themselves; the illusion of a successful return to the old world of Shona politics was very strong among the paramounts of western and central Mashonaland in July 1896. Those few white patrols which tried to disturb it were roughly handled; on July 29th, for instance, Mangwende's militant son, Mchemwa, ambushed a white force at a narrow point of the road two miles from Marendellas and nearly overwhelmed it.

[1] Vintcent to Grey and Carrington, telephone conversation, 24 June 1896, C.O., C.P., S.A., No. 520, pp. 253–4.
[2] Taberer to Grey, 17 June 1896, LO 5/6/1.

The campaigns which followed are difficult to describe since they lack any single focus. It will be best to concentrate upon the fate of some of the outstanding rebel leaders. For the fighting of 1896 an account of two of these—Makoni and Mashiangombi—gives as good a picture as any; both men were regarded as key leaders of the rebellion; both possessed strong forces; both occupied positions athwart or adjacent to the main roads to Salisbury. Many of the rebel paramounts, whose territories were remote from these roads and who were content to stand on the defensive, scarcely saw fighting in 1896. Makoni and Mashiangombi, on the other hand, bore the main brunt of the imperial counter-attack.

This counter-attack fell on Makoni first. We have already seen how paramount chief Mutota Cirimaunga Makoni moved into opposition to the whites; how the manifestations of this opposition were the first overt signs of trouble in Mashonaland; and how despite the internal opposition of Ndapfunya and Chipunza he brought into the rebellion a formidable fighting force. His initiative met with instant success. During the two weeks or so when the administration was aware that Makoni was planning to rise but unaware of the general preparations for rebellion an immediate attack on his kraal at Gwindingwi hill was planned. Makoni, it was known, had called a meeting of all local chiefs and headmen as early as June 9th; on June 16th messengers had been sent out from his kraal to alert his allies for an attack on the Native Commissioner's station at Rusape; on the same day rifles were seized from three native policemen who were threatened with death. 'Police cannot now move,' cabled the Native Commissioner on June 17th; 'I think Makoni should be dealt with without delay. . . . I consider the matter too serious to be overlooked.'[1]

So also did Judge Vintcent in Salisbury: on the 17th he phoned Bulawayo to say that he was mustering 40 men in Umtali and proposed 'going for Makoni without delay. In fact we must.' But before this expedition could set out the whole of western and central Mashonaland came out in rebellion and the situation was changed. 'Our position here now will have to be . . . sit tight,' explained Vintcent on June 19th. 'Umtali is not strong and naturally means sitting tight. Pray do not think I am alarmed or I should

<hr />

[1] Vintcent to Grey, telephone conversation, 19 June 1896; Vintcent to Grey and others, telephone conversation, 21 June 1896; Vintcent to Grey, telephone conversation, 22 June 1896, LO 5/6/1.

rather say in the funks. I want to deal quickly; I mean on the defensive.' On June 21st he reported that the inhabitants of Umtali, now in laager, had held a public meeting to protest against the idea of men being taken from the town to attack Makoni. The whites at Headlands were still keen 'on going for Makoni at once' but Vintcent wisely over-ruled them. 'I feel very strongly that we must teach the niggers a lesson,' he wrote, 'but my view is that the slightest reverse . . . will encourage other natives to join the rebels.' Therefore, as we have seen, the stations at Rusape and Headlands were evacuated, a fighting retreat was made to Umtali, and the country abandoned to Makoni.[1]

For more than a month Makoni ruled undisturbed over his ancestral area. As a precaution he strengthened the defences on Gwindingwi hill, storing food in the great caves which ran below it, and throwing up a loopholed wall, some seven feet high, around the limits of his 'town'. But he also took the offensive. All the cattle of the neighbouring white farmers were driven to Gwindingwi. Moreover Makoni's men fortified and held the Devil's Pass on the Umtali road. 'The Devil's Pass is very difficult country,' testified Native Commissioner Ross at Makoni's court-martial, 'and the natives would have come down very quickly there.' Meanwhile the whites were helpless. At the end of June an attempt was made to persuade his old rival, Mutassa, to attack Makoni's kraal. 'What reward shall I offer Mutassa?' asked Vintcent on June 25th. 'Make it big.' 'What do you call big?' returned Grey, cautiously. 'One thousand pounds.' 'I should have thought £500 was ample,' said Grey, still obsessed with the expense of the rebellion. In the event Mutassa proved unwilling to move against Makoni for either sum; he was not confident enough of his own people's attitude to the rebellion to risk such an attack. So Makoni remained unmolested.[1]

At the end of July, however, the situation was transformed. On July 28th Lieutenant-Colonel Alderson's force, having landed at Beira, proceeded through sensitive Portuguese territory in civilian clothes, and become a military unit once again in Umtali, left that town to march on Salisbury. 'It is to be hoped that he will have smashed up Makoni on the way,' wrote the administrative secretary in Bulawayo.[2]

Alderson did, indeed, attack Makoni on the way. He was warned

---

[1] Vintcent to Grey, telephone conversation, 25 June 1896, LO 5/6/1.
[2] Secretary, Bulawayo, to London Office, 31 July 1896, LO 5/6/2.

of the ambush waiting at Devil's Pass by Ndapfunya, and decided to march through the bush around the Pass and then to launch an attack on Gwindingwi. On the early morning of August 3rd his force, guided by Native Commissioner Ross, made across the rough ground north of the road towards the hill fort. Alderson was equipped with seven-pounders and machine-guns, a force more formidable than the Gwindingwi fortifications had been designed to resist. The encircling wall, however, was manned by Makoni's warriors, armed with old muskets and a few recently captured rifles and after the first surprise of the attack 'the natives began to fire from the walls . . . the fire was at times heavy and fairly accurate'. Alderson faced his task with some caution—it was after all his first experience of Shona warfare. 'Not knowing the exact nature of the defence and the obstacles or how many men were in the kraal I decided to work up to it gradually.' But at 7.30 a.m.—the attack having begun with the shelling of Makoni's huts at dawn—he ordered a general advance; the walls were scaled at two places and white troops for the first time entered Makoni's kraal. Fighting still continued, however. 'Numerous other walls and stockades had to be taken one by one while natives hidden inside the huts continued to fire on our men.' Eventually the interior of the kraal was cleared but Alderson then discovered that the problems were just beginning. Makoni and his people had retired into the caves which ran 'under the east side of the kraal like a rabbit warren'. 'I did not consider that I should be justified in incurring the loss of men which must have resulted from entering them,' wrote Alderson. 'I therefore evacuated and burnt the kraal.'[1]

Native Commissioner Edwards, who was returning to his district with the Alderson column, was scornful of its first engagement. 'The surface of the kraal was taken;' he wrote, 'the natives, however, retired to their caves and made good their position; finding it impossible to dislodge them the Colonel retreated and continued his march towards Salisbury, leaving the natives in full possession, not so much as a sack of grain, which was very plentiful, being taken or destroyed.' Much the same was true, he thought, of the subsequent engagements fought by Alderson on his way to Salisbury. At Marendellas he left the road to attack Mangwende's kraal at the 'rocky fortress' of Maopo, which was held by Mangwende and Mchemwa. 'None of the enemy was killed,' wrote

[1] Alderson report, 17 Aug. 1896, BA 2/8/1.

Edwards, 'as the kraal was found to be abandoned after continued artillery fire at long range. No search was made for grain, only a small quantity being destroyed in the firing of the kraal.' At Gatsi's Alderson found the rebels already in their caves and 'after one or two futile efforts with small dynamite bombs to dislodge the natives from caves many hundreds of yards in extent, withdrew his men, again leaving the rebels in full possession of their kraal and grain'. Marondera, closer to Salisbury, was allowed to escape without loss of life. 'The effect of the above described operations by the imperial troops', concluded Edwards, 'towards the final suppression of the rebellion must, in my opinion, be looked upon as being very small indeed, as except at Makoni's, very few of the rebels were killed and little damage was done in the capture of arms, cattle or grain, and there is no doubt that the natives did not in any instance consider themselves defeated, as they were left in possession or else effected their escape with trifling loss.'[1]

These criticisms were justified in so far as Alderson's actions had not destroyed the rebel strength nor disposed them to surrender as it was widely and erroneously assumed. On the other hand he had cleared the road; Mchemwa and his men withdrew to the north, where they remained unmolested for the rest of 1896; the posts at Rusape, Headlands and Marendellas were re-established and garrisoned. As for Makoni his position had been seriously weakened. Chief Chipunza, who escaped from Gwindingwi during the confusion of the first attack, reported that 'there was complete disorganization among Makoni's men remaining in the caves, that numbers were leaving . . . at least 200 men were killed and many wounded, among the former being the chief witch-doctor and 10 of Makoni's chief counsellors'. Makoni's enemies were encouraged by the sight of 'the vultures passing overhead towards Devil's Pass in thousands' to show themselves more actively against him; Mutassa and Ndapfunya both provided men for further operations against Gwindingwi. Makoni withdrew his men from the Devil's Pass and held counsel to decide what course to follow.[2]

On August 18th Vintcent received the sensational news that Makoni was offering to surrender on promise of amnesty and that his messengers were waiting at the newly built Fort Haines in

[1] Edwards Memorandum, undated, N 9/5/6.
[2] Alderson report, 17 Aug. 1896, BA 2/8/1; Moodie to Longden, 1 Aug. 1896, DM 2/9/1.

Rusape for a reply. It was one of the great missed opportunities of the Shona rising. Makoni emerges from all the evidence as the paramount least influenced by the Kagubi medium and the other religious leaders of the rebellion who were later to prevent the other chiefs from accepting surrender overtures; he was perhaps the one rebel leader in a position in August 1896 to carry out a genuine surrender and his example might have been widely influential. After some initial hesitation—'Makoni is a man who deserves death if any man does'—the Company officials decided that they should parallel the negotiations currently going forward in the Matopos with acceptance of Makoni's surrender. 'We could, of course, wipe Makoni out,' wrote Vintcent, 'but Alderson thinks it means a loss of life on our side in view of the fact that the caves in which the natives have taken refuge are veritable death traps. . . . We consider that the possession of Makoni's person and the coming in of his people will have a most beneficial effect generally and would probably induce other chiefs to konza. It must not be forgotten that we are to a large extent dependent upon the natives for grain supplies [and] any lengthening of military operations unless absolutely necessary will mean a shortening of grain supplies next season. Moreover the sooner this rebellion is ended the better for our prospectors and farmers.' Rhodes agreed—'Give Makoni whatever terms he asks.'[1]

The event showed how necessary it was for Rhodes to present the imperial authorities with a *fait accompli* in his Matopos negotiations. At this moment, which was just before news of Rhodes' first *indaba* was to transform the situation, Martin and Goodenough were insistent that the rebel leaders should be proscribed; they feared in Mashonaland as in Matabeleland a conspiracy of guilty men, with the Company and the rebel chiefs agreeing at the expense of the settler and the ordinary African alike. 'Makoni's surrender on condition that life be spared' declared Martin, 'would be regarded as weakness and have a bad effect. . . . His surrender should be unconditional and he should throw himself upon the Queen's mercy.' Goodenough told Grey on August 20th that no conditions should be offered to Makoni whatsoever. The best that Grey could do, by promising that on Makoni's surrender and conviction he would be sent 'to some gaol in Rhodesia or . . . to

[1] Vintcent to Grey, telephone conversation, 18 Aug. 1896 and 19 Aug. 1896, LO 5/6/3.

Robben Island or Breakwater, Capetown, via Bulawayo, as his passing through here would have a good effect', was to persuade Goodenough to agree that Makoni should be allowed to surrender on the promise of 'a full and fair trial before a court of law', on the result of which would depend any decision on whether his life could be spared or not.[1]

As we have seen Martin was unable in Matabeleland to carry his view that the *indunas* should be given no promises of amnesty but be told instead that they had to face trial. There was no second Rhodes in Mashonaland, however, and the imperial orders were followed. On August 25th the High Commissioner's terms were communicated to Makoni's envoys. Makoni received them with dismay. On the 26th he sent in another messenger to hear the terms again from Native Commissioner Ross, and asked that Ross should come to Gwindingwi to discuss the whole matter. Ndapfunya, who had been assuring Ross from the beginning that the whole surrender offer was a trick, now told him that Makoni was merely planning to lure him to Gwindingwi and to kill him; Ross refused to go and instead presented a 24-hour ultimatum. This was Martin's recipe for the Matopos with a vengeance. After 48 hours no reply had been received and the second attack on Gwindingwi hill was launched.[2]

In preparation for this attack a good deal of military thinking had been done. 'The best method of dealing with the rebels', opined Alderson, 'was to send columns out against them, drive them into the caves, leave a guard on them of 50 men with plenty of supplies, and one or two wagons to gather in all surrounding grain stores. But for this there were not enough men available, nor food, nor transport.' In Makoni's case, however, there were Ndapfunya's and Mutassa's men available to picket the caves and to gather and transport supplies for the besieging force. Moreover a new weapon had been developed; if the men in the caves refused to surrender they would be compelled to do so by the use of dynamite.[3]

[1] Grey to Vintcent, telephone conversation, 19 Aug. 1896, LO 5/6/3; correspondence between Grey, Goodenough, Carrington and Alderson, Aug. 1896, LO 5/6/3 and BA 2/8/1.
[2] Staff Diary for 28 Aug. and 1 Sept., BA 2/8/1; Watts to C.S.O., 9 Sept. 1896, LO 5/4/1.
[3] Alderson to Carrington, telephone conversation, 1 Sept. 1896, BA 3/8/1.

Edwards tells us how this method had been developed between Alderson's first attack on Makoni and the second assault. At Gatsi's kraal during Alderson's march to Salisbury a couple of 'bully beef tins filled with dynamite were dropped into the cave but needless to say they did no damage to the rebels'. A few weeks later more effective techniques were pioneered. Manyepera's kraal in the Marendellas district was under attack by Captain Pease with 80 men, Edwards in attendance. Manyepera took refuge in his caves—'it would have been suicide to have tried to rush the entrance to the cave where there was only room for one man at a time'. It was noted, however, that 'along the flat rock which formed the roof of the cave there was a narrow crack which ran practically the whole length of the rock and this had been filled with stones and ground. We could tell that this fissure went right down into the cave as smoke from the fires inside came out at different places. One night we quietly removed some of the stones and found that we could see light from the fires of the natives in the caves below.' Some 7-lb. shells were obtained and Lieutenant Fichat, later to figure in the story of Makoni's death, 'lit them and dropped them one by one down the hole . . . They went off with a tremendous bang and there was great commotion in the cave but no one came out. It was decided that this was much too dangerous a game to go on with, as there was a good chance of some of us getting hoist with our own petards. We next tried smoking the rebels out; we pulled down all the huts from nearby and piled the poles and grass at both entrances to the cave. The wind was not favourable to our fires and did no harm to the rebels but it must have made them uncomfortable.' Then a wagonload of dynamite arrived from Umtali. 'One case was fixed up with a long fuse and lowered down against the downstream entrance. I again warned the natives but as before was laughed at. The fuse lit and we ran for safety. The explosion blew in the poles and rocks at the entrance and a rebel who must have been on guard there came staggering out. He was a terrible sight. He was skinned from top to toe, but still grasping his rifle.' Despite this experience the men inside still refused to surrender, though they sent out of the caves about sixty women and children. 'Next day several cases of dynamite were laid along the fissure on top of the caves and fuses timed so that they all went off at once. Again I spoke to the rebels and warned them that this was the last chance they would get, but without any result. The fuse was fired and we retired to a safe distance. The explosion rent the cave from end to end. It was the end so far as the rebels in the cave were concerned. Two natives only escaped.'[1]

This terrible encounter became the pattern for many attacks on Shona strongholds, despite humanitarian outcry in England. And when Major Watts set out for Gwindingwi on the morning of August 30th, together with Ndapfunya, Chipunza, two of Mutassa's sons, and their men, he took dynamite with him. Again the kraal was reached at daybreak, though this time surprise was not achieved. 'I would ask my readers', wrote Lieutenant-Colonel Harding, some 40 years after the stirring events in which he took part as a young officer, 'to imagine an irregular miniature mountain composed of huge boulders on which were perched hundreds of native huts inhabited by lazy Mashona men and industrious Mashona women. Near the base are to be found huge caves which had been enlarged by the wily Mashonas to protect themselves against the attacks of the Matabele. . . . As is usually the case with these night attacks something or other gives the show away, and in this case it was the seven pounder with its rumbling wheels, and long before we got to the kraal we heard the Mashona cry of 'Mawe! Mawe!' which . . . in this case meant "Go to your caves!" '[2]

No attempt was made to defend the ruined walls of Gwindingwi; the caves were at once occupied by Makoni and his men and invested by Watts and Ndapfunya. There was plenty of food and running water in the caves and it was virtually impossible to starve the defenders out. More forceful tactics were used. The seven-pounder gun was brought to bear against the main entrance to the caves and machine guns moved from smaller entry to smaller entry. Dynamiting was begun though with little effect on the first day, since the position of the caves was hard to discover. On the second day 'as the position of the caves was ascertained with more certainty heavy charges of dynamite were employed with good effects'. Dynamiting continued throughout the four days of the siege. 'The effect produced by the dynamite had been terrible', wrote the Mashonaland correspondent of *The Times*, 'and the stench from the dead bodies was over-powering.' Gradually the strain became too much for the men in the caves. On the early morning of September 1st one of Makoni's sons and a senior

[1] Reminiscences of 'Wiri' Edwards, ED 6/1/1.
[2] C. Harding, *Far Bugles*, Croydon, 1933, chap. XII.

headman came out to surrender; later in the day some 30 women and children emerged from a cave mouth low down on the hillside; during the night some 30 men, including Makoni's eldest son Miripiri, broke out through Ndapfunya's pickets and escaped. On the 2nd most of the remaining women and children staggered out of the caves. But by nightfall Makoni and the remainder of his fighting men were still in the upper caves. Then at about 2 a.m. on September 3rd Makoni either surrendered or was captured at the mouth of one of the caves; his followers then surrendered *en masse* and the fighting was over.[1]

There was considerable controversy at the time on Makoni's alleged capture. During the siege Watts had sent interpreters five times in all to promise Makoni his life if he would surrender; strange though this seems in view of the High Commissioner's instructions there is no doubt from the evidence that the offers were made. In this context we should read the account of Native Messenger Mandishona. 'Towards dawn,' he tells us of the morning of September 3rd, 'when the waning moon had risen, a light appeared at the cave's entrance and out came two of Makoni's wives followed by one of his sons carrying a candle. Tom Dlamini went towards them. They said: "Mambo a no da kubuda. Nga va regera kuridza pfuti dzazo"— "The chief wishes to come out. The firing should be stopped." This message was sent back to the officer commanding the troops, but he refused to stop the firing and instead gave orders for it to be intensified. The din of the guns became a frightening sound, and the women fled back with their escort. We returned to our watching and, suddenly, the tall bearded figure of the chief appeared at the mouth of the cave, hesitating, afraid of the gun flashes. He said fearfully: "Ndi ka buda a ndi urayiwe here?"—"If I come out will I be killed?" Tom Dlamini went forward and said: "There is nothing to fear, father. Chinyere [Native Commissioner Ross] is here to help you." But Chinyere was not there. Makoni stepped from the cave and as Dlamini took him by the hand we left the boulders and got quickly behind him to prevent him from going back.'[2]

At this point Lieutenant Fichat, who made the 'capture' of Makoni, appeared on the scene. 'Round the corner inside the caves some natives appeared,' testified the lieutenant later. 'A

[1] H. C. Thomson, *Rhodesia and its Government*, London, 1898, chap. VIII.
[2] R. E. Reid, 'The Capture of Chief Makoni' *NADA*, Vol. 32, 1955.

policeman who was standing behind me said, that's Makoni, pointing to an elderly man. I went up and caught hold of him with my
left hand . . . just then heavy firing started on the other side and
Makoni tried to pull away from me. I immediately pulled my
revolver out of my right tunic pocket and held it to his head and
told him another attempt like that and I would blow his brains
out. I told the man holding the candle behind Makoni that if he
blew the light out I would shoot Makoni and loose my revolver
among the remainder of them . . . I took him along, fearing that
he might break away at any moment and handed him personally
over to Major Watts.' Watts cabled later that day that Makoni
'was captured, did not surrender'.[1]

Watts now decided to put Makoni on trial straight away. At
3.30 p.m. on September 3rd he convened a court-martial before
which Makoni was charged with rebellion under arms, the inevitable Fichat prosecuting. The proceedings were irregular; the High
Commissioner had demanded a trial in a properly constituted court
of law and Watts had received no authority to hold a court-martial.
Moreover, there was no warrant for the sentence of death which
the court proceeded to pass on Makoni; the penalty for armed
insurrection laid down by the Matabeleland Order in Council of
September 10th, 1894, which had not yet been superseded, was
merely 'a reasonable fine'.

All this had disturbed not only the prisoners but also the 'friendlies'. Ndapfunya's son when ordered to handcuff Makoni had
refused to do so; and the trial was watched with horror. 'Indap-
funya, a loyal chief, was present with some 200 to 300 men armed
with guns,' testified Native Commissioner Ross. 'They were much
excited when they heard that Makoni was condemned to death
and it was doubtful what they would do in the event of an attempt
at rescue.' Meanwhile 'there were a large number of Makoni's men
watching us from the hills'. Considering these factors Ross sat down
and wrote a formal letter to Watts advising him that there would
probably be a rescue attempt if Makoni were removed to Umtali
or Salisbury for execution and that in this event the loyalty of the
friendlies was not to be relied upon. Watts therefore decided to
proceed with Makoni's execution. At 12.15 on September 4th, in
the presence of all the troops and some 400 of Ndapfunya's men,
Makoni was shot at the uppermost edge of his kraal. 'He was

[1] Evidence of Lt. Fichat, 18 Sept. 1896, BA 2/3/1.

placed with his back to a corn bin,' wrote *The Times* correspondent, 'on the edge of the precipice on which his kraal stood, and died with a courage and dignity that extorted an unwilling admiration from all who were present.'[1]

'The Major asked Makoni if he had anything he wished to say,' relates Mandishona. 'The chief, standing on his "ruware", cried out to one of his followers . . . who was still hiding in the cave to come out and speak for him, but there was silence and he would not come. The chief then called to his brother, Masare, who was sitting among the Vaungwe gathered there, to speak for him. But this Masare had not fought against the white men and now he hung his head and remained silent. Makoni cried, "Zwa pera. Nda fa", and called out to the Vaungwe to see to it that he was buried with his ancestors. The chief was bound to his own "dura" with his arms outstretched whilst a serjeant-major . . . tied a hand-kerchief round his eyes. The soldiers stood in line. They fired their guns together like a thunder-clap and there it ended.'[2]

The death of Makoni was at once condemned by the High Commissioner who had demanded unconditional surrender and supported by the Company officials who had wished to guarantee him his life. It was received rapturously by the settlers—the sub-sequent surrender of arms in Maungwe, noted the *Bulawayo Sketch* with a side-glance at the proceedings in the Matopos, was 'the result of a good sound thrashing not of an indaba'. The admin-istration also came to believe that Makoni's death had 'had a most salutary effect'. 'In savage wars', pontificated *Rhodesia*, 'the severer the lesson administered is in the end often the greater mercy. The Decalogue and all the moral codes ever elaborated, unless admin-istered in a physical shock form, would convey nothing to wild animals. . . . Short and summary measures are the most effective in dealing with savage races, whose laws are founded upon force. Makoni's execution during the Mashonaland campaign saved several hundreds of native and European lives, for it effectively disposed of the impression that rebellion was at a premium and white lives at a discount.'[3]

This conviction was almost certainly wrong, though together with Alderson's belief that he had broken the spirit of the rising it contributed to the mistaken idea at the end of 1896 that the Shona rebellion was virtually over. In December 1896, during the peace

[1] Thomson, op. cit.   [2] Reid, op. cit.   [3] *Rhodesia*, 25 Feb. 1899.

offensive which is described below, Harding went out to parley with a chief near Salisbury. 'The chief was asked to leave his armed men and come unarmed to talk. No, the chief would not come, as he was afraid we should capture him and take him to Salisbury. We had shot Makoni when he surrendered and we might also shoot him.' This, as Rhodes had foreseen, was the real result of Makoni's death which appeared to the other paramounts not as justice but as treachery. It was a main factor in the breakdown of peace negotiations and the continuance of the rebellion into 1897.[1]

Just as the story of Makoni has allowed us also to give an account of the significant actions generally in the area east of Salisbury, so the story of Mashiangombi will complete our account of the campaigns of 1896. Mashiangombi himself perhaps needs a little more introduction. Sinyenkundu Mashiangombi and his people were a branch of a group which had originally come from the Marendellas area and which had moved through many districts in the confused late nineteenth century period before settling in Hartley. Maromo, the rebel chief of Charter district, was a cousin; Chiveru, chief and patron of the Kagubi medium, was a close ally and had shared much of Mashiangombi's wanderings. Sinyenkundu had eventually settled down close to the Matabeleland border in a position of considerable strength.[2]

We have a pleasant account of his villages as they were before the rising from the American prospector, 'Curio' Brown. Mashiangombi's people, he tells us, engaged in a varied and successful agriculture in the sandy forest soils of the area; 'fields of mealies, kaffir corn, rukwaza, sweet potatoes, pumpkins, pea-nuts, rice-beds in the marshes', 'Mashiangombi's numerous small kraals were scattered along the broken granite kopjes on both sides of the Umfuli river. They contained from 25 to 100 huts each' and each was governed by a sub-chieftain. Near them were kopjes 'among which were caves and recesses, partly natural but partly supplemented with artificial stone walls, thus making an excellent refuge and fortress in case of attack'. Brown describes his visits to the villages and the hospitality offered to him by the chief's wives. 'White men were looked upon by the Shona as anomalies who do

[1] Harding, op. cit.
[2] Notes on the history of Hartley district, N. C. Jackson, 1903, N3/33/8–N 3/33/8.

not come under the rules of ordinary humanity', so he was relegated to the women's huts. There he was offered *sadza* and pea-nut sauce, zebra meat, marrow, and engaged in conversations which have an ironic echo in the light of the future of Mashiangombi's community. 'What were the white men doing at Harare? [Salisbury] . . . What the white men intended to do with the gold they were digging and how soon they would have enough of it and all return to Diamond [Kimberley]. They said if we remained very long the Matabeles would come over and kill us while we were working in the mines.' Brown answered their questions with the round assertion: 'We are here for all time, and in a very few years thousands of white men will come with their wives and children and build big towns out of burnt red mud—towns larger than all Mashiangombi's villages put together.'[1]

Gradually their amusement at the activities of 'a lot of harmless lunatics who were temporarily wandering about, shooting game and searching for gold mines' gave way to an alarmed speculation that perhaps Brown was right after all. The paramount's kraal became the headquarters of a Native Commissioner and the centre of tax collection and labour compulsion; Mashiangombi began to plan to free himself of these no longer harmless but still incomprehensible lunatics. We have already seen how he made contact with Mkwati—Brown tells us of the annual visit to Mashiangombi's kraals of 'an old witch doctor from Matabeleland'—and how he brought the Kagubi medium to his kraal in April 1896. We have seen how his kraals became the headquarters of the Kagubi medium, of Bonda and of the Ndebele soldiers brought by Tshiwa; how the first killings in Mashonaland took place there. Until the end of 1896 if there was a single power-house of the Shona rising it was situated at Mashiangombi's.

Mashiangombi's men rapidly earnt themselves the reputation for unusual aggression. The gave the whites in Hartley laager a most unhappy time. On June 18th they opened fire on the laager and thereafter maintained a close siege of the place, harassing water parties and preventing communication with the outside world. On July 5th two messengers from Salisbury, carrying despatches, were killed by the rebels within sight of the fort. It was the nearest thing to a siege proper in the Shona rising.

Naturally the attention of the whites was forcefully drawn to

[1] W. H. Brown, *On the South African Frontier*, 1899, Chap. XIV.

Mashiangombi and he became the object of a series of punitive expeditions in 1896. The first was an attack by Captain White's patrol of 210 whites and 40 Zulus which relieved the laager on July 22nd. This patrol attacked the kraal which the Kagubi medium had chosen as his headquarters, killing 20 of its defenders, and discovering rather to their surprise that it housed some 500 head of cattle, and 'a huge quantity of limbo, blankets and shot', the goods sent in to 'Kagubi' from all over western and central Mashonaland. The next was early in August when the Mashonaland column from Matabeleland under Colonel Beal, engaged in the task of clearing the road to Salisbury, attacked and burnt Mashiangombi's own kraal. As a result of these two attacks Mashiangombi and the Kagubi medium withdrew into positions adjacent to the strong caves; Mashiangombi's continued to be the centre of rebellious activity. Indeed, it became more so as time went on since refugees from kraals destroyed elsewhere in the Hartley and Charter districts took refuge there and since towards the end of the year intransigent Ndebele also made it their refuge.[1]

The third—and supposedly final—assault was Colonel Alderson's on October 10th, the last major action of Alderson's campaign against the Mashonaland rebels. A patrol under Major Jenner had previously attacked other important kraals in Hartley and Charter, driving the occupants in on Mashiangombi's; on the night of October 9th he and Alderson made contact by signal and on the 10th a joint attack was launched. The kraals were taken and 'subsequently all the caves which could be located were blown up'; Mashiangombi and the rest took refuge in a stronghold on the Umfuli and were attacked there on October 16th. Then Alderson left for Lomagundi, which had so far seen no whites since the rising, satisfied that Mashiangombi's had been knocked out.[2]

In fact it had not. It was during this fighting that Mkwati arrived from Matabeleland and it was in this context that his command to fight on was issued: 'The soldiers turned up', recalled Tshiwa, 'and killed 16 natives, wounded some. It was arranged that if we were driven away as we certainly expected to be Mukwati would make for the Zambesi, passing through Sipulelo

[1] N.C., Mazoe, to C.N.C., 30 Oct. 1897, NI/1/6; *The Times*, 7 Aug. 1896–N 1/1/6.
[2] Jenner's report; Alderson's report; Nov. 1896, BA 2/8/1.

district. . . . He accused me of wanting to go back to make peace with the whites and would have killed me had his wife Tenkela not interfered. . . . There were no whites taken prisoners, all were killed when Mukwati was told that Mlimo will kill all natives who made peace and that we were going to fight again when the soldiers go away.' [1]

In this spirit the various occupants of Mashiangombi's reclaimed caves—their authority strengthened by the arrival of Mkwati and Tenkela-Wamponga—settled down to see through the dry season and to prepare for further fighting in 1897. They planned to use the loot still left with the Kagubi medium and that brought by Mkwati to buy food to see them through the next few months and they planned also to use their influence to prevent surrenders by the western and central paramounts and to devise new and more effective military arrangements for 1897. As their continued importance became clear so Alderson was bitterly blamed. 'Alderson committed two great blunders,' wrote Grey in January 1897; 'after his third attack on Mashiangombi he should have blown up his cave and left a fort behind. He did neither and the result is that Mashiangombi believes we are afraid.' 'Mashiangombi . . . has been attacked three times by the white troops,' wrote Grey a few days later; 'the last time by 700 men under Alderson. Father Bieler tells me on this occasion Alderson retired after three days' fighting which in his opinion were inconclusive and rather a successful repulse by the natives than a victory over them. The natives say we have been three times to Mashiangombi and have never been able to beat them. . . . I cannot understand Alderson's action. Father Bieler says he was influenced by Arthur Eyre who was anxious to go to Europe and to secure a visit of the imperial troops to his farm on the way to Lomagundi before his departure, and that this advice being most acceptable to Alderson who was afraid of losing lives if he remained at Mashiangombi's and blew up his caves, he took it and skedaddled.' [2]

At the time, however, Alderson's haste to finish off the Mashonaland rising was fully shared by Grey and Rhodes who wanted to get imperial troops out of that province as well by the end of the year. In late October it certainly looked as if the Shona rising had been broken. Makoni was dead; Mashiangombi in flight; the

---

[1] Tshiwa's statement, 10 Jan. 1897, LO 5/4/1.
[2] Grey to Lady Grey, 3 Jan. 1897 and 10 Jan. 1897, GR 1/1/1.

roads were cleared; most of the rebels were quietly planting crops for the coming wet season. It was hardly to be believed that the Shona would resist longer than the Ndebele had done. Rhodes and his party, travelling in late October from Bulawayo to Salisbury, found themselves 'here in the veld in the heart of a rebellion in perfect safety'. On November 10th Rhodes sent Grey a highly characteristic letter. 'As I told you we found the rebellion all along the road practically over except for a few natives here and there in the caves, e.g. at Charter the people told us they had not seen a native for three months and Taylor, the Native Commissioner for the district comprised in Charter and Enkeldoorn, stated he could go anywhere and that the only rebel Mashona chief was Sango who was living about 7 miles from Enkeldoorn in a granite kopje and as I daresay you have heard we went out and destroyed his kraal, killing a good many natives. It appears therefore to me useless to place Mounted Infantry at Charter and the same remark applies here [Enkeldoorn]. The two patrols that have been to Mazoe and Lomagundi districts are just in and have met with no natives. There are still two or three Mashona chiefs left in caves in granite kopjes but it appears to me they will be a matter for police rather than a large force. . . . With these facts before us I think it would be possible to wind up matters and get the police before the rainy weather.' [1]

Carrington, also anxious to get home now that the Matabeleland fighting was over, was disposed to agree. On November 19th the Staff Diary noted that 'no organized rebellion exists any longer' and that the Shona were anxious to surrender. In this atmosphere peace overtures were made to the Shona chiefs of western and central Mashonaland who were offered their lives in return for the surrender of arms and the evacuation of strongholds. At the end of November Major Jenner held *indabas* with paramounts Chiquaqua and Kunzwi-Nyandoro. They were edgy, rather comic affairs. Jenner's first meeting with Chiquaqua was conducted by shouting over a distance of 200 yards; Chiquaqua asked for the gift of a spade to symbolize the government's readiness to let him grow crops but would not come down to meet them to be given it; 'I did not consider it good policy to thrust it into his hands without receiving any quid pro quo', reported Jenner. But the optimistic major also reported that he was convinced that

[1] Rhodes to Grey, 10 Nov. 1896, BA 2/1/1.

Chiquaqua really wanted peace and would conform. A few days later Jenner met Kunzwi-Nyandoro's brother—Kunzwi himself was diplomatically sick—and although he got no tangible results he again reported that 'Kunzwi's people will be loyal in future'. 'The other chiefs will now come in,' he wrote confidently to Alderson on November 21st.[1]

These *indabas* went on but Jenner's optimism was enough for Carrington. 'After full inquiry I am of the opinion that the rebellion is at an end throughout Mashonaland,' he cabled on November 23rd. There was no further need for troops and the new police to be commanded by Martin could now take over. By December all imperial troops in Mashonaland had left save for 100 to make up the shortfall in the ranks of the new police.[2]

The only man who did not share the general optimism was Sir Richard Martin, who feared that the Shona might be pretending a readiness to surrender in order that they might fight again in 1897; but the success of Rhodes' negotiations in Matabeleland had discredited Martin's views on such matters. He turned out to be perfectly right as far as Mashonaland was concerned. No sooner had the imperial troops gone than evidence began to come to hand which showed that the peace talks had been a conscious comedy on the side of the Shona. This evidence also showed how important still was the concentration of leaders at Mashiangombi's.

On December 18th Chief Native Commissioner Taberer wrote to Grey to state for the first time the central importance of the Kagubi medium in the rising. 'I have no hesitation in saying that the rebellion was, and the present attitude of the Mashonas north of the Macheke river is, governed by the Mondoro, or witch doctor, and that the future attitude of the Mashonas depends upon our manner of dealing with the chief Mashiangombi who, having the Mondoro resident among his people, acts on the Mondoro's direct advice and command and transmits his orders to other districts. . . . The Mondoro exacts tribute and taxes from all the Mashonas; hence his advice to Mashiangombi not to come to any terms unless the Government remove the forces from the district. Provided that they can get good supplies from other quarters, which they can, they are not over anxious to sow their seed. The

---

[1] Reports on *indabas* with Chiquaqua and Nyandoro, 18 Nov., 19 Nov., 21 Nov. 1896, LO 5/4/1; BA 2/8/1.

[2] Grey to Secretary, Cape Town, 23 Nov. 1896, LO 5/2/52.

Hartley Hill natives blindly follow the advice of the Mondoro and although interviews with sub-chiefs such as Chiquaqua, Kunswi and Nyameda are to a certain extent satisfactory my firm belief is that it admirably suits them to comply with our desires that hostilities should cease and the natives sow their crops. They have got to live and have further to supply their Mondoro.' Taberer's assumptions were later confirmed. 'When Kunzwi and Chiquaqua were visited by Major Jenner', wrote Armstrong in February, 'they both sent to Gargoobi and were told not to give up their guns. The messenger sent by Kunzwi was named Panash and took down two pieces of limbo.' 'I am told that when I went and interviewed Kunzwi and Chiquaqua last November,' wrote Campbell, 'they really meant to surrender but each was unwilling to be the first to lay down his arms and afterwards under threats from Kagubi, Mashanganyika, Gonto and Zhanta again became defiant.' In Matabeleland the senior Ndebele *indunas* had been able to defy the religious leaders and to pursue a policy of negotiation. In Mashonaland the religious leadership retained control.[1]

Father Richartz's intelligence report of January 10th 1897 summed up the Chishawasha mission's findings: 'They much hope in an extraordinary intervention of that mysterious power of their chief Mondoros, as they did in the beginning of the rising. . . . Our boys have always asked me whether the Mulenka or Witch Doctor at Mashiangombi's had given in and assured me that the war would be over and the people would come and work at once, as soon as he allows them to approach the white people and gives orders to stop hostilities.' [2]

As this picture grew clearer so the *indabas* grew less reassuring. Talks with Mashiangombi himself broke down in his insistence that the whites must withdraw their police and administrators entirely from his area; and in an *indaba* with paramount chief Soswe on January 15th the authentic voice of Shona resistance was heard. 'I have nothing to talk to the white man about. . . . What do you want to return for? Are you leaving anything behind you? Go away and remain away. I wish to have nothing to do with you white men. Go and live in Chimioio and I will send boys to

[1] Taberer to Grey, 18 Dec. 1896, LO 5/4/1; Armstrong to Taberer, 20 Feb. 1897, LO 5/4/2; Campbell to Taberer, 15 May 1897, N 1/1/9.

[2] Father Richartz, 10 Jan. 1897, LO 5/4/1.

work for you there if you want them. Why did you burn my kraal? Did I ever interfere with your wagons on the road? Go to Chimioio. I don't want any white men in my district.' [1]

It was clear, then, that hostilities would be resumed in 1897 and that in Mashonaland Rhodes' gamble had failed. In January Grey told Rhodes, who was inclined to talk too much in London of how peaceful Mashonaland was, that in fact it looked as if a wholesale resumption of the rebellion was in preparation. 'Ross has warned me distinctly that unless we can impress Mashonas with our strength during the next months we shall have renewed troubles after rains and perhaps on larger scale. Makoni's successor and other friendly chiefs say the Mashonas intend to rise after they have secured their crops. N. C. Morris, Marendellas, informs me has no friendly in his district owing to influence paramount whose kraal only three miles from road. . . . Further Makoni's sons and Mangwende have joined 30 miles N.E. of Marendellas and are 700 strong causing much worry and anxiety to natives supposed to be friendly. In the Hartley district Mashiangombi, supported by witch-doctors and Matabele is waiting. Brabant and Taberer both convinced unless we can make things unpleasant for him I shall have trouble next year.' [2]

Both sides were preparing new forces for the coming struggle. On the side of the whites there were the new Police, most of them raw and untrained and extremely susceptible to fever. 'The police were totally untrained,' wrote Thomson of *The Times*, 'and unused to the country and its ways. They had been enlisted in England and when Captain De Moleyns assumed command they had, as a matter of fact, not arrived, but were on the way from Beira to Salisbury.' When they did arrive Martin at once decided that with such a force 'it would not be safe to take the offensive until the rainy season was over and the men under Captain De Moleyns' command had become in some measure habituated to the climate and to the nature of the work before them'. Grey confessed to Rhodes on January 10th Makoni's sons and Mchemwa could not be dealt with 'at present. . . . We must have force.' And on December 25th, Hopper, commanding the new police in Hartley, admitted that with them he could not move against 'this head of the Mashona rebellion', the Kagubi medium. 'Had

---

[1] Morris to Taberer, 16 Jan. 1897, LO 5/4/1.
[2] Grey to Rhodes, Jan. 1897, Rhodes House, Mss. Afr. s. 228, C. I., Vol. I.

I sufficient number of trained men I would immediately place them in a fort close to Mandora's kraal ... but I saw quite enough of my men the other day to come to the conclusion that to risk any chance of an engagement until their training is considerably progressed would be exceedingly foolish and dangerous. I shall therefore put them through a hurried course of those movements which are absolutely essential in native warfare.' There must have been moments when even Grey wished that the imperial troops were still in Mashonaland.[1]

This state of affairs gave Mkwati and Kagubi a chance to attempt a scheme of their own to make the fighting of 1897 more effective, and to find some substitute for the Ndebele military system. This was nothing less than an attempt to revive the political institutions of the Rozwi. We have already seen how Mkwati exploited the memory of the Rozwi empire during the rising in Matabeleland by his links with Uwini, by his use of Taba Zi Ka Mambo, and inevitably by his use of the machinery of the Mwari cult itself. We have seen also how the spiritual prestige of the Rozwi still extended deep into Mashonaland and how even the memory of their past military might was not dead. The whole area of Mashonaland which was now in revolt had once been part of the Rozwi confederation; groups of Rozwi lived scattered throughout the area and some of them still exercised a ritual superiority over the Shona paramounts. It may be, indeed, that we have understated their role in the outbreak of the rising. They were probably important in the Maungwe area, for example. There lived the holder of the Rozwi title, Chiduku, who himself claimed descent from the royal line and whose presence was necessary at the installation of a Mangwende; the holder of the Rozwi title, Tandi, whose presence was necessary at the installation of a Makoni; and the holder of the Rozwi title, Mavudzi, a man of considerable spiritual power who appears in Rozwi tradition as a 'priest' at the court of the Mambo and who could still be described in the 1920s as 'the great rain-maker of the VaRozwi and indeed of all the tribes in this district'. These Rozwi 'chiefs' were certainly all out in rebellion in 1896 and they may well have played a part in the coordination of the rising. Mavudzi, for instance, is said by Rozwi oral evidence to be the traditional

[1] Thomson, op. cit; Hopper's report, 25 Dec. 1896, C.O., C.P., S.A., No. 517, p. 409.

intermediary between the Nehanda medium and the Mwari cult; and there is evidence that both Bonda and Tshiwa paid visits to the Rozwi title-holders after the rising had broken out.[1]

All this, then, lay behind the decision now taken to install a Rozwi paramount and to gather under his command Rozwi fighting men from the various districts of Mashonaland including those which were not up in rebellion. Such a paramount might even be recognized as a central authority by the Shona chiefs themselves but even if he was not he would represent an ally more able than any of the other chiefs to mobilize men for attack in the areas chosen by Mkwati and Kagubi. There were a number of people who might claim the Rozwi paramountcy which had lapsed in the dark days of the Ndebele victory and the Rozwi diaspora. One of these was Mudzinganyama Jiri Mteveri, living in 1896 in the Ndanga district, which was not in rebellion. Mudzinganyama claimed to be the great-grandson of Mambo Gumbo-Remvura and the great-nephew of Mambo Dlembeu and regarded himself as the rightful heir to the Mambo-ship. In 1901, some years after the events described below, the Native Commissioner, Belingwe, met him travelling through that district. 'He informed me, inter alia, that he was the eldest male descendant of the Mambos and therefore should be king of Rhodesia. He appears to be an intelligent native and is evidently feared and respected by the local natives.' [2]

It was this man who was chosen by Mkwati and Kagubi, with the assent of other leading Rozwi figures, to revive the Mambo-ship. Bonda was the go-between employed to broach this project to the Rozwi chiefs generally and late in 1896 and early in 1897 he made many journeys from Mashiangombi's to the Sabi, to Wedza, and to Maungwe, where he consulted with Chiduku, Tandi, Mavudzi and Mbava. Perhaps surprisingly the Rozwi were more ready to recognize Mudzinganyama as Mambo than the Ndebele had been to accept any claimant as king. In December 1896 an impressive delegation waited upon Mudzinganyama

---

[1] Marodzi, 'The BaRozwi', *NADA*, 1924; E. Lloyd, 'Mbava', *NADA*, 1925; Muhlanga, 'Mbayva and others', *NADA*, 1926; Abraham, 'The Principality of Maungwe', *NADA*, 1951; interview between Mr Solomon Nengubo and Chihoya, a Mwari cult officer, in Bikita, Feb. 1963.

[2] Report for Belingwe, April 1901, LO 5/7/6. Von Sicard gives a genealogy for Mudzinganyama in *NADA*, 1933. Mr. Nengubo's interviews suggest that this genealogy is telescoped.

to invite him to assume the Mamboship. The delegation consisted of Bonda and 'several of the Mlimo's messengers'; of the Rozwi chiefs Chiduku, Mbava and Mavudzi; and of the Njanja chief Gambiza's son with others of his people. 'I learnt', wrote the Native Commissioner, Ndanga, reporting this in March 1897, 'that Mtebera was the head of all the VaRozwi and that he had taken the title of Mambo, this being the name of the VaRozwi chief who lived at Ntaba Zakamambo and who was killed by the Matabele at the time they first invaded the country. After the death of Mambo the VaRozwi scattered all over the country; the head chief discontinued to use the name Mambo and was only known by the name of Mtebera. Why after all these years should the name Mambo be revived now? The natives say that the Mlimo is endeavouring to get the VaRozwi to return to their old country at Ntaba Zaka Mambo but for what purpose I have not been able to ascertain.' Later in March he reported that some of those who had left with chief Mudzinganyama Jiri Mteveri and accompanied the delegation to the north had returned to tell the Karanga that 'it was no use working their lands' as Mwari was preparing another effort 'to wipe out all whites and friendlies'.[1]

The plan appeared to be working. Mudzinganyama had been recognized as Mambo and was waiting in a temporary kraal on the Sabi river in Charter district for his followers to assemble. Rozwi fighting men were being promised by Bonda and other emissaries that 'all WaRosi killed by white men were to come to life again'. But the authorities were for once aware of what was being planned; the report of the Native Commissioner, Ndanga, alerted them to the danger. In March the Native Commissioners of Hartley, Charter and Victoria reported on Bonda's movements—'the Mlimo has sent one Bonda to incite the AbaRosi to rise,' wrote the Native Commissioner, Charter, who instituted a close watch on the local Rozwi and on any movements of strangers in his area. 'The Mlimo had sent Bonda to incite the AbaRosi to rebellion', echoed the Native Commissioner, Victoria, and he also 'placed spies among the AbaRosi to watch for the advent of the messengers'. These precautions did not result in Bonda's capture, but they did, almost incidentally, result in the detention of

[1] N.C., Ndanga, to C.N.C., 2 Mar. and 24 Mar. 1897, N 1/1/8; Armstrong to C.N.C., 20 Feb. 1897, LO 5/4/2.

Mudzinganyama at the office of the Native Commissioner, Charter.[1]

The scheme was not a complete failure, however; the Rozwi were at least partially mobilized. In April 1897, when fighting had broken out again throughout central Mashonaland and Martin's new police were ready for their job, Native Commissioner Armstrong reported from the Mrewa area that 'we found quite a lot of WaRosi gathered there under a MaRosi chief, some having come from Mangwendi's, Makoni's and even from Charter'. In May he wrote: 'I have been astounded by the number of WaRosi rebels and believe the WaRosi were the main support of the rising in every district and our bitterest enemies.' And Rozwi commitment to the rebellion continued to the end. 'None of the BaRozwi have surrendered yet,' noted the Native Commissioner, Marendellas, in June 1897 as others in his district began to come in, 'and I do not think they will unless a patrol is sent to their district and a fort built there.' On December 31st, 1897, he wrote that the only chief in his district who was still defiant was 'a BaRozwi chief named Mbava. . . . This chief has openly resisted my messengers and attacked a neighbouring kraal. The patrol, however, was unable to punish him as he anticipated our arrival and crossed the Sabi river into the Charter district.' Even as late as March 1900 the same officer was writing: 'I should not be at all surprised if there was a disturbance amongst the natives the BaRozwi would be the cause of it.'[2]

This scheme to revive the Rozwi power was linked with the departure of Mkwati and the Kagubi medium from Mashiangombi's kraals in January 1897, 'Kagubi' with the intention of 'going to garden and collect food at Chinamora's; then going down to the Chidukwi district on the Sabi river below Mount Wedza where he intended bringing up a party of MaRosi to fight next dry season', and Mkwati perhaps with the intention of bringing the Rozwi of eastern Matabeleland into the scheme. Grey had the agonizing experience in that month of knowing perfectly well the importance of Mkwati and discovering that of the Kagubi medium; locating both of them and knowing their

[1] N.C., Charter, to C.N.C., 9 Mar. 1897, N 1/1/2; summary of work done during week ending 19 March 1897, LO 5/4/2.

[2] Armstrong to Grey, 29 Apr. 1897, LO 5/4/3; N. C., Marendellas, to C.N.C., 30 June and 31 Dec., 1897, March 1900, LO 5/4/6, LO 5/4/8, LO 5/5/3.

intention to move from Mashiangombi's; but being unable to do anything about it.[1]

On January 8th it was reported that Mkwati had been discovered moving away from Mashiangombi's with a small party into eastern Matabeleland, 'driving people away from them so as not to attract attention'. Grey and Martin agreed that he should be captured but on January 10th the Officer Commanding, Bulawayo, strongly advised against any attempt. 'The patrol under present conditions would be too expensive in lives and material for the result obtained. The present swollen state of the rivers presents serious obstacles to the quick movement necessary.' Mkwati was left alone, therefore, and managed later to join the Kagubi and Nehanda mediums to the north of Salisbury.[2]

Even more humiliating was the failure to capture the Kagubi medium in the first trial of strength between him and the new police. The medium was under observation by Hopper; he had quarrelled with Mashiangombi who regarded his planned departure as a desertion and was refusing to allow him to leave; a reward was put on his head early in January by Grey. Hubert Howard, one of Grey's young aristocratic assistants, was anxious to earn the reward and the distinction of a capture and went off to Hartley but he found it frustrating work. 'It was necessary to capture the God of the Mashonas,' he wrote, 'the Mondoro, at Hartley. De Moleyns did not like the responsibility and waited orders, so in I came from Hartley, rode to the Deputy Commissioner [Martin] who read the despatches and sat irresolutely— moulting is the only true image; up to the Administrator who galvanized the old lady into instant action and in a couple of hours he had doctor's orders and everything ready and despatched. On the orders De Moleyns was again irresolute—made a night march to within a mile of the enemy and then right about to build a fort instead of instantly putting the matter to the touch. I came back in despair.'[3]

It was once again a matter of the weakness of the new police and the strength of Mashiangombi's defences. De Moleyns explained that he had called off his night attack on January 12th

[1] Armstrong to C.N.C., 20 Feb. 1897, LO 5/4/2.
[2] Martin to Rosmead, 4 Jan., 8 Jan., 14 Jan. 1897, C.O., C.P., S.A., No. 517, pp. 383, 401.
[3] Howard to Lady Grey, 17 Jan. 1897, GR 1/1/1.

because 'I was informed by spies . . . that the natives were awake, occasionally firing off guns, shouting, etc., and had men on the look-out, and under the circumstances I considered that even if I could effect an entrance into the kraals it was very doubtful whether I could capture the Mondoro.' On January 16th when it was discovered that the Kagubi medium had left his kraal De Moleyns found it so well protected that it was 'difficult to get in . . . even without resistance'; his African police, moreover, 'had to be driven forward and would not go on without the white men . . . and showed none of the eagerness to get in which I was told to expect'. On the 17th it was discovered that 'Kagubi' had merely moved to another fortified hill but De Moleyns was no more anxious to attack that. 'I hardly think His Honour the Commandant General appreciates the difficulty of surprising their kraal,' he protested, 'when they are barricaded and expecting attack day and night.' On the next day the medium at last slipped away from Mashiangombi's and escaped from De Moleyns' pursuing patrol.[1]

The lessons of these events were spelt out by Father Biehler in an intelligence report on February 15th. It was clear, he wrote, that 'far from any peaceful settlement' the Shona 'mean to be independent'. If Jenner had insisted on an immediate and strict observance of surrender terms from Chiquaqua and Kunzwi something might have been achieved 'but to rely on Mashona promises is mere foolishness'. Two main reasons could be put forward for the fact that even after the operations of the imperial troops the Shona were still able to resist. One was that 'nowhere the natives have received a lesson. . . . At Mashayangombe we have not even been able to take real possession of the witch-doctor's kopje; and more we probably had more casualties than the natives. In any case, our present situation at Hartley sufficiently proves the case. Kagubi is boasting everywhere now that four times the white men came to attack him and they have never been able to get hold of him.' The second reason was 'the untouched power of the witch-doctor Kagubi and the Mazoe witch Nehanda. Kagubi has passed through Seki, Mashanga-nyika, Gondo, Kaiya, Bururu, etc., where he has given orders not to give in, and he is now in a good position called Zwiwa . . . not

[1] *Rhodesia Herald*, 20 Jan. 1897; De Moleyns to C.S.O., 14 Jan ., 17 Jan., 19 Jan. 1897, LO 5/4/1.

very far from Nehanda. If attacked they can easily clear from kopje to kopje.' Biehler went on to lay down the necessary measures to break Shona resistance. 'Our mode of fighting is not the proper one for Mashonas; even the natives laugh at it. They know a long time before hand when we are coming; then they have plenty of time to send away both their women and their cattle, and the men sit in their caves where they have the best chance since they see us and we do not see them. . . . The different method of fighting when dealing with these coward Mashonas in their rocks must be adopted. It seems to me that the only way of doing anything at all with these natives is to starve them, destroy their lands and kill all that can be killed.' And it was essential to capture or kill the mediums: 'as long as those witch-doctors in the country are not disposed of there is no hope of peace'.[1]

White attempts to carry out this programme and to destroy Shona resistance piecemeal were little reported at the time and have been little studied subsequently. The books on the risings which were hastily produced by the soldiers who took part in their suppression dealt exclusively with the events of 1896 and assumed that the rebellions had ended in that year. The English press paid little attention to events in Mashonaland in 1897. To that extent Rhodes' luck held—and the sort of fighting which went on in 1897 did not really threaten a white disaster in the field of the sort which Chamberlain had warned would mean the revocation of the Charter. Nevertheless the continued resistance of the Shona was important at the time to the whites of the eastern province, whose economic activities were hardly resumed until 1898 and who saw their Matabeleland rivals drawing still further ahead. Above all the fighting was important to Shona society in the rebel areas. In some ways this was the really heroic period of the Shona risings. The effort required to renew the war after the privations of 1896; the effort of faith required to maintain full commitment to the rising; the refusal to negotiate—all this exhausted Shona society for years to come. The best way to follow the story of 1897 will be to complete first our account of Mashiangombi and then turn to trace the fate of the Kagubi medium and Mkwati in central Mashonaland.

Hopes of Mashiangombi's surrender faded rapidly in January

1 Intelligence report, 15 Feb. 1897, LO 5/4/2.

1897 and it was decided to follow a policy of harassment: 'I do not propose to attack any strongholds,' wrote Martin, 'but to establish forts, harass him and threaten his crops.' For his part Mashiangombi adopted a similar policy with respect to the forts erected near his kraal. In February African police—the so-called Black Watch under our friend Brabant—destroyed many of Mashiangombi's gardens; he in return made a series of attacks on Fort Mondoro, where the garrison were very heavily hit with malaria and kept awake at night by rebel fusillades. By early March the strain of the white presence was beginning to tell on Mashiangombi. 'I am occupying a kopje 1800 yards from Mashiangombi's own kraal,' wrote Captain Nesbitt, 'this very much against the chief's wish. Mashiangombi is . . . very uneasy at having the white man so near his kraal. This fort is impregnable and the best possible place and will have the desired effect. Mashiangombi himself says he does not want the white man here; one of his terms of surrender is that I evacuate the place and return to Hartley where he will send me labour.' [1]

These renewed surrender negotiations soon proved to be as much a tactic to buy time as the ones in December had been. On March 17th Mashiangombi took more direct methods of ridding himself of the white man. That morning he attacked Fort Mondoro in force, striking at dawn with 400 men; three hours of hard fighting followed before they were repulsed. Nesbitt called in some alarm for fresh supplies and ammunition. 'Escort must be very strong . . . please don't delay one minute but send assistance. Niggers now firing on fort.' 'There has been a lot of fighting in the country during the week,' wrote Milton in Salisbury, thus noting the real beginning of rebel activities in 1897. 'The Mashonas at Hartley—with whom there were certainly many Matabeles—actually attacked the fort for three hours. They were beaten off but killed 3 Cape boys and many mules. A patrol which went out to Mtoko's, N.E. of here, to raise some native levies among the friendlies had 7 days' fighting on the march. . . . The police are doing very well but the Mashonas are stubborn and decline to hold any communication with us. They want a good hammering first. It is very disheartening not to be able to stop the fighting. Lots of men are waiting to go out prospecting and mining but you

[1] Nesbitt to Officer Commanding, 1 Mar. 1897, LO 5/4/2.

cannot go 8 miles from here without risking the chance of being potted at from a kopje.' [1]

Mashiangombi's 'good hammering' came at last in July. A strong patrol commanded by Martin himself left Salisbury to great public acclaim, laagered some four miles from Mashiangombi's on the night of July 23rd and launched a dawn attack on Mashiangombi's kraal. At the same time the Hussars, who had been brought to Mashonaland from Bulawayo, attacked the Mondoro and Mwari kraals, which had once been occupied by 'Kagubi' and Mkwati. The attack was a complete success and the defenders took to the caves. 'As we got into the main kraal,' wrote the *Rhodesia Herald* correspondent, 'we found the fires burning and food simmering, but the natives had made themselves invisible . . . from sundry small fissures around the kraal the rebels kept up a desultory fire but so far no casualties had happened. All day long a heavy fire was kept up to and from the caves. . . . The rebels were asked to come out and surrender but Mashiangombi only returned insulting replies. . . . At night the rebels were still blazing away at us from their inaccessible position, many narrow escapes being witnessed. A very strong picket was then placed around the caves . . . and the camp prepared to eat and rest. But it appeared that there was to be no rest for the weary, for the rebels attempted to pick off the pickets and heavy firing was kept up by both sides right through the night. . . . At daybreak the rebels made a determined effort to dislodge the pickets, seeing that it was their last chance of escaping from the caves and a number of rebels were shot.' One of those shot was Mashiangombi himself. 'We discovered the body of Mashiangombi today at 2.30,' wrote Native Commissioner Scott. 'He had marks of dynamite on his body. He was also shot at daybreak this morning in trying to escape from one of the caves. He was lying about 15 yards in front of the mouth of it. . . . From what I can gather it was Mashiangombi, backed by his brother Chifamba, who was determined to see it out to the last. They both were killed.' [2]

[1] Nesbitt to C.S.O., 17 Mar. 1897, LO 5/4/2; Milton to his wife, 22 Mar. 1897, ML 1/1/2.

[2] *Rhodesia Herald*, 21 July, 28 July, 4 Aug. 1897; reports by Captain Rivett Carnac and N.C. Scott, LO 5/4/5; Scott to C.N.C., 25 July and 6 Aug. 1897, N 1/1/3.

The death of the main rebel leader in western Mashonaland was also recorded in one of those enthusiastic girlish letters which are a strange feature of the surviving records of the risings. One of the troopers present at the attack was Frederick Thomas Blyth and on September 8th 1897 his sister Elizabeth wrote to another brother, Charles, to record a family triumph. 'Oh Charlie, of course you have not heard about Fred's last letters. We were awfully excited when we first read them but it is some days ago and it has worn off. The great excitement is that he actually had the honour of shooting the big chief Mashiyangombi himself. I will tell you a little how it come about; it seems rather less noble when examined closely. Well, this big chief's kraal was five days march from Salisbury. The Police . . . attacked the place. The enemy were in great caves out of which they kept firing heavily. The English could only fire at the openings where they could see firing. The only way to get them out was to blow the caves up with dynamite. This was done and no doubt heaps killed and buried alive. Then about 300 women and children surrendered and afterwards a good many men. Well, Fred was on sentry one night and a dreadful night it must have been as the Black Watch (on our side) were somehow behind him and kept up a constant fire on the caves, being excited and having too much of some native brandy stuff. The bullets were whizzing all round poor Fred's head. He was sheltered by rocks tho. Well, as I was a saying, in the morning just as it was getting light he saw a nigger in an old great coat come strolling out of the enemy's camp as if he were "monarch of all he surveyed". He thought at first it could not be a Mashona venturing out. Then he knew he must be so fired according to orders. The chap was evidently hit but hid behind a rock and then came out again. Then Fred fired again and he went head over heels down the hill. He was afterwards identified as the great Mashiyangombi and Fred was much congratulated. The body was carried into camp amid great rejoicings. Last year there was a reward varying from £100 to £500 offered for him alive or dead. So Fred ought to get something now, oughtn't he? I wish he might be in luck at last, dear old boy.' [1]

Whether or not Blyth got his reward, the luck of the Hartley rebels had come to an end. The sight of the dead paramount 'much affected' his people and as news of his death spread the

[1] Elizabeth to C. W. Blyth, 8 Sept. 1897, MISC/BL 5.

resistance of those still in the caves ended. His caves were now carefully dynamited; the walls of his strongholds pulled down; a small police post was established on the site. His allies were killed or arrested. Bonda was killed some time in July or August during attacks by the Hussars on chief Mzitzwe's people. Dekwende was arrested and sent in for trial in April 1898. The rising in western Mashonaland had come to an end.[1]

To complete the story of the rising in Mashonaland we must turn to events in the central districts of the province. Through the move there of Mkwati and the Kagubi medium and their partially successful deployment there of the Rozwi this area became the really important one in 1897. Mashiangombi's which had once been perfectly situated between the two rebellious provinces was no longer a suitable headquarters, stoutly though it was defended. Central Mashonaland offered many advantages now that the rising had become an exclusively Shona affair. It was 'Kagubi's' old area of operation where he might hope to rally waverers and to encourage opposition to 'friendly' chiefs. Moreover it was possible from there to retreat north-east into the old area of the Mwene Mutapa confederacy, so far not involved in the rebellion but an area which would certainly provide a refuge and which might possibly be brought out in arms through the joint influence of Mkwati, Tenkela-Wamponga and the Kagubi medium. (It was, as we have seen, Mkwati's intention to make for the Zambesi through Sipolilo if he was driven out of the rebel area.)

There were many signs in the first months of 1897 of the importance of the return of 'Kagubi'. As we have seen he at once made a tour of the paramountcies around Salisbury urging them not to consider surrender. Once he had settled in 'his old home at Gonto in the Chikwakwa's district . . . on two almost inaccessible rocky promontories overlooking a small stream hard by Chikwakwa's old kraal', messengers began to come in from the more distant paramounts seeking for advice. On January 20th, for example, Morris, Acting Native Commissioner of Marendellas

---

[1] Bonda's death is referred to in N.C., Hartley, to C.N.C., 12 Sept. 1897, N 1/1/3; the operations against Mzitzwe are described in LO 5/4/5, N 1/1/2 and NS 1/1/1. Dekwende's arrest is reported in N.C., Hartley, to C.N.C., 19 Apr. 1898, N 1/1/3.

in the absence of Edwards, reported that two women had managed to escape from a party bound for 'Kagubi's' and come in to
his office. The party, consisting of seven women 'kept by white
men or colonial boys' who had been seized by the rebels at the
outbreak of the rising, were being taken to the Kagubi medium
as tribute. They were under the care of Mchemwa himself
who wished to ask the medium 'whether they were to go to
the main road and kill white men again'. In this way 'Kagubi's'
authority was recognized by the rebels of the Mangwende paramountcy.[1]

The medium began to exercise the same sort of role in relation
to the Shona paramounts that had been exercised in the Matopos
by the Mwari priests but without arousing the same resentment.
He nominated a successor to paramount chief Seki, when the first
rebel paramount was killed in January during the storming of his
kopje by Lord Grey himself while setting an example to the new
police. He made it plain that any paramount who surrendered
would be 'deposed' and have to face the rival leadership of a more
intransigent nominee; and he apparently planned to overthrow
the hated Ndapfunya in Maungwe and to replace him by Miripiri, the dead Makoni's eldest son. And over and above these
attempts to create a paramountcy structure favourable to continued resistance he and his allies exercised a profound influence
generally over rebel conduct throughout central Mashonaland.
'Gargoobi, Mali and Nyanda are at present holding a conference,'
wrote Native Commissioner Armstrong on May 26th, 'and what
they decide will be implicitly obeyed. In my opinion not a native
in Mashonaland is to be trusted and extra care should be used in
those districts which did not rebel last year as they firmly believe
in the man Gargoobi.'[2]

As this sort of evidence and speculation mounted, so the administration came to narrow down its targets. The original
despondent belief that the Shona rising was so fragmented that
only an assault on every kopje could end it gave way to the belief
that certain paramounts were key figures and that the mediums,
especially the 'Kagubi' mediums, were at the heart of the rebel-

[1] Morris to C.N.C., 20 Jan. 1897 and C.N.C.'s minute, LO 5/4/1.
[2] Campbell to C.N.C., 22 July 1897, N 1/1/9; Grey to Rhodes, 23 Apr.
1897, Rhodes House, Mss. Afr. s. 228, C.1, Vol. 1; Armstrong to C.N.C., May
1897, N 1/1/7.

lion. Of the paramounts Mashanganyika and Kunzwi-Nyandoro were picked out as especially important to deal with. As for the 'Kagubi' medium he increasingly became a prime target. Lord Grey himself had come to see the fighting as a contest between systems of belief. Africans near Chishawasha, he noted on January 23rd, would not work for the Jesuit mission because 'their priests' had forbidden them to do so. 'This you will say is an honourable motive,' he told his wife, 'and so it is; it shows their conduct is controlled by their religion which is more than can be said of many of us whites. We are at present engaged in the most difficult of operations, the bursting up of their faith by chevying their Witch Doctor from point to point and proving him to be a liar.' By June Native Commissioner Campbell, who had at first believed that the paramounts should be the main target had come to see the Kagubi medium as 'the head or king of the rebels'. It was all very well to plan a final attack on Mashiangombi's, he wrote, but 'the better course would be to attack and capture Kagubi first. Although we may gradually subdue the Mashonas by attacking and conquering one chief after another we will arrive at a solution of the native question far sooner by striking at . . . Kagubi. The Mashonas are aware that they cannot wipe us out without help and I believe would surrender but for the fact that Kagubi has promised to exterminate us. . . . It therefore stands to reason that as soon as Kagubi is caught that the spell, so to say, will be broken and the war over but not until then unless every chief is taken in detail and thoroughly crushed which with our present force may take from two to four years, as there are hundreds of strongholds yet untouched. If Mashiangombi is thoroughly beaten and a lot of his people killed he may give in in an unsatisfactory manner but he will nevertheless be in communication with Kagubi all the time and will rise again on the first opportunity, should Kagubi be at large. I read in one of the local papers a short time ago that there was no head to the Mashona rebellion and that each kraal was its own empire, hence the difficulty of subduing it; but there can be no greater mistake. The Mashona war has as clearly defined a head as the last Zulu war: catch Kagubi and it will mean the same thing as it meant when Cetewayo was caught with regard to the Zulu war. . . . Mashiangombi's was the centre of the rebellion last year because Kagubi was there. The centre of the rebellion is now the hills around the

Umvumi river, 35 miles N.E. of Salisbury. If we capture Kagubi the war is over. If not, unless there is a famine among the natives, or we get a few thousand troops up, it may drag on for several years.' [1]

Several attempts were, in fact, made to capture 'Kagubi'. In February De Moleyns besieged Chiquaqua's stronghold—'if you want to kill us', said the defiant paramount, 'get an *impi* large enough and come and do it'. The kraals of both Chiquaqua and Gondo were taken and the caves blown up but the medium had left shortly before. In June another attempt was made which also failed. In August the Hussars and police, hot from their victory at Mashiangombi's, attacked 'Kagubi the witch-doctor, Nyanda, the Mazoe witch-woman, and Mquati, the Matabele prophet of the Mlimo . . . about 40 miles north-east of Salisbury in very difficult granite country'. 'Kagubi's' kraal was reached on August 15th; 'unfortunately Kagubi was found to have fled two or three days previously'; and the patrol had to be satisfied with burning the five hundred huts which had housed the mediums and their supporters. 'Had we come to Kagubi's before going to Mashiangombi's as I advised,' mourned Campbell, 'we should have had him for certain as his kraal was no stronghold . . . I feel very sick at not getting Kagubi.' [2]

The elusiveness of the mediums was, indeed, becoming the subject of a white myth as well as a Shona one. 'Eighteen months ago,' wrote Marshall Hole in *The African Review*, 'hardly anyone except the Native Commissioners knew this Kagube, even by name, but during this year so much time and many valuable lives have been sacrificed in futile efforts to effect his capture. He is such a remarkable man, has fomented so much trouble and has baffled the British South Africa Company's troops for so long. . . . He has proved a most elusive enemy and on more than one occasion when Sir Richard Martin, and his troops thought they had laid hands on him they have captured a nest of rebels only to find that their bird had flown.' Hole commented sourly on his influence on the Shona: 'In Matabeleland,' he wrote, 'they are

---

[1] Grey to Lady Grey, 23 Jan. 1897, GR 1/1/1; Campbell to C.N.C., 15 June, 1897, N 1/1/9.

[2] De Moleyns to Chief Staff Officer, 8 Feb. 1897; Roach to Officer Commanding, 16 Feb. 1897; LO 5/4/1. De Moleyn's report on operations in August 1897, LO 5/4/5; Campbell to C.N.C., 19 Aug. 1897, N 1/1/9.

more reasonable, and, if prone at times to fanatical outbreaks, know at any rate when they are beaten.' [1]

The paramounts proved in the end to be easier to engage than the Kagubi medium and they were eventually persuaded that they were defeated. It was a complex process of innumerable small actions and the relentless destruction of crops and the best way of illustrating it is to take the example of one paramount—Kunzwi Nyandoro, whose discontent with the Company regime we traced in Chapter Two, and whose refusal to pay tax was the first evidence of Shona discontent in 1896. Kunzwi had been left alone for most of 1896 since his kraal was known to be 'a natural stronghold having been brought to perfection by well thought out artificial fortifications, the stockades being of hewn stone, ten feet high and at least three feet thick and loop-holed so as to command every approach'. As we have seen, he had been one of the paramounts who flirted with Jenner's peace negotiations but with no intention of surrendering. In 1897 he was still in regular contact with the Kagubi medium through his son, Panashe, and very ready to join in the new offensive planned for the end of the wet season.[2]

In March, at much the same time that Mashiangombi was astonishing Captain Nesbitt with his assault on Fort Mondoro, Kunzwi-Nyandoro also took the offensive. In the first week of March a patrol set out from Salisbury to put into effect an ingenious scheme for making up white deficiencies in manpower. This was to recruit the warlike Budja of Mtoko, who had themselves thrown off administrative control in 1896, but who had repudiated messengers from 'Kagubi' and who had 'a grudge against the very central Mashonas around here who helped Captain Brabant to subdue the Mtokos'. The idea was that these 'friendlies' would move towards Salisbury, destroying crops and driving the rebels before them like 'a pheasant drive'; Kunzwi-Nyandoro was one of the paramounts who was intended to be caught by this movement. The patrol had not expected to meet resistance on its way to Mtoko but it was soon disillusioned. On March 5th it was attacked by Kunzwi's men 'with some resolution' and had to fight its way through to Mtoko in the face of constant ambushes and night attacks. On the return journey a

[1] H.M. Hole, 'Witchcraft in Rhodesia', *The African Review*, 6 Nov. 1897.
[2] Gosling to Officer Commanding, 19 June 1897, LO 5/4/4.

more serious attack took place. On the morning of March 15th the patrol and its accompanying friendlies were suddenly met with 'a heavy fire . . . more accurate and uninterrupted than I have yet seen in this country', as the adventurous Hubert Howard reported. The Budja took to their heels and there seemed a danger that the patrol would be overwhelmed. This attack also was attributed to Kunzwi's people.[1]

Not surprisingly these encounters drew white attention to Kunzwi. 'From the bold way in which the natives have attacked us', wrote Native Commissioner Armstrong, now in command of the Budja friendlies, 'I feel that Kunzi should at once be dealt with and the other districts I have mentioned. A better opportunity will never occur as we are now here with the Budja and the crops are nearly ripe.' But Armstrong's plan was frustrated by one of the most interesting events of the rebellion—the triumph of the pan-Shona teachings of the Budja mediums over the raiding policy of the chief. Taking advantage of chief Guripila's death while storming a Shona stronghold, the mediums told their people that he 'had now been killed for taking the *impi* to fight with the whites although against the wish of the witch-doctor. More than that', so Armstrong lurking anxiously in the bush near the Budja camp overheard them say, 'there were very few white men left in the country, the Mashonas spoke truth; they had nearly killed the lot . . . if it were not for the black men who were fighting for the whites, the Mashonas would easily kill the few whites left. . . . There were only a few whites there, let them be killed and Mtoko's people would no longer be slaves to the white man.' The Budja turned against Armstrong who made a forced march through the bush for ten days, for three of which he and his party survived on the meat of a pointer dog. The great 'pheasant drive' had not turned out quite as he had expected.[2]

Kunzwi-Nyandoro was still a main target of the white offensive —'the chief Kunzwi is the only chief who must be dealt with', Chief Native Commissioner Taberer went so far as to say, 'as he is powerful and independent and is not likely to surrender unless forced to do so'. But the attack would now have to be delivered

---

[1] Armstrong to C.N.C., 25 Feb. 1897; Howard to Grey, 12 Mar. 1897; Armstrong to C.N.C., 19 Mar. 1897; Howard to Grey, 20 Mar. 1897; LO 5/4/2.

[2] Armstrong to C.N.C., 26 May 1897, N 1/1/7.

by the police themselves. His stronghold was still regarded as so formidable that this attack was delayed for as long as possible. Sample attacks were made on the more accessible kraals of adjacent chiefs, Mashanganyika's among them, in the hope that Kunzwi would be sufficiently impressed to sue for peace. At the end of May Father Richartz sent out messengers from Chishawasha with an offer of terms and Kunzwi again flirted with the idea of negotiations. 'Kunzwi has not the slightest intention of surrendering,' grumbled Campbell, 'but simply wishes to gain time to get his crops harvested; he is one of Kagubi's staunchest supporters. . . . After our last *indaba* with him he sent his son Panashi and several of his men to Kagubi with presents and boasted how he had talked us over and I have no doubt he has done the same since Father Richartz' messenger left him. I am convinced that he has at present no more intention of surrendering than we have of making Kagubi King of England.' And, indeed, when it came to the point Kunzwi refused to talk. 'He would not *indaba*,' Grey told Rhodes; 'said it was unbecoming for a King to leave his kraal. Of course there is only one King in Rhodesia and that is the Govt. of the Queen and so he has been informed. He has sent away his women and prepared to fight.' [1]

The overthrow of Kunzwi's kingdom came on June 19th. On that day the police rushed his kraal in the fiercest action of 1897. 'The fire for an hour was something awful,' wrote Campbell; 'the niggers only left their walls after we were over them.' On June 22nd Campbell wrote a rejoicing epitaph. 'Panashe (Kunzi's son) came back from Kagubi the night before the fight, and said that Kagubi had told him that they were quite safe as the white men would all die as soon as they got to the walls. I would like to know how he is going to explain it to Kunzi after this. Ganyeri [Kunzwi's own medium] at the same time sang out, "Run, run, run, nyika wa parara, nyika wa parara—the country is torn up." A few men however still remained in the rocks below the lower wall and fought for a long time. Kunzi hid in the rocks till dark and then bolted.' [2]

For two months Kunzwi lived the life of a fugitive, moving from one stronghold to another, dependent upon the hospitality of

[1] Campbell to C.N.C., 29 May 1897, LO 5/4/4; Grey to Rhodes, 19 June 1897, Rhodes House, Mss. Afr. s. 228, C. 1., Vol. 1.
[2] Campbell to C.N.C., 19 and 22 June 1897, LO 5/4/4.

other chiefs. It was no life for a king. On August 28th Kunzwi sent in 2s. 6d. to Native Commissioner Campbell, then on patrol in Mrewa, offering to surrender. On September 15th Campbell described his negotiations with Kunzwi-Nyandoro, 'a different man now but still as proud as ever'. 'He said, God and Kagubi had done all this. I said, why do you not catch him then? He said, we are afraid to touch or offend Mlenga, so I said, well, Mlenga may do the same thing again so either bring me 72 more guns or leave our country. He said, you are killing me, where am I to go? I said, you had better ask Mlenga that, you still believe in him. . . . He said, what am I and my people to eat? I said, ask Mlenga that too.'[1]

By the end of August and the beginning of September the surrenders were coming in thick and fast—Mangwende, Soswe, Zwimba, Chiquaqua, Chinamora, Seki, and many others. But Campbell was still not satisfied. 'We are being fooled by the Mashonas and only getting guns that are practically useless while the good ones are hidden. I am thoroughly convinced that this country will never be properly settled till Kagubi and the other chief instigators are either hung, shot or sent to Robben Island.' In fact the Kagubi medium and his associates were not now many months away from one or other of these fates. Although they escaped the Hussars' attack in August, 'Kagubi' and Mkwati soon after ran into a patrol on the Mazoe; they escaped but in the confusion the party broke up and it seems that Mkwati and the rest of the mediums were now separated. The end of Mkwati's extraordinary story was now near. Until August he had continued to speak as the interpreter of Mwari; Campbell described 'the cave that the Umlimo is said to talk out of . . . walled up in front with poles and grass' which the police found and burnt in that month. But there had been reports as early as July that Mkwati's life had been threatened by the disillusioned Shona. He appears now to have gone into the Korekore area to try to raise it in revolt and it was there that he met his death some time in late September or early October 1897. 'The Mashonas killed him,' Mhlope tells us. 'The reason why they killed him was that they had already had news that he was causing trouble and when he came there the *indunas* ordered the people to kill him. . . . They killed him in a curious way. They cut him up in pieces while he

[1] Campbell to C.N.C., 15 Sept. 1897, N 1/1/9.

was alive with choppers. They said if he was the man who was sent by the Mlimo they had better make sure he could not come to life again and make more trouble.' Mkwati's gift for extending the area of the rebellion had at last deserted him.[1]

His consort, Tenkela-Wamponga, lasted longer and had better luck. She at first planned to escape into Portuguese East Africa with the Nehanda medium but that project was foiled by Native Commissioner Kenny's raid on their camp on November 4th. She then withdrew into the north and into the area of the old Mutapa confederacy. Her reception there was evidently a cordial one but she was captured in 1898 during Kenny's 'pacifying' patrols; she had been responsible, it was said, for 'some trouble in the district'. 'She was sent for trial in Bulawayo,' the Chishawasha mission journal tells us, 'and as apparently there was not sufficient evidence to convict her, her life was spared. To this day natives of the Chishawasha district express amazement that Vamuponga was spared and declare that she was the prime mover of the rebellion.'[2]

Neither the Kagubi nor the Nehanda mediums were likely to be spared. Early in October Native Commissioner Kenny's police attacked 'Kagubi' and his entourage in the north Mazoe district; the medium escaped again but 'had all his women captured with the exception of about four'. Kagubi then fled into Sipolilo's country where he was given rather reluctant sanctuary. But the net was closing in. Kenny was in Salisbury preparing a patrol to capture him; Native Commissioner Jackson was on a sweep through Lomagundi district and approaching Sipolilo. His new society in ruins, at long last 'Kagubi' decided to surrender; on October 27th Kenny took him into custody. 'When Kagubi was 20 miles from my camp I sent out 5 of my messengers to escort him into camp which was done,' reported Kenny. 'I must mention that Kagubi's envoys when they came in wanted to know the terms of his surrender. . . . I sent messages to Kagubi that I would give him no terms whatsoever, that he was to surrender

---

[1] Mhlope's statement, 20 Nov. 1938, WI 8/1/3. See also a remarkable story in the *Rhodesia Herald*, 13 Oct. 1897, which held that Mkwati had been murdered by his nephew and ward, Mihe, who was the true 'high priest' of Mwari and who now resumed direction of the cult. There is no other evidence to support this story.

[2] Mhlope, ibid. *Zambesi Mission Record*, Vol. 3, No. 40, Apr. 1908.

unconditionally or otherwise be captured.' In December the
Nehanda medium, still determined not to surrender, was also
captured by Kenny's police.[1]

The capture of the two mediums was greeted with relief and
enthusiasm by whites as a sure indication that the Shona rising
was finally at an end. The week after the Kagubi medium's arrival
in Salisbury 'under guard of the Native Police, who heralded his
arrival in town by a lusty song of triumph', the Salisbury *Nugget*
celebrated the event with its own triumphant verse, under the
heading, 'Kagubi Vinctus'. Indifferent as verse it still breathes
the spirit of white Rhodesian victory:

> How are the mighty fallen! Aye, mighty in bloody deeds;
> The Witch Doctor's wives and women will soon wear widows'
>   weeds.
> Their Lord is fallen—his power is done,
> His rule has set—as the setting sun,
> But—never to rise again.
>
> How are the mighty fallen! Go look at him in his cell,
> Stripped of the bracelets and doctor's charms,
> Stripped of his rank as well.
> A convict waiting to know his doom,
> Like a withered flower that has lost its bloom
> On a sandy desert plain.
>
> Spirits of innocent victims, look down on your vanquished
>   foe;
> Let not your friends who are living forget the revenge they
>   owe.
> As others have learned long years ago,
> So the young generation must learn to know
> That the White Queen means to reign.[2]

Kagubi did not have long to wait to know his doom. Two days
after his arrest a preliminary examination into a charge of murder

---

[1] The surrender of Kagubi and the capture of Nehanda are described in
detailed correspondence between N.C. Kenny and the C.N.C., Oct. to Dec.
1897, N 1/1/6.
[2] *The Nugget*, 2 Nov. 1897. The editorial is a threat that the people will
lynch 'Kagubi' if he is not given the death penalty.

against him opened in Salisbury. The trial was delayed while further arrests were made and more evidence taken but at last he and the Nehanda medium were both brought to trial on the same day—March 2nd, 1898. He was charged with the murder of an African policeman on June 20th, 1896; Nehanda with the murder of Native Commissioner Pollard. Both were found guilty, and sentenced to death. The date for the execution was fixed as April 27th; on the same day 'Kagubi's' father-in-law and ally, paramount chief Mashanganyika was also to die.[1]

Between the sentence and the execution the last act in the drama of 'the war of heathenism against Christianity' took place. Father Richartz of Chishawasha mission attended the prisoners in their cells and strove to convert them. At first when he spoke to 'Kagubi' of religion 'he would say, "Go to the others; I refuse." ' But one of the medium's daughters was, remarkably enough, a pupil at Chishawasha school and she now added her pleas to those of the priest. Under her persuasions the spiritual leader of the rising assented to this last transformation. On Tuesday, April 26th, Richartz was asked to tell the prisoners that they were to be executed the next day. 'Kakubi showed fear and began to cry. Mashanganyika and Mzampi took the news quietly.' The Nehanda medium, however, 'began to dance, to laugh and talk so that the warders were obliged to tie her hands and watch her continually, as she threatened to kill herself'. Next day he made an attempt to talk to her about religion 'but she refused, called for her people and wanted to go back to her own country—the Mazoe—and die there'.

Father Richartz then went down to the Kagubi medium in the death cell and received him into the Catholic church while 'Nehanda' was being executed above. 'Nehanda was taken out onto the scaffold. Her cries and resistance when she was taken up the ladder, the screaming and yelling on the scaffold disturbed my companion, Kakubi, very much, till the noisy opening of the trap-door on which she stood, followed by the heavy thud of her body as it fell, made an end to the interruption. Though very much frightened, Kakubi listened to me and repeated that he would no longer refuse baptism. After he had made the necessary acts of faith, repentence, etc., I baptized him, giving him the

[1] Regina versus Kagubi, HC/M, No. 253; Regina versus Nehanda, HC/M, No. 252; *The Rhodesia Herald*, 9 Mar. 1897.

L

name of the good thief, Dismas, with whom he was to share the great blessing of forgiveness in the hour of death. . . . The hangman came and did his duty . . . Kakubi did not give the least trouble nor did he make any lamentation. He died . . . quiet, resigned and, as I hope, in good disposition.' Thus by a final irony the Kagubi medium died as Dismas, among the first score of baptized Catholics in Mashonaland.[1]

'Everyone felt relieved after the execution,' confesses Father Richartz, 'as the very existence of the main actors in the horrors of the rebellion, though they were secured in prison, made one feel uncomfortable.' With their deaths, it was universally felt, the rebellion was finished; 'their bodies were buried in a secret place, so that no natives could take away their bodies and claim that their spirits had descended to any other prophetess or witch-doctor'. The younger generation, it was hoped, now knew that the white Queen meant to reign.[2]

[1] Richartz, 'The End of Kakubi', *Zambesi Mission Record*, Vol. i, No. 2, Nov. 1898.
[2] Notes by A. H. Holland, HO 7/4/2.

CHAPTER NINE

The Aftermath of the Rising:
White Attitudes and White Power

THE TERRIBLE events which we have been describing had profound effects upon the future of Southern Rhodesia. Although the
rebels were defeated or forced to a settlement which involved
submission to colonial rule their rebellions compelled whites to
take Africans seriously in a variety of ways as they had not done
before 1896. It also brought about significant changes in the
character of white colonial rule itself, so that although it survived
the challenge of the risings it did so in substantially different form.
Many of these changes, though not all, were to the benefit of the
African population in Southern Rhodesia. Thus their rebellion
was not a futile gesture nor merely an incident in Southern
Rhodesian history. In many ways it was a watershed; after the
risings few things were the same as they had been before.

We have seen how before 1896 whites believed that Africans in
Southern Rhodesia had no concepts of religion, no coherent
ability to act and no significant capacity to resist the pressures of
the new colonial society. These attitudes could hardly be maintained by intelligent or sensitive people after rebellions which had
come to be seen as wars of religion, which were conspicuously
coordinated and which showed a determination to preserve
African ways of life.

The experience of the risings was crucial to missionary attitudes
and missionary hopes. For some missionaries at least the realization that Shona concepts of the divine could exercise such an
influence on behaviour was a way into a more fruitful and optimistic relationship with their African flocks. The example of the
Catholic mission at Chishawasha is a striking one. Before the
rising their work had been painfully slow and they had often
given way to expressions of despair. In June 1896 the mission
station was attacked, on the direct orders of the Kagubi medium
in whose original area of operation it was sited, 'by natives of

Chishawasha themselves, who had been allowed to settle on the land rent free'. The disillusioned Fathers believed that from their first occupation the Shona had planned to allow them 'to develop their resources so that at a convenient season they might murder them all and fatten on the loot', a plan displaying 'a depth of blackness in the native heart, a meditated perfidy and a treachery rare even, one would hope, among savage races'. During the rising Chishawasha became a very important intelligence station; its few converts played an important role as go-betweens. One of them, Minyonanyane, now Joseph, was sent ahead of the Mtoko column to persuade Gurupira to provide friendlies in March 1897; another, Benyura, now Victor, was used as an intermediary in surrender negotiations with the Shona paramounts and was partly instrumental in the conversion of the Kagubi medium. The Chishawasha community, then, was fully committed to the white side during the rebellion and committed also to total defeat and severe punishment for the rebels.[1]

But out of these experiences there gradually came an appreciation, even if expressed in somewhat grudging terms, of the spiritual motivation of the rebels. This was very interestingly stated in May 1899 by Father Boos in a jubilant article entitled 'The Springtime of the Mashona Mission'. He began by recalling the depressing prospect which faced the mission at the end of 1897. 'The thousand natives we had gathered round us with such patient toil . . . had been scattered like sheep, and driven from stronghold to stronghold by the victorious army; we had even lost our little flock of neophytes, catechumens and school-children, who had been compelled to depart with the rebels. . . . Our own people, who had received such innumerable acts of kindness at our hands, had done their best to butcher us.' It was little wonder that the Fathers despaired. And yet, wrote Father Boos, 'the storm which has just blown over, so far from having proved the destruction of Christianity in Mashonaland, has in no slight degree aided its propagation'.

The rebels, after all, acted under 'a religious duty to take up arms against the white usurpers' and that fact 'ought to go furthest towards exculpating them in our eyes'. 'The incredible

[1] Viator, S.J., 'A Visit to Chishawasha at the end of 1897', *Zambesi Mission Record*. Vol. 1, No. 1, May 1898; 'The history of Chishawasha Mission', *Zambesi Mission Record*, Vol. 3, No. 40, Apr. 1908.

happened. The degraded, cowardly race which for so many years had proved an easy prey to the Matabele actually dared, at the bidding of their prophets, to engage in a war of extermination with the white colonists; and though defeated again and again, they continued to offer a stubborn resistance from their rocky strongholds, buoyed up with their unwavering belief in the promise of the witch-doctors. If, then,' concluded Father Boos, 'the influence of superstition is capable of converting the weak and degraded Mashona into a strong and daring foe may we not with reason hope that, once thoroughly imbued with the truths of the Catholic faith, he will prove a sturdy soldier of Christ?' Surely this mission was on the threshold of a great breakthrough, able as it was to offer an enduring inspiration to those now disillusioned with the failed prophets of Mashonaland.[1]

To Lord Grey also the fact that the Shona had appeared as 'a strong and daring foe' demanded a revision of white estimates of their potential; in his case he was thinking more in terms of their potential as workers and craftsmen. He was in fact much influenced by a visit to Chishawasha which he made soon after his arrival in Mashonaland. Like Rhodes he admired the Jesuits for their discipline and saw the Fathers as 'willing parts of an admirable machine set in motion by brains for the service of humanity and God'. He was deeply impressed by what remained of their achievement—two little Shona boys who could sing 'God Save the Queen' in perfect tune; an absurd enough little token but one which convinced Grey of Shona educability. If only, he thought, the whites of Mashonaland could model themselves on the Fathers of Chishawasha—'light-hearted, gay, profoundly unselfish and hard-working to a degree which no white man in Mashonaland outside their order can easily comprehend. No work is too hard or too menial for them—manual labour in the fields as gardeners, farm labourers; the menial occupation of cooks, brewers, bakers, etc.; the handicraft of farriers, carpenters, etc.; the higher but more aggravating role of schoolmasters and music teachers. . . . Before this order of the R.C. Church, producing as it does the most admirable results, one must stand hat in hand; and when one contrasts with it the vulgar individualism of our Protestant churches one is obliged to admit that from the policy and action

[1] Father Boos, 'The Springtime of the Mashona Mission', *Zambesi Mission Record*, Vol. 1, No. 4, May 1899.

of these powerful and historical orders one has very *very* much to learn.' [1]

Grey came away from his visit with a faith in the potential of education for the Shona greater than that of the Fathers themselves. They had almost despaired; but they had only failed to produce results, he was convinced, because of the political circumstances in which they worked. The Shona had been cowed and intimidated, ruled exclusively by fear and not by justice, let alone love. The Chishawasha schoolboys equally with though differently from the Shona rebels illustrated what might be done once fear was set aside. So Grey aspired to set up a form of government in which Shona potential could be realized. 'If I were to remain here', he told his wife, 'I sometimes think I might do something to better this state of things—so long as I remain here my endeavour will be to teach the natives that my Govt. is strong enough to punish them when they do wrong and to protect them when they do right and the white population that the employer who ill treats his native dependents and defrauds them of their just rights is a scoundrel.' [1]

Grey's attitude, so different from that of former white governors of Mashonaland, found practical expression in his attempts to encourage educational experiment. 'I want to teach the native boys blacksmithing, carpentry, tin-making, gardening and the girls washing, ironing and domestic handiwork,' he told one of the Company Directors in May 1897. 'Many people take a most gloomy view as to the possibility of doing anything with the Mashonas but I am not a pessimist on the subject, and it is our duty *to try* to make something of them.' Grey's plan, in fact, was a revolutionary one in its context; nothing less than a government attempt to emulate the Chishawasha approach and to take the lead in the transformation of Shona society through education. The rebellions had given the opportunity—'as the trouble the country is now passing through will in all probability produce a number of orphan children towards which the Administration may stand in loco parentis the necessary material for a promising experiment will be forthcoming'. The Company should set aside the buildings at Old Umtali with adequate capital to run 'a native industrial mission' on a large scale—'I shall control it as far as possible on healthy pagan lines, i.e., much industrial occu-

[1] Grey to his wife, 23 Jan. 1897, GR/1/1/1.

pation and little religion, instead of all prayer and no work, and keep it under control of Govt.' Grey also did his best to encourage more conventional mission activity in the same field. 'You will find the natives quick and teachable,' he told the American Methodist Episcopal Church, in flat contradiction to general white belief.[1]

Grey, then, came out of the risings with compassion for the Shona; Rhodes came out with respect for the Ndebele. The former, totally defeated and compelled to surrender uncondition-ally, were dependent altogether on the good will of their rulers— 'Thank God that you did not succeed in killing us', the Chisha-washa missionaries told the crowds to whom they distributed food during the famine that followed the rising. The Ndebele, how-ever, had proved that they had to be taken into account; they had surrendered on terms and Rhodes was anxious that those terms should be kept. Gone was his old assumption that African atti-tudes didn't matter very much; the rebellions had taught him that they could matter a great deal. Gone also was his old in-comprehension and lack of sympathy; the *indabas* with the Ndebele had caught his imagination and he kept up his relation-ship with the *indunas* not only out of necessity but also through a large romantic enjoyment. At any rate the contrast between the totally neglected condition of the *indunas* before 1896 and the priority Rhodes set upon maintaining good relations with them after 1896 was a very striking one. In May 1897 he expressed his sense of that priority when he informed the High Commissioner that he was unable to give evidence in the Charter inquiry in Britain because 'I have arranged to visit all the Matabele chiefs and fulfil my pledge that I would return to them and see that my promises had been fulfilled'.[2]

The Ndebele chiefs were assiduously wooed in the years that followed the rising. Rhodes addressed a great *indaba* on June 23rd, 1897, and patiently discussed problems of bride price and land settlement. In July he held a huge feast at his farm near the Matopos to celebrate his birthday; it was attended by some 1200 Ndebele, including many of the ex-rebel leaders. The *Bulawayo*

[1] Grey to London Board, 8 Feb. 1897, LO 5/4/3; Grey to Cawston, 26 May 1897, Rhodes House, Mss. Afr. s. 77.
[2] Rhodes to Stevens, 20 May 1897, Rhodes House, Mss. Afr. s. 227., letter book 6.

Chronicle's report of the event made a strange contrast with its usual social columns. 'Scattered in groups about the kopje sides were picturesque groups of natives . . . including Lobengula's witch-doctor, Bosaman, two of Lobengula's queens, and one of his young daughters. . . . Mr Rhodes and his friends passed continually in and out of the Matabele host holding a little indaba here and a little court there. . . . The aim of Mr Rhodes seems to be to inspire confidence in the natives, to make them believe that he has their welfare at heart as well as that of the whites.' And so the *indabas* continued. In November 1897 the Ndebele *indunas* were given a ride on the newly opened railway and taken afterwards to the circus prior to another *indaba* in Bulawayo—'a marvellous performance in their eyes and probably made them appreciate the superiority of the whites more than anything else had done.' And after another meeting on Rhodes' farm in 1900 the local Native Commissioner reported that it was characterized by 'profound respect on the one side and open hearted friendliness on the other. . . . I do not remember ever having seen a body of natives impressed in quite the same way as they were that day. It seemed to me that were he so to desire he might become their own elected leader.' [1]

Rhodes played this new role with great success until his death but it was not enough in itself to meet the situation. More tangible promises had been made and had to be kept, partly because of the need still felt to pacify the Ndebele and partly because of the pressures upon the Company for reform which the rebellions coming as the climax of its hectic career had brought into being. Rhodes and Grey had promised a new system of native administration in which would be employed more and better qualified commissioners; this was also the demand of the imperial authorities, and especially Milner, now High Commissioner in South Africa. Sir Richard Martin, charged with producing a report on the administration of Rhodesia, had found the Company guilty of maladministration and injustice, and although Grey and Rhodes hotly contested his findings in detail there was no doubt that reforms would have to be made. It was for this reason that Rhodes had brought Milton up in August 1896 and Milton was soon possessed by a dislike of the adventurism of the Jameson period as great as Sir Richard Martin's.

[1] Report of the Native Commissioner, Malema, Sept. 1900, LO 5/7/4.

'It is of immense importance to the future of South Africa that we should use the present opportunity to get the administration of Rhodesia into something like order,' Milner told Grey in June 1897. 'As far as I can make out . . . there is a great improvement going on in this respect. I think . . . everybody must admit that there *was* great need of improvement.' In the months that followed Milner and Grey discussed the regulations appropriate to the Native administrative system; the scrupulous care of both men over the matter was in striking contrast to the settlement which followed the 1893 war. In November 1897 Milner went to Rhodesia to see things for himself. He found it 'an eye-opener'; 'things in Rhodesia are in a *pretty handsome mess* administratively'. 'Between ourselves', he wrote on December 1st, 'it is a bad story. On the one hand land alienated in the most reckless manner to Companies and individuals, on the other hand a lot of unfit people were allowed to exercise power, or at any rate did exercise it, especially with regard to the natives in a manner that cannot be defended. I know the difficulties were enormous. Perhaps they explain the failure but failure it was, and the rebellion was largely due to it.' 'On this difficult and most important question of the Native Commissioners,' wrote Milner, 'I took it upon myself to speak very strongly to both Milton and Rhodes.' [1]

Rhodes himself had at last been convinced that the days of adventurism in Rhodesia were over; convinced by his talks with the Ndebele *indunas* as much as by his talks with Milner. 'The Company—or in other words Rhodes and his principal agents—recognize this administrative weakness themselves', wrote Milner; 'they *almost* admit it—and they are certainly trying to get things right'. The new Native Department was a very different place from its predecessor in the days of Colenbrander and Brabant. Brabant himself, conspicuously a figure from another age, having been officially cleared of allegations of cruelty to African prisoners during the rebellion, was now planning a filibustering raid on the cattle of Barotseland; detected by Milton he was quietly sent packing with a small gratuity as a remembrance of the old days. It was the spirit of his successor, Taberer, which triumphed now. In 1897 Native Commissioner Staples, who had been placed in charge of Umlugulu's district, was dismissed on the

---

[1] Milner to Grey, 6 June 1897; Milner to Selborne, 29 Dec. 1897; Milner to Chamberlain, 1 Dec. 1897; Headlam, op. cit., Vol. 1.

grounds that he was neglecting his African charges: 'He does not appear to have studied their interests to that extent which would prove conducive to the progress of the country, as far as the Native question is concerned.' 'The importance of the native question is at present so great', Staples was told, 'that the Government is able to retain only those officials who prove themselves fully qualified for the work.' [1]

As for the administration generally the spirit of that 'red-tape' which Rhodes and Jameson had scorned now dominated. Milton, succeeding Grey as Administrator, laid the foundations of a regular civil service. 'I can hardly describe the thin, evasive, official atmosphere of this place', wrote a correspondent nostalgic for the days of Jameson describing Milton's Salisbury in July 1898, 'in which there is none of the robust commercial vitality and imagination of Bulawayo. It is an air so rarefied that new ideas fall to the ground like birds in the high mountain regions of Thibet, unable to obtain support for their wings.' It was to him 'of all mental attitudes the most discouraging. . . . It is like returning to the High Table at College where all goes easily and the storms of the outside world sound far away.' Milner, more appreciatively noted that '*there is great amendment* and . . . the position of the black man in Rhodesia is now probably more hopeful than in any part of South Africa not under direct imperial control, except Natal.' [2]

These good intentions extended even to the vexed question of land. Once again it was a compound of Grey's interest in reform, Rhodes' promises to the Ndebele, and the pressure of the imperial authorities, especially Martin. Rhodes, as we have seen, promised adequate land to the Ndebele at the second *indaba* and later allowed the senior *indunas* to settle on the land which they had occupied before 1893. Martin, although he did not mention the question in his report, had become convinced that the land reserved for the Ndebele after 1893 was quite inadequate. In April 1897 he wrote a scathing memorandum. The areas 'appear never to have been inhabited by the Matabele . . . the districts in

---

[1] C.N.C. to Rhodes' Secretary, 25 July 1898; C.N.C. to Deputy Administrator, 19 Dec. 1897; Deputy Administrator to Staples, 22 Feb. 1898; Rhodes House, Mss. Afr. s. 228, C. 1, Vol. 1. Staples argued in his defence that he had only neglected the interests of Basutos and Makalangas and not Ndebeles!

[2] Sargent to Rhodes, 30 July 1898, ibid; Milner to Asquith, 18 Nov. 1897, Headlam, op. cit.

question are not looked upon as desirable places for settlement'; most of the land, in fact, was 'unsuitable for native locations'. Grey and Milton were both anxious to tackle the problem. 'Land is our great difficulty,' wrote Grey in May 1897; 'it has all been given away. I will not give away another acre until the Native question has been settled, so those people who have not pegged out the land they are entitled to peg or have not got provisional titles must wait until I have the native reserves all tied up.' [1]

In the same month Grey wrote at length to Rhodes on the subject. 'We must secure for the native some means of escaping from a farm where the conditions of his tenancy prevent him from choosing his own employer to a bit of land where he can live under conditions which secure him freedom of choice as to his employer, and this opens up the whole question of Government Reserves. As a first step it will be necessary to inform owners of rights to titles who have not exercised their rights and obtained title . . . that we cannot give titles until we are satisfied that the land so pegged would not be required for Native Locations. . . . The second step will be, I fear, the quiet buying up for the Company of farms recommended for the purpose of Native Locations by the Chief Native Commissioner. Unless we can provide a government farm or two in each Native Commissioner's District for Native Reserves, Martin will insist upon an independent report by some Imperial officer as to the suitability of the Guai and Shangani Reserves for natives and it would be a nasty shock for us if a report were to come out at this time condemning the Guai and Shangani Reserves as wholly unsuitable. . . . This makes an additional reason why we should establish Native Reserves in every district but the real reason to my mind is that this policy is required in the interests of the country and of the native also. This buying up of Private Farms for Native Reserves means a big expenditure but I do not see how it can be avoided—an inquiry into the character of the Guai and Shangani Reserves will bring out the fact that they are regarded by the natives as *cemeteries* not homes. . . . It will cost a lot of money, I fear about £50,000, to get the land we want. The question is can our finances stand it? If it can I have no hesitation in saying, and Milton agrees with me, that we ought to face it.' [2]

[1] Grey to Cawston, 26 May 1897, Rhodes House, Mss. Afr. s. 77.
[2] Grey to Rhodes, 26 May 1897, Rhodes House, Mss. Afr. s. 228, C. 1, Vol. 1.

So the titled fortune-hunters found that the climate of 1897 and 1898 had become as chilly for them as for the Brabants. In November 1897 the Hon. H. F. White, Colonel commanding the Mashonaland Mounted Police during the Jameson Raid, and very much one of the aristocratic supporters of Jameson whom Milton so much disliked, appealed to Rhodes. 'I pegged out 70,000 morgen in the Inyanga district. . . . After a delay of 2 months, I being £100 out of pocket, one of the Trinity who are supposed to rule these territories informed me that the land was required for natives and he would see me d . . . d if I should have it. This was one knock down blow only to be followed by another. I distinctly understood in my interview with yourself, Grey and Lawley, that I might peg land in Matabeleland if I could find it; well it was found, pegged and approved of under Lawley's signature, surveyed and provisionally registered. I am now informed that my syndicate . . . must pay for it. . . . They say the Council cannot *give* land in Matabeleland. . . . I am sick of trying to deal with the Chartered Company. We poor devils who had anything to do with that accursed Transvaal affair get all the kicks.' White felt very much out of his element in a world in which, as he wrote bitterly in the same letter, 'the *Indunas* are staying at Government House; Babyan is very irate at not being allowed to take Lady Hely Hutchinson down to dinner; the Kaffirs are having mealies ridden out to their kraals and dumped there by British South Africa Company wagons'. It was all very different from the days of Jameson.[1]

On these matters—native administration, land, support for industrial education—Rhodes, Grey and Milton were prepared, with varying degrees of enthusiasm, to push reforms themselves. But the new atmosphere after the rebellion extended further than that. The question of how Africans were treated in Rhodesia had become a matter of wide public interest in Britain. Before 1896 the Company administration had certainly had its critics but there was little interest or knowledge about its routine administration. After the rebellion there runs throughout Milton's correspondence in his early years as Administrator a constant sense of the vigilance of the philanthropic groups in Britain and of the limitation which this implied. This limitation was felt most in the field of measures designed to procure African labour. Sir Richard

[1] H. F. White to Rhodes, 9 Nov. 1897, Rhodes House, Mss. Afr. s. 228, C. 27.

WHITE ATTITUDES AND WHITE POWER

Martin had accused the Company of forcing labour before the rising. After it the British Government showed an unusual vigilance on the question. Rhodes and Grey had originally proposed that the salaried *indunas* should be given a bonus according to the number of men they sent in to work; this was the one aspect of their proposed new administrative system that was vetoed by the Secretary of State. Subsequently various projects were mooted for ensuring a supply of labour. Settler pressure was strong—'You cannot conceive how near the brink of disaster we are,' wrote one of Rhodes' correspondents. 'There is abundance of labour in Rhodesia to satisfy *present* requirements but it will not turn out and I fear the Govt. feel that their hands are tied by the Colonial Secretary and Exeter Hall.' But Milton's administration was unable, though anxious, to meet the demand of the employers for 'a really good man who should be appointed Secretary of Labour for Rhodesia' or for an increase in hut tax to compel Africans to work. 'I received yesterday a cable from the Board saying that the Imperial Government had finally decided that we should have nothing to do with recruiting of labour,' wrote Milton to Rhodes on January 2nd, 1902, 'so that is settled. Everyone here agrees that it will have a bad effect on the native mind but of course no-one at home is influenced by such considerations.' 'I asked the Board some time ago,' he went on, 'whether they thought that I should try to get the labour tax of £2 through this year. Fox told me that in deference to Chamberlain's wishes Grey did not refer to it in his speech to the shareholders. I have had no reply.' A few days later he commented on a despairing suggestion from Rhodes that one way to get African labour for the mines would be to provide kaffir beer at them—'I am sure that in reasonable quantities and under regulation it would be good for the natives but the mere mention of supplying "beer" would give Fox Bourne and Co. a fit. If we could only call it "Rapoko Tea" they would be charmed.' Milton resented but was always very well aware of the fact that even his reformed administration was regarded with suspicious vigilance; to the philanthropists, he wrote bitterly, his administrative record was four years of 'tyranny and oppression to which the wicked administration has subjected the natives'.[1]

[1] McDonald to Rhodes, 23 Apr. 1901; McDonald to Jourdan, 18 Feb. 1901; Milton to Rhodes, 2 Jan. 1902, 25 Jan. 1902; Rhodes House, Mss. Afr. s. 228, C. 1, Vol. 2.

On this issue of labour Rhodes was violently indignant with the philanthropic and imperial stand. On January 20th, 1898, he gave an interview to the *Daily Chronicle*. 'The report sent to England by Sir Richard Martin, and the faddists of Exeter Hall and amongst the Aborigines Protection Society have stopped our original plan of obtaining black labour, and the result you see before you, as although I have at least a couple of hundred able-bodied native men on my farm I cannot get a dozen to work in the garden or fields. . . . Their ancestors have generally been warriors, who but rarely did menial work except to help their women plant enough corn to support them and their families. "Now," they say, "the white men want to make us work in their mines and fields. But no—we do not want their money. We have done without it in the past—why should we work unless we wish to?" Until recently we could have got them to work for us in return for permission given them to live on our land, but even that is stopped now; and beyond collecting a hut tax of ten shillings a year, we are powerless. It is really too absurd and the British faddist has dealt us—and me personally—the worst blow that has yet fallen on Rhodesia.' 'With these misguided enthusiasts,' echoed *Rhodesia*, 'there is no medium between idleness and slavery; honest labour under the guiding and protecting hand of their own fellow countrymen is strictly condemned.' But much as Rhodes might fret at the intolerable spectacle of African idleness —'the native lives the life of a retired gentleman and ruffles it with other braves at the different beer drinkings without a thought for the future'—there was little that could be done in the aftermath of the rising. For a period at least the Rhodesian administration *was* 'tied by the Colonial Secretary and Exeter Hall'.[1]

Finally, in addition to Grey's compassion for the Shona and Rhodes' respect for the Ndebele, to the missionary glimpse of unsuspected African potential and Milton's zeal for an efficient administration, to the Company's realization that it must set its house in order and the pressure of the philanthropists upon the imperial and Rhodesian governments, there was another very important emotion produced by the rebellions and sustained by their memory—fear. Gone for a period at least was the armour of self confidence which had carried the handful of whites through before 1896. The sudden unsuspected risings in which the house-

[1] *Rhodesia*, 18 Dec. and 12 Feb. 1898.

servants, the customers in the stores, the respectful old men, suddenly turned into killers, burnt themselves deep into white Rhodesian consciousness. The settlers bitterly resented what they regarded as the new coddling of Africans. 'Some little disgust is being expressed by the Bulawayo citizens at the growing familiarity adopted by the natives in town, who coolly take possession of the footpaths and calmly jostle the white settlers, their wives and daughters, in calm disregard of class distinction and propriety,' wrote *Rhodesia* in February 1898. 'On a platform at Exeter Hall, with a crowd of dainty ladies around, and a sea of bespectacled faces beaming philanthropically on the spokesman, one will hear such sentiments expressed as equality for black and white, the noble example of sharing your room and crust of bread with your black brother or sister as the case may be, but it would be rather curious to note the effect of a sudden contact between a dirty, greasy, woolly-headed, naked, flat-footed and thick-lipped, raw Mashona and a dainty old lady of benevolent appearance and cleanly instincts. The long, deep and wide grin of the nigger cavity, called a mouth by courtesy, would be a strange contrast to the puckered corners of the lady's rosebud mouth drawn down in prim disgust. Imagine in future an Exeter Hall erected in Cape Town or Bulawayo, wherein shall assemble all the well-to-do settlers and with strong denunciations protest against the downtrodden race of coal-heavers, who are considered unfit to associate with fashionable ladies in England.' This sort of thing did not show either compassion or respect, but it concealed fear, and fear could sometimes have the same results.[1]

In the months after the rebellions there were several panics in rural districts in both Matabeleland and Mashonaland in which whites went into laager on rumours of renewed rebellion. This happened in Melsetter in the far east of Mashonaland where there had been no rising in 1896; it happened in Enkeldoorn, the area which Rhodes had declared totally free of rebels in 1897, where the farmers refused to leave the laager in January 1898 unless their families were allowed to stay there and all Africans were forced to live under observation in locations; it happened in the same area again in July 1898 when a rumour of a rising in Chilimanzi was widely believed, and another laager was set up; it happened in the Inyanga district in March 1904 when it was

[1] *Rhodesia*, 12 Feb. 1898.

believed that Makoni and Mutassa—the 'loyal' Ndapfunya and the 'loyal' Mutassa of 1896–7—had agreed to initiate a general rising. 'During the past few months', wrote the Chief Staff Officer, 'there have been scares amongst the white inhabitants in several districts, resulting from reports that have gained currency out of all proportion to their importance, and in some cases these scares have been augmented rather than allayed by the ill timed precautionary measures of the British South Africa Police. . . . Their *normal* condition should be one of preparedness for any emergency so that no action calculated to invite comment or create alarm will be necessary in the event of rumours or unconfirmed reports of native unrest.' [1]

Town dwellers shared these fears also. Throughout 1897 Bulawayo felt very vulnerable to a sudden Ndebele attack; nine years later the new settler population of Livingstone, just over the border from Southern Rhodesia, demanded rifles so that they could defend themselves from any sudden rising. Supposing, the *Livingstone Pioneer and Advertiser* asked, with vivid memories of 1896, the Lozi were to rise or the tribes in the northern part of Southern Rhodesia; 'How would we stand then? Alone, and if thus isolated and inadequately equipped another dark page would be added to the already dark-enough history of Africa. Our stations would be wiped out, murder (and worse) rampant, and each man fighting desperately for his life—nor could all the courage and heroism of the white man avert the calamity. It was only the other day that things looked ominous in Natal—a day may dawn when we are confronted with the like.' [2]

Nor was it possible to dismiss these fears as absurd. Africans continued to demonstrate readiness to hit back. There was a rising in north-eastern Mashonaland in 1900 which we shall discuss in the next chapter; there was a rising in the Zambesian territories of Portuguese East Africa as late as 1917 which the Native Department feared might spread into Mashonaland. And, of course, there were risings in other parts of East and Central Africa, notably the Maji-Maji outbreak in German East Africa in 1905, to remind anyone who had forgotten of the possibility of insurrection. Moreover, though they tried not to reveal it, the Native Commissioners themselves were by no means confident in

[1] See files DE 1/2/9, A 11/2/12/11 and A 11/2/12/12.
[2] *The Livingstone Pioneer and Advertiser*, 10 Mar. 1906.

this period that another revolt was out of the question. Native Commissioner Hulley of Umtali district, who made a bland public statement in November 1903 that there was 'no foundation whatever' for rumours of unrest, was at the same time writing confidentially: 'I am firmly convinced that we are in for such a row as we have not had up here yet. I do not say that there are any tangible facts to lay hold of. . . . I do not believe that I am a coward or a pessimist . . . yet I never travel now without being armed. There are things which cannot be explained yet the whole attitude of the natives leads one to believe that they are going to have another slap at us.' In December he wrote again: 'I have arrived at the opinion that the natives in this country intend to rise. . . . There are looks which natives give white people which cannot be expressed; there are tones of voices and gestures.' Morris from Marandellas agreed that 'certain Mashona tribes will again rebel. . . . The natives, though outwardly satisfied and peaceable, object to our rule. It only requires a witch doctor who has been fortunate in the past and has obtained a footing as a true prophet to prophesy destruction of the whites to get the majority of the tribes to rise.' Edwards from Mrewa expressed his un-easiness: 'There is some unexplainable feeling of unrest amongst the natives. Superstition is at the bottom of it without a doubt . . . the natives blame us for the last dry season, we having killed their principal rain doctor in Nyanda who was hung in Salisbury after the rebellion, and from conversations I have had with some of the natives I am of opinion that another dry season and a famine was prophesied by some leading witch doctor and a method of preventing this happening was no doubt also given by the same authority.' Similar fears were expressed in 1915 when the Super-intendent of Natives, Salisbury, commenting upon Mwari activity and suspected links with the Germans, wrote: 'I do not wish to pose as an alarmist [but] those well acquainted with the natives of this territory know how easily their superstitions can be worked on by a bold and clever witch-doctor, and if the Mlimo in the Matopos and Nyanda were to persuade them to rise, they would, I believe, do so.' Even as late as 1923, at the time of the change from Company rule to Responsible Government, reports of instructions by Mwari messengers to hide grain in the hills was causing official concern.[1]

[1] The views of Hulley, Morris, Edwards and many other Native Com-

As for the police the lessons they drew from 1896–7 were set on paper in the Staff Officers' memorandum from which we have quoted before. 'It cannot be said that rebellion is a thing of the past. Sporadic and local revolts may take place in the future. Some supposed wrong or grievance, some law that is irksome, or some fanatic with more brain than usual, may easily fan the flame of discontent into revolt. A general rebellion, in the sense that all tribes throughout Southern Rhodesia will rise simultaneously, is out of the question in future. . . . What may, however, be anticipated is some local outburst, followed by others in adjoining localities, which if not quickly quelled may lead to their spreading rapidly throughout the country.' In future the Africans must be 'closely watched for signs of discontent, and any evidence of large desertions from employment, removal of grain and cattle, etc., etc., be at once investigated. To have some knowledge of the probable strength and fighting method of the native, as well as the nature of his armament and the locality of his strongholds is essential, as well as the probable grouping of tribes in an emergency and the likely leaders.' [1]

Fear of rebellion, then, meant that the whites, or some of them, had to seek to understand the Africans, at any rate at this sort of level. It also acted as a restraint on the enforcement of measures which might provoke a rising. While before 1896 it was believed that whatever provocation was given the Shona especially would never rebel, after 1896 it was realized that they might rebel again if provoked too far. This at least was gained by their commitment to the risings. We may give one concrete example of the way in which this factor worked to protect Africans in Southern Rhodesia after the rebellion from the extremes of exploitation.

As we have seen the Company and also industrial employers of labour in Southern Rhodesia wished to increase the hut tax and to force Africans to seek paid employment. In 1903 the new Legislative Council passed an enactment raising the tax from 10s. a year to £2 a year. At once voices were raised against this increase from some unexpected quarters. 1903 was a year of rumours of renewed African preparations to rise; of meetings near Great Zimbabwe; of the emergence of a new religious leader. These

missioners may be found in file A 11/2/12/11; S/N, Salisbury, to C.N.C., 24 Apr. 1915, N 3/33/3.
[1] Staff study of the 1896 rebellions, PA 1/1/3.

rumours were linked with the proposed tax increase. Many settlers remembered 1896 and what they regarded as the sacrifice of their interests to the immoral considerations of capital and feared a repetition. Rhodesia, wrote a local correspondent to the *Financial News* in November 1903 was 'on the eve of another of those sanguinary revolts which have twice broken out in that still half conquered piece of South Africa'; the revolt was being planned because of the new tax demand, and what was more, so the correspondent asserted, 'a revolt would be welcome to the promoters of most of the Rhodesian gold mining companies. These ventures are now in a bad way and a native rising would give them an excuse for reconstruction.' The farmers of Melsetter, of all Rhodesians the least likely to harbour sentimental negrophile views, protested against the tax on the grounds that it would pro-voke unrest. And protests came also from white South Africa. 'It will be remembered that the Legislative Council of Rhodesia not long ago increased this tax from 10s. to 40s. per hut per year. To increase such a tax by no less than 300% at one stroke of the pen,' wrote the *South African News*, 'does not indicate commonsense administration, to say nothing of statesmanship. . . . The Rho-desian Government owes it to the rest of South Africa to investi-gate the circumstances, weigh the natives' view of the case and set its house in order. . . . It is hardly necessary to point out that it behoves all governments in South Africa to keep an alert eye upon any possible source of native complications.' [1]

In this context the imperial authorities were able to present the argument of African unrest as a decisive one in refusing to accept the tax increase. On July 29th, 1903, the Colonial Secretary minuted that he could only approve the increase 'on being assured that no serious trouble is to be feared from the increased tax. I shall require definite assurance of the Resident Com-missioner to this effect before I assent.' Such assurance was not forthcoming. The Resident Commissioner expressed the view that the increase would have an 'unsettling effect on the natives calcu-lated to endanger security and good order in the country'. So, acting on the principle that 'the governing consideration is that there should be no risk of native disturbance', the Colonial Secretary refused to sanction an increase of more than ten shillings

[1] *The Daily News*, 5 Nov. 1903; *South African News*, 5 Apr. 1904; N.C. Melsetter, to Administrator, 13 Nov. 1903, A 11/2/12/11.

a year, and imposed a year's delay upon the collection of that additional ten shillings.

The lessons of this incident as they emerge from the correspondence of the Colonial Secretary and his High Commissioner may be taken as an expression of the lessons of the 1896–7 risings generally. Writing to the High Commissioner on June 8th, 1904, about the reports of African unrest which had preceded his decision on the hut tax issue, Colonial Secretary Lyttelton remarked that in future business of this sort 'the attitude of the natives will have to be taken into account'. To this High Commissioner Milner assented. Africans in Southern Rhodesia still hoped, so the Resident Commissioner informed him, that 'the white man has not come to stay and that the day will come when they will regain their country and their independence. This emphasizes the expediency to avoid giving the natives of the territory any common grounds for considering themselves wronged or unjustly treated.' [1]

Thus in all kinds of ways after the rebellions expression was given to a new realization that 'the attitude of the Africans will have to be taken into account'. Much though they had lost through the rebellions the Africans of Southern Rhodesia had these gains to show. It was not only a matter of the good bargain struck for their caste by the senior Ndebele *indunas* but also a matter of mingled white fear and guilt and compassion which resulted in some efforts being made to reform, in some efforts being made to understand, and in a reluctance to push Africans too far in future. All this was very important. And yet the rebellions were great and complex events occurring in an infinitely complex situation. Their effects were not simple nor did they all point in the same direction. If in many ways the effects of the risings strengthened the African position in Southern Rhodesia—by comparison, that is, with their position under the Company regime between 1890 and 1896—they also strengthened the position of the white settlers.

Perhaps the best way to approach this is to recall the definition of Grey's new native policy which we quoted above. The rights

[1] Chamberlain to Milner, 29 July 1903; Resident Commissioner to High Commissioner, 29 May 1903; Lyttelton to Lawley, 7 Nov. 1903; Graham to London Board, 4 Dec. 1903; C.O., C.P., S.A., No. 717, pp. 351, 413–14, 615, 655. Lyttelton to Milner, 8 June 1904; Milner to Lyttelton, 25 July 1904; C.O., C.P., S.A., No. 746, pp. 239–40; 327; 407–8.

and powers of the Ndebele *indunas* were to be restored in so far as was compatible with white supremacy. We must now ask what white supremacy meant in the context of the period after the rebellions and to what extent meaningful reform and redress of African grievance was compatible with it. Which whites—to begin with—were to be supreme?

It is a commonplace that what most distinguishes the history of Southern Rhodesia from that of, say, Kenya is the success of the Southern Rhodesian settlers in obtaining political control. For this difference between the two colonies there are, of course, many reasons. One reason emerges from what we have already said of the early history of Southern Rhodesia. From the very beginning the settler element was of crucial importance there; unlike any other colony in East and Central Africa it began with the arrival on its soil of settlers—the Pioneers of 1890. From the very beginning its economy was dependent upon white enterprise; what opportunities there were of cashing in on existing African trade or gold washing or of creating an African cash crop economy were ignored. From the beginning, also, the settlers were deeply involved in the processes of administration; they had no control over policy and no representation politically but their armed support was essential to the success of the colony. Kenya, of course, was very different in all these respects; by the time settlers in significant numbers were established there the Southern Rhodesian whites already enjoyed representation on the legislative council. Moreover, the Southern Rhodesian enterprise had from the beginning a more forceful thrust; it was a projection out of the South African colonies and drew men and money from them as well as from Britain; compared to the German or British Companies in East Africa we have said the British South Africa Company could draw upon greatly superior resources. So, in the last resort, could the white settler community. As the *Cape Times* wrote in June 1896 the interest of the whites of Rhodesia in defeating the Ndebele and Shona risings was the interest of all white South Africa. There was a danger, it wrote in a call for aid to the Rhodesians, that 'the handful of whites might be swept away by the flowing tide of savagery, a deluge which the whole civilization of South Africa was interested in staying at all costs. Would we do the same for the Free State or the Transvaal as for Rhodesia? We answer, with Mr Innes, Against the black foes—yes!' It may be that with this sort of support available 'against the black foes' the white settlers of Rhodesia were destined from the beginning to achieve supremacy in the territory.[1]

Nevertheless, there can be no doubt that the situation produced by the rebellion resulted in the acceleration of white settler advance. As we have seen the settler communities of Matabeleland and Mashonaland were bitterly resentful at the Company's failure to protect them and their families—'There is a bitter feeling among many in town about the incompetency of the British South Africa Company to rule the country,' wrote Carnegie from Bulawayo in May, 1896. That bitter feeling became stronger as the rebellion continued and as most whites reacted against Rhodes' negotiations with the Ndebele and the evacuation of the Imperial troops. In November 1896, for instance, it was reported that in Bulawayo 'people are asking "What is to prevent an attack? What precautions are being taken to prevent an attack? What show would men and women have in the outskirts of the town should even a hundred rebels attack with their knobkerries alone? Are we altogether dependent on the forbearance of fully armed rebels, who are well aware of our defenceless position. . . . Is the Government so impressed with the Matabele desire for peace that they take no precautions whatever? Is there another town from Cape Town to the Zambesi so utterly defenceless as Bulawayo is at this moment?" '[2]

Feeling in Salisbury was even more bitter. There, after all, the whites had to face the consequences of the failure of Rhodes' policy of conciliation and withdrawal, while in Matabeleland in 1897 most settlers came gradually to realize that it had been successful there. In April 1897 the Salisbury Chamber of Mines unanimously passed a resolution that 'misleading statements have been officially made as to the condition of Mashonaland, causing a totally erroneous idea of the state of the rebellion to be entertained in Europe'. It was in Salisbury that the most vocal critics of Company rule were based in 1896 and 1897.[3]

And at this time, of course, the existence of such criticism was highly dangerous to the Company. As Carnegie wrote in December 1896 the great question was, 'Is the Company to continue? It's

---

[1] *Cape Times*, 30 June 1896.   [2] *Cape Times*, 18 Nov. 1896.
[3] Resolution of the Salisbury Chamber of Mines, Apr. 1897; C.U., C.P., S.A., No. 517, p. 544.

part imperialism now which rules the country and it's very difficult to state how far they are distinct or how near they are to be related to one another.' As a result of the Jameson Raid and the rebellions investigations into the Company's affairs were being made by Parliament and by the British government. Clearly the constitutional position would be changed in some way and clearly there was a distinct possibility of the Charter being revoked and direct imperial control being asserted. As we have seen Rhodes managed to avoid one threat to the Charter by coming to terms with the Ndebele and getting the imperial troops out. But this made the settler threat all the more acute. A good deal of sympathy was felt for the settlers in Britain even amongst the most convinced critics of Company maladministration; if anything like a unanimous settler demand for imperial rule were to be voiced the Company's position would be gravely endangered. In short for Rhodes to complete his rescue operation the settlers had to be "squared" as well as the Ndebele.[1]

In so far as this could be done in fiscal terms it was done; very generous compensation was paid to settlers who had lost property in the risings. But this alone was not enough; the settlers were determined to extract payment in constitutional terms. 'The reform, we take it, towering above all others,' wrote the *Rhodesia Herald* in November 1896, 'is that of the present constitution of the Government and the administration of the country. The Government of this country is unique. No other civilized nation in the world can furnish us with a parallel. It is a deplorable fact that the white inhabitants of the country who have shed their blood and risked their lives in fighting the battles of the Chartered Company . . . are placed politically speaking on a level with the blood-thirsty Matabele and the cowardly, treacherous Mashona, their deadly enemies. We have hitherto had no voice in the affairs of the country and we venture to state that the interests of the Company have suffered severely in consequence. . . . Of course . . . we must creep before we can walk and walk before we can run. The rule by the Chartered Company can be regarded as the creeping, the semi-elective system the walking and ultimate responsible government as the running stage.' The opportunity

[1] Carnegie to Thompson, 12 Dec. 1896, L.M.S., Matabele Mission, Vol. 5, No. 102.

had now come, it was seen, to move from the creeping to the walking stage.[1]

It is in this context that we must see Rhodes' speech to the leaders of settler opinion in Salisbury on November 10th, 1896. 'The Salisbury people are all in an excessively discontented state,' wrote Lady Victoria Grey. 'They say they are neglected in having neither Father or Mr Rhodes there (the truth is they are jealous of Bulawayo), so Daddy feels he ought to go as soon as he can possibly leave here.' In the event it was Rhodes who went to hold, so to speak, his *indaba* with the whites. In Salisbury Rhodes committed himself to the view that 'we should get as quickly as possible into the semi-elective system preparatory to final formal self-government'. 'Mr Rhodes said that he was cordially for the propositions in connection with having an elective system in the Council,' reported the *Herald*, and committed himself to the view that 'he did not think that they would permit themselves to be amalgamated either with the Transvaal or the Cape Government. Therefore they must look at the future and that future would be a change to the semi-responsible body; that was to say, certain elective members in the Council, and finally complete self-government. They could not expect to have a majority of votes in the Council unless they were prepared to pay the expenditure. . . . It was frequently said of the present system that they had no voice in the government of the country and also frequently considered that things were done of which they complain. It was therefore better that they should be represented and through their representatives point out any abuses, preparing for the time when they would have full self-government. This was necessary for the progress of the community, because if the Imperial Government were to take over the Administration they would not be in so good a position. . . . He was glad they were going as early as possible to get elective representatives. . . . He was exceedingly pleased that the community had had the intelligence and energy to bring these matters before him in the form they were. Although he was no longer an official he still had a great—the greatest interest in the country and the Company were still good enough to consult him in regard to these matters.'[2]

With this speech and his later advocacy of the principle of settler representation Rhodes won back majority settler support

[1] *Rhodesia Herald*, 18 Nov. 1896.   [2] *Rhodesia Herald*, 11 Nov. 1896.

'We are far from desiring the abrogation of the Charter,' wrote the *Rhodesia Herald* on the day after Rhodes' Salisbury speech, 'which if suitably modified will provide a golden mean between Imperial red tape and unrestrained financial tyranny and selfishness. Our aim is, after all, sound and wise government. . . . If the Chartered Company can "tumble" to this wish of the public and of the Home Government and prove by acts that it is bent on this excellent course we shall be among the first to give them full credit and support.' 'There is one more point I should like Mr Fairbridge to undeceive himself about,' wrote a Rhodesian settler in December 1896 in an attack upon those who still persisted with the call for British intervention, 'namely that Rhodesia is tired of Company rule and would rather favour Imperial control. . . . The settlers of Rhodesia are satisfied with the promise, many times publicly announced by Mr Rhodes, that when the country becomes more settled and populous the Government shall be handed over to the people and the country ruled responsibly by those who shall doubtlessly by that time have earned the suffrage of the citizens.'[1]

By no means every member of the Company's London Board was ready to accept the implications of these promises. George Cawston, for example, a persistent critic of Rhodes, who had been outraged by the Jameson Raid and who thought Rhodes' part in the negotiations with the Ndebele was 'nothing but duty as whole revolt due to taking police out of country,' was determined that the Company's share-holders should lose nothing because of the follies that had been committed. He objected that under Rhodes' proposals for settler representation and Rhodes' readiness to accept some imperial supervision 'Rhodesia is to be a Crown Colony, governed by the High Commissioner at the cost of the Company, the Directors of which have but little control over legislation, taxation or administration. No doubt it is right to have local Administration but the change is very radical.' But Rhodes was right to claim that his word still carried weight; in the end his proposals were accepted and Cawston resigned.[2]

In advocating the concession of settler representation to the Company Rhodes was able to use powerful arguments over and above the urgent need to conciliate white opinion. 'I consider

[1] *The Cape Argus*, 16 Dec, 1896.
[2] Cawston correspondence, Rhodes House, Mss. Afr. s. 77.

time has arrived for elective system in Council,' he cabled the London Board in May 1897. 'I suggest two representatives for Mashonaland, two for Matabeleland. British South Africa Company should keep majority as being responsible for expenses. This is what I call second stage, namely semi-responsible government; final stage will be full responsible government at some time hence when people can pay the cost of administration. This course will be similar to Natal, British South Africa Company taking place of Crown. . . . Great point is to propose elective system in Council as it meets desire all Rhodesia inhabitants and sooner it takes place the better. It also makes buffer between us and English people who do not mind pummelling British South Africa Company directors but funk to interfere with British South Africa Company directors supported by elected representatives of people.'[1]

Moreover, in making this concession Rhodes was in no sense departing from his own vision of Rhodesia's future. Milner described this vision in June 1897. Rhodes looked 'to making the territory of the British South Africa Company into a separate Colony ultimately self-governed (the Company keeping its mineral and other valuable rights but giving up administration). The Colony (which I may remark in passing though nominally self governed, will be virtually an absolute monarchy, with Rhodes as monarch), he means to unite with the Cape Colony and Natal, and then the three combined will bring peaceful pressure upon the Republics to drive them into a S. African federation. . . . They are pressing for "representative government" and I think myself a representative element in the Council is desirable. Rhodes is going for it "hot and strong", avowedly with the object of strengthening his own position in any difference with the Imperial Govt. They may bully the Company, he says frankly, but they won't dare to bully a representative Council.'[2]

As far as Rhodes was concerned, then, the situation of 1896 and 1897 merely decided him to move towards settler representation more rapidly; the importance of the effects of the rebellion were more that they predisposed both the Company and the imperial government to accept the idea. The Company did so because it believed that it was the least price which it could pay

[1] Rhodes to London Board, 27 May 1897, LO 5/2/54.
[2] Milner to Selborne, 2 June and 15 June 1897, Headlam, op. cit., Vol. I, pp. 105–8, 109–11.

in the circumstances to satisfy the settlers and also offer to the British public the appearance of significant reform. The British government did so for a variety of reasons. There was first of all the point made by Mr Gann in his recent studies of Rhodesian history—namely that to the British philanthropic public it was the Company that was the villain of the piece and the settler who was the small-man victim of immoral capital; from the 1890's to the 1920s the assumption was that settler democracy must necessarily provide better government for all than the Company regime. Hence settler representation was regarded as a progressive step. In the second place, though Milner warned that 'the representative Council will simply be Rhodes even more completely than the Company is', Chamberlain saw the idea of representation as a restraint upon Rhodes' grandiose and alarming designs. 'He certainly does not come out well in connection with the South African inquiry,' he wrote of Rhodes in July 1897. 'In any case the British Government cannot take their policy from him and public opinion here will undoubtedly require considerable changes in the administration of the Chartered Company. The sooner some kind of local government of a popular kind can be established in Rhodesia the better.' Finally, of course, there was the reluctance of the British government to become in any way financially responsible for Rhodesia which powerfully induced them to accept any reasonable looking settlement negotiated between Rhodes and Milner. As Milner reminded them in December 1897 if further native troubles were to bankrupt the Company it 'will throw an impecunious, undeveloped country bigger than France upon your hands'.[1]

Because of all this the question of settler representation presented no difficulty in the negotiations between Milner, Milton and Rhodes in November 1897 out of which the constitutional settlement finally emerged; argument was confined to the details of the new Native Administration and to the exact character of imperial supervision of the whole system. So in October 1898 the Legislative Council came into being consisting of the Administrator, the Resident Commissioner, five members nominated by the Company and four representatives of the settlers. And though formally the least powerful element in the new set-up there was

[1] Chamberlain to Milner, 5 July 1897; Milner to Chamberlain, 1 Dec. 1897; Headlam, op. cit., vol. 1, p. 90, pp. 139–46.

little doubt in anybody's minds that the settler element was the most potentially powerful. It had the promises of Rhodes which laid down a movement to full self-government; it enjoyed an advantage with British public opinion over the Company. Already in 1899 'Curio' Brown was able to describe Rhodesia as 'in a state of transition from the rule of the Chartered Company to that of a self-governing Colony. Not many years will elapse', he confidently predicted, 'ere the establishment of a self-governing Colony will have been completed'. As Brown saw clearly, the settlers were in a very strong position under Company rule. 'By threatening to carry their grievances to the Home Government these people have been able to gain their points in all cases except those where diplomatic measures were resorted to on the part of the Chartered Company's officials.' The settlers were 'better able to gain any desired change under the present system than they would be with the red tape inseparable from the management of a Crown Colony'.[1]

So from 1898 onwards Southern Rhodesia moved steadily towards settler supremacy; in 1903 they achieved parity of representation in the Legislative Council; in 1908 they attained a majority there; even at that early date no one questioned that Company rule would be followed by settler rule. This mixture of Company and settler power, was the form that white supremacy took in Rhodesia after 1898. The question now is—how far was this sort of white supremacy compatible with a new deal for Rhodesian Africans or the working out of the promises made, the realization of the potentialities perceived?

There can be no question that this settler advance, powerfully stimulated though it was by the events of the rebellions, ran counter to the advantages which it can be argued were derived by Africans from their readiness to resist. Milner was in no doubt in 1897 that the elective element in the Council would prove illiberal in its attitude to native policy; Rhodes was correspondingly in no doubt that it would support him in his attitude to the labour question. 'Before everything we must have self-government for Rhodesia,' he exclaimed in January 1898 when contemplating humanitarian interference in the labour field; if he got self-government, commented the *Daily News*, 'then he would get his labour fast enough'. In 1913 the Belgian scholar, H. Rolin, set

[1] W. H. Brown, *The South African Frontier*, 1899.

out with a nice precision the balance of the results of the changes which had followed the rebellions. 'There can be no doubt', he wrote, 'that numerous acts of oppression were committed to the detriment of the natives', before 1896. 'The Company was com-pelled following the rebellions and under the pressure of public opinion to adopt a less harsh approach and to soften the regime to which the natives were submitted. Today there are no more "atrocities" with which to reproach the Government or the settlers. But is the black race over-all treated with justice? . . . The rights of the natives are protected in the sense that pillage, massacre, acts of injustice or of obvious cruelty are effectively prohibited. But is a people well governed merely because it is not exposed en masse to crimes of this kind?' Positively, for all the restoration of rights to *indunas*, Africans were powerless to look after their own interests. 'The Bantu peoples of Rhodesia are at the mercy of their European conquerors. The fear of rebellions and that of compromising by an oppressive policy the economic prosperity of the conquered lands, prevents us from unbounded exploitation'. But the system is conceived totally in the interests of the whites. 'It is, without doubt, a good agency for defending the economic interests of whites in Rhodesia. . . . What dominates all is a pre-occupation with the interests of the whites and the absence of a genuine social policy inspired by the interests of the blacks.'[1]

It is possible to show in some detail how this atmosphere in which already in 1897 and 1898 the interests of the whites were predominant frustrated some of the developments outlined above. Let us take them in the order in which they were set out. There *was* a great missionary breakthrough in Southern Rhodesia after the rebellions just as Father Boos had hoped, though it was per-haps based on more material foundations than missionary realiz-ation of Shona religious sense. 'The opposition of the older people to the education of their sons and daughters has been broken, especially by reason of the famine which followed the war; belief in superstition and witchcraft has received a severe blow which is a great assistant to us in convincing the young people of their futility. The Divine protection which was so evidently over us is acknowledged even by the natives themselves, while, on the other hand, the evil consequences the rebellion brought upon the people

[1] H. Rolin, *Les lois et l'administration de la Rhodésie*, Brussels, 1913.

—poverty, starvation and misery of all kinds—are felt by them too severely to admit of denial. . . . The miserable state in which our people returned, being without food and quite helpless, threw them into our arms for help and protection . . . . We had to take advantage of the favourable moment at any cost and we have made the best of our opportunity.' The centuries long Shona resistance to Christianity broke down at last—'On the one side were missionaries with their oft-repeated threats of God's punishments; on the other the prophet of their God with his war-cry "Murenga". By a wonderful dispensation of Divine Providence our victory was complete in the eyes of the people.' The missions now entered upon a period of great power and influence during which they were, as sour Native administrators remarked, the real rulers of large areas of rural Mashonaland.[1]

The consequences of this break-through were very great but they were not quite what was hoped in 1897. The grand opportunity which Grey saw to exploit Shona educational potential was not fully exploited; the Company did not agree to spend money on African education though it did go so far as to donate the Old Umtali site to the American Methodist Episcopal Church. Above all there was the ambiguity for the missionaries themselves of operating within the context of white supremacy from which they could not and often did not wish to dissociate themselves. It is perhaps not too far-fetched to see this dilemma at work even in Father Richartz's opposition to the increase in hut tax in 1903. He attacked the prejudice shown against Africans by the members of the new Legislative Council whose conduct would 'certainly convince thinking men that the entire management of native affairs cannot be left to such a population', but at the same time he voiced his opposition mainly in terms of the injury the increase would do to the white farming industry. 'Farming will not pay in this country if average wages are higher than 15d a month'; the increase was 'a very heavy indirect taxation on the white population . . . and especially on the farming population'. In this sort of context, for all the educational work that the missions had done by 1913, Rolin's expressed doubts in that year still had point. 'We doubt whether the native, apparently "Christianized" by

---

[1] Richartz, 'Chishawasha after the Rebellion', *Zambesi Mission Record*, Vol. 1, No. 2, Nov. 1898; Boos, 'The Springtime of the Mashona Mission', *Zambesi Mission Record*, Vol. 1, No. 4, May 1899.

the missionaries and superficially civilized is happier or better than his fathers. . . . We are not sure that the poor man who works on the fields of a white owner for a few shillings a month, or labours in a mine to extract gold, represents a superior human type to the "savage", agriculturalist and warrior, of the pre-Conquest period.'[1]

What, then, of the powers given to the Ndebele *indunas* and later to the officially recognized Shona chiefs? Rhodes successfully created the feeling that the *indunas* were important but Rhodes died in 1902; after his death the illusion that white and black interests could be combined could not be sustained by the smaller figures who survived. And in reality the powers which the official chiefs possessed were very small. Gann tells us the Rhodesian philosophy saw tribal institutions as retrograde and Africans not as members of pre-European systems but as 'the privates of the industrial army in every department of work'; accordingly 'the law gave few rights to chiefs. The Administrator in Council was stated to wield all political power and authority over the natives. The Administrator in Council could remove chiefs subject to the consent of the High Commissioner, or even divide or amalgamate different tribes. The chiefs themselves had no recognized powers of jurisdiction. They were simply regarded as subordinate officials responsible for the good conduct of their tribes, for notifying crimes, deaths and epidemics to the Native Commissioners, for giving help with the collection of taxes and for the apprehension of criminals.' This was the extent to which the restoration of the powers of the Ndebele *indunas* turned out to be compatible with white supremacy.[2]

It was, in fact, never the intention of Rhodes and Grey to give the Ndebele *indunas* greater powers than these. But they did intend, as we have seen, to provide enough land in Matabeleland for Ndebele needs; to set up a Reserve system in Mashonaland; and to bring an end to the era of unrestricted white land exploitation. The Order in Council of 1898 placed a statutory obligation on the Company to provide enough land for Africans in both

[1] Richartz to Resident Commissioner, 6 July 1903, C.O., C.P., S.A., No. 717, pp. 420–23; Rolin, op. cit.

[2] L. H. Gann, *A History of Southern Rhodesia*, 1965, pp. 149–50. Chapter Five of Mr Gann's admirable book treats the same range of topics as this chapter in a more detailed way and with some difference of emphasis.

provinces. In Mashonaland, indeed, where white pressure on land had not been so great and where large areas remained unallocated a Reserve system was set up which met Shona requirements in the short run in a more or less satisfactory way. But in Matabeleland the situation was very different. Here Grey's good intentions fell down in the face of Company reluctance to spend money to purchase land already granted to whites and in the face of white resistance to the idea of African settlement in white ranching or farming districts. Rhodes had fulfilled his promise that the senior *indunas* could return to the land which they had occupied in Lobengula's day only by coming to a temporary arrangement with the new white owners. A series of agreements were worked out by which the Ndebele were allowed to settle on privately owned white land rent-free for the first year but paying thereafter 'such portion of native crops as may be suitable', the owners to have the first use of labour drawn from the settlements on the land through official labour recruiting channels. The Ndebele settlers were guaranteed undisturbed possession for two years after October 1896. Whether or not the surrendering rebels understood these terms it was on this basis that most of them were resettled and for the first two years no doubt they were satisfied with their return to their old territories. But as Grey wrote to Rhodes in January 1897 some additional provision was urgently needed for those who did not wish to continue paying rent in kind or in labour to white owners or who wanted greater security than a two-year guarantee of possession. This additional provision was not made in central Matabeleland. In June 1897 Grey was informed by the Assistant Deputy Administrator of Matabeleland, Townshend, that 'we could only obtain lands outright in these districts at very heavy cost as owners would immediately put up price if we offered to buy or demanded to expropriate'. All that the Company were prepared to do in the key central areas was to lease blocks of land for a five-year period on which the Company would allow the Ndebele to settle under the terms of the October 1896 agreement. In any case the Chief Native Commissioner was prepared to assert that 'lands reserved are far in excess of any possible requirements of native population for next 20 years' and that the 'greater proportion of native population will come to some arrangement with private owners to remain on land they at present occupy rather than move to other locations'. Thus in central Matabeleland

X   A cartoon from the Salisbury *Nugget* of July 12th, 1897, contrasting
the fate of the Ndebele and the Shona rebels.

IX   Ndebele leaders gather in Bulawayo after the conclusion of peace 1896.

virtually nothing was done to improve the land situation. Once their two-year guarantee of occupation was up the Ndebele found themselves at the mercy of their landlords. 'White men of varied origin and race become in a day their landlords,' wrote the Superintendent of Natives, Bulawayo, in that account of Ndebele land grievances which we quoted in Chapter Three; 'their over-lords, with power to dispossess and drive forth. To an aristocratic race the delegation of such power has appeared unseemly in many cases. The word "amaplazi" . . . meaning "farms" stands, it may be said, for almost all that is most distasteful in our rule. Almost it stands for helotage and servitude to a chance-made master.'[1]

If Company parsimony prevented the realization of Grey's plan of land reform in central Matabeleland, other attempts to reverse some of the mistakes of the past ran into the resolute opposition of the vested interests which those mistakes had created. Late in 1897 Rhodes told Milton that the 'time has now come when we must enforce the [occupation] clause. The large com-panies have had time enough and now the railways are in they must occupy or abandon'. But in fact most of the great investment land holdings continued to lie unexploited for decades, offering to embittered Africans the spectacle of flagrantly under-used white land; the companies concerned contained too many in-fluential people whose friendship to the Company was valuable. Milton also attempted to check upon the grants made in Jameson's time which had been founded on 'bogus' surveys; he suggested legislation offering final title to people who were prepared to have a resurvey at their own expense. At once there was loud opposition: 'Certain people at Bulawayo . . . claim that we shall recognise surveys which may be faulty or bogus and issue title thereon. They resent the determination of the Government not to tolerate any longer the practice which has led to the present chaos.' This resentment of Company land policy under the new regime was, indeed, the occasion for the first clash between Com-pany and settlers within the framework of the new Legislative Council. 'Instructed by representatives of all public bodies in Rhodesia,' cabled the Representatives Association to Rhodes in June 1899, 'we transmit resolutions unanimously passed at mass

[1] Townshend to Grey, June 1897, Rhodes House, Mss. Afr. s. 228, C. 1, Vol. 1; S/N, Bulawayo, to C.N.C., 1 June 1920, N 3/16/9.

meeting last night. The inhabitants of Rhodesia count upon you to see that right and justice is done. First, resolved that this meeting whilst making recognition of the services to the Empire rendered by the British South Africa Company in opening up Southern Rhodesia to colonization is of the opinion that the legislative powers enjoyed by that Company are inequitable because the past session of the Legislative Council has shown that the business of the Council has been to forward the commercial interests of the Company as distinct from the interests of the community, by the invariable vote of the seven nominee members against the vote of the four elected members. . . . Means should be taken to obtain some considerable modification of the existing constitution until the community is prepared to assume Responsible Government, if possible by means of a conference between His Excellency the High Commissioner and representatives of the inhabitants and of the British South Africa Company. Second that an appeal should be made to the High Commissioner to withhold his approval of the Southern Rhodesian Land Ordinance 1899.' Milton was not willing to ignore opposition of this kind; in October 1899 he was suggesting to Rhodes that it might be wise for the Company to nominate a settler to the next Council so that the disparity in voting strength was less obvious.[1]

When it was so difficult for the Company to secure its own interests over land in the face of settler opposition it was not to be supposed that it would make a very great effort in African interests. Thus the one way in which Ndebele resentment might have found relief—by the communal purchase of land—was tacitly blocked. In the 1898 Constitution the free right of everyone, black or white, to purchase land anywhere in Southern Rhodesia was stated; but by the time that Nyamanda and the other senior *indunas* were coming round to the idea of land purchase as the only way of securing possession of land a convention had already grown up that the Company would not sell to Africans.

This convention, of course, arose from the increasing white settler demand for segregation. We have seen that one enduring legacy of the rebellions was fear and that this fear was a sort of

---

[1] Rhodes to Milton, Nov. 1897, Rhodes House, Mss. Afr. s. 227, Letter Book 13; Milton to Rhodes, 8 Aug. 1898; Representatives Association to Rhodes, 30 June 1899; Rhodes House, Mss. Afr. s. 228, C. 1, Vol. 1.

guarantee that the African population of Southern Rhodesia would no longer be subjected to 'atrocities'. But the accompaniment of fear was hate. During the 1903 debates in the Legislative Council the elected members showed, in Father Richartz' words, 'a bitter hatred against natives and their protectors. I am so disgusted at the outburst of rude hatred against the natives', continued Richartz, beating already against the bars of that prison of white supremacy in which his missionary lot was cast, 'that I am considering whether it is becoming for me to have anything further to do with men who are not ashamed to speak as some members did, or applauded such utterings. . . . We have the sacred duty to teach them obedience towards God and Government but it is a crime to throw them away and deal with them as if they were less than slaves.'[1]

An editorial in *Rhodesia* might seek to argue that the settlers were really concerned only with the improvement of the African and to deny that statements of the sort objected to by Father Richartz 'failed to denote any sense of duty to our fellow men. A Kaffir is a man and a brother, in theory, but when dealing with him you cannot treat him as your peer, but must use the best and most effective methods to make him so. . . . There is as little inconsistency in loving through thrashing your nigger as there is in birching a child of your own flesh and blood. Only practical colonial experience can adequately prove the correctness of this.'[2] But it was not difficult to see beneath the surface of this sort of love the hatred and the fear. It was this mixture of emotions which produced the phenomenon later on of the Black Peril, the threat to white womanhood detected on the slightest of evidence by so many Rhodesians; which produced the notorious decisions of white Rhodesian juries; which produced the colour bar in all its manifestations. Writing in 1932 Marshall Hole admitted that racial prejudice and discrimination were 'more deeply seated' in Southern Rhodesia 'than in the older colonies of South Africa'; it was the result, he said, of the experience of the rebellions and the folk memory of them which every Rhodesian inherited. Even in the passive and peaceful years of the 1920s and the 1930s when every Rhodesian knew the Africans to be totally

[1] Richartz to Resident Commissioner, 6 July 1903, C.O., C.P., S.A., No. 717, pp. 420–3.
[2] *Rhodesia*, 12 March 1898.

contented—or believed that he knew them to be so—the memory of the rebellions and of what was done on both sides during them persisted.[1]

In this complex variety of ways, then, the effects of the rebellions ran through Rhodesian life, helping to shape the relations of white and black. And if they were remembered at the back of the minds of the whites we may suppose that they were not forgotten by the blacks. We need now to turn to their place in the African history of Southern Rhodesia and specifically in the history of African politics.

[1] H. M. Hole, *The Passing of the Black Kings*, London, 1932, p. 306. Hole thought that; 'the danger of a widespread revolt of South African natives against white men cannot be entirely excluded. One can never predict from experience what African natives will do in any given circumstances. Their ways and motives are not ours and they are more liable to mass hysteria which may be induced—as in the case of the Mashona rebellion—by panic or superstition or some imaginary grievance.'

CHAPTER TEN

The Risings in African Political History

WHITES IN southern Africa saw the Shona and Ndebele risings exclusively in terms of imperial history, of the onward march of the white man and the inevitable but doomed resistance to it. But the risings had, of course, another context—that of the African history of Southern Rhodesia. The chronological limits of this other context were not bounded by the arrival of the whites in the 1890s nor even by the bursting out of South African whites into the interior earlier in the century. Even if they are seen exclusively as anti-colonial reactions the risings had much earlier precedents. The Shona people, after all, had experienced intermittent colonial pressures from the sixteenth century onwards, and if their rising was comparable, as we shall see, to other resistances in southern, central and east Africa in the later nineteenth century it was also comparable to their own rising in arms against the Portuguese in 1629–30. Mr Gann describes this earlier rising in terms strongly reminiscent of many of the things we have said about the 1896–7 upheaval. 'Poor administration, the appointment of unsuitable officials, and the absence of any effective central control all contributed to a major African rising. Portuguese traders and their followers were slaughtered, and even Quelimane itself came under siege. Nyambo Kapararidze, the leader of the anti-Portuguese faction, effectively wiped out Lusitanian influence . . . some 300 to 400 Portuguese and some 6000 Africans were killed, the Christians suffering the greatest military disaster that had yet befallen them in South-East Africa.' This was a disaster for the whites closely comparable, even in terms of the numbers killed, with the Rhodesian disaster some 250 years later. It was an example of momentarily successful African reaction which also has its similarities with the organization we have described. It took the form of a war of religion against the Christian missionaries, their converts and the Mutapa who had become their puppet; in this sense, too, it was revolutionary, directed against the administrative machinery of the Mutapa empire as well as against the Portuguese. It was, of course, easier to organize since it took place in a setting in which Shona political institutions still retained great vitality and since it did not involve co-operation with a society as different as the Ndebele; nevertheless it would be fascinating to know more of its details and to see what light they might throw on the risings of 1896–7.[1]

And this rising, though the most spectacular, was only one of the incidents in the long struggle of the Shona and the Portuguese. It was suppressed, just as the risings of 1896–7 were suppressed, and Portuguese influence restored; there was even a breakthrough of missionary influence after it. But the Portuguese recovery was temporary and by the end of the century the Rozwi power, which we have seen in its decline and in its attempted re-establishment, had driven them out of what is now Southern Rhodesia. No doubt it is in this context of the long sequence of Shona resistance to European pressure that the 1896–7 risings will be seen in nationalist historiography rather than as an episode in the triumphal rise of the British imperial system in Africa.

But legitimate and illuminating though it is to set the risings in this different perspective, it needs also to be said that they should not be seen as exclusively anti-colonial phenomena. They must also be seen in the context of the African history of Southern Rhodesia as such; of the relations between the Shona and the Ndebele, both before and after the risings; of the tensions operative within Ndebele and Shona societies themselves; of the long history of 'church-state' friction between the Mwari cult and the successive political authorities of Matabeleland. And as the African history of Southern Rhodesia develops in the second half of the twentieth century it may well be that one or other of these themes will emerge as more lastingly important than the theme of black-white relations itself. It may be that the risings will then be looked back upon as an important stage in the shifting balance of power between Ndebele and Shona; or as the source of significant changes within African society; rather than as a demonstration of African hostility to colonialism. Finally, even if we concentrate on the risings as examples of resistance we should not forget that resistance was offered in Southern Rhodesia to African regimes and to African invaders as well as to European ones. If the example of Kapararidze is illuminating to the student of the 1896–7 risings

[1] Gann, op. cit, pp. 23–5.

so also is that of the great mediums of the Chaminuka spirit who rallied the western and central Shona at the time of the Ndebele raids upon them. In addition then, to the colonial and the nationalist perspective and to the unpredictable perspectives of the future there is the perspective of the Chaminuka medium in 1903: 'I am Chaminuka. I know everything. I am all powerful. I caused the downfall of the BaRozwi and the Matabele and I will cause the white man to leave the country.'[1]

It would be a mistake, therefore, to isolate the risings from the African past of Southern Rhodesia and to treat them as if they were a response to a totally new situation. There is no question but that the colonial pressures of the 1890s were much more intensive and also extensive than anything which the African peoples of Southern Rhodesia had experienced before and so compelled them to produce a retort which involved more people and at a more committed level. But there is much reason to suppose that the answers found to the problems of how to organize more people and how to commit them deeply had parallels in the past of Southern Rhodesian Africans. There is also reason to suppose that they have a continuing relevance to the problems of resistance in the contemporary African context. In short, we must try to see the nineteenth-century resistances as part of a stream of development beginning before and running through the colonial period: it is not enough, as some Africanists are inclined to do, to shift the emphasis away from the Scramble and the 'pacification' and on to the African resistance to them, since this still puts an incorrect emphasis upon the early colonial period as a radical breach with the past. But important though these considerations are, here we are chiefly concerned with the relevance of the risings of 1896–7 to the colonial and nationalist history of Southern Rhodesia, and in the history of African politics from the 1890s to the present day.[2]

Before we can understand how the risings are related to later African politics in Southern Rhodesia, we must grasp their significance in their own time by comparing them with other resistances

[1] Morris to Taberer, 12 Dec. 1930, A 11/2/12/11.
[2] I have discussed these themes further in, T. O. Ranger, 'African Reaction and Resistance to the Imposition of Colonial Rule in East and Central Africa', to be published by Stanford University Press in a symposium on Imperialism edited by L. H. Gann and P. Duignan.

to the imposition of European colonial rule in East and Central Africa. From such a comparison two important points emerge, one as the result of the dissimilarity of the 1896–7 risings to most of the other resistances of the late nineteenth and early twentieth century, the other as the result of their similarity to a few of these resistances. The Southern Rhodesian risings are distinguished from the great majority of attempts at resistance because of their effectiveness. However much it may have appeared that they were doomed to be defeated, and whatever their internal weaknesses, they cannot be evaluated adequately without a realization that the challenge they presented to the whites was the most formidable, and the scale of their organization the greatest, of any of the east, central and southern African resistances. From this point of view what is important about them is not their eventual failure but the degree of success that they were able to achieve. This was no doubt the result of the past traditions of resistance and the past traditions of charismatic leadership, combined with the past history of political centralization which both the Rozwi and the Ndebele had experienced. At any rate there were few risings which attained a similar degree of effectiveness and fewer still that managed to do so on a supra-tribal or supra-linguistic scale.

But the second point that needs to be made is that the few other risings which *did* manage to attack the problem of scale in a comparably effective way present striking parallels with the Shona and Ndebele risings and that these parallels at once help us to understand the significance of some of the phenomena characteristic of those risings and also to realize that they were not in any sense peculiar. Let us take, for instance, the greatest of the East African resistances, the Maji-Maji rising of 1905 in German East Africa. Superficially the background of the two upheavals appears very different. The Maji-Maji rising broke out in an area which had not known any significant degree of political centralization in the past and it broke out in an area which was not occupied by white settlers; those districts which had traditionally enjoyed the degree of coherence given by the institution of the *ntemi* chiefship stayed out of the rising and so did those areas which were being opened up for white settlement. In Southern Rhodesia, of course, the reverse was true; the risings were more or less co-extensive with white settlement and within the area of white settlement it was those peoples with a tradition of centralized political institutions who took the leading part. But this difference, although suggestive in many ways, is less important than the essential similarity. In both cases the area which rebelled was that under the heaviest economic pressure and facing the greatest challenge to 'traditional' economic methods. We have already see how this pressure and challenge operated in settler Southern Rhodesia: in German East Africa it was not applied so much by the relatively weaker settler population but by government-enforced schemes in what became the rebel areas for the collective growing of cash crops. It is probably true to say, indeed, that it was in these two areas that the pressures of colonialism were most acutely felt in this early period and this is no doubt one reason why they were the two areas of strikingly vigorous resistance.

And in both cases the rebels faced the problem of bringing together many different groups, some of them bitter enemies in the past. Maji-Maji managed to combine an intrusive Nguni raiding group with its indigenous enemies just as the risings of 1896–7 managed to combine the Ndebele and the Shona. It did so without the help—except in the case of the Ngoni themselves—of pre-existing political centralization and for that reason it was undoubtedly less articulated than the Rhodesian rebellions, but that it was able to do so at all is a testimony to the importance of the other factors that were common to both movements. Dr Iliffe, who is working towards a major study of Maji-Maji, has remarked that it was a 'post-pacification revolt, quite different from the early resistance. That had been local and professional, soldiers against soldiers, whereas Maji-Maji affected almost everyone in Tanganyika. It was a great crisis of commitment.' This is, of course, the same distinction that we have drawn between the Ndebele war of 1893—'soldiers against soldiers'—and the risings of 1896–7. A great deal more work needs to be done on the mechanics of this commitment in the case of Maji-Maji before we can make confident generalizations. But one explanation which emerges from the German sources is of particular interest in the context of a comparison between Maji-Maji and the Rhodesian risings. This concerns the Kolelo cult, an observance centring around belief in a great snake sent by God to restore order and innocence to a corrupted earth. Like the Mwari cult the Kolelo system possessed a 'priesthood'; operated from a number of oracular cave centres; and attracted pilgrims from all over southern and eastern Tanganyika with gifts and with problems. Like the Mwari cult the ordinary operation of the Kolelo system provided a wider network of contact and communication than any secular political system or combination of systems in the rebel area. But there is also some evidence to suggest that in addition to the use made of this 'normal' cult organization there were developments in the cult structure and theology immediately before and during 1905 which paralleled the innovations of Mkwati and Kagubi. Contemporary German observers believed that there had been a change within the cult from a concern with fertility and sickness to a millenarian pre-occupation. Cult leaders promised the overthrow of the colonial system through direct divine intervention. They offered protection against witchcraft and against bullets; rebels entered the community of the faithful and invulnerable by drinking the holy water distributed by the priests of Kolelo and demonstrated their membership of that community by observing its new rules of conduct and using its passwords and greetings. There was a promise of resurrection and there was an appeal to all Africans. 'Be not afraid,' ran the message; 'Kolelo spares his black children.' In this spirit an appeal could be made across the frontiers of old animosities, just as the spirit medium of the Budja appealed to them against their old rivalry with the Zezuru. 'We received an order from God', wrote chief Songea of the Tanganyika Ngoni to his old enemy chief Mataka of the Yao, 'to the effect that all white men had to quit the country. . . . This war ordered by God must come first. Send 100 men with guns. Help me in taking the boma. . . . Once we have taken the boma of Songea we shall move against the stations on Lake Nyasa, you and I together. Let us now forget our former quarrels. This bottle containing the medicine was sent by Kinjala himself [one of the Kolelo prophets] the leader of the war.'[1]

The parallels here with what happened in Matabeleland and Mashonaland are obvious. And these parallels, with the same mixture of the traditional and the innovatory appeal of a religious leadership, can be found in other resistances which were effective because they involved an extension of scale. Sometimes, indeed,

[1] J. Iliffe, 'The German administration in Tanganyika, 1906–11', Cambridge University Ph.d. thesis, 1965; Fr Elzear Ebner, *History of the Wangoni*, mimco, 1959, p. 171.

they can be found within the context of a tribal or linguistic group. This is the case with the Nandi of western Kenya whose resistance against the whites began as a traditional, soldiers against soldiers, affair and developed over a decade into the struggle of the whole of Nandi society, united in action for the first time. The figure around whom they united was the *orkoiyot* or prophet, a figure originally derived from another people, whose authority grew as the colonial pressure grew. But more striking are the supra-tribal and supra-linguistic examples. For our purposes one more must suffice. It concerns the Nyabingi movement of the Bantu-speaking peoples of northern Ruanda, the Belgian Congo, British Ruanda and Kigezi. These peoples had historically been organized on a very small scale and before the colonial period had experienced the pressure of the non-Bantu state systems of Ruanda and the inter-lacustrine area. During the nineteenth century the Nyabingi cult arose in northern Ruanda to become the focus of opposition there to the Ruandan monarchy. It was derived theologically from the religious belief and practice of the Bantu peoples of northern Tanganyika and celebrated the power of the spirit of a Bantu queen figure, overthrown in legend by usurpers from the north; it presented a powerful pan-Bantu appeal. Mediumistic, giving full scope to innovation and charismatic leadership, it first served as the basis for resistance to the pre-colonial monarchy of Ruanda and of 'heretical' opposition to the state cult, many of whose practices it had borrowed and modified; then it provided some coherence to the politically fragmented Kiga people; then became the vehicle for an organized attempt to overthrow the German regime in Ruanda and its royal Ruandan ally; then encouraged the Kiga to attack the Ganda agents of British rule; then mobilized forces during the first world war which impartially attacked German, British and Belgian troops alike. It cut across the frontiers of both pre-colonial and colonial state systems; promised immunity to its adherents if they observed its rules of conduct; and survived into the post-war period to harass the colonial regimes. 'It has everywhere proved itself revolutionary in method and anarchic in effect,' wrote the Assistant District Commissioner, Kigezi, in 1919. 'Fanaticism and terror are everywhere inculcated. . . . The whole appeal is to fear and to the lower instincts; to the masses, Bahutu, against the classes, Batussi. . . . The whole aspect of the Nabingi is of a fanatic anarchic sect as opposed to the liberal and religious principles of the indigeneous Kubandwa cult.'[1]

We can now begin to see the Mwari cult leaders and the Kagubi medium in better perspective. They were not the fraudulent agitators of Company legend, whose leadership of the risings was held to make those movements by definition so irrational that any attempt to understand them was bound to fail. They were very successful exponents of a type of leadership which appears to have been associated with most of the striking attempts to solve, on however impermanent a basis, the greatest political problem of pre-colonial Africa; the problem of scale. They were not uncomfortable oddities whose involvement in the rising is a source of embarrassment to rational modern nationalists. We shall not understand the risings, indeed, unless we approach them in a spirit which finds the Kagubi medium sending his daughters to Chishawasha school no more strange—or perhaps as strange—as Father Richartz 'converting' the Kagubi medium on the scaffold. Although all religious enthusiasm has an element of the suprarational, the services of the religious leadership to the 1896-7 risings, as to the Maji-Maji and the Nyabingi movements, were eminently utilitarian. The resistances were a defiance of a power which enjoyed great technological superiority and began with a superiority of morale based upon it and upon confidence in its ability to shape the world. The religious leaders were able to oppose to this a morale which for the moment was as confident, if not more so, based upon *their* supposed ability to shape the world; and they were able to oppose to modern weapons the one great advantage that the Africans possessed, that of numbers. In no other way could the African peoples of the late nineteenth and early twentieth centuries, especially perhaps those peoples involved in the movements we have discussed have offered a challenge to the Europeans. Moreover the so-called 'superstitious' injunctions of the religious leaders not only served the purpose of creating a sense of the new society but also ensured the minimum of discipline essential in movements such as these. The great injunction —not to loot European goods but to deliver them to the servants

[1] Report by Capt. J. E. T. Phillips, A.D.C., Kigezi, 31 July 1919, National Archives, Dar es Salaam, Secretariat file 0910; M. J. Bessell, 'Nyabingi', *Uganda Journal*, Vol. VI, No. 2, Oct. 1938; P. W. T. Baxter, 'The Kiga', in *East African Chiefs*, ed. A. Richards, London, 1959.

of God—prevented the risings from breaking up into a series of fragmented raids for property, and gave the religious leaders, through their control of the modern weapons seized from the whites, a stronger hold still upon the military side of the rebellions.

This fact—that the risings of 1896–7 represent a particularly successful example of mass commitment under the sort of leadership most appropriate to the circumstances—is one of the important ways in which those risings were looking to the future. Before we leave them, we must make one further point. This concerns the attitude of the rebels to 'modernization'. Through all these risings there ran a strain of repudiation of the white man's way of life and of his goods; of prophetic warning against their seduction. Thus in Mashonaland we have the famous story of the Chaminuka medium's prophecy that the Shona would be able to preserve their independence only if they could resist the temptation to acquire the goods of the whites; we have the Nehanda medium in June 1896 urging her followers to fight only with spears and sticks and to repudiate European weapons; we have in the decades after the rising a series of commands from the Mwari shrines to use only African utensils and to reject enamelware, or from the north-eastern spirit mediums to kill all pigs as 'non-traditional' animals. During Maji-Maji, we are told, the rebel name for the Europeans was Walutupilukere, meaning the men made of red clay, and orders were given that all red goats, pigeons, hens, etc., be killed. It is tempting to contrast the inevitable attitude of the traditional religious leader with the potentially innovating African secular authority; the one having nothing to gain from the arrival of mission education and technology, the other often seeing in them a way of strengthening the government and economy of the state. It is tempting to see the risings which had such religious leadership as essentially reactionary, turning their backs on the new.

Yet it is not as straightforward as that. Even in these early resistances there is apparent that ambiguity towards European ideas and technology which is so obvious in later millenarian and mass nationalist movements. There is repudiation but also desire; a rejection of white mastery but a longing for African control of modern sources of wealth and power in an African environment. We have already argued of Mkwati and Kagubi that they were not reactionary in the simple sense of looking to the restoration of the *status quo* of 1890; their programme was in some ways revolutionary in its vision of a new society. This was true also of Maji-Maji and the Nyabingi movement. But in addition to this the new society involved, at least at times and in some of its aspects, control of European goods. If the Nehanda medium instructed the abandonment of guns, Mkwati and the Kagubi medium made a great point of collecting the modern rifles taken from whites killed in March and June 1896 and distributing them as rewards for particularly loyal or effective service. In the same way we may not absurdly see in their creation of their own 'police' force—'they were like the white man's police officers', said an African witness at the trial of the Kagubi medium, describing his personal following; 'their only work was killing people'—an imitation of white power. This comes out quite strongly in the evidence presented in 'Kagubi's' trial; how he himself instituted a sort of trial of Africans who had served whites; how he found them guilty as 'rebels' and ordered their execution. And the Kagubi medium himself, after all, had allowed his daughters to attend the mission school. Mr Gann tells us that his personal 'police' force, the 'hands of the Mondoro', 'included men who had been in touch with Europeans and picked up some of their skills'. As for Mkwati, in his millenarian promises there was a strange mixture of return to the past and control of the new. Lobengula was to return from the dead—and to reign from Government House, Bulawayo. When Mkwati was trying to rally the north-eastern rebels in August 1896 it was reported that he promised them that they only had 'to wait until all the whites are dead or fled and then they will enjoy the good things of the town and live in palaces of corrugated iron'. 'Directly the white men are killed', a police inspector was told during the Inyanga scare of 1903–4, 'we will occupy your houses; all these nice things will be ours.' These hints justify us in finding in the risings of 1896–7, though in different proportions, the same elements which are so clearly detectable in the twentieth century millenarian movements with which they are in other ways so comparable.[1]

These, then, are the features of the risings of 1896–7 which are most important in considering their relationship to the future.

[1] Gann, op. cit., p. 136; Regina versus Kagubi, HC/M, No. 253; *The Daily Chronicle*, 13 July and 10 Sept. 1896; intelligence report, Inyanga, 26 Mar. 1904, A 11/2/12/12.

Let us now turn to the events which followed the risings. Here we need to discuss three aspects: first the direct continuance of the tradition of armed resistance after 1897; then the immediate legacy of the risings in Matabeleland and in western and central Mashonaland and the way in which politics there developed as a result; finally the remoter legacy of the risings in the period of modern mass nationalism.

We have been hinting already at ways in which the 1896-7 risings looked forward to the sort of opposition that developed once armed 'primary resistance' was over. But these risings were not the last in the long sequence of Shona 'primary resistances', if that term can sensibly be applied to a series of contests stretching over several centuries. The Kapararidze tradition was still vital; the combinations of memories of older centralizing institutions with the continuing authority of the spirit mediums was still able to produce challenges to European rule. Risings so organized did not break out again in the area of the 1896-7 revolt, even though whites certainly thought they were planned in Mashonaland, but they did break out on a large scale in areas which had not been involved in that rebellion. The significance of these later upheavals, the first reaching its peak between 1900 and 1902 and the second erupting as late as 1917, has been obscured for historians of Rhodesia because they took place mainly in Portuguese territory, with some significant overspills into north-eastern Rhodesia. But they form an integral part of Shona history, being to the nuclear area of the Mutapa dynasty what the 1896-7 risings were to Ndebele and Rozwi political tradition. For us their interest is partly that in them we have another opportunity for comparison and one nearer home than the Maji-Maji or Nyabingi movements and partly that these risings appeared to demonstrate the continued practicality of this sort of organization right up into the years of the First World War. This was one of the reasons why Shona opposition to colonial rule in central and western Mashonaland took so long to express itself in new terms; the exploits of Mapondera in the north-east in 1900 and 1901 or the saga of the Makombe paramounts' defiance of the Portuguese still exercised a powerful hold on the Shona imagination.[1]

[1] For fuller accounts of these two upheavals, indicating the sources on which the following paragraphs are based, see. T. O. Ranger, 'The last days of the Empire of Mwene Mutapa', *Conference of the History of the Central African Peoples*,

Both resistances covered a large area—a great crescent of territory between the Zambesi and the Rhodesian frontier, running east from Zumbo along the river almost up to Tete itself and then south to the Barwe, the paramountcy of the Makombe. In the earlier upheaval the revolt was extended into Rhodesia. The Rhodesian Korekore and Tavara were involved and it was rumoured that the Budja of Mtoko and the people of the Inyanga district opposite Barwe also intended to come out in arms. In 1917 there was no rising inside Rhodesia but numbers of Rhodesian Africans crossed the border to fight against the Portuguese and some of the rebel leaders planned an invasion of the Mount Darwin district. If they covered a wide area these risings also offered a considerable challenge. Both between 1900 and 1902 and in 1917 Portuguese administration collapsed throughout the whole crescent of the rebellions; in Rhodesia at the turn of the century there was fighting in both the Korekore and the Tavara areas which reached its climax in Mapondera's raid on the Mount Darwin township in February 1901. The suppression of both required considerable military activity on the part of the Portuguese.

Thus even if these resistances did not succeed in combining such disparate elements as the 1896-7 risings—for rebel hopes of bringing in the Ngoni and the Shangaan were disappointed; nor display the same degree of coordination; nor put into the field so formidable a fighting force; they were nevertheless important examples of African armed opposition to colonial rule. The Makombe rising of 1917 is particularly interesting because of its late date and because it represented by all odds the most vigorous African response to the pressures of the First World War. Their organizational pattern is a familiar one. Thus the fighting in 1900 to 1902 revolved around two political leaders whose traditional influence had been very extensive and who were able to revive it in the situation of colonial pressure. One of these was the titular Mutapa, reduced to a small chief in Portuguese Tavara, who now became the focus of resistance in the northern half of the crescent of revolt; surrounded by 300 men armed with modern rifles Mutapa Chioco Dambamutupe showed himself 'really hostile' to Portuguese and British alike, stimulating tax refusal, armed raids and other manifestations of rejection of administrative authority in both British

Lusaka, 1963; 'Revolt in Portuguese East Africa; the Makombe rising of 1917', *St Antonys Papers*, No. 15, 1963, ed. K. Kirkwood.

and Portuguese territory until his death in 1902 and the defeat of his followers in Coutinho's campaign. The other was the Makombe paramount, ruler of the WaBarwe principality. The 1917 risings once again focused on exactly the same positions or rather on the claimants to them striving to revive their authority through rebellion. In both upheavals the evidence is strong that the supra-tribal religious authorities were deeply involved; the mediums of the Dzivaguru cult, which had existed before the Mutapa dynasty in Tavara country and which had then become closely associated with the Empire, joining with the mediums of the dead Mutapas and the senior mediums of WaBarwe to bring about what coordination the risings possessed. Even in 1917 the fighting spirit of these rebel mediums was as fierce as ever; in the Zambesi valley the fight against Christianity still did not seem to be lost. We read of them taking command of *impis;* leading the attacks on Portuguese garrisons; planning to invade north-eastern Rhodesia to 'liberate' the headquarters of the Dzivaguru cult. The involvement of these religious leaders helped to give the rebels something of the same high morale that characterized the 1896-7 risings, and their influence was felt deep into Rhodesia, drawing men across the border to fight. In both upheavals, but especially in the Makombe rising of 1917, there was apparent the ambiguity of attitude towards modernization and the European way of life. If the Kagubi medium was served by wagon leaders and carpenters, the leaders of the 1917 fighting included ex-waiters from the hotels of Salisbury, ex-policemen and other migrants to the towns of Rhodesia and South Africa. And though there were the same injunctions to throw aside European products, to kill pigs and so on, there was no doubt in the minds of the Makombe claimants that they wanted profitable trading connections with Rhodesia and even the protection and advice of the Rhodesian administration once they had achieved independence.

Thus these characteristically Shona movements continued into the second decade of the twentieth century, exercising a powerful hold on the imaginations of the ex-rebels of central and western Mashonaland and being, in fact, linked with them in a variety of ways. Some of the most intransigent of the central Shona rebels of 1896-7 went after their defeat to assist the Makombe in his war with the Portuguese. The Inyanga scare of 1903-4 was caused by the repercussions of Coutinho's defeat of the Makombe and by the flight of his successor to Rhodesian territory at the end of 1902. 'Makombe is coming soon,' said the Chaminuka medium in 1903. 'Why he is one of my children. He will not stay away.' The Native Department believed that this medium was telling the people of the Hartley district that 'Makombi's people in Portuguese territory are coming down and going to drive the Europeans across the Inyati river'. And most of all there was the connection created by the career of Mapondera.[1]

This Rozwi warrior was one of the last citizens of the old Shona world. In 1894, unwilling to endure the restrictions upon his power which resulted from the establishment of the Company administration, he left his home in south Mazoe and moved out of the Company sphere eastwards. During 1896-7 he was fighting for Makombe in Barwe against the Portuguese; returning after the risings to find his cattle seized and his relatives shot, he raided for revenge into south Mazoe early in 1900; driven from there he fell back into Korekore country where he allied himself to the chief spirit medium and ambushed a white patrol; driven from there he fell back into Rhodesian Tavara where he allied himself with Chioco Dambamutupe and marched on the Mount Darwin township in February 1901 with a force drawn from the whole area of Chioco's influence, intending if he took Mount Darwin to send messengers south to call the central Shona once more into revolt; defeated outside Mount Darwin in pitched battle he fell back into Portuguese Tavara, continuing his alliance with Chioco and raiding over the border; then back again to Barwe to help Makombe fight against the Portuguese attack of 1902; then after Makombe's overthrow deeper into Portuguese territory. But the old Shona world, of which he made so free, was falling apart; there soon seemed to be nowhere to go to avoid the intrusive influence of the whites. 'Kadungure was then running away from Rhodesia,' his grandson tells us. 'He went on and one day he walked a whole day without covering an inch of ground. He was still in one place and when he thought he had sighted a place where to spend the night it was only to discover that it was the same place where he started.' So Kadungure Mapondera determined to run no further and in August 1903 returned to south Mazoe. On the night of August 30th 1903 police surrounded the hut where the old warrior was resting. 'Kadungure was taken out,'

[1] Morris to Taberer, 26 Nov. and 12 Dec. 1903, A 11/2/12/12.

so his family myth runs, 'whereupon he flew all over the place until he was tired and gave himself up.' In the police report the capture of this old-style Shona hero and magician is reduced to administrative prose. 'Surrounding the place as much as my party would permit, on entering I found Mapondera at the fire and arrested him. By his manner he seemed surprised. The following appeared to be his sixteen wives. He had a Martini-Henry rifle laying across his knee and four rounds of ammunition in an old stocking.'[1]

Mapondera's career ended with a seven years' hard labour sentence which the old man did not survive. But even after his imprisonment and death bolder spirits could still be tempted by the continuing disorder on the Portuguese frontier, which went on between the two great outbreaks of 1900-2 and 1917, to try to emulate his career in the now very much shrunken world of the Shona warrior.

Against this background let us turn to the next question. Where did the risings of 1896-7 leave the societies which participated in them? And how could continuing opposition manifest itself within those societies? Let us turn first to the Shona. As we have already seen the rising ended in Mashonaland very differently from the negotiated peace of Matabeleland. Out of that negotiated peace most of the senior Ndebele *indunas* preserved their lives and even their leadership. Out of the unconditional surrender of the Shona many of the most important rebel paramounts lost their lives. The administration went carefully at first: 'It has been found desirable,' wrote the Chief Native Commissioner, Mashonaland, in September 1897, 'in order to expedite the surrendering of the various chiefs, not to take too hasty proceedings against murderers, but as soon as the chief and his followers have been quietly located and the necessary evidence obtained, the guilty ones are arrested and lodged in gaol.' In Matabeleland, meanwhile, the Chief Native Commissioner had given the opinion that the Ndebele understood from the terms of peace 'that no action would be taken against any induna or headman who may have been instrumental in instigating the rebellion or murders, but who were not actually on the spot when the murders were committed, though they ordered them'. Grey had urged that 'if those rebels were prosecuted who were accessories or instigators it would be regarded by the natives

---

[1] Interview with Alexander Mapondera, 21 Jan. 1963; Goodyear to Commandant, Salisbury, 4 Sept. 1903, RC 3/3/8.

as a breach of faith or of the arrangement arrived at and would seriously disturb the feeling of confidence which is rapidly growing up'. No such considerations applied in Mashonaland. In March 1898 the Chief Native Commissioner was able to report that 'wherever it has been possible murders have been brought home to the paramount chiefs who in most cases give the orders for certain men to be killed. I have insisted on this being done wherever possible and it has resulted in seven paramount chiefs being arrested for murder, of whom five have been sentenced to death and two committed for trial.' Paramounts Makoni, Mashiangombi, Soswe, Maromo and others had died during the rising; now paramounts Mashonganyika, Chiquaqua, Wata and others were hanged in its aftermath. The sons of other paramounts, who themselves could not be proved guilty of ordering the death of whites, were put on trial or hunted—this was the case with Kunzwi-Nyandoro and Mangwende. The whole Shona paramountcy system was shaken profoundly.[1]

The Matabeleland idea of salaried chiefs was also extended to Mashonaland but while in Matabeleland salaries and recognition were given to rebel leaders, who formed an actual majority of the district heads, in Mashonaland the great majority of the newly recognized chiefs were either men who had been loyal during the rising or successors to dead rebel paramounts chosen by the Native Department. 'In the morning Umtaza came into town to be made chief', recorded Lady Victoria Grey from Umtali on December 15th, 1896. 'Of course, he was chief already but to be made a responsible one with a monthly salary of £5. Father held a little indaba with them all squatting on the floor through an interpreter and formally made him a chief.' Other 'responsible' chiefs in that eastern area were Ndapfunya, now paramount chief Makoni at £5 a month, and Chipunza at £3 a month. And so it went in the other districts. Men like Kunzwi-Nyandoro, who survived their leading part in the rising continued as chiefs but were denied subsidies.[2]

In Matabeleland men like Sikombo commanded the respect of the ex-rebel faction which felt that through the district *induna* system it had a voice in the new administrative order. In Mashona-

---

[1] Chief Native Commissioner's reports for Mashonaland, 30 Sept. 1897 and 31 Mar. 1898, *Reports on the Administration of Rhodesia, 1896–7*, 1897; C.N.C. to Public Prosecutor, 29 Apr. 1897; Grey to Rosmead, 31 May 1897, LO 5/4/4.

[2] Lady Victoria Grey's diary, entry for 15 Dec. 1896, GR 4/2/1.

land the paramountcy system which emerged from the reorganization of 1897 and 1898 could hardly be felt representative of the old rebel majority. Abundant evidence exists to show that the 'loyal' paramounts, rewarded for good service during the rising, or the new successors to dead rebel paramounts, and even paramounts like old Mangwende, whose commitment to the rising had always been half-hearted and whose decision to surrender was taken against the wish of a strong intransigent faction, experienced many challenges to their authority during the years after 1897. In Salisbury district, for instance, where many of the rebel paramounts had been prosecuted for murder, the Assistant Native Commissioner reported at the end of 1899 'the great want of control the Mashona chief has over his people. A paramount chief in Mashonaland does not get the respect or civility that an ordinary headman gets in Zululand, and I don't altogether blame the Mashonas, because with the exception of Kunzi and Seki, the paramount chiefs in the Salisbury District are very weak and do not assert their authority.' It was no accident that the two exceptions were both survivors of the risings, Kunzwi-Nyandoro whose career we have followed already, and the Kagubi medium's nominee for the Seki paramountcy. In Mrewa Native Commissioner Edwards found the chiefs reluctant or unable to capture and bring in the men wanted for murder: 'to have done so would have been beyond their power. It must be remembered that most of the wanted natives were men of some standing in the tribes, and for the Chiefs and Headmen to have rounded them up would have been committing suicide.' One of the fugitives was Mangwende's son, Mchemwa, who had urged in 1897 that the whole tribe migrate into Barwe and throw in its lot with the Makombe, and who now offered a challenge to the leadership of his father. 'From the time of the rebellion onwards', writes Edwards, 'Mangwende's power over his people was on the wane. . . . In October 1898 Mangwende sent to complain that Mchemwa was usurping his power and causing trouble amongst his people.' Mchemwa then took to the bush, moving between Barwe and his father's area. It proved almost impossible to capture him. 'Mashemwa during the rebellion', wrote Edwards in December 1898, 'was leader of the natives in this district. He had in fact far more power than his father Mangwende and it is not in human nature for them to turn round and now hunt him down. It may also be remembered that

the Mashonas will not believe that we intend remaining in the
country for good . . . and it would take a very strong minded native
to give his chief's son away when he believes that the whites are
only here for a time.'[1]

Mchemwa operated with a band of similarly disposed men,
drawn from all over the area of the rising in central Mashonaland.
Among them was Miripiri, son of Makoni Mutota Cirimaunga,
who pursued with his brothers a blood feud against Ndapfunya.
In September 1900 Miripiri raided Ndapfunya's kraal but found
the new paramount away at the Native Commissioner's office.
'This man, Miripiri,' wrote Native Commissioner Hook, 'is the
son of the old Makoni and the others are either relations or followers of the old chief who was killed in the rebellion. They have
always been very bitter against the present chief as they consider he
is not the lawful paramount and helped the white man to kill the
old chief. They openly stated their reasons in the kraal and said
they would have their revenge soon.' The sons of the old Makoni,
who continued their harassment of Ndapfunya until 1903, certainly enjoyed wide support in Maungwe. In November 1903 Native
Commissioner Ross reported that there was certainly a feeling of
unrest there; a number of headmen 'hostile to the present Makoni'
had applied for passes to visit Kunzwi-Nyandoro in order that
they might discuss with him instead of with their own chief what
their reaction to the proposed tax increase should be. In 1917 the
Native Commissioner admitted that Ndapfunya had very little
authority over the tribe and had always been regarded by a majority as an usurper; he thought it possible that the Makombe rising
of that year might stimulate attempts in Maungwe to overthrow
the hated paramount.[2]

The Shona, then, faced a real leadership dilemma after the
rising. They could not accept the majority of the paramounts as
representing adequately their feelings, nor did they have any
reason to suppose that the views expressed by these paramounts
were taken seriously by the whites. Thus in February 1904 Edwards
reported from Mrewa that he had called all chiefs and headmen

---

[1] A.N.C., Salisbury, quarterly report, Dec. 1898, LO 5/5/1; Reminiscences
of 'Wiri' Edwards, ED 6/1/1; Edwards, 'The Wanoe: a short historical sketch',
NADA, 1926; Edwards, quarterly report, Dec. 1898, NSI 1/1/1.

[2] A. N. C. Hook to C.N.C., 27 Sept. 1900, N 3/1/10; N.C. Ross to C.N.C.,
28 Nov. 1903, A 11/2/12/11.

together to inform them of the new tax increase. 'Most of the chiefs took the information quietly. Mangwendi and a few of his headmen objected to the increase but their arguments were weak and childish. . . . A firm hand with the chiefs and headmen is all that will be required.' On the other hand there was no future in the kind of leadership represented by Miripiri or Mchemwa, both of whom were murdered in the course of their inter-tribal feuding, or in the kind of leadership represented by Mapondera. It would certainly be interesting to investigate how far there continued to exist over the decades a rival leadership in the paramountcies, tracing back its claims to positions taken up during the risings, and to ask, for example, how far such considerations combined with the normal rivalry of chiefly houses to produce the complex politics of the Mangwende reserve during the paramountcy of Mchemwa's son fifty years later. Certainly in Maungwe the administration were careful not to allow a descendant of Makoni Mutota Cirimaunga to attain the paramountcy for more than fifty years; the present chief is a son of his, given into the care of the whites at Gwindingwi just before his execution and brought up ever since in the service of the native administration. But though it is interesting to speculate whether this sort of opposition tradition continued to exist within the paramountcies and whether it ran into later manifestations of rural radicalism, it is clear that it had nothing to offer at a provincial or national level.[1]

The one man who emerged from the rising still in a position of authority and prestige was Kunzwi-Nyandoro, 'the most self possessed and strongest chief in the country', as the Chief Native Commissioner described him in 1898. 'Now that so many of the big chiefs who were hostile to us in 1896 are dead', wrote Native Commissioner Ross in November 1903, 'nearly the whole of the Mashona nation look to Kunzi for information and advice.' It is worth while, then, completing his story. It is a story which shows how difficult it was for the Shona to move out of the context of their old traditions of opposition. Kunzwi-Nyandoro continued to oppose but still in association with the mediums; in the new circumstances of twentieth century Mashonaland his opposition merely brought him a series of humiliations.[2]

[1] Edward's report for February 1904, LO 5/5/25.
[2] C.N.C. to A.C.N.C., 3 June 1898, LO 5/4/9; Ross to C.N.C., 28 Nov. 1903, A 11/2/12/11.

Even in the immediate aftermath of the defeat and surrender Kunzwi remained 'as proud as ever'. In June 1898 the Chief Native Commissioner held an *indaba* with the chiefs of the Salisbury district, emphasizing that 'their great witch-doctors had been brought to justice' and calling upon them to regard the rising as a thing of the past even though 'it might be that some of them whose relations had been hanged for murders . . . felt aggrieved'. Kunzwi-Nyandoro, that faithful supporter of the mediums whose son was at that moment in hiding in the bush after his escape from Salisbury jail in February 1898, was singled out for special treatment. 'I felt it my duty to inform Kunzi that I was sorry to see that he had not shown the submissive spirit evinced by other paramounts since the rebellion. I told him that his attitude must change or he would before long get himself into trouble.'[1]

Kunzwi did, indeed, find himself in almost continual trouble. In 1900 he was showing a suspicious interest in the progress of the Boer War. In March one of his headmen told the administration of a meeting in Kunzwi's kraal at which the prospects of a Boer success were discussed; the loyal headman objected that 'if the Boers beat the British we will be killed' and was silenced by his chief, who 'turned on him and told him to hold his tongue; that he was a friend of the English and would die when the Boers came'. In April the same informant declared that the mediums and especially Kunzwi's medium, Ganyere, were spreading rumours that it was now the turn of the British to be beaten and telling the Shona to store their grain and be ready to rise. According to the African policemen in the area Kunzwi's men were saying 'that the English were cheating and that the Mrenga was going to rise a second time', that 'the English have taken our country; we don't get sufficient food, the English won't allow us to drive out the witches'. These reports were taken seriously. Kunzwi was watched and in May 1900 he was taken with other chiefs to see Carrington's camp and the imperial troops then stationed near Salisbury; 'they seemed to be very struck by the size of both men and horses', and the rumours thereafter stopped.[2]

Kunzwi was watched through 1901 and 1902; his area was still

[1] C.N.C. to A.C.N.C., 3 June 1898, LO 5/4/9.
[2] Gilson to C.N.C., 6 Mar. 1900; Gilson to C.N.C., 2 Apr. 1900; reports by Native Messengers, Mar. 1900; Acting C.N.C. to Chief Secretary, 4 Apr. 1900; Gilson to C.N.C., 1 June 1900, N 3/1/18.

the source of rumours and he was endeavouring to bring together all his people from the districts in which they were scattered 'and by so doing have greater power as a chief'. Then in 1903 administrative suspicions flared up. In November of that year the appearance of a Chaminuka medium in the Hartley district was reported; the medium was said to be predicting that the whites would be driven out of Mashonaland. In December Native Commissioner Morris reported that Kunzwi-Nyandoro was 'evidently the witch's right hand as three of his sons are living at Gabaza's kraal, also Sanga, a nephew of his. These natives are the witch's bodyguard and messengers.' Kunzwi himself attended meetings and was reported by spies to be 'only too willing' to join in a rising. The medium was detained and examined by the Chief Native Commissioner who reported in January 1904 that 'she had already given me information about Kunzi of such a nature that should it be correct Kunzi will have to be arrested and charged under the Peace Preservation Ordinance of 1901'. In fact the woman committed suicide before any sworn statement could be taken, as a result, so the Chief Native Commissioner thought, 'that I knew of Kunzi's dealings with her'.[1]

In 1904 Kunzwi remained the centre of suspicion—'there is no doubt that the Chief Kunzwi is the ringleader and the originator of any discontent that exists'. He had, or so the Administrator alleged, 'for some time now' been exchanging messages with Makombe and Mapondera in Portuguese East Africa; 'I have strengthened all the police posts in the neighbourhood of this chief and if I can get any evidence at all that could be brought before the court I shall at once issue a warrant for his arrest.' In May a strong police patrol was sent through his territory; it was reported to 'have had a wonderful effect. These patrols invariably make a good impression on the native mind.'[2]

Kunzwi was not arrested but he was harassed in every way the administration could devise. His own desire to move with all his people to Charter district was refused; about 1907 he was moved out of the Kunzwi reserve when that land was sold to European

[1] Morris to C.N.C., 26 Nov. and 12 Dec. 1903; Ross to C.N.C., 28 Nov. 1903; Edwards to C.N.C., 4 Dec. 1903; C.N.C. to Chief Secretary, 12 Jan. and 16 Feb. 1904, A 11/2/12/11.
[2] Administrator to Joint Manager, London, 31 Mar. 1904, A 11/2/12/12; Native Commissioner, Salisbury, report for May 1904, LO 5/5/27.

farmers and placed under the authority of his hated rival, Samuriwo, whose men had been sent as spies to the meetings at the kraal of the Chaminuka medium in 1903. As late as 1915 he was still hoping to escape from Samuriwo's over-lordship and reports were coming in of the same repetitive kind; presents to the mediums; contacts with Mashiangombi's kraal and with a suspected Mwari messenger from Jiri's area in Ndanga; a sort of automatic running through, either on Kunzwi's part or on the part of the Native Department's informants, of the pattern which had produced the rising in 1896. The Native Commissioner, Marendellas, urged upon an administration which had somewhat melodramatic visions of a link between Kunzwi, the Mwari cult and the Germans, that they should allow him to wait and watch events. 'Through the agency of Samrewo, the most influential chief in that district, and in whom he has absolute confidence, he is being kept informed of Nyandoro's movements. Nyandoro has always been regarded as a man of some influence and wanting in loyalty to the Government, and for these reasons he was some years ago removed from Goromonzi district to Marendellas and placed under Samrewo.' In May 1915, when two 'witch-doctors', one from Charter and one from Gutu, were found at Kunzwi's kraal the Native Commissioner cabled to the Superintendent of Natives, Salisbury, suggesting that he 'come down and deal with Nyandoro on charge of trying cases and other offences'.[1]

And so Kunzwi-Nyandoro passes out of the records, persistently proud, persistently attempting to live the life of the Shona paramount, admirable in this persistence but quite ineffective. He was not completely limited by the horizons of Mashonaland; he sought to keep informed of developments elsewhere in southern Africa and he was capable of implying a shrewd distinction between Company and imperial rule. 'Paramount chief Nyandoro said they had heard more about the Chartered Company than Her Majesty the Queen,' runs a report of a meeting with the Salisbury district chiefs in January 1901 after the news of Queen Victoria's death, 'but all that they had been told about the latter was good.' But he could not break out of the old traditions or find new allies; and like the paramount 'nearly the whole of the Mashona nation' which had looked 'to him for information and advice' also remained within the old Shona intellectual universe.[2]

[1] Correspondence between N.C. Morris and the Superintendent of Natives, Salisbury, 1915, N 3/14/5. [2] N.C., Salisbury, report for Jan. 1901, LO 5/5/6.

Thus for some twenty years after the risings the Shona made no significant move into new kinds of opposition. Nyasa clerks and mine-workers brought various kinds of independent Christianity into Mashonaland; educated Africans from South Africa formed associations to watch their own interests. But there was no contact between them and the mass of the rural Shona. Things were very different in Matabeleland where the Ndebele equivalents of Kunzwi-Nyandoro were able to move into more modern politics fairly rapidly and to assume leadership of movements of opposition which contained not only the old rebel factions but also the educated young of the Ndebele nation, modernizing African migrants from the south, and African clergy of the so-called "Ethiopian" independent church movements which had entered Matabeleland from South Africa. There were, of course, many other differences between the Ndebele and the Shona situation, but some part of this contrast is explained by the different legacies of the risings in the two provinces.

The first difference is already clear enough. The Ndebele emerged from the rising of 1896 with most of the chief rebel leaders in positions of influence, relatively well placed to act as spokesmen for future Ndebele discontent. Although, as we have seen, the powers of the salaried *indunas* were very limited and although *indunas* who quarrelled with the administration could be removed—as Somabulana was, for instance—there was nevertheless a big difference between the position of a man like Sikombo or Nyamanda and that of the hunted Mchemwa or Miripiri. This gave the erstwhile leaders of the rising a foothold in the new system.

In the second place, while men like Kunzwi-Nyandoro were still tied to their belief in the spirit mediums and their loyalty to the great concepts of Chaminuka and Nehanda, concepts which it was difficult if not impossible to reconcile with the ideas of a new age, the Ndebele aristocracy had decisively broken with the Mwari cult during the last days of the rising. There are numerous references to the activities of Mwari messengers after 1897, of their carrying instructions for the boycott of European goods or advice to stand ready to exploit the friction between English and Afrikaaner, of their being received with honour by chiefs—but these references are all to the Shona areas of Matabeleland, such as Belingwe district, or to western Mashonaland. This continuing

Shona respect for the cult was another aspect of the conservatism we have already described. But the aristocratic Ndebele alliance with it was over, and no insuperable problems arose to prevent an alliance with other forms of religious belief if such an alliance seemed profitable.

The whole Shona political system had been committed to the rising and emerged from it shaken up and transformed, with no sort of focus for supra-tribal loyalty except still for the senior mediums. But the major institution of the Ndebele—the monarchy —had not really been involved in the 1896 rising; all plans for its restoration had fallen through; and different authorities had usurped during the risings its central position. The main claimants to the kingship, Njube and Nguboyena, had been in South Africa throughout the risings; their claims, if not advanced, had not been compromised by the events of 1896. Lord Grey, indeed, had planned in June 1896 to bring Njube to Bulawayo in the hope that his return would induce the Ndebele to make peace. In the event he had decided that 'the Mlimo, who is very clever, might tell people that *he* had brought Umjube up to Bulawayo' and had not gone through with the scheme. But it was not unreasonable to hope that once the Mlimo's power was broken the administration could be persuaded to complete their 'restoration' of Lobengulas's system by restoring the kingship also.[1]

From the beginning, therefore, the rebel faction had a clear target for renewed political action. It is clear that it was pre-eminently the rebel faction who were pushing for the restoration of the kingship, even though loyalists also joined in the demand for 'one head, not half a dozen heads' at the third *indaba*. In 1904 Njube's support was described as coming from 'those who rebelled in 1896 . . . while the "loyal" portion of the nation does not desire his return'. In December 1898 the first signs of disillusionment with the settlement was accompanied by a demand for Njube's return. 'There has been some little trouble with the natives in the Matoppos', wrote Rhodes' farm manager in December 1898, 'due to the stupidness of 2 native commissioners, Stewart and Moodie. The indunas want your boy Jube back—you ought to lose him'. In 1900, when Njube did in fact visit Bulawayo, those most eager to visit him were men like old Umlugulu, who hastened into Bula-

[1] Secretary, Cape Town, to Secretary, London, 17 and 24 June 1896, LO 5/2/49.

wayo at Njube's summons without notifying or seeking the permission of the Matabeleland Native Department.[1]

And yet at the same time as being the obvious cause for the ex-rebels to support the restoration of either Njube or Nguboyena was also the cause of the young, educated and forward looking men. Njube and Nguboyena were themselves the most highly educated and westernized of all Ndebele at that time. Njube was a student at the premier South African secondary school for Africans. Nguboyena was even more gifted and in 1908 began to prepare for the English bar. They had connections with the political *élite* of South Africa—the lawyers, the independent church leaders. In South Africa the historic kingships and paramountcies were being made the focus of the new politics at this time; their treaties with the European powers being made the object of a legal offensive. A restored Ndebele kingship held out the same possibilities. In this way Umlugulu and the rest found themselves as allies of the Ndebele modernizers. In 1905, for instance, a collection was held for Njube in Bulawayo organized by 'Natives of known good character', the educated town dwellers. In 1908 Nguboyena's visit to Bulawayo was welcomed by the senior *indunas* but also by this other element. 'Nguboyena does undoubtedly receive sympathy from the educated natives (Matabele and others) in Bulawayo,' wrote the Chief Native Commissioner, 'and it is from this direction that he is likely to obtain support in the event of his wishing to give trouble.' And Nguboyena proceeded to adopt a line which was likely to unite both elements in his support. 'Nguboyena is an extremely intelligent youth. He is at present studying the conditions of native life in this country, and has asked for varied information regarding the Native Reserves, the terms on which the natives reside thereon and has applied for a map showing the Reserves.'[2]

Neither Njube, who died in 1910, nor Nguboyena who suffered a nervous breakdown in the same year survived to work out fully the implications of this new sort of politics. Nevertheless their candidature for the kingship was an important episode in Ndebele political history. It enabled the rebel faction to move into a new sort of political activity and into cooperation with new allies. The

[1] McDonald to Rhodes, 19 Dec. 1898, Rhodes House, Mss. Afr. s. 228, C. 14; A.C. Mlugulu, report for Aug. 1900, LO 5/7/4.
[2] C.N.C. to Secretary, Administrator, 9 and 16 Sept. and 10 Nov. 1908, A 11/2/11/8.

prestige of the two sons of Lobengula and the impression made by their relative mastery of the white man's world was one of the factors in the readiness of the Ndebele *indunas* to send their children to school, as Nyamanda, for instance, sent his son to an Ethiopian church school in South Africa; this Ndebele approach to education was often contrasted by the Native Department with the lack of modern preparation enjoyed by the possible successors to the Shona paramountcies. And the fact that the old leaders of the rising were in positions within the new administrative system and at the same time able to lend their support to the kingship movement meant that the Ndebele imagination did not remain obsessed with thoughts of another rising, even though the tradition of violent resistance was shown to be alive in the wider Nguni world by the Zulu rising of 1906. Although there were fugitive murderers in Matabeleland there was no parallel there to the challenges offered by Mchemwa and Miripiri to the authority of Mangwende and Ndapfunya.

Of course this contrast should not be pushed too far, nor should it be suggested that there was in the first decade of the twentieth century any unbridgeable gulf between armed resistance and 'new' forms of opposition. If the Shona peoples were connected by history and sentiment to the continuing resistances in Portuguese East Africa, the Ndebele were connected in the same way with the story of the Zulu response to white pressure. On the one hand this connection with the Zulu meant that the Ndebele came into contact with the Zulu intellectuals and church leaders who were among the pioneers of modern African politics in South Africa; on the other hand it meant that the Ndebele were touched by the news of the Zulu rising of 1906, a resistance to pressure that combined old and new elements. There was during this period a complex interaction between Ndebele and Zulu political history— the treatment of the Ndebele in 1893 and 1896 helping to harden the attitude of Zulu intellectuals towards the whites, experience of Zulu churches helping Ndebele migrants to develop new forms of protest, and so on. Certainly at the time whites in Rhodesia did not imagine that further armed opposition by the Ndebele was out of the question and when the Ndebele did not follow the Zulu example in 1906 it was explained in terms of the deliberately fostered divisions within the Ndebele nation rather than in terms of an Ndebele transition to new political forms.

In fact the memory of the rising and the whole tradition of Nguni resistance had not ceased to be important in Ndebele politics. But as time went on it began to be distanced and made use of in a way that could not at that period happen in Mashonaland. This comes out very clearly in the later career of Nyamanda, Lobengula's eldest son, whose involvement in the rising we have already seen. Nyamanda went through a characteristic progress; given a place in the new establishment as a salaried district head he was nevertheless increasingly disillusioned by the fruits of the accomodation with Rhodes. Given both the position and the dissatisfaction, and enjoying the prestige of his showing in 1896, he was able to assume leadership of radical Ndebele politics after the death of Njube and the withdrawal of Nguboyena.

It was the breach of what he, together with the other *indunas*, regarded as Rhodes' undertakings over land which precipitated Nyamanda into political activity. After the risings he had been re-settled in the Insiza area but had been forced to move when the owner began to develop the land; he then settled in the Bubi area but was told 'to remove by the Company owning the land'. Turning to the idea of offering to purchase land he was given no encouragement in this by the Company administration which consistently answered his complaints by telling him that he could choose an area to settle in one of the Reserves. 'Being landless and at the mercy of any purchaser of land', complained Nyamanda, 'was a difficult and bitter pill for a man of his standing to swallow and . . . he felt that the Government had no sympathy or regard for his difficulties or troubles.' In this way the Company reaped the results of its failure to follow through Grey's land reform policy.[1]

The issue of land was one on which it was easy to rally the radical Ndebele faction. 'The well-founded and growing discontent by an important section of the community cannot be ignored,' wrote the Superintendent of Natives, Bulawayo. 'It can be foreseen that the land difficulty becomes more acute Nyamanda's policy of constantly harping upon it is certain to augment his following with the effect of consolidating native opinion in an undesirable manner.' And Nyamanda moved from expressions of personal grievance to a demand on the behalf of the Ndebele as a whole. 'All we want', he insisted, 'is for the Government to say,

[1] N.C. Inyati, to S/N/Byo., 16 Mar. 1920, A 3/18/18/6.

"This is a tract of land for Lobengula's people." ' He demanded a great block of Matabeleland as a national home—'I know that some of the land within these boundaries is already occupied,' he told the Chief Native Commissioner in 1920. 'It is for Your Honour to decide how I am to acquire it. We will find the money.'

Once again the administration believed that support for Nyamanda came from the ex-rebel factions among the Ndebele. Nyamanda's appeal to them was couched in terms harking back to the days of 1893 and 1896. 'I write this paper of mine to you, all Chiefs of the Regiments,' runs one of his letters in 1919, 'I say to you, all nations that have been conquered by the English, the Government gave them Chiefs to whom they pay their tax. Look at Khama! He has his country, and Lewanika, he has his plot. His country is settled well, and Mosheshe, he has his land. Also the son of Dinizulu has his country. All natives have their bit of ground where they pay their taxes. They pay taxes they know and are not like you who pay for what you know not. You do not know what is done with your money. It is like money that is lost because you pay so greatly and do not know what your money does. At the same time you undergo tribulation.' 'I want to hear your word,' ran another letter. 'We remain in a scattered state all the time. Even if people have been conquered may they not abide in one place? For myself, I ask of you, ye owners of the territory, inasmuch as you are the nation. I do not say it is war, my compatriots, I only inquire. You also know that all black tribes in great numbers were overcome by the white people, but they have their piece of land to stay on happily. We, forsooth, pay only for staying on white men's farms, and for what reason?'

The theme of Ndebele defeat in 1893 and 1896 dominates Nyamanda's thinking; but even in these letters his response is not that of Kunzwi-Nyandoro, still seeking to set himself up as an old style paramount with the aid of the mediums. It is not for renewed war that he appeals but for support for an attempt to petition the imperial authorities and to lobby overseas; the *indunas* were being called to contribute money 'so that I can essay across the Ocean and go to the king over the Water in England and talk with the Big King George. I say to you, O People! A child who does not cry out dies at labour.' And in this approach to the political problems of the Ndebele Nyamanda was able to draw upon a whole range of sophisticated allies. The connections with South African

XI   The Kagubi medium under guard 1897.

XII   The Nehanda and Kagubi mediums in Salisbury prison awaiting
execution, 1898.

modern politics which had existed in Njube's day were easily re-established; especially to the Zulu politicians Matabeleland seemed an extension of South Africa in a way that Mashonaland did not. Thus Nyamanda counted among his allies Congress lawyers and Ethiopian church leaders. He also counted Ndebele teachers, ministers and migrants and South African settlers in Rhodesia who also wanted a chance to purchase land and were prepared to attach themselves to the idea of a revived Ndebele state. In this way the grievances of the Ndebele nation were expressed in petitions of startling modernity and even represented at the Versailles Conference by the Ethiopian church chaplain to the South African National Congress, Reverend Ngcayiya. In this way the idea of a Matabele Home enjoyed the support of many non-Ndebele while the Ndebele radicals gave their weight to petitions attacking the move to settler Responsible Government and calling for imperial intervention.[1]

In this movement, which I have described in greater detail elsewhere, the transition from the politics of rebellion to the politics of protest was clearly made. Nor was it the only sign of Ndebele ability to see the risings in the context of the twentieth century. In 1919 an abortive attempt was made to found a Rhodesian Native National Congress. Its moving spirit was an Nbedele migrant living in Johannesburg, the Reverend P. S. Ngwenya. Ngwenya had earlier founded the African Mission Home Church, which largely catered for Ndebele migrants and had ministers at work in Matabeleland as early as 1914; then the Matabele Rhodesian Society which was intended to act as a focal point for Ndebele exiles in South Africa. Very much a modern man he now attempted to extend the congress movement to Southern Rhodesia, calling for funds and delegates to be sent to a great inaugural meeting in Johannesburg. And his appeal was essentially similar to Nyamanda's; a tale of conquest and of white unforgivingness. 'From 1893 until 1919 the Government has been bad towards the brown man of Rhodesia. Even if I had killed a man, after such a lapse of time I would be forgiven for having done so. If I have not been forgiven what am I to do? It is good that you should contribute money and ask others to do so, money being a sword and

---

[1] For a fuller account see, T. O. Ranger, 'Traditional Authorities and the rise of modern politics in Southern Rhodesia, 1898 to 1930', *The Zambesian Past*, Manchester, 1966, eds. Stokes and Brown.

buckler, for without money you can do nothing and you cannot open your mouth. . . . Contribute money so that we can speak to the Rhodesian Government as to the rule under which we are ruled.'[1]

This comparison, then, of the effects of the risings in Matabeleland and Mashonaland and of the place which the memory of the risings held in the thinking of Ndebele and Shona leaders would seem to indicate that the Ndebele negotiated settlement had allowed them to make a much more effective transition into the new political world than had the Shona resistance to the end. Even if their readiness to negotiate had perhaps saved Company rule and so led on to the white settler march to political supremacy, at least the Ndebele leaders were able to speak out against the idea of Responsible Government at a time when Shona reaction was still limited to the warnings of the Mwari cult. 'Referring to Native laws and treatment,' ran Nyamanda's petition of March 10th, 1919, 'Your Petitioners have experienced with great regret that High Commissioners and Governors General, who are the true representatives of Your Majesty, have merely acted as disinterested spectators whilst Responsible Government parties of various names and associations are interpreting the Laws in class legislation to suit their purpose. Your Petitioners pray that in case Rhodesia is granted any form of Government the Imperial Government take over the Administration of Native Affairs in that Country as is the case with regard to British Basutoland, British Bechuanaland and Swaziland.' 'We would most respectfully request Your Royal Highness as High Commissioner', ran another petition in August 1921, 'to make representations on our behalf to His Majesty's Government, that the Natives of the country be given an opportunity to express their wishes in the Rights and forms of Government they would prefer and on the Safe Guards that might be made in their welfare and protection.' It was all much more sophisticated and to the point than the reaction of the Shona in Belingwe, where the Native Commissioner reported in 1923 that 'natives are killing cattle and hiding grain and saying that the Dutch and British are preparing to fight.' 'There appears to have been talk of anticipated fighting between the Europeans (English and Dutch),' wrote the Superintendent of Natives, Gwelo. 'It is probable that this is due to the change of Government, the peaceful

[1] See N 3/5/8; N 3/5/3.

effecting of which is something foreign to the native mind. . . .
It appears to be true that some natives hid their grain in the hills,
but this has, I believe, ceased. The precaution was probably taken
with the idea of having food supplies available should it be necessary
to take to the hills when the Europeans were fighting.'[1]

And yet the story of the inter-action of the risings and of modern
politics in Southern Rhodesia is more complicated even than this.
Despite the contrast which we have drawn for the early 1920s the
energy and driving power behind modern mass nationalism in
Southern Rhodesia has come from the Shona rather than the
Ndebele. Almost none of the leading figures in contemporary
African nationalism are drawn from the ranks of the superior
Ndebele castes; the movement both in Matabeleland and in Masho-
naland is essentially a spectacular Shona renaissance. And in this
Shona renaissence the themes and memories of the risings have
once again come flooding back into Southern Rhodesian politics.
How is this apparent paradox to be explained?

One part of the explanation is that the relevance and effectiveness of the new Ndebele politics was only theoretical rather than
practical. The sort of movement that Nyamanda was trying to
build; the sort of issues that he and his allies were raising; these
were certainly to the point. But the whole movement had profound
weaknesses and limitations. If the Ndebele had emerged from the
rising with some radical leaders still in positions of authority they
had also emerged in a seriously divided state. From 1896 onwards
it was the policy of the Rhodesian administration to balance factions
within the Ndebele nation, loyalists against rebels, intransigent
rebels against accommodating rebels, district against district. As
time went on there was not only the difficulty of achieving a
single candidate, acceptable to the majority, around whom all
the protagonists of a restored monarchy might group themselves
but also the difficulty of the threat offered by the idea of a restoration to the *status quo* in which so many had come to possess a
vested interest. It was precisely for this reason that the Nyamanda
campaign to restore the monarchy was in many ways more of a
radical than a conservative movement. 'Our steadfast policy has
been', wrote the Chief Native Commissioner in 1929, 'to oppose

[1] Petition to the King, 10 Mar. 1919, A 3/18/18/11; Petition to High
Commissioner, 16 Oct. 1921, A 3/18/11; N.C. Belingwe, to S/N/ Gwelo,
26 Sept. 1923, S/N/Gwelo to C.N.C., 10 Oct. 1923, N3/14/5.

the building up of a unity among the Matabele which would have been a danger; the policy of *divide et impera* was, in effect, adopted; and because of our more or less direct rule and scattered Reserves, we were able to avoid the evils which followed the Zululand settlement.' Even though it possessed a greater national coherence than the Shona an Ndebele community thus divided was no match for the single-minded pressure of the settlers for Responsible Government.[1]

Another part of the explanation, however, lies still in the survival of the Ndebele national ideal, despite these weaknesses and divisions. Long after the 1920s, Ndebele politics continued to revolve around the idea of the kingship and the idea of the national home, and the Matabele Home Society remained their main vehicle. But while in Nyamanda's time such a programme had enjoyed the support of a wide range of non-Ndebele allies it soon ceased to do so. After 1923 the chances of appealing on the basis of the legal rights of the Lobengula family seemed slim indeed; the 'alien' African allies of Nyamanda turned instead to agitate for Land Purchase and to explore the possibilities of working within the new Responsible Government system. In this way the Nyamanda programme continued to obsess the Ndebele but became more and more irrelevant to national politics.

Leadership in the sphere of national politics appeared to pass to the new *élite* associations—the Southern Rhodesian Bantu Voters Association, the Southern Rhodesian Native Welfare Association, the Southern Rhodesian Bantu National Congress, and the rest—or to rising trade union movements. Many of the key figures in these movements were Nyassa or South African and Southern Rhodesians involved were consciously turning their backs on the Ndebele and Shona past, seeking to educate Africans and to co-operate with Europeans. Except to the radical trade unionists of the Industrial and Commercial Workers Union the tradition of armed resistance and the memory of the risings meant nothing to them; the tradition of millenarian enthusiasm was totally foreign to their spirit. Thus, as Mr Shamuyarira tells us, 'The Matabele Home Society survived as a tribal society long after the trade unions had taken over the role of political pressure groups, and it kept alive the image of Matabele kingship. . . . Mashona reaction also looked to the past for comfort, and took as a tribal hero the

[1] C.N.C., to Minister of Native Affairs, 18 Nov. 1929, S 84/A/262.

tall, bearded prophet Chaminuka'; the only people expressing 'themselves in anything like modern terms' were 'an obedient group of educated men', important in the history 'of Southern Rhodesian nationalism because of their supra-tribal approach but committed to the programme of 'constitutional resolutions and peaceful propaganda and . . . consulting the Native Affairs Department, MPs and Missionaries'.[1]

Now, this new sort of association *was*, as we have said, important in the history of nationalism and the Shona masses *were* looking to the past for comfort. But the history of the development of modern nationalism in Southern Rhodesia has been more than a matter of the gradual evolution of a more militant educated supra-tribal *élite* and the diffusion of its ideas to a wider and wider audience. Modern nationalism is characterized by its desire to create a modern supra-tribal national identity; but it is also characterized by mass membership. The struggle between the nationalists and the white establishment in Rhodesia is, to use, Dr Iliffe's phrase 'a great crisis of commitment'. And any student of nationalism in Southern Rhodesia has to ask again, how was this commitment achieved?

The answer, necessarily superficially given here, seems to be that commitment has been achieved by bringing the mass of the Shona peoples and of the Ndebele subject peoples of Southern Rhodesia into the nationalist movement through its presentation to them as a radical, almost millenarian, movement which looks to the past for inspiration but promises mastery of the future. The mood of Southern Rhodesian nationalism is closer to the ambiguity towards the white world which characterized the risings and subsequent millenarianism than to the total acceptance of its values which characterized the new associations of the 1920s and 1930s. It seems to me to be possible to argue that it was partly because the African peoples had espoused in 1896–7 a movement of revolt which was not merely a reaction in defence of the *status quo* but which involved an attempt to attack the problem of scale; because their imaginations remained captive to this ideal of entry to the new society through upheaval—an idea perhaps in the end more realistic in Southern Rhodesia than 'constitutional resolutions and peaceful propaganda'—that it was possible to mobilize them so effectively behind the modern mass nationalist parties.

Modern nationalism, I would argue, has tapped the same sort

[1] N. Shamuyarira, *Crisis in Rhodesia*, London, 1965, pp. 28–31.

of energy that flared up in 1896–7. It is interesting before examining in more detail the way in which this has been done to look at earlier attempts to do so and to divert such energy into new channels; attempts which did not lead anywhere but which throw considerable light on the process we are discussing.

Up to the early 1920s, we have said, the current of opposition among the Shona still sought to run in the old channels represented by Chief Kunzwi-Nyandoro's post-rebellion career. By about the time that the settlers achieved Responsible Government despair was beginning to prevail about the ability of the old powers to bring about the sort of radical changes which was felt to be needed. The atmosphere within the Mwari cult for instance was already that of the cult song collected by the American scholar, R. Werbner, in 1960; a despairing lament for the ruin created in the Shona world by the white man and the powerlessness of the defeated to do anything about it.

> Ay, this world fails one,
> Ay, the unburnt pot has entered here,
> Ay, the unburnt pot (the white man) has spoilt the world.
> He has cut the world in the middle . . .
> The unburnt pot has entered the world and killed it. . .
> Yelele, fellow men, to be defeated brings one to eat shit,
> Yelele, the world I no more understand it as long ago when
>   I grew;
> Yelele, the unburnt pot just handles the world, twisting it.
> Yelele, we are troubled. . .
> Yelele, the god who is in heaven has given us his back;
> The God who is at the roof has thrown us away like dogs,
> Yelele, the Mwali in heaven has given us his back.[1]

In Belingwe in 1923, where the cult still exerted a 'political' influence, this sort of despairing passivity characterized the Shona reaction to the new age of white Responsible Government. 'There can be little doubt that the natives in Belingwe, as in many other districts, are not in a contented frame of mind,' wrote the Superintendent of Natives, Gwelo, 'This may be attributed mainly to the difficulty experienced in meeting their financial obligations such as Government taxes, repayments for famine relief, dipping

---

[1] The translation of this song is Werbner's own. I am grateful for his permission to use it.

funds and, on farms, rent. They have no market for their cattle and the old men show signs of despondency. The younger men show indifference amounting to almost passive acceptance of the penalties incurred by failure to fulfill their obligations.' The consequences of 'the cattle slump and the general financial depression, the talk caused by the change of Government and the somewhat numerous cases of non-payment of wages' were an apparently 'quite callous' and fatalistic attitude. But as the Superintendent remarked, this was 'fertile soil. . . prepared for any seditious seed'; it was the passivity productive of millenarian belief and action.[1]

No doubt there were still many dreams of old-style rebellion. In an account of a similar situation of depression and financial pressure in the Inyanga district Wulf Sachs writes of 'ugly rumours of a general revolt; rumours and stories multiplied—wild tales of thousands of natives killed and imprisoned because they refused to pay the tax. Young blood preached revolt, recalling feverish sagas of old wars against the whites.' But there were also attempts made to offer a new sort of millenarian solution. In a situation in which, according to Sachs' account of Inyanga, the mediums and *ngangas* professed themselves unable to assist, telling 'the people that the diseases came from the white folk . . . not sent by the midzimu or by the Mwari but by the white people', there was a logic in turning to millenarian forms of Christianity.[2]

Two such attempts to transform the tradition of revolt may be noticed here. One was an attempt at the level of a paramountcy—the Church of the White Bird founded by Matthew Zwimba mainly for the people of the Zwimba Reserve. An independent Christian church, Zwimba's movement nevertheless grew out of Shona tradition and especially out of the tradition of the risings. The white bird stood for both the dove of the Holy Spirit and the traditional messenger of Mwari, which it will be remembered from Native Commissioner Edwards' reminiscences had carried the news of revolt to the Africans of Mrewa in 1896; the saints and martyrs of the church were those who had been killed in the Zwimba area during the fighting of 1896 and 1897. There are parallels to Zwimba's attempt elsewhere in eastern and southern Africa— Isaac Shembe's Nazarite Church in Zululand, Elijah Masinde's *Dini Ya Msambwa* movement in western Kenya, both of which

[1] S/N/Gwelo to C.N.C., 10 Oct. 1923, N3/14/5.
[2] Wulf Sachs, *Black Anger*, 1947.

appeal back to the memories of the resistant dead—which taken together make clear the potentialities of this sort of use of the resistance tradition. To appeal to the resistant and the rebel dead was not to appeal to the past only but to appeal to the predecessors in search of the new society.[1]

Zwimba, for all his eccentricities, did become the mediator between the Zwimba chiefs and people and the modern world— he gave evidence as their spokesman to the Land Apportionment Commission of 1925. But his horizons were too limited for any really spectacular success. It was an alien millenarian movement, which made no direct appeal back to 1896 and 1897, but which effectively presented itself as a successor that swept the rural districts of Mashonaland in the late 1920s. This was a version of the Watch Tower movements of Malawi carried to the Shona by Nyassa mine workers and domestic servants. In 1925 the movement suddenly appeared in the Sinoia district; in 1926 it spread into the whole of the Lomagundi district, into Urungwe and Sipolilo as well as Sinoia; by 1929 it was supported by thousands of people in the Zezuru and Korekore rural areas. The teachings of the movement were millenarianism of an undiluted kind. The Nyassa heroes of the cult were 'to rise out of the water and come to the people in the "Mbudzi" moon. They will give the people a potent to drink from a cup. This will send the recipient to sleep for seven days. When they awaken they will be white and have amassed wealth. They will not need to work.' The promise of the new society went hand in hand with an attack on the customs of the old. 'Their respective totems have been supplanted by the single totem of "Israel". . . children, men, women, and even mothers-in-law are shaken by the hand by all and no modesty, as of old, is shown . . . Shawe charms and ornaments and all medicinal charms are to be discarded. People not dipped are to be shunned and referred to as "Nyoka". An Israel cannot eat food with a Nyoka or live close by one or come into bodily contact with one.' 'All our customs have been abandoned,' complained chief Bepura 'so that we elderly people who retain our old laws are apart now from those of my people who have dipped. They are shameless in their familiarity with their mothers-in-law and they do not even salute us, their elders. They have taken European names', and say 'Our King is now America . . . America is black and not white . . . We shall take

[1] For Zwimba see, A 3/6/9.

the white people's stores and we shall own them. We shall be the people who remain.'[1]

This movement, again, did not lead anywhere. Marshall Hole, who saw the millenarian leaders as 'only witch-doctors in another guise' feared for some time that they might play the same part in a new rising that the old religious leaders had played in 1896. But, he concluded with relief, 'their demonstrations have been short-lived and confined to localities and it would seem that the Bantu people have not the necessary cohesion to maintain any prolonged agitation or to make it general'. 'What do they think they can do?', asked an African opponent of Watch-Tower. 'They have no guns. The Maswina listen too easily.' But the movement revealed once again the radical supra-tribal potentialities in the Shona tradition of resistance. It was, in a sense, a half way house between mass commitment to the risings and mass commitment to the African nationalist parties of the 1950s and 60s.

It would be wrong to suggest by the term 'half-way house' any simple or straightforward progression from one form of expression to another. In the late 1950s, just as the sort of mass feeling we are describing began to find expression in the new nationalist move-ment, it was still welling up in the most remarkable of the post-war Shona independent churches, the Guta Ra Jehovah of Mai Chaza. Despite Mai Chaza's own attempt to keep within the mission church and to keep out of political activity, her movement was rapidly infused with notions linked to the Shona religious world of the nineteenth century and with millenarian expecta-tion. Her followers believed her to call forth voices from the air, from rocks, from trees—even from the Zimbabwe ruins themselves. They organized themselves into khaki uniformed troops and ex-pected the aid of 'spirit soldiers'; they regarded the water blessed by Mai Chaza as a medicine of salvation and invulnerability; and after her death in 1961 Mai Chaza was regarded as a messianic liberator, whose return would bring about the new Jerusalem. It was little wonder that looking at these phenomena and at a fol-lowing which spread over the Mondoro, Chiweshe, Salisbury, Zwimba and Zimunya areas, an apprehensive African correspon-dent wrote to the *African Eagle* in March 1957 to warn the Shona

[1] See files S84/A/259 and 293. For a fuller treatment of this episode see, T. O. Ranger, 'The early history of Independency in Southern Rhodesia', *Religion in Africa*, ed. W. Montgomery Watt, Edinburgh, 1964.

that Mai Chaza was following in the footsteps of another woman—presumably either Nehanda or Wamponga—who had led them into defeat in 1896.[1]

But by the time of the Mai Chaza movement mass emotion could find an outlet of a more directly political kind in the new nationalist parties, and it was in these that memories of the risings most importantly revived. A newly militant *élite* had come into being, no longer obedient and acceptant of all things European; and this *élite* was able to reach and to tap the latent energy of the Shona. The new leadership brought to the people a much more coherent and practical ideology, an evolved concept of the nation state, a knowledge of twentieth century political and constitutional procedures. In this respect they were very different from Matthew Zwimba or Mai Chaza. But at the same time they brought essentially the same promise of radical change—'We shall be the people who remain'.

Thus the new nationalism appeared to the rural masses as a sort of millenarianism, offering membership of a new society with its own customs and costumes, leading them against their own chiefs and discredited establishment as the mediums had sometimes done in 1896–7 and the Watch Tower leaders had done in the 1930s. The new nationalism was also able to 'maintain a prolonged agitation' and 'to make it general'. At the same time the character of this new nationalism was profoundly modified by its discovery of the potentialities of the traditions of resistance of the rural masses. The nationalist leaders, hitherto chary of appeals to the tribal past, discovered that it was possible to appeal to the great supra-tribal spirits or to the heroes of the risings because they had been in a real sense forerunners in attempting to create, by however ephemeral means, a larger society. They discovered that the rural masses, while profoundly steeped in the Shona tradition, would follow urban nationalist leaders against their own chiefs in the very name of that tradition. They discovered that their own critical and selective attitude towards the life of the West, very different from the emulative acceptance of the early associations, was oddly mirrored in the ambiguities which had existed since the risings, and no doubt before, in the reactions of rural society. Thus the leaders of the new parties gave the rural Shona a programme,

[1] I owe this information on the Mai Chaza movement to Mr David Wiley of Princeton.

an organization, a purpose; but they were given in return the energy of rural radicalism and were able to place the nationalist movement, apparently so sudden and rootless an affair, firmly in the context of the African political history of Southern Rhodesia.

One of the results of this new sense on the part of African politicians of the importance of the rural masses was a revival of the political influence of the Mwari priests and the spirit mediums. Nationalist leaders discovered that they still possessed influence and courted them; the religious leaders regained some of the confidence lost in the 1920s and 1930s. Thus, for example, in 1954 a number of Bulawayo trade unionists, later to become leading figures in the nationalist parties, visited the Mwari shrine at Matonjeni to seek the blessing of the god on a proposed strike. They reported to the kraal at the foot of the hill and remained there until the hour given for their interview came. Then, just before dawn, they went up to the cave and told the old woman who was acting as the 'ear' of Mwari their errand—the white people were troubling them; they wished to act to obtain fair wages. Their message would be passed on to the god, they were assured; now that they had remembered their own religion all would go well with them. Field workers report that many of the Mwari officers played an active role in the nationalist politics of the later 1950s and early 1960s.[1]

The spirit mediums, or some of them, have been equally involved. Professor Gelfand records that when he tried to question the medium, Hore, while possessed with the spirit of Nyanhehwe-Nosenga, about the Dzivaguru cult he was told, 'I don't want to talk to you about Dzivaguru because my people have no land to plough. Give them good land. My people have not enough room. I have been paying tax. You have taken the guns of my people. You rule my people. All these, however, we do not mind, but you have now taken the land of my people. The land is so small that they cannot get enough crops to sell and get money.' 'This interview', Gelfand comments, 'is a good example of the influence the tribal spirits may have on the general population. There can be no doubt that while the tribal spirit is much concerned with the religious practices and observances of the people under its care, there can also be a political character to the pronouncements made by the spirit.' Some of the mediums, indeed, like the Gwangwadza medium in Sipolilo, became known as Z.A.P.U. mediums during

[1] This account was given to me by one of the trade unionists concerned.

the time of the Zimbabwe African Peoples Union; this medium urged the Shona of his area to accept the leadership of Mr Joshua Nkomo on the ingenious grounds that the Ndebele had overcome even Chaminuka and that Mr Nkomo as an Ndebele speaker would be able to overcome the whites; he was arrested and imprisoned, and the traditional song of his spirit which he sang while on his way to jail—'Men can die while dreaming'—became one of the most popular of the old spirit medium songs which replaced modern nationalist choruses as the favourite music of party members.[1]

But the point is not so much that the influence of the priests and mediums revived; the new parties also made use of the influence of independent church leaders and of eminent African members of the mission churches. A characteristic meeting might begin with the invocation of Chaminuka or Nehanda and be followed by a prayer to god in which all members of the audience raised both their hands to heaven in the fluttering motion of the Pentecostal sects. The point really is that what was happening was the involvement of the ordinary man and the encouragement of his morale to an extent which had not been paralleled since 1896. Mr Shamuyarira tells us something of these developments. The legends of Chaminuka 'took on an extra significance . . . after the formation of the City Youth League', the first of the radical nationalist movements in Mashonaland. 'George Nyandoro particularly dwelt upon his memory in speeches as a binding factor in resisting the settlers'. Mr Shamuyarira goes on to describe how the National Democratic Party, founded in 1960, 'added one important factor that had been singularly missing in Rhodesian nationalism: *emotion*'. He describes their mass meetings, the prayers to Chaminuka, 'thudding drums, ululation by women dressed in national costumes and ancestral prayers'. 'In rural areas meetings became political gatherings and more—social occasions where old friendships were renewed and new ones made, past heritage was revived through prayers and traditional singing with African instruments, ancestral spirits were invoked to guide and lead the new nation. Christianity and civilization took a back seat, and new forms of worship, and new attitudes were thrust forward dramatically. Although all attendants wore western clothes . . . and cars and loudspeakers were seen everywhere as signs of the

[1] M. Gelfand, *Shona Religion*, Cape Town, 1962, pp. 48–50.

scientific age, the spirit pervading the meetings was African, and the desire was to put the twentieth century in an African context.' These meetings, he tells us, had an emotional impact 'that went far beyond claiming to rule the country—it was an ordinary man's participation in creating something new, a new nation.'[1]

'Remember our dear friends,' sang a popular township harmony group in July 1960, when the leaders of the National Democratic Party were arrested:

> Remember our dear friends,
> That day of suffering
> When all the leaders
> Of the African Party were arrested
> Suffering was experienced
> Many people died
> We are fighting for Freedom
> In our Country.
> Father have mercy on us
> Listen to our cries.
> Our Continent of Africa
> Has many riches
> Nehanda represent us
> So that we can be freed.

And in July 1962, Joshua Nkomo, leader of the National Democratic Party's successor movement, the Zimbabwe African Peoples Union, was met at the airport by a ninety year old survivor of the 1896–7 risings who presented him with a spirit axe as a symbol of the apostolic succession of resistance and so that he might 'fight to the bitter end'.

So in these infinitely complex ways the memory and effects of the risings have interacted with a host of other factors, necessarily neglected in this chapter, to influence the African political history of Southern Rhodesia. Nor can one suppose that the story is yet over.

As I write this concluding paragraph Southern Rhodesia is entering upon a new phase of the struggle between black and white, a phase of violence which the nationalists are calling once again by the Shona name for the 1896–7 risings—*ChiMurenga*. It

[1] N. Shamuyarira, op. cit.

remains to be seen what the issue of this contest will be and in what ways the risings of 1896–7, and the whole tradition of which they form a part, will be regarded in the Southern Rhodesia—or Zimbabwe—of the future.

A Note on Sources

I DO not propose to give a detailed bibliography of published material relevant to this book. There is a very full bibliography of books, pamphlets, periodical articles, theses, official publications of the British South Africa Company, the Southern Rhodesian Government, and the United Kingdom Government given in L. H. Gann, *A History of Southern Rhodesia*, London, 1965. Those published works which I have used and which are not included in Mr Gann's bibliography are fully described in the footnotes to the text.

The bulk of the sources used in this book are deposited in the National Archives of Southern Rhodesia in Salisbury. There is a full description of most of the government material available to scholars in *A guide to the public records of Southern Rhodesia under the regime of the British South Africa Company 1890–1923*, Central African Archives, 1956. Some of the files cited in this book have recently been removed from open access. Sources of private provenance in the National Archives form the Historical Manuscripts Collection. There is a typescript guide to these at the Archives in Salisbury.

As stated in the introduction of this book all references in the footnotes which give no indication of place refer to documents deposited at the National Archives of Southern Rhodesia. It may be useful to indicate the meaning of the main code numbers. Files coded A are those relating to the Administrator's Office; under B those relating to the Defence and Police; under N those relating to the Chief Native Commissioner and the Native Department; under HC those relating to the correspondence of the High Commissioner for South Africa; under RC those relating to the correspondence of the Resident Commissioner; under CT those relating to the Cape Town office of the British South Africa Company; and under LO those relating to the London Office of the British South Africa Company. Files coded under S are those relating to the years after the attainment of Responsible Government in 1923.

No further description is needed for most of this material. The London Office letter books, containing in-letters to the London

Office of the British South Africa Company, are such an important source for this book, however, that some account of them may be useful. The letter books, stout volumes of several hundred pages each, form a constant series from 1889 to 1908. At first all communications to the London Office from Mashonaland went through the Kimberley/Cape Town office first and were forwarded to London with covering comments from there. Series LO 5/2/1–58 covers these forwarded reports from 1889 to 1899. The last volumes in this series, however, are mainly press-cutting books since from 1896 onwards material began to be sent direct from Salisbury and Bulawayo to the London Office. The direct Salisbury reports are in series LO 5/4/1–17, covering the period November 1896 to November 1899. The direct Bulawayo reports are in series LO 5/6/1–19, covering the period May 1896 to November 1899. After 1899 there was a division between administrative and commercial correspondence. Salisbury administrative correspondence between 1899 and 1908 is in series LO 5/5/1–36. Bulwayo continued to correspond directly between 1899 and 1901; the correspondence is in LO 5/7/1–6. Cape Town continued to communicate directly between 1899 and 1907; the correspondence is in LO 5/3/1–4. In all, therefore, there are some 140 volumes of correspondence from Rhodesia amounting in all to scores of thousands of pages. There is also a series of out-letters from London, LO 3/1/1–82 and LO 3/2/1–50. These letter books have no index or guide to contents.

Most of the material in these very valuable volumes takes the form of type-written copies of the original correspondence or reports and African names are often very oddly rendered. This is true also of the material reproduced in the Confidential Prints series of the Colonial Office. For this reason I have often given a reference to the original letter or report rather than to the copy.

Some comment is necessary, too, on the material relating to the trials of the rebels which has been used in this book. The notes of evidence collected together under the code HC/M, (High Court, Matabeleland), refer in fact to the proceedings at preliminary inquiries before a magistrate rather than to the proceedings in the High Court itself of which no official record appears to have survived. For the proceedings in the final trial I have depended upon press reports. The preliminary inquiry reports are very full, however, and often contain evidence which was not made use of in the final trial, notes of re-examination of witnesses, and so on. The records of the Matabeleland trials appear not to have been preserved in the same way; at any rate I was unable to trace the notes of the preliminary inquiries into murders committed in Matabeleland. For the rising in Mashonaland these records constitute a source of extreme value, only a very small part of which has been cited in this book.

The only other major archival sources used were found in the manuscript collection in Rhodes House, Oxford. The papers of Cecil John Rhodes which are deposited there have frequently been used by scholars but the material relating to Rhodesia has been very little exploited. There is in fact a good deal of material in the collection of little interest to a biographer of Rhodes but of considerable interest to a historian of Rhodesia. There is also, it may be added, a good deal of material of interest to the biographer of Rhodes in the Company records in the National Archives in Salisbury which has so far not been made use of. For this reason the account given in this book of Rhodes' negotiations with the Ndebele is much fuller than that given in any biography of that remarkable man.

In the few cases where I have cited oral evidence I have given the name of the informant and the date of the interview. Full transcripts of these interviews are in my possession.

In general it may be said that the common view that the early history of Rhodesia is very thinly documented owing to the destruction of records at the British South Africa Company offices in London during the last war is very much an exaggeration. Abundant documentary material still survives, only a very small proportion of which proved of direct use to this study.

Appendix

Oral Traditions of the Rising in the Mazoe District of Mashonaland

AT a late stage in the production of this book I was sent a copy of an Honours Seminar Paper given at the University College in Salisbury in June 1966 by Mr C. G. Chivanda. Mr Chivanda's researches into the oral history of the rising in his home area of Mazoe are still uncompleted; nevertheless his work represents by far the most effective and co-ordinated attempt to piece together a picture from a wide range of oral sources and to compare it with the available archival material. The results obtained make such a fascinating commentary upon the themes of this book that I have asked Mr Chivanda for permission to quote from the first part of his paper—'The Mashona Rebellion in Oral Tradition: Mazoe District'—in which he summarizes the oral accounts still current in Mazoe.

The Mazoe district was one of especial importance to the Shona rising. It was the headquarters of the Nehanda medium on the one hand; on the other hand it was close to Salisbury, attracted early concentrations of white miners and farmers, and was exposed to very considerable white pressure. Mr Chivanda's picture of the district before the white occupation is one of the interaction of numbers of rival clans and their chiefs—Wata, Chiweshe, Madombwe, Negomo, Nyamweda, and so on. 'One feature which seems to have characterized the tribal life of the tribes around present day Salisbury is warfare. There was a lot of raiding and counter-raiding, for instance, between Chiweshe and Nyamweda, or Chiweshe and some Rozvi group from Zvimba. . . . The tribes seem to have been of about equal strength, or at least none was strong enough to force a combination. The lack of co-operation against the Matabele, who were often in smaller numbers than the local people, is a weakness which is freely and readily admitted in oral tradition.'

Into this divided area came the whites. They were regarded

initially as traders to be exploited to the advantage of whichever group was able to strike up relations with them. The Nehanda medium, so Mr Chivanda tells us, 'said to each of the chiefs under her: "Don't be afraid of them—they are only traders. But take a black cow to them and say, This is the meat with which we greet you."' This the chiefs did and their messengers were told by the whites that 'they were looking for gold and asked for help in prospecting'. Some chiefs readily entered into relationships with the new-comers, accustomed as they were to the gold-trade with the Portuguese. Chiweshe's brother in law, Guyo Marimo, served as a gold prospector; chief Wata, the special guardian of the Nehanda medium, sent some of his family to serve the whites.

But the favourable impression created by the presents at first given to the chiefs by the newcomers was rapidly dispelled. The whites showed no signs of wishing to establish normal trading relations or of leaving the neighbourhood; they did not respect the customary authority of chief or medium. 'They couldn't listen to the talk of Africans as owners of the land,' Mr Chivanda's informants told him. 'The whites coveted our land, its resources and riches.' More than this. The whites began to press labour and to flog those who ran away or who refused to work. Native Messengers, drawn often from the so-called Vanyai, a group of unfree servants to the chiefs who had taken advantage of the coming of the whites to break away, were used to enforce labour recruitment. The complaints of chiefs Wata, Chiweshe and Negomo were ignored; Chiweshe himself was flogged later for not reporting the death of cattle from rinderpest.

Yet the Mazoe Shona refused to accept that the whites were in any sense their rulers. 'Wata and Chiweshe refused to pay tax to Europeans because they were strangers. For three or four years Europeans were demanding tax, and it didn't seem logical that one who wasn't acknowledged as a ruler should demand tribute. This informant further states that they couldn't pay tax to the English when the Portuguese used to pay tax (44 guns a year) to the Shona. . . . Most people interviewed state that taxation was attempted and rejected by Africans and only came as a result of defeat.'

'All this was happening in the eyes of Nehanda and Mwari, and both could not bear to see their people suffering as they were doing. Chiefs and headmen brought their troubles to Nehanda, and she in turn reported to Kagubi at Mashayamombe. She said her people were ill treated and were ready to fight. . . . Messengers and presents were exchanged between Nehanda and Kagubi, messengers travelling mostly at night . . . the role of Kagubi and Mashayamombe is clearly remembered in this refrain sung by the people of Mazoe: "Wakarigona Mashayamombe akati mhungu chena ngaiurayiwe" (Mashayamombe was just right when he said that the white cobra must be killed). Kagubi seems to have been prominent in the organization of the rebellion. Messages and preparations had been going on for some months in secret and to small groups of people. Kagubi gave orders and advice from Mashayamombe and there developed a close network of communication. Kagubi said whites must be killed—but it would not be said in this manner. Rather than say "White people must be killed", messengers were to say "Nhapi! Nhapi!"; "Nhapi" or "dapi" is a Rowley's otomys, and the general idea which Kagubi conveyed was that people should talk of murdering white men as though they were talking of going for a big hunt. This use of hunting terminology seems to have been extended to tactics as well. The rebels as much as possible preferred to attack from cover, as if afraid of frightening off big game. The long grass in June, and the dense forests and the rocks to be found in the Mazoe district afforded excellent cover. The rebels knew the roads frequently used by the Europeans, and when they thought the enemy would be coming a particular way they dug pits across the road, laid sticks, soil and grass on top or did anything to increase the effectiveness of the trap, or "hunza".'

Mr Chivanda gives a valuable insight into the role of the mediums in Mazoe. 'Nehanda was, of course, the overall Mhondoro. She not only gave information of the whereabouts of the enemy, but gave orders and kept up the people's morale by predicting victory and doctoring the rebels. Under Nehanda there were less Mhondoro who carried out the more detailed planning and preparation. Just to give an example: every chief had a principal mhondoro in his clan who co-operated closely with him and established communications with greater spirits like Nehanda. . . . The Chiweshe clan had one called Chikukwa . . . himself a reputed warrior in his day; he was once a chief and the father of Chandaengerwa, the Chiweshe at the time of the rebellion. The spirit or Mhondoro of Chikukwa spoke through the medium, vaTakai, wife of Chandaengerwa (and mother of Gondo, my informant). Thus there was the greatest possibility of co-operation between the chief and the spiritual leaders who kept the people in fighting mood. "Chikukwa used to tell us what to do and where to go." The preparations for battle were carried out at night: the war-song was sung, accompanied by Mbira music; a goat or other sacrificial animal was offered to the dead ancestors who had been warriors in their days, and the dance would go on throughout the night, usually in the thickets and forests, preferably near a mountain, far from the village. . . . It is important to understand the confidence of people if we realize that the presence of the mhondoro, who was a warrior himself, was constant and reassuring. People felt safe because the mhondoro were believed to be able to prophesy and ward off danger.'

At the same time the intending rebels also sought protection in the 'ndudzo' medicine, a powerful war medicine brought into Mazoe from the Mutapa area by the Rozwi of Negomo. 'Men would form a queue, dip first the right hand then the left into the prepared ndudzo, and finally make a mark on the forehead with some special piece of grass, oiled.'

Thus prepared, the Shona of Mazoe were ready to attack the whites. 'The main target was of course the white people but any policeman or Africans who co-operated with whites, as well as Africans who were not Shona were to be attacked. Secrecy was to be observed, and orders from Nehanda were usually obeyed satisfactorily. Any pretext to get near the enemy was employed; trade, looking for work, hunting together, or just the usual kindness or conversation. The adoption of these tactics necessitated the employment of agents who were acquainted with certain Europeans. The method required extraordinary friendliness and normal behaviour, and there is no doubt the Europeans were taken by surprise.'

However, as the surviving whites gathered in the Alice Mine laage so the peoples of Mazoe came together to attack it. 'Most of the people in the district were fighting together. . . . Each chief would send his own contingent under himself or an officer to join in the attack.' And the high point of the combined Mazoe attack came with the ambush on the Salisbury road of the Mazoe Patrol returning with the whites rescued from Alice Mine. This fight was an epic of white memory of the rising; so also of black. 'Then we saw them coming along the road to Salisbury,' recalls one of Mr Chivanda's informants. 'There they were, we could see them in a long line. Meanwhile we hid ourselves in dead silence behind rocks and in the long grass. We could see them approaching, their heads moving up and down and could hear the sound of horse shoes. We let the leader go by a little. Then suddenly one gun was let off! Ndogo! One bullet for the horse, another for the white man. Then came general shooting. Man! You should have seen it for yourself. The guns really gave them a hard time that day.'

But 'the offensive by the united rebels' ended with this engagement; it was now a matter of defending the strong points of the chiefs from white counter-attack. As might have been expected Mr Chivanda's oral evidence is not very clear or helpful on the complex of detailed clashes over the next months. But it becomes vivid again with the surrender and the death of the Nehanda medium and provides a fascinating oral comment on her struggles on the scaffold. The medium was taken in company with Wata and Gutsa and tried for murder with them. In the view of the Mazoe Shona they were at serious fault in not assuming all the blame themselves and their treachery to the medium whose protection was their special responsibility is held accountable for her death. 'At the scaffold Nehanda is known to have somehow defied death. It is said that the first two attempts to take her life failed. But Wata's people who were present pointed out to the Europeans why she was able to resist execution: she had her snuff with her, which she took just before going for execution. The people of Wata advised the executioner to remove the snuff from her and Nehanda, disappointed, but courageous, gave it away and went to meet her death.'

It will be seen, I think, that this compilation of oral evidence broadly confirms the picture which it is possible to derive from the written evidence. But it will also be seen how the oral evidence provides incomparably vivid details and insights. I can perhaps end this Appendix as I began the Introduction to this book by expressing once again my hope that the work of Mr Chivanda, Mr Chigwedere and others will be carried to completion so that we can build up a picture of the rising district by district.

Index